What To Do About Your Brain-Injured Child

**Or Your
Brain-damaged,
Mentally Retarded,
Mentally Deficient,
Cerebral-palsied, Epileptic,
Autistic, Athetoid, Hyperactive,
Attention Deficit Disordered,
Developmentally Delayed,
Down's Child**

OTHER WORKS BY THE AUTHOR

The Gentle Revolution Series:

   HOW TO TEACH YOUR BABY TO READ

   PATHWAY TO WELLNESS

   HOW TO MULTIPLY YOUR BABY'S INTELLIGENCE

   HOW TO GIVE YOUR BABY ENCYCLOPEDIC KNOWLEDGE

   HOW TO TEACH YOUR BABY MATH

   HOW TO TEACH YOUR BABY TO BE PHYSICALLY SUPERB

   THE UNIVERSAL MULTIPLICATION OF INTELLIGENCE

Children's Book:

   NOSE IS NOT TOES

What To Do About Your Brain-Injured Child

Or Your
Brain-damaged,
Mentally Retarded,
Mentally Deficient,
Cerebral-palsied, Epileptic,
Autistic, Athetoid, Hyperactive,
Attention Deficit Disordered,
Developmentally Delayed,
Down's Child

Glenn Doman

SQUAREONE
PUBLISHERS

Square One Publishers

115 Herricks Road • Garden City Park, NY 11040

(516) 535-2010 • (877) 900-BOOK • www.squareonepublishers.com

Appendices:

DETOXIFICATION FROM ANTICONVULSANTS
Copyright © 1999   The Institutes for the Achievement of Human Potential

CHILDREN WITH SEVERE BRAIN INJURIES
Copyright © 1960   American Medical Association

THE INCLINED FLOOR INSTRUCTIONS
Copyright © 2002   The Institutes for the Achievement of Human Potential

The Institutes for the Achievement of Human Potential, The Institutes, The Gentle Revolution, How To Multiply Your Baby's Intelligence, What To Do About Your Brain-Injured Child, and the *"Boy on Hand"* logo are trademarks of The Institutes for the Achievement of Human Potential and Registered in the U.S. Patent and Trademark Office. *Glenn Doman* is a registered trademark and service mark of Glenn Doman (Registered in the U.S. Patent and Trademark Office) and is used with his permission.

Library of Congress Cataloging-in-Publication Data

Doman, Glenn J.
  What to do about your brain-injured child : or your brain-damaged, mentally retarded, mentally deficient, cerebral-palsied, epileptic, autistic, athetoid, hyperactive, attention deficit disordered, developmentally delayed, down's child / Glenn Doman.— "30th anniversary edition"—Ack.
     p. cm.
  Includes bibliographical references and index.
  ISBN 0-7570-0186-6 (pbk.) — ISBN 0-7570-0187-4 (hardcover)
  1. Children with mental disabilities—Care. 2. Children with disabilities—Care. 3. Patterning therapy. I. Title.
  HV891.D65 2005
  362.19'7481'0083—dc22

                             2005001031

ISBN 0-7570-0186-6 (pbk.)   •   ISBN 0-7570-0187-4 (hdbk.)

Printed in the United States of America

10   9   8   7   6   5   4   3   2   1

CONTENTS

DECADE OF EXPANSION—1960 to 1970

THE FUTURE—1970 to The Present

To my family, who believed in me,
To the staff, who held down the fort,
To those endlessly determined people, the parents,
and
To the brain-injured children—who live in
a threatening, frightening, and even dangerous world,
and who somehow manage to survive it all until help comes.

ACKNOWLEDGMENTS

There are four groups of people without whom there would have been no book and, for that matter, no Institutes for the Achievement of Human Potential. They have my love and respect which go far beyond the book; they make me the most fortunate of men. I list them with love.

The Staff of The Institutes for the
Achievement of Human Potential
The Kids
The Parents
My Family

In regard to the first edition, I thank beyond measure Dr. Raymundo Veras and Dan and Margaret Melcher who made me tackle it again for the ninth time. For the illustrations, I am indebted to David Melton, father, artist, and author who made it easy by understanding it all. For the research, I am indebted to my assistant, Greta Erdtmann. For the preparation, I thank Vicki Thornber. The endless manuscript changes were made efficiently and cheerfully by Irma Kieslich, Cathy Ruhling, and Sherry Russock. The original version was instigated and carried out by Lindley Boyer.

For the 30th anniversary edition, I am indebted to the very capable team that undertook the task of updating the book: my daughter Janet, my son Douglas, and Susan Aisen. In addition, Dr. Mihai Dimancescu, Dr. Denise Malkowicz, and Dr. Coralee Thompson contributed invaluable advice for which I am very grateful. I thank Dr. Ralph Pelligra for writing the Foreword for the book. The Institutes editor, Janet Gauger, deserves special mention for the many hours of love and care she put into this new edition and without which it would never have been completed.

FOREWORD

This book is a precious gift for thousands of brain-injured children who drift perilously on a sea of ignorance and misunderstanding, for beleaguered parents who desperately seek guidance and refuse to give in or give up, and for medical professionals who can find within its pages scientifically sound and intellectually satisfying answers to a difficult and perplexing clinical problem.

It is not a medical text in the classic sense, nor has it been sanctified on the holy altar of the "prospective, double-blind, controlled clinical study." But, like all seminal scientific discoveries, it uncovers fundamental, deceptively simple truths that have been obscured and subverted by prevailing dogma.

Glenn Doman and his team anticipated by several decades the discoveries of modern neuroscience—that the human brain has remarkable abilities for self-repair (neuroplasticity) and regeneration (neurogenesis), that the brain is easily accessible and modifiable by intense sensory stimulation, that the protean symptoms of brain injury are just symptoms, and that treatment should be directed at their cause, the injured brain itself.

Glenn Doman looks at the commonplace and sees the profound. He looks at the floor and sees not a floor, but a landscape of opportunity for the developing infant. He looks at human mobility and sees not just a mode of locomotion, but a key to unraveling the complexity of a pathological process. He questions the obvious "What is normal?"—and asks, provocatively, "Who is not brain injured?" He extracts scientific truths from insights and observations, and, not content with theoretical explanations alone, he incorporates them into a practical and meaningful manual for parents.

This book contains all these things and more. It is a nemesis for the arrogant who cling to callous authority and a lesson for anyone who fails to question, to challenge, and to remember from history the unreasonable personal toll we exact from those who dare to innovate.

I was deeply honored when Glenn Doman asked me to write the Foreword to the 30th Anniversary Edition of this rare literary and scientific gem, but I would not have agreed had I felt unqualified to do so. I have worked side by side with Glenn and the staff of The Institutes for the Achievement of Human Potential for more than a quarter of a century.

Under Glenn's direction as senior researcher, we have conducted research programs that validate the basic premises put forth in this book, particularly those regarding respiratory and oxygen availability programs. I have been a researcher for many years and know well the gratifying feeling of publishing the results of good research. But there is nothing to compare to the intellectual and emotional excitement of seeing scientific premise come to life—to see a formerly paralyzed child doing handstands and other gymnastic feats, or to see a presumed "mentally retarded" child reading and comprehending above the level of his chronological peers. Even today there are still children who fail to progress, but the work set in motion by this book continues and the results improve steadily.

For all its science and innovation, this is a moving story of human dedication and devotion. It is told with warmth and honest directness by a decorated war hero whose battlefield has changed but whose cause has not. Tyranny and the threat to human dignity come in many forms, but none so devastating as the innocent child who is imprisoned in his own body, labeled with false deficiencies, and often warehoused and forgotten. Glenn Doman, a scientist, humanitarian, and tireless warrior has given us a battle plan—a fighting chance for the brain-injured child. He provides an end to false despair and a beginning for hope.

—RALPH PELLIGRA
CHIEF MEDICAL OFFICER
NASA AMES RESEARCH CENTER, MOFFETT FIELD, CALIFORNIA, USA

CHAIRMAN OF THE BOARD OF DIRECTORS
THE INSTITUTES FOR THE ACHIEVEMENT OF HUMAN POTENTIAL

PREFACE

This book by Glenn Doman is in many ways a very bad book. Upon my sober reflection, I see it to be the least good book of major importance I have ever read. However, perhaps this is so because I have not read many so-important books in my lifetime of reading. It is not so important to all people alive, but only of major importance to the parents of children.

This is not a bad book because to read it is difficult, for truth dictates that I report that it is very easy to read. Glenn Doman does not address himself to professionals but writes only for the parents, whom he so admires and respects. This makes it a marvelously easy book to read.

This is not a bad book because it is unexciting. His descriptions of the early discoveries of "the team," such as those which revealed the importance of the Floor to hurt children and normal infants, the reader will find exciting.

This book is not bad because it is not emotionally moving. The reader may find himself enraptured even to tears while reading the chapter *on motivation*, as I found myself moved.

I find this in many ways to be a bad book, because having started a New Age, he tells us so little about it in a doctrinal sense.

Glenn Doman gives us only the slightest glimpse into the years of unrelenting work through the brightness of days and the darkness of nights. It is a heroic story of a group of people who would in no case accept defeat and most especially when they *were* defeated.

This book tells us nothing of the years upon years of exploration into the lives of children all over the world. Glenn Doman does not tell of his expeditions and explorations into the wildest areas of the world, and they were many. He went so that he and his beloved "team" could see with their own eyes, while living with children, what no child expert had ever seen before since the beginning of time. He does not tell us how they have lived with children in more than fifty different countries, from the most highly sophisticated to the most wild. They have circled the globe at the Equator and lived with the great Masai in Africa and with the very small Bushmen in the Kalahari Desert in Africa. They have wandered over Africa, living with many tribes, and through the Middle East, the Holy Land and Asia. It was sometimes not very safe. It has almost always been uncomfortable. I know this because sometimes I have been privileged to be with them.

I remember a day, deep in the Xingu Territory of my own Brasil, where live the people who will one day come to the Stone Age, but who were not there yet by a long time. On this day, when the Brasilian Air Force had left us eight hundred miles from the nearest road and had flown away, we had marched for many hours toward a tribe called Kalapolo. The temperature was very high and there were clouds of biting mosquitoes. I remember looking at Glenn Doman, Dr. Bob, and Dr. Thomas. Their blood, from thousands of mosquito bites, joined with their perspiration to run down their bodies in rivulets, making of them a sight most fearful. They did not complain as they pushed through the tall jungle grass to see children and childbirth and child-rearing practices no child expert had ever seen before. Delacato and I, being more dark complexioned, suffered little from these nasty little creatures. But I have suffered elsewhere, having been with them to the Arctic to live with and study Eskimo children. The Arctic at 56 below zero F is not the natural place for a Brasilian from Clara. Of these storybook adventures, the book tells nothing.

Nor does this book tell us about the vicious attacks and terrible libels of fearful and jealous societies which the staff had to endure and fight off during the pioneering years. These unworthy enemies retarded for some years the work of the group, while they were developing the doctrines, the philosophy, and the techniques which would give new lives to thousands of children and their families, not only in their own country, but here in Brasil and in other countries in South America, Europe, Africa, and Asia. Although they have collected the fruits of victory, their continuing struggle for new knowledge and techniques give them no time to enjoy them. They have only tasted them. Of all this, the book tells us almost nothing.

This incomplete book tells us nothing of the worldwide search, in the beauty of their enthusiasm, for a single piece of the puzzle as to why it was that a certain group among the children, called athetoids, were failing to learn to walk even after years of treatment. It does not tell us of the brilliant deductions that led to the discovery of brachiation [using gravity to straighten rather than bend the body by using arms to swing from rung to rung on an overhead ladder] as a solution to the problems of those children and many others. In fact, it does not tell us of brachiation itself as the most important advance in treatment in twenty-five years, which has added an entire new dimension to the world of brain-injured children.

For everything this book says, there are a hundred things of importance it does not say. For every story it tells, there are a thousand stories it does not tell.

It is these things which make me say that in many ways it is a very bad book.

In contrast, I am forced to say that if this book told all the marvelous stories of the "team" and the rich, glorious days of The Institutes, which are worth telling, it would be a grand library instead of a small book.

I can't say that Glenn Doman knows more about children than any man alive, because I don't know every man alive, but I can say that he has *done* more about children than any man alive. I can say as well that he knows more about children—little ones and big ones—hurt ones and average ones—civilized ones and primitive ones—poor ones and rich ones— and how to make hurt ones well and well ones weller than any man I have ever read about or heard about or met. I know of no other person or group of persons who knew about all those kinds of children except him and the people he has taught.

Yet, Glenn Doman believes that every mother in the world knows more about her child than he does. Not only does his mouth say it and his heart feel it, but his brain knows it and he believes it.

He believes some unusual things for a professional. He believes in parents. He believes in children. He believes parents are the answer to children's problems, while everybody else believes they are the problem. It is easy to understand why he makes unhappy all professional organizations which earn their money from brain-injured children. He believes in fixing the children. Worse, he believes that parents can fix the children better than professional people. He teaches parents how to fix their children, not because to do so makes it economically feasible—although it does—but instead because he is sure that parents get better results than *does* any professional, including himself. This book does say these things.

He exists within a philosophical base very different from what we have formed through the example of our predecessors.

Most of all, he believes in results, and this book is the first book in history, to my knowledge, which tells how to treat brain-injured children, why to treat brain-injured children, and most precisely what happened to a group of brain-injured children when they were so treated.

It is not only appropriate but also typical that he should write the first book in history which gives results of treating brain-injured children by a particular method in a straightforward, easy-to-read way. No other book in history has done that. Moreover, no precise results have ever been given of *any* treatment of brain-injured children before, with one exception. In 1960 an article appeared in the *Journal of the A.M.A.* on the treatment of brain-injured children with precise results. The reader may not be surprised to learn that Glenn Doman and his staff wrote that article also.

When we sum up this book we find that this is a book about brain-injured children and their parents. It tells *why* brain-injured children should be treated. It tells *how* the human brain can be treated and it tells exactly what happens to brain-injured children when you do it.

It is true to say that it is the worst such book ever written. But we must remember it is also true to say that it is the best such book ever written. The reason for this is that it is the *only* such book to be written.

It is very good for children—I think—that when it was finally written it was written by the man who knows more about the subject than any other man.

I think perhaps, in the beginning, the people who make books will not like it so much. Perhaps as well the people who are paid to criticize books will not like it so well. And, as I said earlier, in many ways it is a bad book.

But I believe that many parents will find within this not-so-perfect book the knowledge and the courage they need to make their severely brain-injured children well without any further help.

I believe that many thousands of parents of the brain-injured, brain-damaged, mentally retarded, mentally deficient, cerebral-palsied, epileptic, autistic children will find their own child within the pages of this book and will also find inside it the confirmation of their own heart's belief that he must have his chance to be free and will find the road to get the help they need to give their child that chance.

I believe this book will be the first true hammer in striking down the horrible institutions in which the brain-injured children of the world have been cruelly and unjustly confined.

—RAYMUNDO VERAS, M.D.

PRESIDENT EMERITUS

THE WORLD ORGANIZATION FOR HUMAN POTENTIAL

RIO DE JANEIRO, BRASIL

1

BRAIN-INJURED CHILDREN TODAY

Periodically one hundred people will arrive at The Institutes for the Achievement of Human Potential in Philadelphia for one week.

They will have nothing in common except that all are the parents of brain-injured children.

They will be mothers and fathers who have in common the refusal to believe that their hurt child cannot be helped.

If it is a typical group, the families will come from the four corners of the Americas and from Europe, Africa, Asia, Australia, or the Middle East.

In short, from everywhere on earth.

The children will range in age from one year to nineteen years.

There may be one young person or adult in the group.

Some will be so paralyzed that they are barely able to breathe.

Some will be so mildly injured that they appear to the eye to be totally well.

Some of the kids will be paralyzed from head to toe. Some will be blind as a bat. Some will be deaf as a post. Some will suffer from recurring violent convulsions. Some will be unable to talk or even make sounds. Some will have all of these problems.

They will come with recorded IQs of 90, 80, 70, 60, 50, 40, 30, 20, 10, or 0. Most of them will be said to have unmeasurable IQs.

They will arrive having been diagnosed as brain-damaged, mentally retarded, mentally deficient, cerebral-palsied, Down syndrome, spastic, emotionally disturbed, flaccid, epileptic, quadriplegic, autistic, psychotic, hemiplegic, rigid, etc.

Almost every one of them, on the basis of lengthy and sophisticated examination, we will diagnose as brain-injured, meaning that the problems are not problems of weak arms or legs, or poor musculature, or malformed organs of speech, or defective eyes as much of the world has believed. Instead, we will conclude that his problems originated within the brain out of some accident which occurred before, during, or after birth and that either interfered with the brain's ability to take in information or with the brain's ability to respond to it.

Of course, if the problem originates in a condition that could be solved by surgery—such as hydrocephaly—we prescribe surgery. However, operable cases will ordinarily have been diagnosed and taken care of before the child reaches us.

In a typical group, about fifteen percent will return home and do no program but will see their children in an entirely different and better way and, as a result, give their children new opportunities to grow.

Fifty percent of a typical group will return home, diagnose their child, design a program for him, and carry it out with varying degrees of frequency, intensity, and duration with commensurate results.

The remaining thirty-five percent, the most determined group, will apply for and be accepted into the aspirant program, with the goal of being accepted into the Intensive Treatment Program.

It is for these parents that this week is designed so that we can teach as fully as possible the principles of brain growth and development and how to design a program to increase brain growth and development.

After this week these families will design such a program and carry it out with the intention of joining the Intensive Treatment Program in the future.

By addressing ourselves this week to the needs of these families we best serve all the families who have come to learn.

We act as if every family here is going to be a part of the Intensive Treatment Program because all of them will have everything to gain and nothing to lose if we do so.

Some of the children will be on the Intensive Treatment Program for a year. Some children will be on the program for five years. Some others will be on the program for longer. Some of the parents will run out of energy and give up. Most will not give up. Some will never give up, even if they lose.

The great majority of children will do better than their parents had dared hope on the basis of prior experience with the conventional methods. With others there will be disappointment.

Sometimes a severely hurt child will make greater gains more quickly than another child whose problems seemed much less serious.

Some of the children who were completely blind will end up reading—

not with their fingers but with their eyes, like everybody else. Some will remain blind.

Some of the children who were completely paralyzed will end up walking, running, and jumping—not with braces or crutches but with their legs like everybody else. Some will fail to walk.

Some of the children who were unable to make sounds will end up talking—not with their fingers by pointing and pantomime but with their lips and mouths, like everybody else.

Some who writhed endlessly or could not remain still will find an end to their writhings.

Some of the children who were paralyzed and speechless and blind and deaf will end up totally well and in the same school and grade as their normal peers. In short, they will be normal.

Others will end up walking, talking, and dancing and perhaps with IQs in the genius area.

The results, therefore, will range from total success to total failure.

It is not surprising that children sometimes fail in a world where most professionals were taught in school that hurt brains are beyond mending. Instead, it is surprising that anyone gets well. To many it would seem miraculous.

And who is it who has accomplished such miracles, if miracles they be, in this new century? It is the parents who have done so, and at home. Parents—those commonly ignored, sometimes despised, frequently patronized, almost never believed people—will have done at home all of the treatment which brought a child from despair to hope, from paralysis to walking, from blindness to reading, from an IQ of 70 to an IQ of 140, from dumbness to speech. Parents.

In some cases, a medical doctor will be closely involved in the home treatment. Hundreds of physicians have come and watched the work at The Institutes—and then enrolled their own brain-injured child. However, more than 20,000 parents, quite without medical training, have brought us their hurt child and then gone home to carry out the prescribed treatments.

How is it possible for parents to accomplish this with their children?

Perhaps to understand such a process, it is best to begin at the beginning, which was more than a half century ago.

That's where we begin in teaching parents about brain-injured children. If one really wants to understand about brain-injured children, perhaps there is no place else to begin.

1950 to 1960

DECADE OF DESPAIR

2

TEMPLE FAY

When I entered the gleaming halls of Temple University Hospital & Medical School in 1941 to take up my new post as assistant chief of the Physical Therapy Department, I was considered by all to be fortunate to receive such an important appointment at a leading medical school at such a young age.

To keep the truth in perspective, however, it should also be pointed out that there were only two full-time therapists, the chief and me.

It should also be pointed out that my salary was ninety-five dollars a month plus meals for a five-and-a-half-day week, which, in all fairness was not bad for a physical therapist in those days.

To put the truth into final perspective, I was an eager but not very good physical therapist. Although I had graduated high in my class and had a high theoretical knowledge, I had had little experience.

There was one area in which I had absolutely no knowledge, either practical or theoretical, and that was the field of brain-injured children. It took me several years to find out that almost nobody else did either. In 1941 there were very few people who even claimed to know anything about brain-injured children.

Fortunately for me and for my future there was a man at Temple who probably knew more about such children than any man alive. His name was Temple Fay, and although Dr. Fay was then only in his early forties, he was both professor of neurology and professor of neurosurgery. He was one of the all-time Greats of Medicine. It was in his service at Temple University that I saw and was fascinated by my first brain-injured child.

In those days, few if any people referred to severely brain-injured children as *brain-injured*. Instead, they were called by names like *feeble-minded*. This was because, being severely brain-injured, a high percentage of them could neither walk nor talk. It was assumed that the fact that they couldn't talk constituted sufficient evidence to prove that they weren't smart enough to talk.

I shall not forget the first brain-injured child I met. Being fascinated by all that went on and being aware of my monumental ignorance, it was usual for me to spend my off hours in the evenings going everywhere in the hospital. Because I was young and pathetically eager, department chiefs and head nurses opened the doors of their departments to me. Now that I am no longer young, I realize how irresistible it is to be confronted with a person who is at once young and eager to learn. How powerful is the alchemy and how mutually marvelous the opportunity when one who is young and eager to learn meets an older person who knows something worth learning.

On this particular day I was in the nursery, not where the newborns (who also fascinated me) were kept, but where the very small, very sick children were kept. The children were in little cribs, and except for them I was alone in the room. I had read some of their histories and was now seeing the children. Most of the babies in the room were asleep, and the room was quiet except for the labored breathing of the babies and the sounds made by my white crepe-soled shoes as I moved quietly from bed to bed.

I was therefore more than a little startled, and I jumped visibly, when a voice said, "Hello," in a room where I considered myself alone except for infants and small babies. While the voice wasn't an adult voice, it certainly wasn't a baby's. I glanced hurriedly around the room and was extremely uncomfortable when I could see nothing but very small cribs.

Just as I was persuading myself that I had imagined the voice altogether, the small voice spoke again. This time I happened to be looking at the precise corner from which the voice came, and, as a result, I started even more violently than the first time. "What's your name?" the voice asked.

By now I was totally confused and more than a little frightened as I took three or four reluctant steps toward the corner of the room from which the talking was coming. I would not, even then, have seen him if he hadn't spoken again as I stood directly over the tiny crib in which he was lying.

"My name's Billy," said Billy, as I looked down at him. If it had been difficult to believe my ears, it was now even more difficult to believe my eyes. No one in neurology or pediatrics had ever taught me that such children existed. Looking up at me from a tiny crib was an extremely strange but not unpleasant adolescent face set in a head as large as any adult's. What shook me to the core was the fact that, although I could see the very large head, the rest of this child's body—covered with a blanket—could not possibly have been more than *two feet* long. I had the horrible feeling that he had no body at all and that I was being talked to by a disembodied head which spoke pleasantly and intelligently.

Although today, many thousands of brain-injured children later, I can honestly say that I have never once since felt horror at contact with a brain-injured child and am, in point of fact, quite upset by people who do, I must admit that I strove mightily to contain the horror I felt then. I now realize that it was not the child I was seeing that so upset me, rather it was not understanding the child I was seeing.

If I was upset, Billy was not, and his next statement gave me time to gain my outward, if not my inner, composure. "I'm eleven years old," said Billy, in a voice that made me think he had often answered that question. I do not remember the conversation that followed, but I do remember that Billy remained entirely composed throughout the ten or so minutes which followed. I have always hoped that I sounded more sensible than I felt.

When finally I managed to escape that room, I paused outside the door to calm myself before seeking out the charge nurse. I tried hard to appear nonchalant when I said to her, "Oh, by the way, what's the matter with that big kid...er...ah...that is, that eleven-year-old kid, Billy?"

I shiver a little as I remember that question and realize how it revealed my total ignorance. The searching look she gave me as she answered made it clear that the question itself completely revealed my ignorance. "He's hydrocephalic," she said steadily. "One of Dr. Fay's patients." She made both of these statements as if either one by itself explained everything.

I wonder now how I got the courage, but without even stopping to look *hydrocephalic* up in the medical dictionary, I took myself directly to the elevator and to Fay's office and asked his secretary if I might see him. It was an impulsive and astonishing thing to do since his appointment list was crowded with famous people. Fay had been called in to examine no less a person than President Franklin D. Roosevelt himself.

While I had made rounds with Dr. Fay, I had never actually spoken to him, and so large was his retinue when we made rounds that I had sometimes made rounds with him without actually seeing him. Since he was at the head of the long column, and I at the very end, I was frequently around the corner from him and received whatever physical therapy orders he gave me at third or even fourth hand.

I shall never know for sure why he agreed to see me and saw me immediately, unless it was his insatiable curiosity, whetted by the unlikeliness of my request.

In addition to everything else, Fay was a formal man in the old-fashioned professor mold, and it was difficult not to stand at rigid attention before his desk as his piercing eyes looked into me and, for all I knew, right straight through me.

I didn't give him a chance to ask me why I had come, but blurted out the question which was driving me to distraction and which had driven me to stand before this awesome person.

"Sir, I have just seen Billy, the hydrocephalic. What the devil is the matter with him?"

"The matter with him," said Fay, not answering my question, "is that he is hydrocephalic. Why the devil were you seeing him?"

Not even the clear rebuke in Fay's question could put me off, and after a brief and not very clear explanation of how I spent my spare time, I asked the question again. What the devil was the matter with Billy?

While I was obviously in trouble for seeing Fay's patient without his consent, it was equally obvious that something in my answer had pleased him. I later learned that nothing was more irresistible to Temple Fay than a young mind that wanted answers and that would dare to come to the right place to get them.

The great man explained briefly that hydrocephalic children had huge heads and tiny bodies because the cerebrospinal fluid constantly being manufactured within the brain was unable to escape, as it does in well people, due to a clogged reabsorption mechanism, and that the consequent increased pressure forced the skull to expand in size and compress the underlying brain. He recommended several books for me to read, although he cautioned me that they weren't entirely accurate.

Having thanked him for his time, I headed for the door. I had already partially opened the door when he stopped me to ask if my training at Penn had included experience in the operating room. I told him that it had.

"Did your experience in the O.R. include brain surgery?" inquired Dr. Fay.

In some intuitive way I knew that this question was a highly important one which could mark a turning point in my life. Fay's question had not been asked in a casual way.

I turned to face him. "I have never seen a piece of brain surgery, sir."

"Don't be so defensive, son, very few people ever have," said Fay, very deliberately. "Would you like to see some neurosurgery?"

Although he watched me very closely, he would not have had to, since the answer was obviously written all over my face. "Go see the head O.R. nurse and tell her you have my permission to come once. If your O.R. behavior suits both her and me, perhaps you can come often." He turned his back and dismissed me.

I couldn't believe my luck. The Dean of Neurosurgeons, Fay himself, had not only answered my question but had invited me to join him in the operating room. I was sure it was the first time he had ever seen me as an individual human being. He had called me "son". Did that mean anything or was it simply a synonym for young?

Fay had daughters but no son. I was to find that it was a term he used very seldom.

Being in an operating room with Fay was sheer delight. Not that he permitted an instant of nonsense. He ran a tight ship and he dominated that operating room for every second his team was in it. He did not dominate the situation because of his very high-ranking position; he dominated it because he was Fay.

Fay was a Teacher. He was a born Teacher, he was a trained Teacher, he was a Teacher by design, he was a Teacher by choice, he was a Teacher by instinct. Most of all Fay was a Teacher because he could no more help teaching than he could help breathing.

I don't mean that he was a teacher, I mean that he was a *Teacher* in the same way that Aristotle and Christ were Teachers.

In the sixteen years of hours, days, weeks, and months that followed, when for weeks on end I virtually lived with Fay, I do not believe there was a period of longer than fifteen consecutive minutes that he was not teaching me.

In all the years that followed, I do not once remember discussing the weather with Fay, even in blizzards, unless the weather had something to do with the brain or with a patient. If that's hard to imagine, I can only say that Fay was a man hard to imagine and impossible to forget. He himself was dominated by his own voracious interest in almost everything that mattered. I would say that he had contempt for all things that did not matter, but that wouldn't be quite true. It is closer to the truth to say that he was completely unaware of what didn't matter, or perhaps that he had some way of totally tuning out what didn't matter.

I had been completely hypnotized that first day in the operating room watching Fay caress a human brain. Fay was a superb surgeon. A few years ago a prominent neurosurgeon told me that he had served under two very famous neurosurgeons, one of whom was Fay. Although he had always been furious with Fay personally, he said that one of those two famous brain surgeons was a true artist in the operating room and the other a bull in a china shop, and that regardless of how he felt about Fay otherwise, it was Fay who was the artist.

Even so, it was not Fay's brilliant surgery or even his love of that marvelous organ, the human brain, which made him the delight he was in the operating room. What fascinated me was his eternal teaching. He taught every moment he operated, beginning with his preparation of the patient, which, in later years, he insisted on doing himself, and ending not before he had personally put the patient back into the patient's own bed. One could learn more practical neurology and neuroanatomy watching Fay in an operating room than from any book or lecture.

There before my very eyes was the "beautiful and wondrous" thing he so respected and loved. Here was no dead, gray, ugly thing in a jar but instead the live, throbbing, coral-colored human brain. Even hurt ones were beautiful to Fay, and so they became to me. In those days, more than a half century ago, there were not a great number of people who had ever seen a live human brain, not even among graduate physicians.

A certain way to arouse Fay's quiet ire was to let him hear an "expert" discuss the human brain familiarly if he had never seen a live one. Fay would note caustically that getting an idea of what the human brain was like from looking at dead ones in jars or photographs of dead ones in jars was very akin to getting an idea of what human beings were like from looking at corpses in caskets.

We had the extraordinary opportunity to see live ones, for in those days it was not unusual for a single piece of neurosurgery to require eight hours.

Apparently my behavior in the O.R. passed muster, because after the first time I was invited back again as often as I liked. Not only did I spend every moment of my off hours watching and listening while Dr. Fay performed his brain surgery, but indeed, I began to use the slow periods in the physical therapy department for the same purpose. By and by, I began to use some of the not-so-slow time in the physical therapy department, and as a result it was not long before I was called on the carpet not only by the chief therapist but also by the physician who was responsible for the department.

What the devil was the matter with me, they wanted to know? Didn't I know I was a physical therapist and had work of my own to do? Watching brain surgery performed by the master himself was interesting and all that, but when you had seen a few operations you had seen them all; but what was most important was that I was shirking my work.

They were right and I promised to reform, at least in terms of my working hours, which I did. But I still haunted Fay's operating room in all my off hours, including full time during vacation.

Still, I had to ask myself what I was doing spending all that time in neurosurgical O.R. After all, I was a physical therapist and a pretty junior one at that. Aside from the fascination of watching an artist work with his hands, aside from listening to a true scientist discuss what he was doing, why indeed was I wasting such a major portion of my life on this subject? There did not appear to be even the most remote relationship between what Fay was doing in the operating room and what I was doing in the physical therapy department.

Why was I gathering such large amounts of knowledge I would never be able to use? I did not know. I knew only that I was compelled, absolutely compelled, to spend every single moment I could steal watching Fay and listening to him. I was hypnotized. I was fascinated. I was intrigued. I was bewitched. I was hopelessly lost in what I was watching. Every day I was learning, although I had not the foggiest notion that ultimately his specialty, neurosurgery, and my specialty, physical therapy, would interact to provide new hope for brain-injured children everywhere.

Although I had no way of knowing it at that time, what I was seeing was the answer to what was wrong in the world of the children who had been written off as being hopelessly retarded. It would be a heartbreaking number of years before we would appreciate the relationship between those "beautiful, throbbing, coral-colored brains" that Fay was showing me and the children the whole world was failing so miserably.

Although I had not the faintest notion that it was so, it was the beginning of the beginning. A team was forming which would some day profoundly alter the lives of brain-injured children the world over and the lives of their families as well. It was a team whose work would lead it deep into the world of brain-injured children and beyond that into the world of children we presently call well. It was the beginning of a journey that would consume the lives of many people, some of whom were not yet born.

There was, however, much to suffer before that team would become a working reality. For one thing, there was World War II.

The morning after Pearl Harbor, I enlisted as a private in the U. S. Army. For the next four years I went from the Medical Corps to the Infantry, from the United States to Africa and back to the United States for infantry Officer Candidate School at Ft. Benning. In the course of infantry combat through France I became an infantry rifle company commander. Through the bloody, icy Battle of the Bulge and the struggle through Luxembourg, Holland, and across Germany and the assaults across the Moselle River and the mighty Rhine and into Czechoslovakia itself, we fought, we maimed, we killed, and we were maimed, and we were killed until we stood victorious. We had wounded, killed, or captured many thousands of young German soldiers. Of an original company of 187 men and 6 officers, I had three times been reduced to 18 men and no officers. In all the world there is no greater pacifist than a victorious combat infantry soldier at the end of a war—unless it is possibly a defeated combat infantry soldier. Except for uniforms they are astonishingly hard to tell apart. The brains I had destroyed sharpened my desire to return as quickly as possible to my practice of healing rather than destroying.

3

I AM PLUNGED DEEP INTO
THE HEART OF BRAIN INJURY
—AND DESPAIR

Although I did not know it, when I was discharged from the army in 1945, plans were being made for me by others.

Since the company whose command I had inherited during the war had been one of the outstanding companies in General Patton's Third Army, I had received a large number of decorations and the press had made much of it.

Back home in Philadelphia, the members of the Physical Therapy Association had read of this, and although they did not remember me, they read that I had been a physical therapist.

As a reward for what they considered my wartime accomplishments, they decided to give me a ready-made practice. All of them were over-worked and so each of them decided to turn over to me some of his patients. It was extremely kind of that group who later became my close and dear friends. I had never even heard of anyone who had been given a busy practice as a gift. It was a great compliment.

My new practice was, in fact, unique. It consisted of thirty-one patients, every one of whom had had a stroke. I would guess that nobody else in history had ever had a practice consisting entirely of stroke cases.

I was once again involved with the human brain—for a stroke is a brain injury, although we didn't think of it in any such orderly way in those days.

The vast majority of strokes are a result either of a hemorrhage due to a broken blood vessel in the brain or of a blood clot that lodges in one of the blood vessels which supply blood to the brain. The location, the extent, and the severity of the paralysis that follows a stroke is determined by the location, the extent, and degree of the brain injury itself.

My new patients mystified me mightily. As time went by I grew ever more successful at keeping my stroke cases alive longer and longer; it was clear that the more active I forced them to be, the more healthy they became. But rarely was I wise enough to get them walking independently, even more rarely could I get the speechless ones to talk, and never was I able to make the curled and spastic fist of the stroke case into a functional hand. It seemed a strange thing to fail so consistently.

I recalled over and over again the first patient I had ever seen. This was before the war and just after I had graduated from school. He kept coming back to my mind unbidden, and at the oddest times, until remembering him came to annoy me vastly because if there had been something to learn from him, I had failed to learn it.

He was pathetic in so many ways. In the first place, he was old. In the second place, he was completely uneducated and poor as a church mouse. He had had a stroke in his left and dominant hemisphere and a bad one. Thus, he was severely paralyzed on his right side and totally without speech. In short, this poor old gentleman had absolutely nothing, which was precisely why he had me. I was fresh out of school and had not a single patient. He was very poor and couldn't afford someone better.

I remember that his house did not have electricity and I remember, as well, that his family was just like him, which is to say that they were also desperately poor, had no education to speak of, and were extremely simple people.

Full of enthusiasm and burning to help, I began to treat him. I did what I had been taught to do. I had seen plenty of people who could not move an arm or leg. They were mostly people who had suffered broken arms and legs and who had just had the cast removed. I had, in school, seen a few stroke cases, and we had been taught to treat them in the same way. So I began vigorously and enthusiastically to heat, to massage, and to move the joints in his paralyzed arm and leg.

His family watched me in what was, I became increasingly aware, puzzled silence. After a half-hour during which his son, his two daughters, and his wife had several whispered conversations, his elder daughter, prodded by the others, finally dared to ask a question.

"We don't understand what you are doing," she ventured.

"Well," I responded magnanimously, delighted that the strained silences and whispered conferences had come to an end, "just ask me, ask me anything you like. I'd be glad to explain to you."

I was simply bursting with inner confidence, based on hard-won knowledge of every muscle in the body as well as its origin, insertion, blood supply, and innervation.

"The doctor said something had happened to Dad's brain right here," she said timidly, pointing to a spot about three inches above his left ear.

"That is absolutely right," I said with complete finality. "A blood clot lodged in your dad's brain at just that point and that's just exactly what a stroke is."

"Then why," she asked, "are you rubbing his arm and leg?"

There followed a brief but thunderous silence. What I said to that poor and ignorant family was in every way inevitable. I was right out of school and filled to the very brim with modern knowledge and erudition. Indeed I was brimming over.

When I think of it now, which I do often, I burn with embarrassment.

"Oh," I said, "I couldn't possibly explain that to you. You have to go to school for years to understand that." It wasn't as terrible that I said it as it was that I believed it.

Who in the world in my position would have dared wonder whether my learned professors could have been so wrong and this poor, uneducated family could have been so right?

What I said to them, I still believe was inevitable. But if only, riding home in my car, I had *asked myself* exactly the same question that they had asked me, namely, *why* in fact I was rubbing his arm and leg, we would have saved more than *seven* years.

I sometimes wonder where our work would have been today if we had known the truth seven years sooner, and my mind boggles at the thought. I know that a severely brain-injured child coming to The Institutes today has a vastly improved chance over a similar child who came seven years ago. I have an extremely active imagination, but I cannot for the life of me imagine what our world of brain-injured children will be like seven years hence. All I'm sure of is that we will know even more than we know today and be able to do more for more children.

But, unhappily, I did not ask myself why I was rubbing his arm and leg. I just continued to do so. I did so three times a week for the next fifteen months at the end of which time he was fifteen months older—but not even a little bit better. There was no real reason why he should have been better. What I was doing to him had a great deal to do with his symptoms, but it had almost nothing to do with the cause of his problem, which was in his brain.

Somebody said once that ignorance did not consist so much of not knowing anything as it consisted of knowing so many things that aren't true.

That family was a perfect example of the former, and I was a perfect example of the latter.

Since I did exactly the same thing for my thirty-one other stroke cases as I had done for the old man, none of them got well either.

Perhaps I am too hard on myself and on those days because one terribly important advance had been made. Prior to World War II stroke cases had been kept in bed since virtually everybody believed that it was physical exertion which had caused the stroke in the first place and that the slightest physical exertion would cause another one. Because the patients remained in bed they very quickly developed hypostatic pneumonia or urinary tract infections as a result of immobility and then they died—not of a subsequent stroke, as almost everyone took for granted, but of hypostatic pneumonia or urinary tract infection.

Back in 1940, one of my relatively young stroke cases had decided that he would rather get out of bed and take his chance on dying than staying in bed and living. He absolutely insisted that I try to walk him. His doctor agreed to accept the terrible risk of letting the patient get out of bed. We did so and he improved vastly. We soon satisfied ourselves that it was the immobility itself that was killing people. So it was that in late 1940 and in 1941 we had gotten a half dozen patients out of bed into chairs. Moreover we had "walked" them around supported by two people. The more activity we had imposed on them, the healthier they had become.

Now instead of dying quickly they lived for years and years. But since few if any actually learned to walk or talk this only meant that they had more years in which to be depressed, despondent, morose, or even suicidal.

These were the years of my discontent. I was now seeing five patients a day. Since each patient required about three hours of my time, it made a long day.

I massaged their paralyzed arms and legs, I used infrared lamps or hot packs or diathermy on their arms and legs to speed up their circulation. I moved all their joints in arm and leg over and over again to *exercise them*, although I always noted with a vague feeling of uneasiness that after I finished vigorously exercising a patient it was I rather than the patient who was tired. And why not? It was in each case I who had done the work. Following this bed treatment I would get the patient up and *walk* him around the room. At least after this walking we were both puffing. Finally, I would spend a long time just talking to the patient cheerfully pointing out how much farther we *walked* each day, discussing the news of the day. This was very difficult if the patient had a speech problem and I had to make a single conversation seem to be a two-sided one. I noted with concern that this business of cheering the patient up seemed to be the most effective thing I was doing. The patients looked forward with apprehension to my treatment but with pleasure to my visit, which roused them temporarily from their depression.

I also noted with distress that it became ever more difficult to pull them out of despair as the hopelessness of their individual situations became clearer and clearer to them.

There was an additional reason why these brain-injured patients had come more and more strongly to rely on me. This was that almost everyone else, including the people who loved them most, believed (covertly or even overtly) that they were either insane or mentally deficient.

I, on the other hand, living as I did with thirty-one *different* patients, had a unique opportunity to observe them.

Strangely enough, the more I observed these brain-injured patients with their agonizing frustrations over not being able to walk or talk, the more my opinion ran contrary to everyone else's. I found myself less and less able to believe them to be either feeble-minded or insane. The more time I spent in intimate contact with them the more I became convinced that they were not only intelligent human beings but also extremely sensitive ones and this despite some apparently peculiar patterns of behavior. Indeed, I gradually became convinced that highly intelligent human beings were more likely to have strokes than less-intelligent ones and that they retained that intelligence after the stroke although they were frequently terribly frustrated by being unable to express it.

It was obvious to these patients that I was deeply sympathetic to their problem and that I, and sometimes I alone, knew them to be intelligent and sensitive. This increased their dependency upon me to dispel their gathering gloom. It also increased tremendously the emotional strain that I was experiencing in the losing battle to keep spirits high. My patients saw ever more clearly the hopelessness of their situation, and so did I.

As it became more and more difficult to dispel their despair I began to feel a despair of my own and to ask myself if I had really done them, or the world, or myself a favor when by getting them up I had increased their life expectancy but done nothing to decrease their frustration.

By now the practice of getting stroke cases out of bed was becoming reasonably widespread, so that now there were tens of thousands of people who had been brain-injured by strokes who were not going to die but who were not going to regain much function either.

My patients spent the better part of each day crying, and more and more, I spent the better part of each night wanting to cry, and on occasion I did so.

It was almost good news when a family called to say, "We wanted to tell you that Mother died this morning and to say how grateful we are to you. Your visits were the high points in her life. They were about the only high points in her life."

Then I would say, "Isn't that nice. I'm glad her problems are finally over."

Then they would say, "Yes, we wanted you to know."

They were real *Alice in Wonderland* conversations, where life becomes problem and death becomes solution.

I was extremely busy, very much in demand, with my practice of stroke cases growing larger every day. I was possibly the most successful therapist around. I was certainly the busiest young therapist in the county. I prospered.

It was the absolute low point of my entire life.

4

A RESEARCH TEAM BEGINS
TO SHAPE UP, 1947 TO 1950

I had not set eyes on Temple Fay, since a few days before Pearl Harbor six years earlier. I had in truth avoided him and I had done so rather consciously. The time I had spent with Fay before the war had been extremely rewarding—but it had also been expensive. All the time I had spent in his operating room was time that I could not be seeing patients, and nobody paid me for learning neurophysiology.

I had always considered it in exactly the opposite way. I had always considered it a superb postgraduate education for which I had paid not a cent of tuition. I would have considered myself lucky if I had had to pay a huge tuition. I had been privileged and I knew it.

Still, after the war I had avoided seeing Fay because a huge change had taken place. I was no longer a blithe twenty-two-year-old given to spending his spare time hanging around neurosurgical operating suites. Quite to the contrary and, I might add, in many ways much to my own astonishment, I was now a responsible married man much devoted to spending every non-working moment hanging around my wife, Katie, and my son, Bruce, age one and a half.

I had met Katie first when she was a child only eight years old and when I was twelve and therefore practically in my teens. She was the pain-in-the-neck little sister of my closest friend, Ray Massingham, who was actually thirteen and therefore actually in his teens.

It was natural that she would therefore become practically my own pain-in-the-neck little sister, and so she remained when I had gone marching off to war.

At Christmas time of 1942 I returned home from the African theater a lean, hard-bitten, bronzed twenty-three-year-old sergeant who had been sent home to be made an infantry second lieutenant. Then, quite as in romantic novels, I met my pain-in-the-neck practically little sister who had suddenly become eighteen years old and who was now a student nurse at Abington Hospital. We were married just before I went back overseas and just before she graduated from nursing school. Bruce was born in the year following my postwar discharge.

As a happily married man I had purposely avoided seeing Fay since I did not wish again to be hypnotized by him and by his work.

In 1947 I was attending a medical convention where I had hoped to learn something useful about stroke patients—but in fact had learned nothing—and where it had occurred to me that I might just run into Fay and get myself hypnotized all over again. I was leaving and congratulating myself on not meeting Fay when I met Fay.

He had me instantly.

I knew the minute he looked at me and through me with those penetrating eyes that if he had plans for me, I was a gone goose. He had made quite a fuss about my war record of which he had heard and said that he was pleased to see me. When he asked me what I was doing I could not resist telling him about my problem with my unique practice in *strokes*. After all, I had not the slightest question that this rather frightening genius knew more about the brain than anyone alive.

He listened to me quite closely and carefully. Fay, despite his genius (or perhaps because of it) was ordinarily a very poor listener, but at any rate he heard me through.

He told me that he too was quite interested in stroke cases and that indeed he had some very good ideas about the treatment of such cases. He had now left Temple University Medical School inasmuch as his brilliant and pioneering work in human refrigeration had become far too controversial for him to be able to remain within the walls of any normal institution of what is solemnly called "higher education."

I cannot resist a very small aside. Today there is no modern hospital anywhere on earth which does not daily use human refrigeration, or hypothermia, in one form or another—usually in many forms—to save human lives, to ease pain, and in other ways to improve the human condition. Hypothermia is the artificial lowering of body temperature in order to slow physiologic processes during surgery or for therapeutic purposes.

There is not the slightest question that Temple Fay is the father of human refrigeration and pioneered it despite the bitter opposition, scorn, and ridicule that the "recognized experts" so often heap upon any advance which they see as undermining their expertise.

He walked without fear in the pathway that had been trod by virtually every medical pioneer before him.

Ignaz Philipp Semmelweis, for example, had been driven to insanity by the prejudiced hostility of his colleagues after he proposed that physicians should wash their hands in a solution of *chlorina liquida* before delivering babies in order to prevent puerperal fever. (In the clinics of that time the mortality rate ran from *10 to 50 or 75 percent among obstetrical patients.*) Semmelweis died in 1865, unvindicated in the eyes of many.

Another young man would begin an experiment in the very year that Semmelweis died which would vindicate Semmelweis posthumously and revolutionize the science of surgery. Indeed, surgery could hardly have been called a science with the horrifying death toll it carried until Joseph Lister introduced antiseptic surgery. Lord Lister died in 1912 but even his right to be called "Your Lordship" did not save him from the ridicule of his fellow surgeons who condemned him for advocating sterile operating room conditions and opposing what they termed *laudable pus.*

Fay with his human refrigeration, or "hypothermia," was as ridiculed and condemned by his medical colleagues as were Semmelweis, Lord Lister, and a score of other medical greats both before and since their time.

I remember that Fay's first human refrigeration machine used to sit in an old barn at The Institutes covered with dirt and pigeon dung and there it remained until he died. Today it is in the Smithsonian Institution where it properly belongs in belated recognition of the acclaim to which he had always been entitled.

Someone has said, brilliantly and succinctly, that "The first condition for immortality—is death." It is indeed.

But this was 1947 and Fay was a long, long way from his death and here I was, spellbound by him as I had been years before.

He had left Temple University in 1943 and moved his office to a spot near his home in the beautiful north Philadelphia suburb called Chestnut Hill. Here in a beautiful old suburban home he had founded an institution called, The Neurophysical Rehabilitation Center. Even the name was typical of Fay. It would be another quarter of a century before any but the brightest of his colleagues would begin to understand what that name really meant.

Fay was already working with several physical therapists of prominence, among them Milwood Mathers, Irene Neider (my boss and chief from Temple Hospital days), Roy Evans, a friend and classmate, and that most regal and charming of physical therapists, Eleanor Borden, whom I had known from Temple University days and who would one day join our team to spend the rest of her splendid life with us.

At any rate, Fay invited me to visit him to see what he termed some "new and exciting developments." It was all that I could do to keep from following him then and there as the children had followed the Pied Piper.

Fay was blessed with rare genius of a type that occurs only about once each century in any given field, but he paid for the blessing with a curse most dreadful.

It was Fay's fate not alone to be *misunderstood*, as is the case with almost all geniuses, but worse than that to be *un-understood*. It took me many years to understand more than a fraction of what Fay was saying. The reason for this I now realize was quite simple. When Fay was making every effort to speak simply and basically (which happened sometimes) he would usually still be speaking over the heads of the rest of us. Fay at his lowest was quite simply higher than his colleagues at their highest. They were his colleagues but they were not his peers. In fact, he had no peers.

As controversial as Fay was all of his life, he virtually never made a speech or taught a class without a *Standing Room Only* situation occurring. I have many times seen Fay speak when large numbers of people could not even crowd into the room or auditorium where Fay lectured and who yet remained to listen to his voice without once laying eyes on him. The audience was invariably enthralled, and despite the most crowded and uncomfortable conditions there was almost always the deepest and most respectful silence when he spoke.

His eagerness afterward to learn how he had done was almost childlike.

"Did they appreciate it?" he would invariably ask on the way home. His eyes would sparkle with warmth and pleasure when I assured him that everyone had enjoyed it vastly and that he had held them spellbound (which was almost invariably the precise truth).

"That's very good because it's important that they understand," he would say.

I would then summon every ounce of my courage, take a deep breath and announce with all the firmness that I could muster, "Oh, they loved your speech, sir, but I don't think that they understood a word you said."

He never did really understand why almost no one understood what he was saying. It always seemed so clear to him.

I left Fay that day at the medical convention enthralled and frightened.

I was genuinely frustrated over my own ineffectiveness in helping my stroke patients and I wanted desperately to know what answers he might have, but I knew I could no longer afford to spend my time hanging around his operating room, what with a wife and family to provide for. On my own, I doubt I would have followed through on Fay's invitation. I was unaware, however, about Woody.

Woody (Milwood Mathers) was an extremely successful physical therapist who had been working with Fay in Chestnut Hill. He had, however, been approached by the Woods Schools to accept a position as the chief of their new department. The offer they had made him was an extraordinary one which he considered far too good to turn down. There was, however, a problem. He felt honor bound to continue his work with Fay until he found someone to take his place who was suitable to Dr. Fay.

I had been elected.

Woody had called me to make the grand announcement. I would not be working *for* Fay but rather *with* Fay. He would rent me office space in the beautiful Georgian building on Germantown Avenue in Chestnut Hill which he owned and which housed his office. He would then refer his patients needing rehabilitation to me. I would treat them and would have the privilege of joining him in the operating room and in daily consultation.

As sorely tempted as I was to learn from Fay, it was out of the question. I lived on the Main Line, which was a western suburb of Philadelphia, while Fay's office was fourteen miles away in Chestnut Hill, a northern suburb. It would require a few hours of driving time daily. I was very busy both in my office and in my home calls. I had bought a lovely home and drove a Cadillac. I was a confirmed young family man and well on the way to becoming a pillar of respectability in my community establishment. I suppose that those days were as close as ever I came or will ever come in my life to being part of any real establishment. I sometimes wonder idly what it would have been like to lead a quiet, respectable, don't-rock-the-boat, establishment kind of life.

But Woody persisted in calling me each week, and it was one of those embarrassing situations which is obvious to all parties. On the one hand I was obviously being complimented by both Woody and Fay himself, and I was truly flattered by their attention. Still I knew in some innate way that even listening to his proposition threatened that whole peaceful way of life into which I had grown and which (after the horrors, intense excitement, physical pain, incredible exhaustion, and acute discomfort of infantry combat) seemed so desirable by contrast.

I knew that what would happen to me if I visited Fay would change the entire course of my life. Why should I wish to change a life which was completely successful already?

Someone has said that conscience is that small part of you that feels so bad when everything else feels so good.

I wish now that I could say that the reason Woody finally got to me on the phone was because of my conscience. In conscience, I must say it was not. I finally acquiesced to Woody's importuning because he embarrassed me into doing so. I had each time pleaded being busy on every date he proposed for a meeting. On the final phone call he simply said that I could meet with Fay on the first date available to me.

Fay was too great a man and Woody far too nice a person for me to put it off any longer.

Dr. Fay's office was huge and impressive. It opened off a tremendous center hall. Just as I had feared, he was prepared to charm me into insensibility and fascinate me into mental flaccidity, which he promptly did.

We would have the opportunity to spend many hours working together (I loved that thought, but where would I *get* the hours). He would rent me the office across the hall for a very small rent (I was at that time paying no rent at all since my office was in my home). The office was very conveniently located for all the patients (but fourteen miles away from me and my present patients). He was sure I could earn more than a hundred dollars a week seeing his patients, which was a lot of money for a physical therapist (I was at that time earning more than twice that much seeing *my* patients).

It was a ridiculous situation for me and whether I liked it or not I simply had to refuse it for the sake of my family and myself.

"It sounds wonderful, sir. How soon can we begin?" I heard myself saying.

I tried at first to work in my new office from nine to five and to see my own patients all night long. It was physically exhausting, but that wasn't the reason my own practice soon began to disappear. For a month I strenuously resisted all temptation to be fascinated by Fay after five o'clock. But after a month this resolution went to hell in a basket. More and more I phoned Katie at five to tell her to cancel my first evening patient, then I phoned to cancel the first two patients. and it wasn't long before all of Dr. Fay's promises had come true.

I *was* spending hours each day in consultation with him (instead of seeing my own patients).

I *was* paying a small rent (as compared to none).

I *was* driving fourteen miles to my office (instead of walking across my own living room).

I *was* earning the hundred dollars a week he had promised (instead of more than twice as much).

I was scared and in certain ways much more frightened than I had ever been during the war. For now I was intellectually frightened. I had never been intellectually frightened before in my life; awed by great people perhaps, but not truly frightened. Petrified that Fay would ask me any one of innumerable neurological questions to which I did not know the answer. Frightened that he would expect me to have treatment answers I didn't have.

But for all of that, I was exhilarated. Excited beyond any excitement I had ever known because now I was intellectually excited for the first time in my life just as I was intellectually frightened for the first time in my life.

Fay led me mentally into fields which I scarcely knew existed, let alone knew anything about. For example, never had anything prepared me to believe that what had happened to early creatures millions upon millions of years earlier might have the slightest thing to do with how human beings behave. All of my professors, all doctors I had met until now, all of my own professional people were extremely pragmatic and so also was I inclined to be.

If someone had a painful shoulder and you applied *diathermy* to his shoulder, and if afterward he felt better, then that was a good enough reason to apply diathermy the next time a patient appeared with a pain in his shoulder. As to *why* putting diathermy on a sore shoulder might make it feel better and thus "cure" it, the simplest of explanations would suffice. It was because diathermy "heated" the internal tissues and everyone knew that "*heat*" was good for you because it speeded up circulation and things like that. It had always been a good enough explanation for "practical" people like me and my fellow therapists and all of the physician fathers who had taught us.

Nobody had taught us to ask questions such as, "Is 'heat' *good* for painful tissues or would our patients have gotten well anyway? Would they have gotten well *more quickly* without that heat? *Did* diathermy, in fact, heat internal tissues at all? Would *cold* possibly be good for painful tissues? Would it possibly be even *better* than heat if in truth heat was good at all?" Most important of all, nobody seriously asked the question "*Why?*"

Fay on the other hand was a master at asking "Why?" and this alone fascinated me. He made me think every instant I was with him, and nobody I had ever met before had made me think to anything like the degree that he made me think. Not only did he, in the end, force me to ask the question "Why?" of everything that I had ever been told and continued to be told, but he taught me that I had a whole endless world in which I might look for answers and that the only limit placed on me as to where those answers might be was the limit of my own knowledge—and he made me realize how very, very, very limited that knowledge was.

He made me realize that the answer to why my *stroke* patients rarely *walked*, almost never *talked* in a functional way, and absolutely *never* used their involved thumbs correctly might not exist in the muscles of the leg, the muscles of the tongue, or the muscles of the thumb. He taught me that the answer to those mysteries were not even to be found in the human being per se. He taught me to believe that those mysteries might be solved by our understanding of how the nervous system worked in a fifty-ton reptile—with a three-ounce brain—who had already been dead for millions of years and whose thunderous tread had not disturbed even the oldest of living things. But in order to look for answers to present human problems in creatures who had died long before the earliest human had existed, one had to know that such creatures had existed and had to know something about them. I alternated between wild hope at the new worlds his knowledge and genius opened to me and deep despair about all the things I didn't know.

I also alternated between getting to bed at midnight and not getting to bed at midnight, as Fay's demands on my time became greater. Even after going to bed, the discussions would often continue, as I poured out my heart and my exultations to my wife, Katie—and received yet other viewpoints and ideas from her in return. Katie had always been an immense help to me in the conduct of my own practice, and I found myself with constantly growing respect for the seemingly endless practical knowledge that she had acquired during her years as a student and graduate nurse. Of course, in addition to being confidante and colleague at 2 a.m., she was also appointments secretary and mother to our children, but before any feminist screams "Unfair" I cannot resist quoting Katie herself. When asked about her attitudes toward Women's Lib she said, "I have always felt myself to be superior to males and I see no reason to accept equality at this late date."

Although I had now lost my own practice, I did feel that something important was growing to replace it, namely, a new and improbable kind of research team consisting of Fay, the world-renowned expert on neur surgery; my wife, Katie, who contributed two oft-ignored viewpoints, those of nurse and mother; and myself, the physical therapist. We were shortly to enlarge the team by a fourth member, my brother, Dr. Robert Doman, who was just about to be released by the U. S. Army Medical Corps.

Dr. Fay had been feeling the need of recruiting a young physician he could mold early into his way of thinking regarding brain injury.

Fay himself was a neurologist and a neurosurgeon.

So it was not a young neurologist that Fay was looking for but rather some cross between a neurosurgeon and an orthopedist with a strong dash of physical therapist thrown in.

Precisely such a creature had just begun to emerge.

These new and strange creatures were called *physiatrists*. There were in the whole world only a handful of them. The few that existed were graduate M.D.s who had specialized in physical medicine and rehabilitation. Following their internship these physiatrists had to serve a residency as stringent and as long as a brain surgeon or any other specialist. Physical medicine and rehabilitation were themselves new terms in the 1940s.

The field of physical medicine was a gathering together of the three primary therapies used to restore function to non-functioning patients (rehabilitation). These therapies were physical therapy, speech therapy, and occupational therapy. The physiatrist was trained in all these as well as in orthopedics, neurology, and general medicine.

A physiatrist then would meet Fay's needs beautifully.

These physiatrists were being eagerly sought by every large hospital since, as a product of the war, new departments called "Rehabilitation" Departments were now a sign of a very modern and advanced hospital. Such departments were very rare, but most such departments were run by physical therapists because physiatrists were even more rare.

My brother, Bob, was such a physiatrist. We managed to get him before any of the many medical schools in Philadelphia could lay hands on him for three reasons:

1. He was eager to work with children, and Fay saw many children.
2. He was eager to learn from Fay himself.
3. He was my brother.

So by the end of the 1940s there were four permanent team members, Fay and three Domans, the last of them Robert J. Doman, M.D., Diplomate, American Board of Physical Medicine and Rehabilitation, and lately Captain U. S. Army Medical Corps.

Bob was a perfect addition to the team not only because he was a physiatrist but because of his temperament. He was the perfect choice to balance me. I was always extremely fond of Bob and we always had a typical "Jack Sprat" relationship with each other. While I am inclined to be quick to enthusiasm—quick to embrace ideas and inclined to solve problems by overwhelming them by immediate, direct, and energetic action—Bob on the other hand was inclined to be more conservative, inclined toward an initial attitude of scientific suspicion toward new ideas, and inclined to attack problems with deliberate regard. I always was inclined to pull my brother along; he was always inclined toward preventing me from injuring myself in pratfalls.

Lest, in describing my brother's more studious characteristics, I make him sound stuffy, let me quickly point out that Bob was instantly beloved of all children—I have watched while Philadelphia children flocked to him, and have also seen him go down under a pile of parka-clad Eskimo kids in the Arctic, and several lapsful of pre-stone age Indian children in the jungles of Brazil's Mato Grosso.

Children the world over took to Bob. He was himself, in the nicest way, childlike. I never saw a kid who got in the pool sooner than Bob or out later.

5

A CATCH-AS-CATCH-CAN
ORGANIZATION

It was a loose organization if one could call it an organization at all.
Fay's Neurophysical Rehabilitation Center was avant-garde in the
extreme. Too avant-garde. It was a patient success but an economic failure, and not even that genius, Fay, was able to act as medical director,
chief, neurosurgeon, chief executive officer, director, and administrator,
all simultaneously.

In the end Fay's dream institute, born a quarter century too soon, died.
The buildings were sold to become a nursing home, although some of
Fay's patients remained and he agreed to continue to see them. So did I.
Dr. Fay, Bob, and I had our offices together in Fay's handsome Georgian
building. I saw Dr. Fay's patients and Bob's as well. Our days began often
in the operating room looking again at beautiful live, throbbing, coral-colored human brains. Our afternoons we spent together seeing patients in
each other's offices or at the bedsides in various hospitals where we
served as staff members. I often saw patients with Fay at the United States
Naval Hospital in South Philadelphia or at the Hospital of The Women's
Medical College or at Chestnut Hill Hospital, where Fay now did most of
his surgery. We saw clinic patients in many hospitals and we saw private
patients in our offices, and I saw private patients in their homes as well.
We saw children and we saw adults.

One thing our patients had in common was that they were all brain-
injured (although we had not yet learned to call them that). Another thing
they had in common was that, except for the acute surgical problems on
which Dr. Fay operated, nobody ever got well. And this was no less discouraging because Fay had such fascinating theories about them.

We had actually founded what is today called a rehabilitation team,
although in those days neither of those words was yet fashionable. Neither
did we think of ourselves as anything so fancy as a rehabilitation team. I

31

think really we thought of ourselves a good deal more simply and perhaps also a good deal more clearly. We saw ourselves as precisely what we were—a small but growing group of people each of whom was charged with responsibility for dealing with some phase of the problem of hurt children. Each of us was convinced he was failing the responsibility. It was for that very reason we had gotten together to form a sort of convoy to protect us from our mutual failures. Today that is generally called a rehabilitation team.

When we had begun our work together we had never seen or heard of a single severely brain-injured child who had ever gotten well. Nor did we meet anyone who claimed he had ever heard of such a child. Indeed, it is still possible to find professional people who become enraged at the mere suggestion that brain-injured children may be made to function.

If a man is going to choose a field in which to work, he cannot possibly pick a more promising field than one in which the success rate is zero and the failure rate is 100 percent. Any slight change he can manage to bring about will of necessity be for the better. We had such a field.

Taken together we were seeing perhaps two hundred and fifty patients privately and more in clinics. All of the time we were learning, although as yet there did not appear to be the slightest pattern to this learning.

Perhaps the most valuable time of all was that which we spent together in the evenings after dinner, generally right in the kitchen of one of our houses. These sessions sometimes went on until it was daylight or until there was no more coffee. They were great sessions. They still are.

1950 to 1960

DECADE OF DISCOVERY

6

A JOURNEY THROUGH FAILURE

By 1950 we had come to a moment of truth. By that time we had been treating a group of one hundred brain-injured children for a number of years. The children themselves ranged in age from one to nineteen years. They represented the types of brain injury that we felt we understood, as well as many types that we were quite aware we did not understand.

Many different methods of treating the disabled children were used then. Generally, a technique enjoyed almost universal acceptance for a period, only to fade a little as a new technique and a new hope was introduced and gained ground. The fact that so many different techniques existed did not mean that any of them were successful; indeed, it meant quite the reverse. The multiplicity of techniques in use was not a reflection of the amount of information available, but rather a reflection of the intensity of the search for a *better* technique.

The methods then in use included such treatments as heat (infrared lamps, diathermy machines, etc.) and massage of the affected limbs; exercise; orthopedic surgery to transplant muscles or to change bone structure to achieve various mechanical results; and electrical stimulation to help maintain paralyzed muscles.

Most institutions which treated brain-injured children used some combination of, or all of, the methods described.

Our team members were also using all of the methods described with great intensity, great dedication, and great energy; yet hope was beginning to die as the years went by and few results could be seen.

The team decided it was time to evaluate honestly the results of our work. We decided that nothing but the brain-injured child himself should remain sacred. We carefully evaluated the one hundred brain-injured children.

The results of this study proved how tragically inadequate were our methods. For one thing, it quickly became obvious that we had never graduated a single child as being well. If one were conducting a school from which no one ever graduated, eventually the question would have to be asked, "Is this school achieving its purpose?" Quite obviously our school was not.

Our hundred children fell essentially into three categories: (1) those children who were *better* following two or three years of treatment, (2) those children who remained essentially *unchanged*, (3) those children who were actually *worse*.

First we looked hopefully at the best group, those children who had improved, to see *how much* they had improved. We found our reports full of such statements as, "Johnny can now raise his head better." "Mary is less spastic." "Billy's balance is better." It was rather obvious that if it had taken two or three years of treatment, two or three times a week, to raise his head "better," Johnny was going to be an old man by the time Johnny could walk, and such treatment was not effective. So the children who were better were not better in any way that mattered. Many of the children had not improved at all. And, worst of all, many of the children were actually *worse*. This latter group of children was large, and there was no question about it, they were actually worse.

With a heavy heart, the team reviewed the question of why all this was so and what to do next. Our egos bruised by the tragedy of these results, we began to search for consolation, any hope, any reason that would justify the years of hard work we had spent on such children. An obvious answer presented itself. If the results of our work were slight, think what shape the children would be in if we had not treated them at all. Obviously, they would be worse. Much worse. We had at least helped some of them maintain the status quo.

Sincerely believing that this was so, we looked for a way to confirm it. There was a way. Over the years we had seen and evaluated many children who did not return for treatment. Mostly they were children who were in some way underprivileged. Some were children whose parents could not afford even our modest charges. Others were children whose parents simply did not care enough to undertake treatment. Searching our records, we found the names of those children and went to the parents, asking permission to evaluate the children again without charge so we might determine whether these children who had remained without treatment had indeed become worse.

We came to an absolutely astonishing conclusion. The children who had been without treatment were almost overwhelmingly *better* than the children we had treated! Among the untreated group of children, the better children had made more improvement than the best children in our group and the worst were not as bad as our own children who had actually gotten worse. The evidence was overwhelming. Not only was our work ineffective, but the children who had been without treatment were better than our children whom we had treated so long and so hard.

We faced a potentially tragic decision. Obviously, we could not justify continuing to treat the children if treated children did not do as well as untreated children. We had two choices. We could either stop treating children altogether and admit that all of our collective knowledge and work was of no avail, or we could find better answers.

We were unwilling to stop treating children. This meant we would have to start again at the beginning, on the assumption that we knew nothing. Indeed, was that not true?

Now each member of the team in turn was called upon to defend his methods and his reasons for using them. Each of the various specialists within the group had to stand still while the remainder of the group tore his field, his background, his techniques, and indeed all of his beliefs to rather bloody shreds, for we had agreed initially that nothing from the past would be held sacred except the brain-injured child himself.

"What," the team asked the physical therapists, "do you do and why do you do it?" The physical therapist (me) explained that he massaged arms and legs, that he gave corrective exercises to arms and legs, either in individual muscle groups or very holistically, that he did something called muscle re-education, and a team member asked, "Why do you do this to brain-injured children?" When the essential elements of his answer were finally bared, it could be said that he did these things for two reasons. First, because he had been taught to do so in school, and second, because physical therapists had always done those things. Perhaps, if one is doing what he has always done, because he has always done it, and is achieving splendid results, he can justify his work. But if he is doing what he has always done because he has always done it and the results are very bad indeed, in fact, worse than the results if nothing is done, he will have a hard time defending himself.

As each of the other team members in turn got up to defend his work, his defense was the same: He was doing what he did because he had been taught to do it and because he had always done it.

Again the team began long sessions of debate. The new series of discussions, however, had a new and somewhat frightening intensity—an intensity that bordered on anger and indeed occasionally erupted into brief but furious quarrels. Only the mutual respect and admiration which the group had for each other prevented its dissolution. In short, the happy, enjoyable scientific discussions of good friends were ended and would not return until this specific question had been answered. For now we were milling about in the midst of a herd of sacred cows, and when a team member pushed a sacred cow aside, in order to get a clearer view of the world around the herd, he found he had best beware that the team's worshiper of that particular cow was not handled too brusquely.

It must, surely, be a difficult time for an African tribesman who has always worshiped the sun when he is being converted to a new and very different religion. Certainly there must come a time, a frightening and difficult time, when he is sure only that the sun is not the Deity but is not at all positive where or who the Deity is. Our team was in a very similar position. We knew with certainty the old ways didn't work, but we didn't know what would work.

We started again by looking at the methods of treatment we had been using and asking ourselves what they had in common. Certainly there seemed a very wide gap between massage, heat, and exercise at one end of the spectrum and orthopedic surgery, bracing, crutches, casts, psychological treatment, and so on at the other end. They had one thing in common, however. With them, every child in the group was being treated from his neck down, while every child in the group actually had his problem from the neck up. In short, we were treating everybody where his problem was not and nobody where his problem was.

We had to conclude that if one was to treat a brain-injured person, one would have to treat the injured brain, wherein lay the cause, rather than the body where the symptoms were reflected. Where did we go from here? Our decision was to begin at the beginning, throw out all existing knowledge and ask ourselves a very basic question: What were we trying to do? Obviously, the answer to this question was that we were trying to *reproduce normal.* Therefore, the only question remaining was: What was normal? To this question we now directed our efforts.

7

WE SEEK HELP AND SO WE GROW

The question of what was normal proved to be a monumental one. In truth, it was a question we were not capable of tackling alone. There were many normals to be considered. All of us were predominantly expert in physical functions such as walking and hand use; we knew little of the fields of speech, psychology, or education.

Help came first from a speech therapist: Dr. Martin Palmer, the founder and director of The Institutes for Logopedics at the University of Wichita. Palmer was an extraordinary man—physically huge, intellectually brilliant, and in many ways as learned as Fay. He knew a very great deal about the human brain and this was what made him astonishing in a day when most speech therapists were orators who taught children how to project their voices. The few speech therapists who concerned themselves with medical problems believed that if a human being was speechless then he was either an idiot or had something wrong with his tongue.

Palmer and Fay were extraordinarily good friends considering that they were both unquestionably geniuses and that Fay was not a man who had many friends since he had virtually no social life. Although Palmer was not an M.D., Fay invited him into the operating room to share his knowledge of the brain. Fay, working from brain pathology which he saw in the operating room, could determine what speech symptoms a patient would have, while Palmer, working from a patient's speech symptoms, could tell what the patient's brain pathology would be. Although I was extremely unsure of myself, I was beginning, under the tutelage of both of them, to be able to do it both ways not only with speech problems but with other physical symptoms.

Martin Palmer flew in from Kansas at least once a month to join us in a brain-storming session. I was personally much impressed with Martin Palmer and his tremendous knowledge. He had a charming habit of saying something extremely scholarly, which was so erudite that I would have to strain to even follow the thought, and then he would look directly into my eyes and say, "Hmmmm?" Since the manner in which he said it left the clear impression that he was asking whether I shared his view (when in truth I barely understood it), I was deeply flattered.

We needed Martin Palmer full time if we were to answer our question as to what normal was. This was patently impossible, so Dr. Palmer did the next best thing. He sent to Philadelphia his most trusted student, a very young midwesterner named Claude Cheek. He was to supply invaluable information for several years as part of the team. Since his relationship to Martin Palmer was in many ways similar to my own with Fay, we had a great deal to teach each other. He was the fifth team member.

As for the psychological and educational aspects of the slowly growing team, these were supplied by Carl Delacato, who was to become my closest colleague for the next twenty years or more. So closely would our names become associated in the future that more than once in more than one nation on more than one lecture platform I would be introduced as Dr. Doman Delacato.

Carl Delacato had just gotten his doctorate at my old school, the University of Pennsylvania, and was the headmaster of the middle school at a local private school. We had heard that he was a psychologist, that he was an educator, and that he was extremely bright.

We issued him an invitation to visit us and he accepted. It was now 1952. Delacato was not yet quite thirty. Cheek was just past thirty and I was thirty-two.

Delacato brought yet another dimension to the team. Like my brother he was bright, mild, and scholarly. Unlike either of us, he brought training and experience focused on the psychological and educational side of the normal child.

We could now find within the team wide and deep expertise of the physical, neurological, psychological, and educational facets of normal and abnormal newborns, school children, and adults.

Since we each knew our own fields reasonably well by now, we proved to be treasure houses of knowledge for each other. We made an exciting, stimulating, and productive combination. For the next ten or fifteen years we fed each other's happy hunger. We did so in the brain-storming sessions over coffee; we did so on long walks. We taught each other in railroad stations and in airports, in classrooms, waiting rooms, and operating rooms. We would in the future do so in South American jungles, African deserts, Arctic wastes, and other unlikely places. We had a lot to talk about and there is no question that the new knowledge bred by this cross-fertilization was more than the sum of our individual knowledge. This was a case where one plus one did not equal two, but instead something a good deal more like ten.

A typical conversation went something like this:

GLENN: "…and so quite naturally the arm won't work."

CARL: "What did you say?"

GLENN: "Well, I don't know, I guess I said, 'So naturally the arm wouldn't work.' Why?"

CARL: "My God, is that true?"

GLENN: "Why, sure it's true. Everybody knows that."

CARL: "Like hell they do—psychologists don't know that! Why if that's true, we could. . ." etc., etc.

or

CARL: "So following Pavlov, the psychologists spent huge amounts of time carefully recording data about reflexes, time lag between stimulus and response and…"

GLENN: "The hell you say. Did they really?"

CARL: "Did who really what?"

GLENN: "The psychologists. Did they really record those data about reflexes?"

CARL: "Sure, tons of it, but everybody knows that."

GLENN: "My people don't! Good Lord, Carl, the therapists barely know that reflexes exist, never mind believing that reflexes have anything to do with their lives or their patients. But if the psychologists have already done this stuff and you can get your hands on it, we'll save years of work. . ." etc., etc.

And so it went for fifteen years or more until each of us had augmented his own expertise with that of every other member of the team.

Carl was the sixth team member.

The seventh team member was stately Eleanor Borden, already in her sixties and older than Fay, with the keenest humor and a true love for people. Eleanor was a physical therapist with the mind of a sixty-year-old and the courage and imagination of a twenty-year-old. She worked every day well into her eighties, when she died. She used to tell Delacato to stand up straight every time she saw him.

The team now grew ever more rapidly as other physicians and therapists, fascinated by the work, came to see and stayed to work.

We were ready to tackle the first positive problem.

What, indeed, was normal?

8

THE SEARCH FOR NORMALITY

In the beginning we sought particularly to understand normal walking and normal talking, since our children, generally speaking, could neither walk nor talk, or lacked at least one of these abilities. It was particularly the period from birth to twelve or eighteen months of age, when the normal child learns to walk and talk, that we wanted to study.

Our study began as most studies do, with a search through the medical literature to learn what had been recorded up to that time on the subject. We were astonished. Having braced ourselves for countless hours of studying the voluminous literature we expected to find, we were dumfounded to discover that virtually nothing had been said on the subject! Gesell was all there was. It appeared that Gesell was perhaps the first man in all of recorded medicine to make his life's work the study of the normal child.

Certain it was that Gesell had studied the well child on a broad scale for that day, not only his movement and speech but also his social growth, etc. However, Gesell had not attempted essentially to *explain* the child's growth but instead had devoted himself to being a careful *observer* of the child and how he grew. But our group had a more focused interest. Where Gesell recorded *when* the child learned to move and speak, we wanted to know *how* he did it, and *why* he did it. We wanted to isolate those factors *significant* to the child's growth. Clearly, we had to seek these answers on our own.

In an initial attempt to do this, the team went first to those people who might be expected to know, "How," we asked the experts, "does a child grow?" "What are the factors necessary to his growth?" We asked pediatricians, therapists, nurses, obstetricians, and all the other specialists who were concerned with the growth of the well child. We were surprised and distressed by the lack of knowledge we encountered, but, on reflection, the reasons for this were fairly obvious. Rarely did the people consulted ever *see* a well child. Quite obviously the reason for taking a child to a doctor, nurse, or therapist is that the child is not well. Thus, the people consulted saw primarily sick children and rarely well ones. Consequently, we found in the literature and in our interviews with professionals that much information existed relative to an unwell child, but very little existed about the well child and why he grows as he does. We realized finally that mothers knew most about this subject. Even they were vague, however, as to the exact times that a child did what he did, and what was significant in what he did.

We decided to go to the source, the infants themselves. The world became our laboratory and new babies our most precious clinical material. We tackled walking first. If someone's cousin was having a baby, we went to that cousin and sought permission to look at the child carefully from the moment he was born until he learned to walk. What, we asked ourselves, were the things which, if they were removed from a child, or denied him, would prevent walking? What were the things which if given to the child in abundance, would speed his walking? We studied many, many newborn *well* children.

After several fascinating years of study, we knew we had rediscovered the pathway we had individually trod as babies. We also came to feel that we understood this pathway. In the dark and formerly unpromising tunnel we were beginning to see a little light.

Most particularly was it evident that this road of growth which the baby followed to become a human being in the full sense of the term was both a very ancient road and a very well-defined one. This road, it was interesting to note, permitted not the slightest variance. There were no detours, no crossroads, no intersections, nothing that changed along the way. It was an unvarying road, which every well child followed in the process of growing up. Anyone who could observe carefully could learn how a well baby learned to walk and then run.

When all extraneous factors, all those things not vital to walking and running, were removed, the essential facts that remained were these. Along the road there were five terribly important stages. The first stage began at birth, when the baby was able to move his limbs and body but was not able to use these motions to move his body from place to place. This we called, "Movement Without Mobility." (See Figure 1.)

The second stage occurred later when the baby learned that by moving his arms and legs in a certain manner with his stomach pressed to the floor, he could move from Point A to Point B. This we called "Crawling." (See Figure 2.)

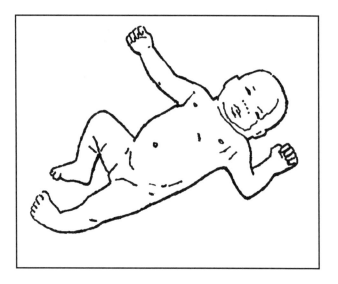

FIGURE 1

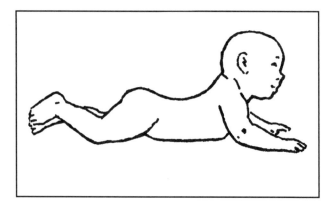

FIGURE 2

Sometime later, stage three occurred, when the baby learned to defy gravity for the first time and to get up on his hands and knees and move across the floor in this easier, but more skilled, manner. This we called "Creeping." (See Figure 3.)

The next significant stage occurred when baby learned to get up on his hind legs and walk, and this, of course, we called "Walking." (See Figure 4.)

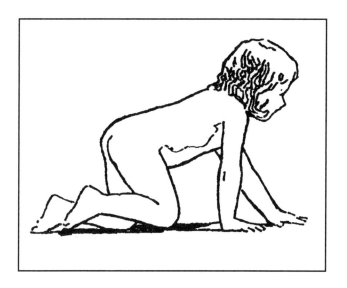

FIGURE 3

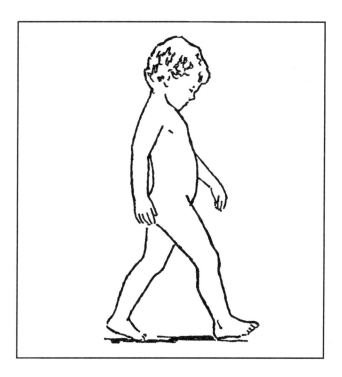

FIGURE 4

FIGURE 5

The last significant stage occurred when the tiny child accelerated his walking into a trot. As his balance and coordination improved, eventually he began to run. Running is distinguished from walking because there is a brief moment when both feet leave the ground simultaneously and the child "flies". (See Figure 5.)

There is no hope of understanding the importance of what this book has to say unless the reader understands the full significance of these five things. If we viewed these five stages as schools, that is to say, if we looked at stage one—that of moving arms and legs and body without mobility—as kindergarten, if we looked at stage two—crawling—as grammar school, if we looked at stage three—creeping
—as high school, if we looked at stage four—walking—as college, and then looked at stage five—that of running—as graduate school, we could see the importance of those factors. No child ever misses an entire school; no child goes to high school before he completes grammar school.

There is an ancient saying that you have to creep before you can walk. We now felt safe in saying that you have to walk before you run, you have to crawl on your belly before you can creep on hands and knees, and that you have to learn how to move your arms and legs in the air before you can move them for crawling purposes.

We became firmly convinced that no well child ever missed a stage along this road, and we became convinced of this, despite the fact that mothers sometimes reported that their children did not crawl. However, when such a mother was asked, "Mother, do you mean that this child simply lay in his crib or pushed himself on the floor until one day he jumped to his feet and then walked?" Mother generally reconsidered and allowed as how the child had crawled for a short period of time. While there was no way to travel this road without passing each and every milepost, there was indeed a difference in time factors. Some children would spend ten months in the crawling stage and two months in the creeping stage while other children spent two months in the crawling stage and ten months in the creeping stage. However, always these four significant stages occurred in the same sequence.

Along the ancient road there were no detours for the well child. So convinced did the team become of this that we also became convinced of two other factors.

First, we became convinced that if an otherwise well child were to miss, for any reason, any stage along this road that child would not be normal and would not learn to walk until given the opportunity to complete the missed stage. We were persuaded, and we still are, that if one took a well child and suspended him by some sort of sling device in midair when he was born and fed him and cared for him until he was twelve months of age and then placed that child on the floor and said, "*Walk*, because you're twelve months of age and this is the age at which well children walk," that the child would, in fact, not walk, but would instead first move arms, legs, and body; second, crawl; third, creep; fourth, walk; and fifth and last, run—and that, therefore, this was not a mere chronology of events but instead was a planned road in which each step was necessary to the subsequent step.

Second, we became convinced that if any of these basic stages were merely slighted, rather than wholly skipped, as for example in the case of a child who had begun to walk before he had crept *enough*, there would be adverse consequences such as poor coordination, failure to become wholly right-handed or wholly left-handed, failure to develop normal hemispheric dominance in matters of speech, failure in reading and spelling, etc. Crawling and creeping, it began to appear, were essential stages in the programming of the brain, stages in which the two hemispheres of the brain learned how to work together.

To this day, we are convinced that when we have seen a child who did not go through each of the major stages in the order in which they are listed, however briefly they may have remained in a stage, we have seen a child who later on gave evidence of having a major or a minor neurological problem.

Now we had our first piece of certain knowledge. We knew what normal was, at least so far as mobility went. The next step would obviously be to determine how this piece of knowledge could be used to the benefit of the brain-injured child.

9

THE FLOOR

We returned to our long-suffering, brain-injured children who had worked so hard and accomplished so little. Where, we asked, are these children along the pathway to normal? The observations that followed left us completely aghast.

We looked carefully at the facts and either did not believe what we saw or, perhaps, it must be admitted, did not want to recognize what we saw. The awful fact was that the brain-injured children *were not being given an opportunity* for normal development.

Gesell had described the floor as the athletic field of the well child. *The awful fact was that not one of our brain-injured children had ever been on the floor.*

No matter from which angle we examined the facts, or how often, or how many excuses we made for ourselves, the fact remained that the brain-injured children had been denied the possibility to be normal.

We had come to realize clearly enough that a well child had to creep before he walked and crawl before he crept and would not learn to walk without the opportunity of working up to it by working his way through these stages. But we, the team charged with making the brain-injured child walk, were actually preventing his development by denying him the opportunity.

The brain-injured child, who had been treated intensively and extensively and with every device that anyone concerned could imagine, was rarely if ever given a single opportunity to be on the floor so that he might try to crawl and subsequently to creep and walk. It was an acutely embarrassing fact, but it was true.

If he was not on the floor with his well brothers and sisters, then where was our disabled kid? The truth is our problem child was almost everywhere except where he belonged. He was in braces, he was in casts, he was in a wheelchair or special stroller, he was in a standing table, he was in custom-made seats, he was in a special crib, he was on crutches, he was in a wide array of orthopedic devices or canes, he was in mother's arms; in short, he was every place except on the floor. Why was he where he was? *We* had put him there.

How could we have been so abysmally stupid?

Let's examine how we could have been so stupid. The arms of the goddess of tradition are enticing and seductive and so very comfortable. It is ever so easy to remain in her tranquilizing embrace and to do things the way she orders because it has ever been so. When one leaves her embrace to explore the region of new ideas, the climate may be brisk and invigorating, but it is also chilly and frightening.

Why had we built, for a child who couldn't move, an external skeleton of steel? It had all seemed so logical at the time. When we had seen a child who was four years old who could not walk, we had held that a child of four should be standing and walking, and if we could not make him walk, we could at least make him stand by giving him total or partial body bracing. This would be at least a step in the right direction. How sensible and seductive was this idea and how reassuring. Having supplied him with an external skeleton of steel called bracing, we could now say to ourselves with satisfaction (having stood him against the wall) that at least he was standing.

Looking at this child now, in the light of our present thoughts, we could ask ourselves whether it had really been true that he was standing, or was it nearer to the truth to say that he could simply no longer fall down? Could not a corpse be said to be standing under the same circumstances? By encasing him in steel braces from head to toe, we had painted an oil portrait of normality, but one devoid of life. It was a Pygmalion-like thing we had done. We had carved a statue of the child looking the way we wanted so desperately for him to be, and then we had tried to breathe life into it.

When we placed a disabled child in a custom-made seat, were we really placing him in a position that favored the improvement of his problem as we sincerely believed, or were we actually putting him in a sort of position of preferred paralysis which would make him easier to handle than he would be if he were in a totally rigid extension or if he were curled up in a ball-like position of complete flexion?

When we placed him in a specially constructed standing table, were we really strengthening his leg muscles and coordination as we hoped to do, or were we instead creating an illusion of normality which was pleasant to behold?

Even in those instances where the child was permitted to lie on the bed, crib or, rarely, the floor, he was seldom if ever permitted to lie in a face-down (or prone) position which might possibly let him crawl, but instead was placed, almost invariably, in the face-up (or supine) position so that we might be sure he was breathing properly and not smothering, and so that he might be amused by seeing the world around him.

How had it been possible for us all to fall into such traps?

It must be realized that at that time there were no more than a handful of specialists alive who had gone beyond the mere treatment of symptoms and explored the origins of the many symptoms of brain injury. Consequently, very little information on how to diagnose such children existed. By the time the symptoms were recognized, the deformities which had resulted were generally very far advanced and the early workers in the field were, in most cases, orthopedic surgeons who quite naturally were thinking in terms of correcting present deformities and preventing future ones, rather than attacking the problem at its source, which was, after all, a neurological rather than an orthopedic one. As new workers joined the field, they had rather naturally learned from those people who had preceded them. For these rather natural reasons, the neurological disorder that had created the problem had received very little attention. A natural, but deceptive, evolution of treatment had resulted.

When we evaluated the brain-injured children who walked poorly and could not run, we found that the pattern of their creeping was poor. In many cases they could not crawl in the prone position at all.

Even the brain-injured children who could run, but not perfectly, did not crawl and creep as well as average children.

When we spoke to the parents of these walking and running children, we found that the children had crawled or crept very little when they were young. In some cases they had skipped these vital stages entirely and had instead rolled, or hopped like a bunny, or "scooted" on their bottom. Thus these walking and running children had never had the opportunity to crawl and creep as their well brothers and sisters had because they had disorganization or injury to the mid-brain.

Having made an error it was necessary to correct it—to put the brain-injured child on the floor, stop all other treatment, and see what happened.

The results of this experiment were dramatic in the extreme and were destined to teach us many lessons we would never forget.

While many additional techniques and methods had yet to be developed, many of them complex and highly scientific in their conception and execution, none to this day has achieved nearly the significance of just putting the child on the floor.

When the children were placed on the floor, face down, we saw a reproduction of the exact stages we had seen in the normal child. The brain-injured children traveled down this road in exactly the normal order that has been described, without further treatment of any kind.

This explained, of course, the underprivileged brain-injured children who, it will be remembered, had done better than the kids we had treated so very hard with the classical treatment methods. Mother had not given us the opportunity to immobilize the child by treatment, but had instead taken the child home—placed him on the floor and permitted him to do as he pleased. It could now be seen that these "underprivileged" kids had pleased to crawl or creep. Underprivileged indeed! The children had instinctively demonstrated better sense than had our highly specialized world.

It was now 1952 and we had found our first method of treatment: *The brain-injured child who could not walk was to spend his entire day on the floor in the face-down position.* The only exception to this rule was that he might be removed from the floor to be fed, to go to the bathroom, to be treated, and to be loved.

The brain-injured child who could walk, but did so poorly, was given crawling and creeping to accomplish daily. The brain-injured child who could walk well, but not run well, would also be asked to do crawling and creeping daily. We would also make certain that he had opportunity to run on a daily basis.

Under this simple program we saw for the first time results we could really take hope from—tangible, significant, unmistakable results. Many of our brain-injured children improved more than they had in years. The results, however, varied, and in highly thought-provoking ways.

Some went rapidly from helplessness to crawling to creeping—but could not stand or walk. Some learned to crawl but not creep. Others learned to walk but not run. And, of course, there were the children who had no purposeful movement at all, and could not take advantage of the new freedom.

In fact, although many children moved up a stage or two, they still tended to fall into one or other of the five categories we had noted earlier, namely:

1. Those who could not move their arms and legs.
2. Those who could move their arms and legs but could not crawl.
3. Those who could crawl but could not creep.
4. Those who could creep but could not walk.
5. Those who could walk but could not run.

The children had stopped in the five precise places that we had earlier determined were essential to the development of normality.

However, they had *stopped*, rather than continuing on in the pattern of the normal child. The question was, what had stopped them?

10

THE ROADBLOCK—INJURY

Now we were in the flood tide of ideas. Ideas flowed more freely and more quickly than they ever had before—so quickly that we could not investigate them all at once. Instead, we found it necessary to examine them one at a time, looking at each carefully while the others waited, containing our impatience to attack on all fronts at once.

The answer to the enigma of the brain-injured child was far from clear, but we had begun to erect the framework on which we could fasten pieces of information as we uncovered them. We now knew how kids who were well grew and developed and what happened to brain-injured kids when they were permitted equal opportunity by being placed on the floor.

We were particularly fascinated by one group of children. These were the children who had wriggled like a fish, crawled like a salamander, crept on all fours like a quadruped, but stopped short of walking.

Why could these children not walk? Certain it was that they crept freely. They could move arms and legs, they had balance, their bodies were good. Why did these children not walk? Certainly it would appear that these children had everything necessary to walk, and yet they did not. Why? Why? Why?

Suddenly, the answer was before us, stark, clear, and beautifully simple.

We had really learned the answer to this years before in an evening or perhaps in the distillate of a hundred evenings with Temple Fay. He was master of language and of storytelling, this brain surgeon, and he could shrink millions of years into an evening for us in explaining the function of the central nervous system. What he said to us went something like this:

"Every creature of the earth has enough spine and brain to perform the functions which he is expected to perform. He also has all of the nervous system possessed by all the creatures lower in the animal kingdom than he is. That is to say, he has what he needs as well as what all of the creatures which preceded him needed.

"If we take the earthworm, who is a simple creature, and therefore easy to explain, it will be seen that from a digestive standpoint he has a simple gut tube which extends from one end of him to the other. At one end he takes in food and at the other end he gets rid of waste products; he has a simple and effective digestive tract."

"Is his nervous system that simple?" asked a young physical therapist named Charles Peterson, who was now my first assistant.

"Perhaps simpler," replied the brain surgeon. "His nervous system is simply an arranged chain of neurons or nerve cells, which also run the length of his body. He puts out one segment of his body, anchors it down and then drags the rest of it up behind. Simple mobility; simple nervous system. It's all he has and it's all he needs because the earthworm is not expected to teach aphasics to talk, as you are," he said, nodding at Claude Cheek, "or to measure intelligence in a speechless child as you are," he said to Carl Delacato.

"Maybe my central nervous system is just an arranged chain of neurons, too," the psychologist grunted, "because I can't measure them either, and I'm trying."

"It is in a sense," the brain surgeon continued, "except millions of years more advanced and complex."

"Let's skip the millions of years in between and get to man himself," proposed Colonel Anthony Flores, a military physical educator who had become intrigued with our work. "What's with him? What's he do that's unique to man?"

"Well, of course, the end product of two billion years of evolution, at least up to now, is man himself, man who added the human cortex with the six functions we know it contains," said Dr. Fay. "It always shakes people up a little bit to come face to face with the fact that there are really only six functions that distinguish man from the animals. We may find someday there are others."

Someone ventured the thought that probably thinking was unique to man.

"Not thinking," said the psychologist. "We did experiments which are now ancient stuff with chimpanzees that not only think but even demonstrate deductive reasoning."

"But certainly one of the things that man does that the other creatures don't do is to stand erect," said someone else.

"Right," said Fay. "Standing upright is a function of the human cortex.

Man has a more fully developed cortex than any other creature, and he's the only creature who walks bolt upright in a way that frees his hands for the use of tools or weapons. This kind of walking is a unique function of the human cortex."

Bob, the physiatrist, added the next point. "There is at least one function of man, and an important one, which I have to consider every day. This is opposition: Man's ability to put his thumb and forefinger together to pick up small objects. Man would be much less man if he couldn't do this, and no other animal can do it, although some of the apes come close."

"That makes the second function of man," said Fay. "Cortical opposition is a cortical function, and man is the only creature with that skill, which results in writing."

"Don't forget man's most important function, that of speech," said Claude Cheek. "None of the other creatures come close to that ability."

"I quite agree," said the brain surgeon, "although calling it the most important is a somewhat parochial view and probably the psychologist and the others might feel that the other functions are equally important. Nonetheless, speech is exclusive to man and is the third function of the human cortex. The fourth is the other side of the same coin, the ability to decode speech. Only human beings hear in such a way as to understand human speech, and that also is a function of the unique human cortex.

"The fifth human function that we presently know is in your areas of interest, Doctor," said Temple Fay, nodding to Delacato. "Know what it is?"

"Sometimes I wish I didn't know what it is," said the psychologist, "because it certainly causes me enough grief. It's the ability not only to see the printed or written word, but also to interpret it in terms of language. Only man can read language, and that too must be a function of the uniquely human layers of the cortex."

"The last human cortical function is the ability to identify objects by tactility alone," said Fay.

"So to recapitulate, there are six functions that only man has, and they all exist in man's cortex. They are:

1. The ability to read.
2. The ability to understand speech.
3. The ability to discriminate objects through sophisticated tactility.
4. The ability to walk upright.
5. The ability to speak.
6. The ability to oppose thumb and forefinger, which results in writing.

"All of these are functions of the cortex, and when you see a damaged cortex you will see the loss of one or all of these functions. This is an important diagnostic tool never to be forgotten," said the brain surgeon.

Now, many years later, Fay's words returned. *All these are functions of the cortex, and when you see a damaged cortex you will see the loss of one or all these functions.*

Was this the answer to why our children stopped at different levels?

We rushed eagerly back to the children whom we had placed on the floor.

Were there children who had pretty much every function that animals have, that is to say all of the subcortical functions, but who stopped short of function at the cortical level?

There were some whose problem seemed to be focused primarily on walking; that is to say they could hear and they could speak but they could not walk upright even though their legs seemed strong enough. If their problem originated in damage to the cortex, it had to be damage affecting only the centers of the cortex controlling walking—so-called focal damage.

However, among those children who could crawl and creep but not walk, there was a larger group that could not talk, either. With growing excitement and enthusiasm we ticked off the things this group couldn't do.

Was this group able to stand upright?

No, they were not.

Was it further possible that this group of creepers-but-not-walkers couldn't pick up small items between their thumbs and forefingers?

No, either they could not, or they did it poorly.

Had this group of children been able to talk, as well kids did, at one year of age?

No, they had not. When they talked at a later age, they usually did it poorly.

Were these children able to understand human language through their ears?

No, they did it poorly or not at all.

Were these children able to read the language which was spoken by their families and which was their native tongue?

No, they read poorly, if at all, even if long past reading age.

Were they able to discriminate objects by tactility alone?

No, they also did this poorly or not at all.

In this group of children, then, we had every reason to suspect damage to the cortex.

Interestingly enough, however, the histories revealed that even for such children who had in common the five symptoms spelling damage to the cortex, their backgrounds were very varied. Some of the children had sustained their brain injury before birth; some of the children had sustained their brain injury immediately after birth; others had been hurt by falls or disease at one, two, or three years of age. Very different backgrounds, but all were damaged in the cortex, that is, in the highest level of the brain.

We now had our first piece of vital information about injury itself. If a child, when given normal opportunities, got to the point where he could move his arms and legs, crawl and creep, but not walk, there was a great likelihood that his injury was in the cortex of the brain.

Likewise we found if a child, when given normal opportunities, got to the point where he walked poorly but could not run, there was a great likelihood that his injury was not in the lower level of the cortex but in the higher levels of the cortex.

Now the logical question that presented itself to the team was this. If the cortex represented walking, were there other stages of the brain that represented the other three functions? Did the brain exist in stages, each stage of which had a separate, consecutive responsibility? After a long period of study, we concluded that this was exactly the case.

There were four essential and important stages of the brain. Many areas of the brain and nervous system may need to work together to produce a particular neurological function. Brain development and maturation occurs along a continuum. However, it became clear that certain structures and their connections needed to be developmentally and functionally intact to obtain a particular level. These areas were predominantly responsible for neurological function, particularly in the motor system, at certain brain stages. The first, and the lowest of these, was the *early brain stem and cord*. This stage was predominantly responsible for the ability to move the trunk, arms, and legs. Fish haven't much brain beyond this stage, in a functional sense.

Next in order, and higher up, was the *brain stem and early subcortical areas*. This stage was predominantly responsible for controlling trunk and limb motion to move the body in crawling motions with the belly on the floor. Therefore, this stage was responsible for crawling. Salamanders and other amphibians, such as frogs, are well-developed in this stage and the one below it.

Above this was the *midbrain and subcortical areas*. The subcortical areas are a functional area that includes such structures as the basal ganglia, thalamus, and cerebellum and their connections. It was predominantly the midbrain and subcortical areas that had the responsibility of getting the child up on hands and knees in the first anti-gravity position. Therefore, the midbrain and subcortical areas were responsible for creeping. Reptiles, such as lizards and alligators, are well-developed in this area, in addition to the lower stages. So are higher quadrupeds.

Finally, as has been said, the cortex, or top of the brain, was responsible, among other things, for the human ability to walk.

The human cortex is physically much larger than all other areas of the brain combined. It requires many years to mature as a child develops from beginning to walk, to walk well, and finally to run and run well.

The team came to these conclusions after a lengthy search of the records. We started with the records of our own children and went from there to hospitals where we spent weeks poking into the records rooms (which were seldom the most attractive areas of such institutions and in those days were generally located in dusty and crowded basements). We sat on the floor of crowded records rooms going over dusty records with the absorption of a Sherlock Holmes uncovering obscure clues. The comparison to a piece of detective work is perhaps an apt one, for a search of medical records can tell a terribly interesting story to people attuned to what may be in them. Although long periods of sitting on a cold floor may result in what we described as double-feature paralysis, it was a small price to pay for the results.

In almost every case where records of test results could be found, they confirmed our belief. Wherever we were able to verify the existence of damage to the cortex (usually through surgery or autopsy), we found a record of loss of one or all of the distinctively cortical functions enumerated by Fay.

Again the team knew the satisfaction of a hard-won victory. Again there was a period of elation and again a rededication to the job ahead with new energy born now of success. We had established another principle.

We called this new method of determining the stage of brain injury by a somewhat fancy but nonetheless descriptive title: *Functional Neurological Diagnosis*. Through the years we would continue to add to, to refine, and to sophisticate the symptoms of varying levels of brain injury, but none of the dozens of future additions, refinements, or sophistication would bring us nearly the excitement or satisfaction that we found in the basic discovery that we could diagnose a brain-injured child's level of brain injury by examining what he could not do.

11

PATTERNING

Now, in addition to knowing that if a child were injured at any of the stages described he would stop progressing at that stage, we also knew that he could not progress beyond that stage even though he was not damaged at higher stages. Therefore, if the child were hurt in the midbrain and subcortical areas, he would not only be unable to creep, but because he was not able to creep he would also not be able to walk, since creeping is necessary before walking can take place, as we had proved in our study of well children.

The team was now faced with *the* question: Must we accept defeat? If a child were hurt in the midbrain and subcortical areas, did it mean that this child could never creep and therefore never walk, or was there something we could do about this? Was it possible, we asked ourselves, to build a bridge, if you like, across this injury? Could we dig a tunnel or beat our way through the injured areas? Could we, perhaps, go back to the point at which Nature had accepted defeat and simply intensify those sensory inputs which had clearly fallen short of doing their job but might not have fallen *far* short?

We knew the lower stages of the brain and cord to be intact because we could check the movements they control. Now, was there a way we could check his higher stages beyond the midbrain and subcortical areas when we had made the decision that it was true that these areas were hurt? If his midbrain and subcortical areas were hurt, he would not walk; therefore did that mean that we could not check to see if his cortex was intact?

Well, we knew that there were six functions of the cortex, only one of which was walking. Therefore, if we checked the other five in a child who could not walk or creep because he was hurt in the midbrain and subcortical areas, would we find that he could nonetheless perform the other five cortical functions? Suppose that he could speak, suppose that he could read, suppose that he could oppose his thumb and forefinger, suppose that he could understand human speech, and suppose that he could identify objects through sophisticated tactility. Did it not seem extremely likely that this child was good in the cortex since five of his six cortical functions were intact? Might it not also be assumed that the sixth, that of walking, was wanting only because he was unable to creep? This did appear to be a logical assumption, and we knew that the only time there might be an exception to this would be if a child had, in addition to the injury to the midbrain and subcortical areas, a highly localized injury confined purely to that area of his cortex responsible for walking itself.

Could we now do something about this hurt midbrain and subcortical areas? (Of course we knew that we never saw a child who was *minus* a midbrain and subcortical areas; a child could not live without them. We were seeing only children who were *hurt* in these areas and, obviously, this degree of hurt varied from a little bit of hurt to a great deal.)

Suppose, we finally asked ourselves, we tried to teach his hurt midbrain and subcortical areas the functions that this stage would have performed had it *not* been hurt?

In the past, we had tried to teach muscles, but the very term *muscle re-education* was a contradiction in terms, in that it implied that a muscle had the capacity to learn. A muscle is simply a piece of meat and is in every sense uneducable. On the other hand, if we tried to teach the hurt stage of the brain its *own* function rather than to attempt to teach the *muscle* an *exercise*. . .was this a possibility? Could we teach the hurt midbrain and subcortical areas the function of creeping?

Again we returned to the well children to study carefully the things that the well child did, in order to determine what creeping looked like. Having watched the normal child creep on hands and knees, we carefully recorded the separate functions of each of his bodily parts in the symphonious whole. We could then proceed to try to superimpose this ability on the hurt brain which, because it was hurt, was unable to perform its own function.

Creeping differs from crawling in that it not only rewards coordination but requires it. A creature that drags along on its stomach can move its four legs more or less at random and still make progress. A creature that has lifted its body from the ground must learn, however, *not* to pick up both rear legs or both front legs at the same time—or it will fall. Efficiency requires picking up the right front leg only in combination with the left rear leg, or vice-versa, in a cross-pattern type of coordination. Only creatures with a midbrain and subcortical areas have this skill.

Temple Fay had long ago used the term *cross pattern* in his studies of how the lizard or alligator (both creatures with developed midbrain and subcortical areas) moved. He had even developed different ways of putting brain-injured children through the same motions, a procedure he called "patterning." This patterning had appeared to help but as applied had not actually succeeded in getting paralyzed children to walk. We decided to try again. We altered his patterns somewhat to represent how a well child moved, in contrast to how a reptile moved, although there were many similarities between the two. We stepped up the frequency of the patternings, remembering how much of his time a well baby spends in going through these motions. We then began the administration of those patterns.

Let me review our logic here. Fay had stated that each creature's brain embraces those capabilities it needs for survival plus those capabilities each creature lower on the evolutionary scale had needed for its survival. The lizard does not reason out the advantages of cross-pattern crawling. He is simply endowed with a brain that lets him crawl in cross pattern without having to think about it. We, as his descendants, still have that built-in instinct for cross-pattern locomotion. With our "patterning," all we were trying to do was to awaken those inherited instincts.

In a well child, the reflexes produce movement which he can feel. What he feels develops his capacity to feel, and matures the sensory portions of his brain. As the brain matures it begins to appreciate the correlation between motor output and sensory response. It becomes able to initiate voluntarily an action that was originally reflex. Each additional cycle matures both the intake and output portions of the brain.

In the case of a child who had failed, for any reason, to complete this cycle on his own, could we perhaps give him external help? Instead of relying wholly on the random reflexes to teach his brain how motion feels, could we perhaps impose the motions from without and thus give his brain an exposure to the feel of motion that would be even more purposeful and greatly intensified?

We decided to try it. In the case of a child with an injury in the midbrain and subcortical areas, who could not move his arms and legs purposefully when on his belly, we decided to try moving those arms and legs for him—and in the exact pattern that the midbrain and subcortical areas were designed for. We decided to "pattern" him.

The patterns were administered by three adults, and were to be performed smoothly and rhythmically. One adult turned the head, while the adult on the side toward which the head was turned flexed the arm and

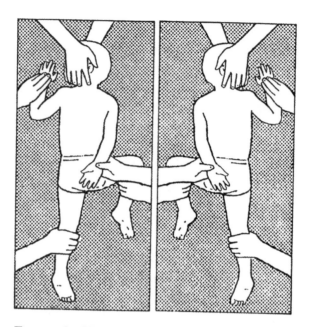

FIGURE 6   CROSS-PATTERN PATTERNING

extended the leg. The adult on the opposite side extended the arm and
flexed the leg. When the head was turned the other way, the position of the
limbs was reversed. (See Figure 6.) Through the years the basic pattern
has remained the same, with only slight modifications. We found eventually that when this patterning was done often enough and consistently
enough, then indeed many a child hurt in the midbrain and subcortical
areas would begin to creep and, indeed, once creeping began, walking followed since it was normal to his well cortex.

We had now answered, at least for those people hurt in the midbrain
and subcortical areas, a terribly important question. Could we actually
treat such people? The answer was an emphatic yes.

If treatment implies actually changing illness itself, then indeed this
was our first *true* treatment method, as opposed to merely giving normal
opportunity, which we accomplished when we put the children on the
floor, important as that is.

Now it remained to be determined whether we could develop like procedures for the other brain areas, by imitating precisely the things a well
child did as he went through each of these stages. With this question in
mind, we now moved back down the scale to determine whether there was
a method that we could use to superimpose the normal crawling methods on

the brain of the child injured in the brain stem and early subcortical areas.

Again we examined carefully the well child, this time as he went through the stage of the brain stem and early subcortical areas, or crawling stage (usually at around five months of age). Again, after many attempts and many failures, we developed a method that was very similar to the method used by Fay, whose brilliant conclusions regarding the amphibians we now paralleled with the normal movements of well children. This pattern of activity he had long ago called *homolateral patterning,* and this appeared to us to be a good name.

This pattern was also administered by three adults. One adult turned the head, while the adult on the side to which the head was turned flexed the arm and leg. The adult on the opposite side extended both limbs. As the head was turned, the flexed limbs extended while the extended limbs flexed. (See Figure 7.) We found that when this pattern was administered consistently enough and frequently enough, in a timed pattern, many of the children hurt in the brain stem and early subcortical areas began to

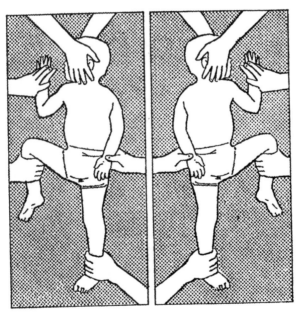

FIGURE 7 HOMOLATERAL PATTERNING

crawl. When they became able to crawl, if their midbrain, subcortical areas, and cortex were uninjured, they would rapidly move through creeping to walking and do well. (It is interesting to note that of all the methods of patterning that had been described by Temple Fay in his study of the growth of the human race, the homolateral pattern is the only one which has remained almost exactly as he described it in his original work.)

Now there remained only the bottom and the top—the early brain stem and cord, and the cortex. We turned our attention first to the early brain stem and cord, the lowest stage, which controlled the very basic first movements of arms and legs that precede crawling.

As has been said earlier, if a well infant, in the days immediately following birth, is placed on his belly instead of on his back, one can observe the normal movement of arms and legs. They are synchronous movements of both trunk and limbs which *aim in the direction of crawling*. Here again we devised a pattern of movement. We called it *truncal movement*. Again the head was turned by one adult while an adult worked on each side of the body. When the head was turned to the left, the left shoulder and hip were lifted a few inches off the table. When the head was turned to the right, the right shoulder and hip were lifted and the left shoulder and hip were placed on the table.

Again success was achieved in many children.

Now there remained only the question of whether or not we could reproduce the final stage of walking in children hurt in the cortex. It seemed strange to us, initially, that this was the most difficult of all the problems to solve, although as time went by the reasons became increasingly apparent.

We had studied walking in the well baby in intricate detail—in particular those things that had followed creeping but preceded normal walking. The well baby, in between creeping and totally well walking, did many things. Among these was getting onto his knees and walking for brief periods of time on his knees. He also pulled himself up by holding onto furniture and walked holding onto furniture. He also experimented by getting up in the middle of the floor all by himself in a position, not of hands and knees, but of hands and feet in a sort of inverted "U" and from there attempted to stand unsupported. This last stage Fay had described as *elephant walking*, and he had felt this was useful since it was a stage that occurred in man's evolutionary past. Although we tried this repeatedly as a technique to precede walking, we did not get useful results even though we saw well children do this frequently. We did find, however, that walking on the knees could sometimes be a helpful prelude to walking itself, and that the device of pulling himself erect on something stable such as furniture and walking holding on was also a useful technique.

Two other techniques used by the well baby also proved useful—walking with arms held above the horizontal as a balancing device, and walking with arms held below the horizontal and used as pistons to pull the body forward.

Finally, the pattern of reproducing "normal" in a child hurt in the cortex took shape as follows. We found it wise to delay the process of walking as long as possible once the child had reached the level of perfect cross-pattern creeping, since we found that the more he crept, the better his synchronous movements became and the easier it then was to introduce him to walking. When walking had been delayed as long as possible the child was then permitted, when he *insisted* on doing so, to pull himself up into the cruising position on furniture or to walk on his knees if this suited him better. When the child then began to take his first faltering steps without holding on to anything, the treatment was then directed at making his walking good.

It must be noted here that sometimes the child who is hurt in the cortex is hurt in only one cortex, and man has two cortices—a right and a left cortex. This is of vital importance to man. When a child is hurt in only one side of the cortex, this results in a paralysis of only one side of his body. We found that the longer such a child could be kept creeping, the more likely it was that he would achieve good control of the paralyzed side of his body, whether through maturation of the damaged cortex or even through a transfer of the responsibility for the missing function to the undamaged cortex. (There are many cases on record where an entire hemisphere of the brain has had to be removed surgically—and yet the remaining hemisphere has learned to take over its functions.)

It seems prudent to point out that the above method of patterning can hardly be called either the method of Temple Fay or of the team itself. Nor can any of these methods be so described because, as Fay had pointed out long before, they were hardly his methods but instead those of the Good Lord himself. We had simply decided to imitate nature as best we could and to perform these motions as had been intended by nature herself.

We had found that if these patterns were applied rigorously, on a specific schedule, and done with a religious zeal, brain-injured kids improved. If all these things were accomplished and additional central approaches, still to be described, were added, virtually all but the most severely involved youngsters showed marked improvement. We had observed nature and had acted as her Boswell in writing down what we had observed. The approach had paid off.

12

THE QUESTION OF RECEPTION AND EXPRESSION

May I point out again that the methods described up to this moment, while employing the use of arms and legs and the movement of the head and body in an imitation of what is normal, were not treatments of the arms, legs, head, and body but instead of the hurt brain itself. It is vitally important to remember that these methods of patterning were in no sense methods of exercise intended to strengthen arms and legs but instead were *organizing the hurt brain* so that it might perform its own functions. They were therefore, in every sense, a true non-surgical approach to the central problem of the brain itself rather than treatment of the periphery wherein the symptoms lay.

Having found one series of methods for successfully treating the brain-injured child, the question now arose as to whether there were other methods by which he might be successfully treated.

Obviously, in answering this question, the sensible approach would be to find out what other limitations there were in the brain-injured child. In what other ways did he vary from the normal child in his inability to perform?

Here, let me pose to you, the reader, a question that the team had posed to itself a long time before. Suppose you passed a personal friend on the street and said to the friend, "How are you this morning?" If the friend did not answer, what would you assume was the reason for the lack of response? Would you assume that he did not answer because he could not talk—or is it not much more likely that you would assume that he had not heard or seen you?

This illustrates an important question. Can a human being fail to function because of a failure in receiving information, just as he can fail to function because of the inability to express himself? The preceding example would certainly imply that this was true. And yet it was important to note that we had always viewed a failure to function as a failure in the inability to express rather than in the ability to receive. We had said, in essence, that *expression* equaled *function*.

Was it not true that when a human being was unable to bend his knee the world would ask, "What is wrong with his knee or with the muscle in his leg?" We had learned, however, that the failure to move the leg might not exist in the leg itself, but might exist in the front part of the brain or the front part of the spinal cord or anywhere in the motor system, down to the leg itself. Up to now, we had not seriously asked ourselves whether failure to function could occur for reasons that existed outside the motor system.

While we had already added much to our knowledge by observing, as we had, that a failure of function might not exist in the leg itself but might exist within the motor portion of the central nervous system, was it possible that such a failure could exist elsewhere in the central nervous system? This was an important question.

Suppose a child was born deaf. It would follow, would it not, that he would also be unable to talk? Even if he had nothing wrong with his speech mechanism, it would be extremely hard for him to learn to speak words he could not hear.

However, this would be a failure of sensory reception (hearing) rather than a failure of motor output (speech).

If it was true that, in this case, a failure to function might be due to a failure to receive information rather than a failure to express information, then a whole new field of understanding the problems of brain-injured children might open up.

More importantly, if this were true, a whole new field of treatment of the brain-injured child might present itself.

Certainly an investigation of how a human being took in information, as well as how he then expressed himself, seemed in order.

Motor and *sensory* are the medical terms assigned to what we have called expression and reception. Let us review their physiology and workings.

Generally speaking, the back (posterior or dorsal) portion of the brain and spinal cord are responsible for processing all incoming information. These are the sensory or receptive areas of the brain. (See Figure 8.)

Generally speaking, the front (anterior or ventral) portion of the brain and spinal cord are responsible for all outgoing responses. These are called the motor or expressive areas. (See Figure 9.)

This is seen clearly in the names of diseases such as tabes dorsalis (dorsalis meaning back) which is a disease that affects the back of the central

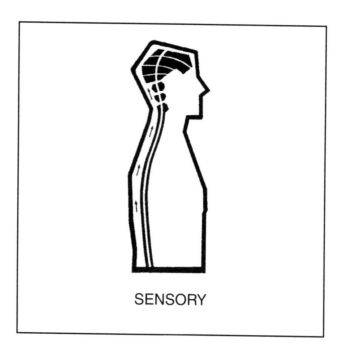

FIGURE 8

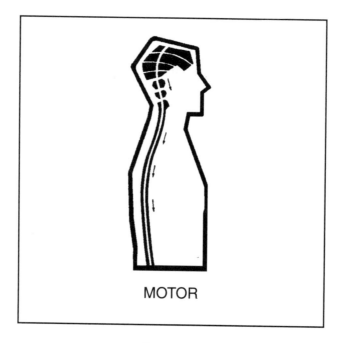

FIGURE 9

nervous system. As a result of tabes, *sensation* is lost, although motor abilities in the front of the central nervous system are untouched. (It is highly significant to note here that, although the tabes patient has all his muscles intact and all motor factors are good, he staggers when he walks as does a drunk and eventually does not walk at all, just because he has lost feeling.) This certainly supported our new line of investigation. It might be said, then, that tabes is a receptive, rather than an expressive, disease.

The motor disability is seen clearly in anterior poliomyelitis (infantile paralysis). Polio exists in the *front* of the spinal cord and is therefore called *anterior* poliomyelitis. Polio is a disease that affects only the *motor* system and in no way disturbs sensation or reception. It might be said that it is an *expressive* rather than a *receptive* disease.

If this is true, and we shall verify that it is as we progress, then the formula that we had previously described would have to be expanded, so that instead of saying *expression equals function*, we would have to say *reception plus expression equals function* or, in the words of the medical world, *sensory plus motor equals function.*

What we have stated up to now then is that in order to perform a function, man must be capable not only of commanding his muscles to perform acts, but must, in addition, have certain prior information upon which to base the movements he intends to make. Without such prior information, movement may exist, but it will not be purposeful or functional.

We should examine this view in more detail since understanding it completely is vital to understanding the next method of treating brain-injured children.

What are the sensory or receptive abilities by which man learns—not only about his environment, but indeed about anything at all? While there are many, they can be reduced to five essential areas.

The five ways in which man gains vital information are: (1) seeing, (2) feeling, (3) hearing, (4) smelling, (5) tasting. Many other very important senses such as balance, position, sense, etc., exist but can be placed within one or more of the categories above.

A simple experiment will illustrate how dependent we are on our senses. If you should seat yourself before a table upon which has been placed a paper clip, you could pick up the paper clip. It could therefore be said that you have the motor or expressive ability necessary to perform the function of picking up the paper clip.

Let's now see which sensory or receptive factors are employed in picking up the paper clip and eliminate them one at a time until it becomes *impossible* to pick up the paper clip even though the muscles (motor or expressive factors) used in picking it up are still normal and capable of picking up the paper clip—or even something that weighs thousands of times as much.

Before you can perform the motor or expressive act of picking up the paper clip, you must first find out where it is. Obviously, until the paper clip is located it is impossible to pick it up, no matter how strong you might be or how capable. The most commonly used of the receptive senses and probably the one you'd use in picking up the paper clip is vision. You locate the paper clip by seeing it. Then you pick it up. Let us now eliminate vision and see what happens.

If you will now close your eyes and attempt to pick up the paper clip from the table, you will find yourself running your hand over the table to feel for the paper clip. Having eliminated the most commonly used of the senses, vision, you resort to the next of the senses, namely feeling, to locate the paper clip. Having felt it, then you pick it up.

Now let us eliminate both seeing and feeling and see how you will pick up the paper clip. The ideal way to eliminate feel would be to anesthetize the fingers by a local anesthesia but, since this would not be easy as a home experiment, let's do the next best thing, which, while it will not eliminate sensation, will reduce it sufficiently to serve our purposes. If you will now take Scotch tape and completely cover your fingertips down to the first joint—so that no unexposed skin touches the tabletop—we will have enough reduction in feeling for the experiment. If you will now pick up the paper clip with your eyes open, you can still pick up the clip. It will be awkward, since you cannot use your fingernails, but nonetheless, you can still do it.

If you will now close your eyes, we can eliminate both seeing (vision) and feeling (tactility). When you try to pick up the paper clip with eyes closed and feeling gone, you will quickly realize that you cannot and will then begin to make sweeping motions across the table with your fingers. Why do you do this? You realize instinctively that in order to pick up the paper clip, you must first learn its location. You know that there are only five ways to do so—seeing, feeling, hearing, smelling, tasting. We have already made it impossible for you to see (by having you close your eyes) and feel (by anesthetizing your fingertips). You know you can neither smell nor taste the paper clip. You have now resorted to the only remaining sense, that of hearing, to locate the paper clip and you are sweeping your fingers across the table, hoping to *hear* the scraping noise of the paper clip should it become trapped under your sweeping fingers.

Even should this be successful, you will still find it impossible to pick up the clip because you will not *know* when you have been successful. It would little matter if you brought your thumb and forefinger together a thousand times and then lifted them hoping to have within them the paper clip since you would not know if you did indeed have the paper clip.

By this and innumerable other experiments, we can establish that sensation is just as vital to function as motor ability and that if all areas of reception or sensation are destroyed, the human being will be totally unable to function. In accidents involving the spinal cord, any resulting paralysis of the lower limbs may be due more to the loss of sensation *from* those limbs than to the loss of ability to send instructions *to* those limbs.

If one could imagine a human being who had *no* ability to see, feel, hear, taste, or smell, one could only imagine the state of death, or of deep coma, or of very deep anesthesia. Under such circumstances, although a human being might have a brain of the rarest genius, of what value would it be?

If a genius were unable to receive any of the five sensations, how could he even verify the fact that he was alive? He could not pinch himself to prove that he was alive, because he couldn't feel it even if he did pinch himself. He could not cry aloud, for even if he did he could not hear himself to verify that he had cried. He could not look to verify the existence of his body, for he could not see. He could not so much as smell or taste himself.

Experiments have been performed on extremely healthy young men who for periods of time volunteered to be isolated in total silence and darkness with all other factors reduced as much as possible without inducing unconsciousness. Although only a few of the five senses were totally eliminated, in a few hours these healthy young men were almost totally disoriented as to time and space and were not able to say how long they had been maintained in this state or what had happened during that time.

From these and hundreds of other experiments we may conclude that man can only be totally complete to the degree that he has his receptive factors intact.

We may further conclude that if all of a man's receptive factors were removed, a deathlike state would follow and remain at least until they were returned.

If, between these two extremes, man's faculties for learning are removed one at a time, we will reduce his ability to function. We could therefore conclude very positively that it was *essential* to man's function that he have sensory intake, or reception.

Helen Keller's fame was not due essentially to the fact of her accomplishments; it was due to what she accomplished *without* two of her vital receptive qualities, seeing and hearing. The world has long recognized the tremendous handicap that such losses bring about.

It soon became clear that brain-injured children are usually deficient in at least some of their receptor functions. Children whose problem is a result of Rh incompatibility are sometimes deaf, others are sometimes blind, and most brain-injured children have reduced ability to feel. We then examined the rest of them carefully through new and more skilled eyes to see to what extent the brain injury might have caused sensory problems as well as motor problems, because we knew that they were equally vital to function.

It was clearly important never to forget for a moment that there are: (1) sensory (receptive) pathways which bring information into the brain, and (2) motor (expressive) pathways through which the brain reacts by commanding motor responses based on the information it has received.

Fay had taught us that all incoming sensory pathways are a one-way road into the brain and are incapable of carrying an outgoing message, while all outgoing motor pathways were equally one-way and are incapable of carrying a message into the brain. This was a long-recognized and well-known fact of neurology, but the world's failure to apply it in the diagnosis of the symptoms of brain injury explained in part exactly why the conventional rehabilitation techniques were so ineffective. Classical methods had tried to treat the brain-injured patient in purely motor terms. The results of that motor-oriented treatment had been that whatever information had managed to reach the brain had been both accidental and incidental.

Dr. Fay, virtually alone in medicine, had been fascinated by the work of that great mathematical genius Norbert Wiener, and had not only understood Wiener's book *Cybernetics* but had also understood its implications for human beings—most especially brain-injured human beings. He had insisted that I read and understand it as well.

It was clear that the human brain, like Dr. Wiener's self-regulating systems, operated like a cybernetic loop—and a superb one.

The normal cybernetic functioning of the brain is completely dependent upon the integrity of all of these pathways. The *total* destruction of all motor or all sensory pathways will result in *total* lack of functional performance of the human being. The *partial* destruction of one or the other will result in *partial* lack of functional performance.

It is also depressingly clear that such lack of function will continue until the former specific pathways are restored to function or until new pathways are established that are capable of completing the total loop.

In human beings this loop, which begins in the environment, follows sensory pathways to the brain and motor pathways from the brain back to the environment. (See Figure 10.)

All efforts in treatment of the brain-injured child would therefore have to be directed toward locating the break and closing the circuit.

Could we find procedures to locate the break and thereafter to close the circuit? We would have to if we were to solve the problems of our brain-injured children.

But how?

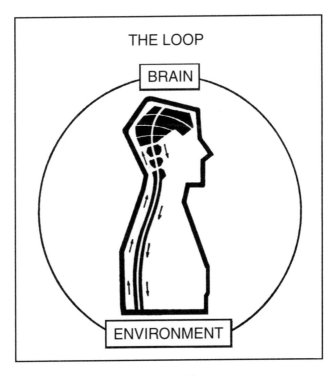

FIGURE 10

13

THE INSTITUTES ARE BORN

Finding the break in the circuit was only one of innumerable problems which faced us. By now we had organizational problems, too.

While I would be reluctant to say that I believe in miracles in the old-fashioned religious sense, I must say that there have been some periods of time during which I have felt that I was being shoved about by forces beyond my control. One such period began in the last half of 1954.

As the team had continued to grow during the early 1950s, it had been necessary that some structure emerge to make functioning possible.

We had agreed years before to continue to see Dr. Fay's patients in the nursing home into which Dr. Fay's Neurophysical Rehabilitation Center had been converted. The original idea had been that we would see his post-operative patients until they had all been discharged from the nursing home. These patients ran the gamut of adult brain-injured patients—from stroke patients to Parkinson's disease—and included many relatively rare neurological disorders. Seeing such patients meant that after Dr. Fay had operated on them I would be responsible for their post-operative rehabilitation.

We had expected our patient population in the nursing home to decline as our patients were discharged and as aged patients coming for domiciliary care took their place, freeing us to spend *all* of our time in our offices seeing patients together.

That is not what happened. After an initial falling off of patients as anticipated, new patients began to seek admission to the nursing home not as a domiciliary care unit but, instead, to receive the treatment services of our team. The United Cerebral Palsy Association also began sending us children as patients. (By this time the team consisted of Dr. Fay as the neurosurgeon, my brother as the physiatrist, Carl Delacato as the psychologist, and me as a sort of director of rehabilitation services since by this time I had several physical therapists and an occupational therapist working for me. Claude Cheek served as speech therapist.)

What had happened was that we had grown into a rehabilitation center, one of the earliest in the country.

We had many problems, and as the director, these problems weighed heavily on me. In the first place, the buildings and grounds were inadequate to the task before us. Since most of the buildings and grounds belonged to the nursing home, we could not make the changes we wished, and since the objective of the nursing home and its owners was to make money rather than to solve problems, which was their right, we found ourselves frustrated in our attempts to do research or to do teaching.

We were beginning to receive requests from physicians and therapists, here and abroad, who wished to visit our "institute" to study the work we were doing. We had neither time, money, nor facility to do any such teaching.

What was needed was crystal clear, but how to come by it was far less clear. What was needed was a nonprofit organization, organized for the purpose of research, training, and treatment in the field of brain-injured patients. It should be organized along the lines of a typical hospital or university. Such an organization should have buildings, grounds, and staff adequate to treat inpatients, to conduct clinical research, and to teach other professional people what we were doing, how we were doing it, and why we were doing it.

A reasonably large amount of ground would be required, certainly no less than several acres, and in Chestnut Hill land sold by the foot. Certainly the ground would cost $25,000.

Also needed would be a minimum of forty beds plus treatment areas, etc. In those days a rule of thumb for the cost of building patient beds was $10,000 per bed, which meant that building would cost about a half million dollars.

In addition, a minimum staff of about ten first-rate professional people would be needed, as well as about ten service people, such as cooks, laundress, plant engineer, etc. By the most stringent economies salaries could not fail to be less than $150,000 per year.

Food, heat, electricity, telephones, etc., would surely cost no less than a hundred thousand dollars for the first year.

In short, we would need close to a million dollars just to get us started.

Dr. Fay, although he could command huge surgical fees, seldom did, and he had not yet recovered from the financial disaster of The Neurophysical Rehabilitation Center. Bob, Carl, and Claude were even younger than I and recently out of school. That left me, and everyone looked to me for a solution. I needed a million dollars and I knew where I could get about forty-three dollars.

It was just about then that the events began which led me to feel that I was being pushed around by forces outside my control.

It was the very day when I had decided that there was simply no way to solve the problem when the first thing happened. Betty Marsh came to see me. Betty Marsh was a very nice, middle-aged, redheaded, Irish practical nurse who worked for the nursing home and who would often bring patients over to my office in wheelchairs when I called for them. Although she and I had often exchanged pleasantries, I hadn't remembered her name. Although she was a registered practical nurse, what she had to say to me was as impractical as anything I had ever heard—and strangely insightful.

She had, she said, been watching the results of the work in the Rehabilitation Center and thought it was the most kind work she had ever seen. She thought that if human beings could be that kind to each other perhaps there was some hope for us all. She had noticed how tremendously busy I was and lately she had felt that perhaps I had not been entirely happy with the circumstances at the nursing home.

Then she dropped her bomb. She felt, she said, that it was very important to the people of the world that my work be continued. While she knew nothing of the situation, she wanted me to know that she had lived very carefully all of her life and that she had saved up six thousand dollars and that these six thousand dollars were in the bank and that I could have them anytime I wanted them, and I could pay them back if I was ever able to do so. There would, she announced, be no paper signing of any kind (a process she mistrusted) and no interest paying, which took all the good out of a good thing.

I mumbled my appreciation of her kind thought and sat stunned as she blithely took her departure pushing her now-empty wheelchair.

What the devil did it mean?

How had she guessed that a problem even existed?

Why in the name of everything sensible would this single little woman without security of any kind offer me her lifetime savings when I was almost a stranger to her?

What in hell was her name?

While I had not the slightest intention of accepting her offer, I was totally overcome by her unbelievable generosity to a man who didn't even know her name. I was seething with conflicting emotions.

On one hand her extremely strange insight and incredible generosity had moved me close to tears. On the other hand she also made me feel extremely selfish and rather cowardly and, in a way, unworthy of the work I was doing. I had been overwhelmed by the need for hundreds of thousands of dollars and had decided to give up such an impossible dream as being out of the question. Yet it was obvious to me that six thousand dollars must represent more money to her than hundreds of thousands of dollars did to me. Yet she had offered it all. While it was unquestionably true that six thousand dollars was more money to her than hundreds of thousands were to me, it was also true that those sums of money had less worth to her than they had to me. I was ashamed.

I got through my work that day in a mechanical way, which was not characteristic, but I was mightily distracted by what had happened. I was not even given the rest of the day to recover.

As I finished work, Mae Blackburn proposed that we sit awhile and talk.

Mae had been a yeomanette in the U. S. Navy in World War I and also, I had been told, a crack secretary. I had seen Mae first as a patient three or four years earlier. She weighed eighty-eight pounds, was a few years older than my mother, and looked old enough to be my grandmother.

Mae's problem needed no psychiatrist to understand. Mae was in her early sixties but she was very young at heart. Her husband had died and so had most of her friends and those that hadn't, had grown old more willingly than Mae. Her son was married and gone and Mae was alone. Mae had not taken care of herself and when I saw her first she had not the strength to walk. Good food, regular hours, no parties, and a sensible program of exercise had set her right in a few months and she had been discharged as well. Six months later she was back and the entire process was repeated. Then she came back for the third time.

It was then that I had put into effect a little scheme that backfired. I had up to that time been my own secretary (I had the virtue of being both cheap and careful.) When Mae Blackburn had returned for the third time, painfully thin, exhausted, and so shaky that she could not light her own cigarette, I had proposed that perhaps she could help me by typing a letter or two. Although the thought obviously frightened her, she had agreed to try. Her letters were absolutely terrible in the beginning, and I would take them home at night and retype them with two fingers. Since that is what I would have had to do anyway, there was no extra work for me and it was clearly good for her. Very quickly her letters improved until they were perfect and so, too, was she. It was obviously time for her to be discharged since she no longer needed me. My clever game had backfired, however, because now *I* needed *her*.

So Mae had gone to work for me at a terribly inadequate salary to become my secretary, my bookkeeper, my second mother, my boss, and my friend.

I sat on the desk and listened in stupefaction while Mae offered me *her* life savings. Since Mae got a tiny salary, she only had three thousand dollars saved, but it was mine.

I saw a plot of some sort and accused her of collaborating with what's-her-name, the redheaded Irish nurse. She obviously did not know what I was talking about, but she did know that the redheaded Irish nurse was named Betty Marsh. I told her with wonder what had happened that morning. She had known nothing about it, but she saw nothing unusual in the story since she also thought the work was kind and wonderful. She thought everyone ought to help. She was surprised that everyone hadn't offered to help, and the fact that no one knew about the problem did not seem to her a good reason not to help. Nobody had told her and Marshy about it, but they knew, didn't they? I agreed in a trancelike way that they did.

Even today I find it difficult to believe my own story, and perhaps I would find it harder to believe, now that many more years have passed, if I did not daily look out my office window across the lovely green lawn to the Mae Blackburn Building. It helps me to remember that amazing woman. It also helps me to remember Betty Marsh when I look out my office window toward the Mae Blackburn Building because my office itself is in the Betty Marsh Building.

Mae Blackburn had insisted also, in addition to lending me the three thousand dollars, that she could, would, and insisted on working free in whatever the "new place" was.

I had difficulty sleeping that night because I did not know what the "new place" was. I had the feeling I was getting pushed around by factors beyond my control. It is a feeling I have had many, many times since, and I have learned to relax and not resist even when I do not entirely understand.

Both of these women, I thought that night, are far older than I. They have no security at all. Yet through some prescience which I did not understand they had both insisted on giving everything they had. What of me? What was everything I had? Was I willing to give it?

Well, I had my equipment and all the furniture in my large house. All of that could be donated to be used in the "new place," whatever that meant. That was worth nine or ten thousand dollars.

Then there was the house itself. Although a large mortgage still remained, I could sell it and realize fourteen thousand dollars and that also could be donated.

Altogether it sounded to me as if I could scrape up about thirty-two thousand dollars. Only a drop in the bucket. It couldn't be done, and so I would tell those two crazy women tomorrow. *How* could I tell them that? They simply wouldn't understand.

Maybe though, with Mae's idea of working free . . . Suppose all the professional people worked free for awhile until we got going? I got out of bed and got pencil and paper.

Suppose by some miracle we had the place in which to work. Maybe we could rent it or something. Could we then make it work? If there were a place to work we might by a miracle make it for a couple of months if we had forty thousand dollars instead of thirty-two.

Two nights later Mr. Massingham, my father-in-law, offered me eight thousand dollars. It was obvious how he knew about the problem. I had told him—but without having the foggiest notion that he might help to solve it. Both he and Mom had been very poor as children in England and although Dad had done well in America he had been unable to forget about his childhood poverty and was extremely cautious with money. He had simply not occurred to me as a source of money.

Dr. Fay agreed to work free. So also did my brother. So, of course, did my wife.

It was then that Miss Galbraith asked to see me. By now I was used to people asking to see me, and I went half expecting her to offer help. Libbeth Galbraith was a patient. She was a fifty-year-old brain-injured kid with the problem that most people call cerebral palsy. These are the people who, when they are severe, are in constant writhing motion. These are the people who look so awful (when they are severe). Most people assume them to be mentally retarded when in truth they are smart, smart, smart.

Libbeth was unlike the severe athetoid cerebral palsy type in that she did not writhe, although she could not walk, but she was like all other athetoids in that she was smart, smart, smart. She was also most insightful. Although she and I spent a part of every day getting her out of her wheelchair and teaching her to walk for the first time in fifty years, we had never discussed my problem.

This night we did. We drove to Fairmount Park and as we drove Libbeth talked. She believed I should go have a talk with her brother-in-law, A. Vinton Clarke, and her sister, Helen Clarke.

I had only met Mr. Clarke once before in my life and that most casually. I was sure he would not even remember me, and when I called to make an appointment this proved to be true. He did not remember me. Nonetheless, he invited me to his house the following evening.

He listened carefully as I told him of our hopes and dreams. Taking a deep breath, I told him that to get started I believed I needed about twenty-five thousand dollars. He slowly shook his head no. You will need, he told me, more like eighty thousand dollars. Having said so, he handed me a check for eighty thousand dollars. Although I had never so much as seen that much money and although I was extremely grateful, I was no longer surprised.

Neither was I surprised when I found the "new place." It was a superb estate in Chestnut Hill. There were eight acres in that original site and two superb buildings as well as lovely greenhouses and a barn. There were more than a quarter of a million dollars' worth of beautiful trees and bushes. The place was obviously worth millions of dollars and was absolutely ideal for our purposes. I wasn't surprised that I had found the ideal place for us.

I wasn't even surprised when I called the agent to find out how much the estate would cost. The firm sale price was exactly eighty thousand dollars.

What do you think of that for being pushed around?

Aside from my work, the only friends I had were military friends. I had, after the war, believed that the world was far from safe and I had remained in the active reserve. I had joined Philadelphia's ancient 111th Infantry Regiment of the Pennsylvania National Guard. The commander of that regiment was Col. Jay Cooke, an outstanding Philadelphian whose great-grandfather, Jay Cooke, had financed the Civil War for the Union.

It was he who had promoted me to captain when I had joined the regiment, and it was his former estate which we bought. Since I had been his guest there I had known about it. He had lived there with his wife and two daughters, and when he had found himself alone with a huge staff of servants after the death of his wife and the marriage of his daughters he had offered the place for auction. The very wealthy man who had bought it had realized quickly that even a wealthy man could not afford to support such an estate, and he sold it to us.

Jay Cooke came to serve as a member of the board of directors of the "new place" until the day of his death in 1963.

On July 22, 1955, after months of work, the Honorable Judge William F. Dannehower of the Court of Common Pleas of Montgomery County, Pennsylvania, decreed that The Rehabilitation Center at Philadelphia be approved as a nonprofit corporation.

The directors were Glenn Doman, Robert Doman, Frank D. McCormick (a military friend), Temple Fay, Claude Cheek, and Martin Palmer.

Thomas R. White, Jr. (a prominent Philadelphia attorney and a senior officer of my regiment) was to serve The Institutes as attorney until his death years later. He did so without pay.

Robert Magee, one of my oldest and closest friends, had served as the first president of the board of governors.

Major General Arthur D. Kemp served as a member of the board of governors from the day of that body's inception, and later as its president, until its service was completed many years later.

Bob Magee's wife, Doris, served several terms as president of the women's board and still remains an active part of that active group.

They served, all of them, because they were personal friends and for the love of the children, and this they found reward enough.

The Rehabilitation Center at Philadelphia would later change its name to The Institutes for the Achievement of Human Potential.

So—with a number of shoves—The Institutes for the Achievement of Human Potential were born—and just in time.

14

SENSATION AND
ITS IMPORTANCE TO MOVEMENT

We have noted that without incoming (sensory or receptive) factors an otherwise well adult human brain will fail to function in even so simple a process as picking up a paper clip. It can be imagined what such receptive losses would mean to the much more complex acts of walking and talking in a brain-injured child who had *never known about such things in the first place.*

We now had to determine where the brain-injured children had suffered such losses, and to what degree. If they had such losses, we then had to determine whether anything could be done about this *since such losses by themselves could prevent not only walking and talking but even far simpler acts.*

We had determined that there are five human receptive abilities that make it possible for a human to obtain information of any kind, from the most complex sort (understanding nuclear physics) to the most simple sort (understanding that the radiator is burning the leg which is lying against it). The five receptive areas in man are: (1) seeing, (2) feeling, (3) hearing, (4) smelling, (5) tasting.

Smelling and tasting are essentially recessive characteristics in man, and our dogs are more skilled in them than we are. For well adults these characteristics are essentially pleasure seeking. They are extremely important to certain specialists, such as wine tasters and perfume sniffers. Adults derive most of their operating information from the other three.

This chapter will deal with seeing, hearing, and feeling.

We had begun to feel that we understood how a child learns to see, hear, and feel in broad terms, and we had as yet spent only a little time on how he learns to smell and taste.

VISION

We again went first to well children to study how they learned to see. We found that they progressed through four important stages, which, generally speaking, corresponded to the four stages we had seen in mobility, stages that were normally completed by the age of twelve months. We were struck with this coincidence, and later events proved that we were wise to have noted what would prove to be a most important relationship.

Much ingenuity was required to test these children and to determine what they saw since visual testing is usually based on the patient's verbal responses to what he sees. None of the children under one year of age could answer such questions, and many of the brain-injured children over one year of age had speech problems. New methods had to be developed and new equipment designed with which we could come to a determination of what a child saw without asking him to answer questions. This was not easy, and even the methods we developed did not tell us all we wanted to know. Nonetheless, we learned a good many things.

The four stages through which well children pass in learning to see are as follows:

Stage 1—In the days that immediately follow birth a child reacts reflexively to light and to darkness. This is called a light reflex. It is not safe to say that he perceives light or that he understands light, for such appreciation is impossible until higher stages come into play. His reaction is completely reflex in nature. When light falls on his eye the pupil constricts; when the light is removed the pupil dilates.

Stage 2—During this stage, the well baby begins to gain outline perception and to differentiate varying degrees of light; that is to say, he can see a human silhouette if the person is outlined against the light, and he will respond to less bright light shined toward his face. He can follow a human being about the room with his eyes if that person is outlined against a light.

Stage 3—During this stage he begins to see detail when a light is thrown on an object itself and to appreciate the differences in detail of such an object. He can now see an object within a larger configuration. Vision takes on added meaning. (He can differentiate the buttons on mother's blouse from the blouse itself.)

Stage 4—During this stage, which begins at about one year of age and which will not be complete in all its human detail until almost six years of age, many, many important things take place. Principal among these is *convergence*, which results in depth perception. In the human being this is another function of the cortex. (Here again was reconfirmation of our original ideas.)

We came to realize that a very high percentage of brain-injured children have visual problems; in fact, we were daily becoming more convinced that virtually all brain-injured children had some visual problem despite the fact that some had eyes that appeared to be normal to external examination and showed no obvious signs of visual deficiencies.

We have also seen many seriously injured children who did not react, either consciously or reflexively, even to a strong light shining in their eyes. This is blindness. For many years we felt that this was a situation where we could do nothing other than pray, for if a child was blind, what was there to do? But as years went by, we began to see a startling phenomenon which we did not even attempt to explain, other than to feel that it was a most fortunate coincidence. Many of the children who in the beginning appeared to be blind began to gain small amounts of vision. Others who had had small amounts of vision began to gain greater amounts of vision. This was exceedingly strange since we were doing nothing whatsoever that we considered to be in the nature of visual treatment.

As more children began to gain ground visually, it became necessary to ask whether this was actually a coincidence or was a result of something that was happening to the children.

Up to this time we had not kept progress notes on children's vision but had only examined them thoroughly at the beginning of their treatment period, since we viewed vision as a static affair—something that would not improve. Now we began to keep progress notes.

We began to see that this visual gain was more than coincidence because it was apparent that the children who were making visual gains were the same children who were making gains in mobility. If treatment stopped for any reason and mobility progress stopped, visual progress also stopped. When treatment was again resumed and mobility again improved, we began again to see visual progress. What was making these visual gains occur?

As I think I have demonstrated repeatedly in this book, hindsight always checks out at 20/20. Looking back now, these startling facts are understandable. Indeed, it is extremely ironic that, in light of the views that the group held, we should have been surprised to see progress in visual areas. It is surprising that people who had devoted so much of their lives to establishing the fact that brain injury lies within the brain did not see this point. We ourselves had said repeatedly: If the problem lies within the brain, it will do no good to treat the elbows, nose, ears, and eyes, where only the symptoms of the problems exist.

We ourselves had fallen into the very trap we had sometimes criticized others for falling into. We had been thinking of blindness as a problem of the eyes instead of a symptom of a problem within the brain. Indeed, why should it be strange that vision improved if we were, in fact, as we intended to do, treating the brain itself? If, in fact, the difficulty that caused the paralysis of the leg existed within the brain as we said it did, then might not the difficulty that caused the visual problem also exist within the brain itself? Here was a question of tremendous import.

Why should such a very high percentage of the brain-injured have visual problems of great magnitude? Did we have a right to suspect that the children who were brain-injured also had had something else happen to their eyes which gave them visual problems? This hardly seemed likely. Was it not much more likely that the children who had brain injury were having visual problems due to the brain injury itself? Could we not say that if a problem existed within the brain then the chances were good that a brain-injured child would also have difficulty seeing for the same reason that he had difficulty moving a leg or an arm?

After all, there was plenty of evidence that a human being could have a visual problem that did not exist in the eye itself. He could, and very frequently did. We repeatedly had seen visual problems in brain-injured adults following a stroke. We knew of the visual problems that beset the adult brain in Parkinson's disease. We knew of the visual problems that could beset an adult when his adult brain was hurt in an automobile or a diving accident.

We were not observing some strange miracle when we saw blind children who could now see outline or detail for the first time, but rather we were observing the only logical course we could expect if, indeed, we were treating a brain rather than an elbow or an eye.

We turned with renewed energy to probing the visual problems such children demonstrate.

In brief, we found that those children had all of the visual problems that confronted the brain-injured adult.

We saw in these children the exact same sort of vision problems that we saw in adult stroke patients. Some of these children saw nothing to the left of the nose or nothing to the right of the nose or nothing above the horizontal or nothing below the horizontal. Some had the visual problem of constricted fields in which the entire cone of a child's vision was greatly diminished, permitting little vision to the sides, top, and bottom.

We also detected scotomas (blank spots) in the vision of some of these children, although these were hard to detect since the children were not capable of telling us about their visual problems and such sophisticated testing as was necessary to determine the presence of a scotoma was difficult to perform.

Some of the children could see at near point (within arm's length) but could not see at far point (beyond arm's length); in others this was reversed. Some children could see fairly well but could not detect detail.

Most common of all, we found problems of fusion in our children. These problems were very easy to detect since they were generally accompanied by an easy-to-see strabismus.

The word strabismus, you will remember, is the medical term for what is generally called either cross-eye or walleye, or sometimes a squint. If one eye turns in, this is called a *convergent unilateral strabismus*. If one eye turns outward, this is called a *divergent unilateral strabismus*. If one eye turns upward, this is called a *superior unilateral strabismus*. If one eye turns downward, it is called an *inferior unilateral strabismus*. If both eyes do so, the unilateral is simply changed to bilateral so that if we saw a child who was cross-eyed in both eyes, this child would be recorded as having a *convergent bilateral strabismus*.

These problems are extremely common, particularly in those children who have problems in the midbrain and subcortical areas starting at or before birth. While a marked strabismus is rather easy to detect, even by the least initiated person, a very small strabismus is not easy to detect and requires careful evaluation. This examination, however, can be performed by parents themselves simply by observation of the child's eyes and the way they move.

If a child has a strabismus, it is quite obvious that his eyes cannot converge on the object being seen. Often one sees a child who has a strabismus fixed, until such time as he looks specifically at an object, at which time the strabismus may disappear and he may actually see that object in proper depth. If a child has a strabismus that is always present, or if he has a strabismus that alternates from eye to eye, he obviously cannot see in depth.

What, then, does the child see who does have a strabismus? We know that he does not see in depth. It is possible also that he actually sees two different visual images. When this is the case, what the child is seeing is called *diplopia*.

Let us say that a child has a right convergent strabismus, that is to say that his left eye looks at the object which he intends to look at, while the right crosses over that axis of vision to see something else. The left eye might therefore be looking at a lamp in front of the child while the right eye is actually seeing a scene far to the child's left.

Is there an alternative to a child seeing two images if the eyes are in fact seeing two different scenes? Yes, there is; it is most likely that if the strabismus is severe, the child will learn very quickly to ignore entirely one visual image. He learns to "look at" (pay attention to) only one of the images, or only one at a time. This process is called *cortical suppression.*

The methods we have since developed to get maximal visual abilities out of a child will be described in a future book, but, in summary, these things can now be recorded. Visual problems in a brain-injured child should not be considered surprising since the visual tracts run the length of the brain from the eye to the occipital area in the back of the head itself. It is easy to see how many different kinds of brain injury can affect this visual pathway, thus creating a visual problem that does not exist in the eye itself but exists somewhere between the eye and the back of the brain.

The team also came to realize that many secondary involvements might occur as a result of brain injury. It would be necessary to treat also these secondary things that had happened as a result of the inactivity brought about by the brain injury. In other words, in the case of the child who was beginning to see for the first time, the team sometimes had to teach the child how to use that new visual capacity.

We now began to ask ourselves an extremely interesting question. Was it possible to treat the brain for one missing function *without* seeing results in all areas? We asked ourselves a question that was more amusing than realistic. Suppose a parent came to us with a brain-injured child saying, "I should like you to make my child walk, but I do not want him to see."

The moral question aside, could we have accomplished this? Could we have hoped to develop movement and walking in this brain-injured child without simultaneously achieving results in vision if both were the result of the same injury? It hardly seemed likely.

It would not be fair to leave this section on vision without pointing out one visual problem which we find in brain-injured children but do not find in adults who were hurt in later life. It is a serious handicap. The adult who sustains an injury that creates for him a visual problem has one tremendous advantage: He *has* known what the world looks like. He knows what seeing is. The brain-injured child has no such advantage.

FEELING

There is no more important system for the preservation of life than the sensory mechanism we call feeling. Without this tactile mechanism we would exist in constant danger of the destruction of life itself. By feeling, we are warned of the dangers that threaten us. The quadriplegic patient who has lost the ability to feel from the neck down as a result of a severely damaged spinal cord may sit with his leg against a radiator and not be aware of the fact that his leg is burning until he actually smells the burning flesh, since in him the sense of smell is intact, while tactility is not.

Suppose that we did not have the pain which we frequently complain so bitterly about. If there were no pain, how would one ever know that appendicitis existed? It is the pain that leads us to perform the laboratory tests which so frequently confirm the presence of the inflammation. Without such pain it is quite likely that few human beings would ever be operated on for appendicitis. They would instead die of the unchecked disease.

Where, in the human, does feeling exist? It would almost be easier to answer the question, where does it not exist? At least in the external covering of the body it exists virtually everywhere, and if you were to close your eyes and ask someone else to touch you somewhere on your body, you could detect this touch even if it were your hair he touched, since even the movement of the hair would make itself felt on the scalp.

We wanted first to look at how feeling or tactile sensation develops in the well child up to one year of age, as we had long since learned was the proper course. We found again a fact that was most interesting to us: In normal children the area of feeling developed in four stages and these four stages again paralleled the four stages we had seen in mobility and in vision. These four stages are:

Stage 1—This stage exists essentially during the first month of life, and has primarily to do with those sensations that are of the most basic and primitive sort. These sensations are entirely reflex in nature. They are skin reflexes, which are present at birth and which do not require decision from the brain at all. These reflex reactions go only through the sensory pathway to the spinal cord and directly from the spinal cord back through the motor pathway to the muscular system. An example of this is the Babinski reflex. Here the examiner scrapes a point such as a key along the bottom of the infant's foot. In the normal infant the toes will turn upward and fan out. This is normal in an infant but abnormal in a well adult. In a well adult the toes will turn downward and come together.

Stage 2—This stage exists from about four weeks of life, during which time the child begins to respond to stimuli from outside the body. However, these stimuli, to affect the child, have to be of a vital nature and must actually threaten the child's existence. He responds during this stage of his life to vital stimuli, to vital feeling, to feeling that, if continued, would actually threaten life itself, such as a pin stick or extreme pain of any kind. This period could be called the period of vital sensation. His response is to withdraw from the pain and to cry for help.

Stage 3—This stage, which comes fully into play by about seven months of age, is the stage in which he comes to understand gnostic sensations. "Gnostic" comes from the Greek root meaning "to know" and includes sensations that are less strong than the vital sensations that might threaten life. During this period of time the well child is able to identify things as being not merely hot but also warm, not merely cold but also cool, not merely very painful but also uncomfortable. The child now reacts to contentment because of pleasant stimuli, such as dry diapers, etc., and reacts unpleasantly to those things that might be uncomfortable, such as wet diapers (which he is now able to recognize). Also during this period of time a factor very vital to his walking begins—the beginning of balance. Balance is a very important product of sensation. It draws from all of the three basic sensory areas but has important ramifications in tactile sensation itself. During this period of life the child's feeling varies a great deal, and if there are areas in which he is undersensitive, there are also areas in which he is oversensitive to certain kinds of stimuli.

Stage 4—This stage begins at approximately one year of age. During this period, which is the beginning of the development of the cortex, the child begins to develop the ability to recognize by touch alone the three-dimensional shape of an object. This is the tactile equivalent of depth perception. By feeling an object between his fingers he begins to appreciate the fact that objects felt have depth just as do those objects that can be "felt" with the eyes. His sense of feeling now becomes highly discriminative. He will be able, in the future, to identify, by touch alone, objects that are remarkably detailed. He acquires, during this period, the heightened sense of balance necessary to the upright or walking position.

In examining our children, we came to the conclusion, as we had with vision, that it was a rare brain-injured child who did not have some problem in some area of sensation. Sometimes the problem was as small as not being able to distinguish mildly warm from mildly cool, even though the ability to differentiate between hot and cold might be present. Sometimes the problem was so severe that the child was virtually devoid of sensation and was in as much danger, due to this factor, as was the quadriplegic. The brain-injured child was also frequently oversensitive, and this was often as large a problem as having too little sensitivity.

It was interesting to note that until a well child reached the age of five or six, even he did not have sensation that was as good, in some ways, as the adult. Perhaps you have had the experience of having your own head butted by a small child's—resulting in a good deal of pain in your head and a good deal of delight on the part of the child who is not disturbed by the tremendous blow.

We frequently saw brain-injured children who could lie, with no apparent discomfort, on top of a large object on the floor, such as a plastic toy. We drew the conclusion that they did not feel the object. We concluded that many of the brain-injured children were not even aware that their arms and legs actually belonged to them or had any connection with their bodies. If a child could be unaware that his legs were his, he could hardly be expected to move these legs in a manner that would teach him to crawl, to creep, and to walk.

Again, as with vision, we came to the conclusion that the problems did not truly exist in the arms and legs of the children but rather existed in that portion of the spinal cord or nervous system that was responsible for all incoming information.

These children were handicapped, indeed, since the child who did not gain information could not possibly function. A child could not put out functional movement if he did not first take in the information on which the functional activities were based. (You will remember your own experience with the paper clip.)

Finding ways of treating this problem within the brain itself was the next assignment we gave ourselves, and over a period of many years sensory techniques have been developed which, while they are applied to arms, legs, and body, are not expected to affect the arms, legs, and body directly, but instead are a method of giving information to an injured brain relative to where its arms and legs *are*.

HEARING

The brain-injured child had problems in hearing, also.

We learned rather quickly that auditory acuity was not the most important element of hearing, just as visual acuity was not the most important part of seeing. While complete lack of auditory acuity (deafness) was often present in our children, it was much more common to find children who could hear but could not hear in a way that permitted them to interpret what they heard.

When we measured how a child learns to hear and what he understands from what he hears, we could define the same four stages we had seen in the other areas.

Stage 1—This stage, immediately following birth, is the period when what a child takes in through his ears is of a purely reflex nature. When a loud noise occurs he jumps in what is called a *startle reflex*. This implies no fright or fear on the part of the child, nor does it demonstrate an understanding of what he hears. It is a simple reflex activity.

Stage 2—This stage, which begins at approximately one month of age, is when a sudden loud noise can be interpreted by the child as a possible threat to his life. Now, in addition to being startled, he cries. It might be said that he is crying for help in response to what could be a threat to his life.

Stage 3—This stage, which begins at approximately 2.5 months of age, is when the child begins to understand the meaning of sounds. Words do not yet have significance at this stage, but the tone of mother's voice is highly significant. If mother scolds, baby cries even though he does not understand her words. At this stage the baby begins to locate the source of the sounds he heard. This helps him to understand the sound. This is the stage of meaningful sound.

Stage 4—This stage, which begins between six months and twelve months of age, deals with a depth factor. This time it has to do with the depth of meaning of words themselves. By now the baby understands not only the meaning of sound but also the meaning of words themselves.

While at this time it would appear that hearing problems are less common and perhaps even less important than those problems existing in the areas of vision and of feeling, nonetheless it is quite true that such problems do exist, and there is reason to suspect that there are aberrations in hearing not only among some specific groups of children who are frequently deaf (such as those who are the result of incompatible Rh factors) but also among those children and adults who are hurt in the midbrain.

We know that those people hurt in the midbrain and subcortical areas, such as children described as having "athetoid cerebral palsy," frequently have a marked startle reflex; that is to say, they respond with huge jumps and body stiffening to sudden noises. These patients also frequently complain that certain sounds are actually painful to their ears—painful, not simply undesirable or uncomfortable. We now realize that in Parkinson's disease there is an over-sensitivity of hearing which makes these patients talk lower since it is not nec-essary to, as they put it, "shout." We also know that in injuries resulting from certain kinds of trauma, such as automobile accidents, the patient frequently talks far too loudly. These three abnormalities in hearing can all be related to the same area of the brain even though they appear to be very unlike each other.

Thus, as the clouds of mystery that hid the truth from us were gradually being blown away by the fresh and stimulating winds of new knowledge, one could see that sensory intake was not only as important to human function as was motor ability, but that all motor ability was *based* on sensory intake.

It was now clear that there could be four degrees of sensory problems (in visual, auditory, or tactile terms) in the brain-injured child.

These were:

1. The total absence of visual, auditory, or tactile intake (blindness, deafness, insensateness). These were disastrous to the brain-injured child if permitted to continue.

2. Too little visual, auditory, or tactile intake (hard of seeing, hard of hearing, hard of feeling). These were overwhelming handicaps to the brain-injured child if they were left unhandled.

3. Too much visual, auditory, and tactile intake (oversensitive reception of such stimuli). This was equally overwhelming.

4. Chaotic visual, auditory, or tactile intake (receiving distorted visual, auditory, or tactile information as, for example, the visual information received by the child with strabismus). This could likewise be discourag-ing, disconcerting, or frightening.

It was becoming daily more clear, as we saw more and more severely brain-injured children, that one or many of these problems was usually in the picture, though the degree of disability could range from the almost imperceptible to total. It was rare that a hurt kid did not have some of them.

In addition, as we began to make more gains in mobility, we also saw more gains in visual, auditory, and tactile areas. There seemed to be some connection, even if we couldn't yet quite explain it.

If true dawn had not yet arrived, perhaps it could be said that first light was upon us and that silhouettes of the shapes of tomorrow's formula-tions could be dimly seen. However indistinct the picture, at least it seemed to be taking shape.

15

BREATHING

The matter of breathing and the manner in which the brain-injured child breathes are also terribly important—and a most interesting story.

It is breathing that supplies the oxygen to the brain which is vital to the well human being and which is at least as vital to the brain-injured.

Not infrequently, it was a temporary lack of this oxygen (a state called *anoxia*) or a temporary insufficiency of this oxygen (a state called *hypoxia*) that caused the original brain injury itself, regardless of the actual incident (such as a fall, a blood clot, a stoppage of breathing, a high temperature, etc.) that set in motion the chain of events that led to the undersupply of oxygen.

We did not begin this research on breathing with any idea that it might in the end be an important answer for brain-injured children. Instead, we began by looking for an answer to one of the big problems in polio (infantile paralysis) and ended up with a more important answer in the treatment of brain-injured children.

Although the first love and prime interest of our little group was, and is, the brain-injured child, it was natural that in the early days we should see many patients who were not brain-injured but who had allied problems. Among them were patients suffering from polio.

It is hardly possible to express our delight at seeing the elimination of the crippler, polio. We here pay tribute to that genius, Jonas Salk, who did a better thing than merely curing those patients who had polio. He prevented polio and thus began the process of stamping it out.

One could scarcely imagine a greater pleasure, unless that pleasure were the elimination of brain injury. Here, however, there will obviously be no single answer since the problems of brain injury have a multiplicity of causes.

In the late 1940s and the early 1950s the treatment of polio was difficult work and frequently discouraging work. Polio could not be solved by treatment directed to the brain because, of course, polio was not an injury to the brain itself but instead existed along the edges of the spinal cord in what is called the anterior horn cell where nerve pathways leave the spinal cord and fan out to the various parts of the body to which they carry motor commands.

Severe polio frequently left monumental breathing problems in its wake in the form of paralyzed or partially paralyzed chest musculature. Frequently the best efforts to save the patient did not succeed, and the patient was lost in a respiratory death. All the work and effort had been to no avail.

Even when the patient did survive, there were monumental problems due to respiratory conditions. If the patient got a cold that would have been only mildly annoying to a well person, it generally resulted in pneumonia; consequently, much valuable treatment time was lost.

Furthermore, during these very frequent periods when the patient missed treatment, the progress that had been made—and it was painfully slow—was generally lost. This discouraging set of circumstances led us to the work on breathing.

What could we do to make it easier for a polio patient to combat respiratory problems? The case simply stated was this: Because of paralyzed chest musculature, the polio patient could not breathe deeply, therefore the chest capacity was bad, therefore the patient was subject to repeated respiratory attacks. It could be said that polio patients had insufficient chests.

How could we build the polio patient a "better" chest? There was already a standardized set of chest exercises to be used to increase the chest girth of well persons. However, these were dependent upon the patient's being able to carry out the exercises, something the polio patient could not do. How could one make a partially paralyzed chest (sometimes close to totally paralyzed) undertake a breathing program? If a severely involved polio patient with great respiratory problems were offered a thousand dollars for taking a very deep breath, the money would be safe because the fact was he could not. How, then, did we begin to build up a chest?

The team had in the past been faced with such a problem, the problem being: How does one make a muscle that doesn't work, work? The patient simply did not have command over the chest muscles. Faced with this problem previously in brain-injured persons, the team had come to the conclusion that, under certain circumstances, reflexes might be used to achieve motion which might be later put to volitional use by the patient. This method, called *reflex therapy*, is now in common use the world over.

Was there, then, a way in which we might have a polio patient take a deep breath by reflex activity beyond the patient's control? If we could find such a method, it was possible that we might be able to build larger chests in polio patients and eventually bring the expanded chest under the patient's command. This was the course upon which we now embarked.

Many of our efforts failed. There were those things that were partially successful but not practical. Among these was an effort to make the patient breathe reflexly by applying ice to the chest. If you simply place an ice cube against your own chest, you will realize that you take a deep breath in a reflex manner, recoiling from the cold. You will have no control over this breath; it will happen whether you want it to happen or not.

The question was, would this also happen in a polio patient? We tried it. Having bared the chest of a polio patient with a severe respiratory problem, we applied ice to his chest. The patient took a deep, deep breath, over which he himself had no control. While this method did in fact work and permitted the patient to take a deep breath without conscious control of the muscles, it did not prove to be a practical method. After three or four applications of the ice, the patient became cold and did not respond continuously to the cold application, nor was the reflex breath he took the deep rhythmic breathing that would be necessary if we hoped to improve his chest and his breathing in any reasonable period of time.

After more attempts which were unsuccessful, the group came to the realization that there was a well-known reflex for inducing deep breathing, although it had never been used in a therapeutic sense. To understand this method, you must first understand something about the way the human body regulates its oxygen supply. The human body is a most magnificent instrument and one cannot imagine a man-made machine that could match it in performance. A good example of this is the action of the chemoreceptors.

The chemoreceptors are small areas within the brain that control a complicated and vital function. These tiny chemoreceptors might be said to be a sort of laboratory, which not only gives constant laboratory reports (somewhere near twenty each minute of life) but finds and quickly solves chemical problems in the body. (At least, such problems are solved within the ability of the chemoreceptor laboratory system to do so.) The purpose of these chemoreceptors is to test every incoming breath of air. In the event that this incoming breath of air does not contain enough oxygen (or too high a level of carbon dioxide) to sustain life, the chemoreceptors not only report this fact instantaneously but *do* something about it. What the chemoreceptors do about it is to set in motion a process within the brain that, since there is not enough oxygen in the air now surrounding the human being, makes this human being breathe deeper and faster. This breathing takes place on a reflex level. As a result of this reflex breathing, the human being takes in a greater quantity of air than usual and thus is able to extract more oxygen to meet his body's needs.

We knew, therefore, that if a group of human beings sat in a room which was very tightly sealed, and thus did not get enough oxygen, as the air became more and more unpleasant and the oxygen content went down and the carbon-dioxide content went up, the people enclosed in that room would reflexly breathe faster and deeper. This is one set of circumstances that causes us to yawn in order to get more oxygen. This would compensate for the lack of oxygen as long as that were possible and therefore sustain life longer.

Now we asked ourselves: If a group of human beings, including a polio patient with a severe respiratory problem, were placed in a sealed room so that as the oxygen was used up and the oxygen content went down and the people in the room began to breathe deeper and faster reflexly, would the polio patient also breathe deeper and faster? If he would, he would be getting great chest movement even though he could not control his chest movements as could the well people. The reason we suspected this was so was that even the well people would not *consciously* be breathing deeper; they would not be breathing deeper because they ordered their chest musculature to do so, but instead because of a reflex action over which they had no control. The question then became: Was this life-saving deep-breathing reflex intact in the polio patient, as it is in well people?

Unable to answer that question in any way except by actually trying this experiment, the staff prepared such a room. The head nurse, Lorraine Bouldin, who was herself a severe polio patient with a severe respiratory problem was brought into this room along with other staff members. The room was then crudely sealed by putting paper strips under the door (it had no windows), using putty to plug up holes and then painting around the edges. Having done this, the staff sat in the room and simply breathed over a period of several hours. Since the room was very inefficiently sealed, it was several hours before there was a significant lowering of the oxygen content, and raising of the CO_2 content, but as this occurred it was easy to see that the staff members began, on a reflex basis, to breathe deeply and rapidly. With fascinated eyes, we watched while Lorraine, in her wheelchair, also breathed more deeply and more rapidly than she was capable of doing on a volitional basis. We were elated.

However, the particular arrangements we had set up for the experiment were not such as would readily permit us to give Lorraine the treatment for (say) five minutes out of every hour, so we went to an engineer and asked him to design for us a room for the purpose. Even though the engineer offered to design such a room without charging for his services, the estimated cost turned out to be twenty-two thousand dollars. Without a special grant it was obvious we could not go this route.

As we moodily discussed this problem one evening, someone came up with a bright idea, or perhaps it would be safer to say that up to now we had been taking a very stupid approach. Why, said this staff member, is it necessary for us to have a large room? Could we not simply take a small closet, put one patient in the closet at a time, and hermetically seal the closet itself? Obviously this was a splendid idea and might reduce the cost to a point where we could afford to try the experiment.

On that happy note we began to consider how this might be done. Suddenly Colonel Anthony Flores, a top-flight U.S. Army physical educationist who had left the Army to join our team, said, "If it is true that a smaller room would not only be less expensive but better than a larger room, why do we not simply arrange a box-like device in which the patient's upper body may be put? Why is it necessary for his lower body to be encased at all?" He had hardly finished speaking before he was interrupted by Dr. Bob, who said, "If this be so, why the upper body? Why not just the head, since it is only the breathing mechanism in which we're interested?" At which time, the speech therapist Claude Cheek quickly interrupted to say, "In fact, why not just the mouth and the nose since these are the only external breathing apparatus that are important to this question?" This was quite obviously sensible; therefore instead of a twenty-two-thousand-dollar room we substituted paper bags into which the patient might breathe.

This had actually been suggested sometime before by Fay himself — but with a different goal in mind related to the diagnosis of certain kinds of brain injury.

The team delightedly tried this approach. We held the paper bag tightly around Lorraine's face to include the nose and the mouth; in thirty seconds the concentration of carbon dioxide in the paper bag was great enough to cause her to begin deep respiratory movements.

Claude Cheek, who had thought of the paper bag, then came to another very sensible conclusion. He suggested that the small plastic bags which had been designed for the administration of oxygen to patients might be used. These bags were inexpensive and were also disposable. This suggestion obviously had much merit since the bags were designed specifically to fit over the mouth and nose of the patient. They quickly proved to be valuable.

Now began a long period of testing. The staff, using itself as guinea pigs, set out to determine what happened, not only to respiration, but to pulse, blood pressure, and so on when this bag was used. It was determined that up to a period of three minutes, at least in well persons, there were no untoward effects other than the effect of deeper, quicker respiration.

Now we began work on Lorraine herself, who, despite an overwhelming paralysis, ran the nursing staff from her wheelchair. Her respiratory problem was, in fact, a rather desperate one and she volunteered herself as a subject. She had little to lose since she was in constant danger of her life as it was. We could hardly control our elation when it became clear that this method did work and that her chest improved tremendously.

Respiratory episodes were cut way down. Her chest began to grow in size, which was startling, as Lorraine was very much an adult and therefore had been assumed to have a relatively fixed chest.

We established, after some months, the appropriate duration for the mask to be both safe and effective.

The mask has since been used for this purpose in many institutions and many countries and is still being used today on the small remaining numbers of polio patients.

In light of the things that we have since learned, the staff now looks back with embarrassment on the period of time when the mask was used exclusively on the polio patients while the brain-injured patient whose chest breathing was as bad or worse sat side-by-side with the polio patient and did not receive this benefit.

It was at an evening conference a long time later that we wondered what would happen if we used the mask on the adult brain-injured patients? In the early stages of stroke, the brain-injured patient sits slumped over in a chair, therefore materially reducing his breathing. His paralyzed arm, if it is flaccid, is held in the midline or, if it is spastic, is held across his chest, causing further restrictions on his breathing. What would happen, we wondered, if we used the breathing mask on the adult brain-injured patient, or the brain-injured child? Brain-injured children always have bad chests. The brain-injured child frequently has colds and respiratory conditions. Generally speaking, such a child had many more colds than his brothers and sisters and these lasted longer. If the colds and respiratory illnesses were accompanied by high temperatures, he frequently had convulsive seizures, as well.

This was a most interesting thought, one which we felt should be approached very carefully since breathing into the mask affected the brain directly. We had more reservations about the complications that might exist here than we did in the case of polio where there was certainly no problem within the confines of the brain.

The more one thought about the idea the more intriguing it became. Certainly the brain-injured did have bad chests, frequently as bad and sometimes worse than many of the polio patients. Improving a child's chest should have good ramifications. His posture, for one thing, should be better and also he should have less respiratory episodes which would reduce his loss of treatment time. Perhaps even more important, he might be less vulnerable to the seizures that frequently followed infections of any kind in the brain-injured child.

We reviewed why it was that Temple Fay had used such breathing measures as the paper bag so long before. The fact was, we recalled from our conversations with him, he had used carbon dioxide, rebreathing, as a test. It was his feeling that, in certain types of brain injury, carbon dioxide would force relaxation and as a result of this one could do a differential diagnosis between two kinds of brain injury. He had described this in the literature and had used tests with carbon dioxide being administered by an anesthetist.

He had also told us long ago of the use of carbon dioxide in the treatment of epileptics, who were subject to seizures or convulsions. His theory had been that an epileptic undergoes a convulsion as a sort of reflex protest against a temporary insufficiency of oxygen to the brain, much as a fish out of water flops this way and that trying to get back in. Fay therefore tried administering *oxygen* during convulsive seizures. As he had stated the result, "The patients promptly had bigger and better seizures."

The experiment was a failure. However, no one knew better than Fay that carbon dioxide is one of the most powerful vasodilators known to man. This is to say, the rich content of carbon dioxide in the blood stream will cause the blood vessels to dilate or open wider thus permitting the flow of a greater *volume* of blood to the brain and, consequently, an increase in the *amount* of oxygen available to the brain. This, of course, was the reason his experiment had failed. By giving the patient oxygen he had cut *down* the carbon dioxide and thus constricted the blood vessels and as a final result *reduced* rather than *increased* oxygen to the brain. Then, of course, Fay performed the exactly opposite experiment.

Fay now gave carbon dioxide to patients while they were having convulsive seizures. He did so with hundreds of patients. He had found that doing so had resulted in reduction in the severity of seizures, in the length of seizures and in the frequency of seizures.

It had long been recognized that the well human being operated well or badly in direct relationship to the adequacy of usable oxygen available at the brain level. If a well human being is deprived of oxygen, he can, in a five-minute cycle, go through the following stages. First, he will become incoordinate. Second, he will have *petit mal* seizures exactly like those minor epileptic episodes that we see so often in the brain-injured child. Next, he will become grossly incoordinate, be unable to walk, speech will become thick, and he will drop objects held in his hands. Next, he will actually have a *grand mal* convulsive seizure, which looks exactly like those seizures that occur in a brain-injured patient. Following this, he will suffer brain damage due to the lack of oxygen to the brain cells and, last of all, he will die. This whole cycle can take place in five minutes in the well human being. It was certain that the brain-injured patient who *already* had a damaged brain needed this oxygen no less than did the well person. Therefore, if we could improve the chest capacity and breathing of the brain-injured patient, this should be of tremendous value.

Following this line of thought, we began extremely cautious experiments on the brain-injured. Having already done these experiments on the staff and having established a very safe treatment level, we now began with brain-injured patients to work on the same thing. Over a period of many months, we worked to establish the safe and effective duration and frequency for this treatment.

The results were even better than we had hoped. Not only did the patient's breathing improve, but his problems with respiratory illnesses decreased. As in the case of polio patients, our brain-injured patient often had *fewer* respiratory episodes than other members of his family.

This breathing program has now been in use for many years at The Institutes as well as in many other institutions in the United States and abroad. Two to three billion maskings have been given to brain-injured children in the United States and the rest of the world.

We had found a technique that not only improved the brain's nutrition, by enriching its oxygen supply, but was sometimes even life-saving.

16

WE PUT IT TO THE TEST

My apprenticeship to Temple Fay really stopped in 1955 when I became the director of The Institutes. Fay continued to work with us for two more years, but now I had the responsibility for forty inpatients, many critically ill, and I had to be director, administrator, chief of staff, and chief therapist. My wife, Katie, was the head nurse, the charge nurse on each of the shifts, and sometimes the only nurse on a shift.

Having sold our house and given all of the money we possessed to The Institutes, we had inevitably moved the family into The Institutes, lock, stock, and barrel. Perhaps if I said that for six months I worked twenty-four hours a day, seven days a week, and that Katie worked longer, you would know how I felt then.

Now for the first time I could no longer give first priority to sitting at the feet of my teacher. I had patients who were counting on me.

Although all or virtually all of the theoretical constructions with which we had begun had been those of Dr. Fay, practically all of our practical applications were developed by the team working together.

Twenty years had passed since I had first met Fay and ten years had passed since I had joined with Fay. The decade of the fifties, our decade of discovery, was drawing to a close.

It seemed to us to be a time for consolidation, a time for thought, a time to decide precisely where we were going and just how we ought to get there. Four questions cried out for answering. (1) Just what *were* we? (2) What did we *believe*? (3) What were we *doing*? (4) What were the *results*?

Here's the way it looked to us in the middle of 1957.

1. Just what *were* we? We were the staff of The Rehabilitation Center at Philadelphia and we numbered about forty—physicians, therapists (physical, occupational, speech), nurses, psychologists, educators, administrators, board members, and so on.

We were a federally tax-exempt, nonprofit organization chartered for the purpose of conducting treatment of brain-injured children and adults. We were a research Institute looking into all problems associated with brain injury. We were a teaching Institute educating other professionals on what the treatment and research had revealed relative to brain function in normal and brain-injured patients.

We had forty inpatients with severe neurological disorders including twenty children and twenty adults. Fay had always been greatly excited by what he described as that "wealth of clinical material."

We had many resident students ranging from all of the senior nurses from five major Philadelphia hospitals (each of whom spent a month in residency at the Center during her senior year where she received forty hours of didactic instruction per week taught by the senior staff members) up to postgraduate students in the therapies, education, or psychology to resident postdoctoral students in medicine or education from the United States and abroad.

Our research was primarily clinical, although we were soon to plunge into laboratory research as well.

Our patients were now referred to us by many physicians including Dr. Eugene Spitz, a top pediatric neurosurgeon and Dr. Edward B. LeWinn, chief of medicine at Albert Einstein Medical Center, Philadelphia, a greatly respected internist, who had earned such respect by the high order of his clinical abilities and research projects. Dr. Sigmund LeWinn, his brother, was our chief consultant in pediatrics and much liked by the staff. There were consultants in orthopedics, urology, ophthalmology, and general medicine as well.

We had earned some national and even international reputation as a pioneering institution in the treatment of brain-injured patients.

2. What did we *believe*? What we believed was by now a great deal clearer than it had been. If today our beliefs sound so simple as to be obvious, I can only say that in 1957 few others found them obvious. We believed:

(a) That brain injury was in the brain. (This has always been our most radical belief.)

(b) That since the brain controls all human functions, if the brain is severely hurt the symptoms of brain injury will be demonstrated everywhere in the body.

(c) That treatment of the *symptoms* which exist in the eyes, ears, mouth, chest, arms, legs, and everywhere else in the body will not alter the basic brain injury.

(d) That if we could successfully attack the problem in the brain itself rather than merely the symptoms, the symptoms would disappear spontaneously.

(e) That there were ways to address treatment to the brain itself.

Perhaps what we believed could best be summed up in a speech I had made in 1953 to Dr. Rusk's Institute for Physical Medicine and Rehabilitation. It had been something of a landmark in our progress that we had been asked to speak there because it was at that time without question the most famous rehabilitation center in the world. My lecturing fee was by far the highest I had ever received up to that time, and I had been excited and flattered at the invitation.

I said in my conclusion:

It must then be considered as a basic principle, that when a lesion exists within the confines of the brain, that treatment, to be successful, must be directed to the brain wherein lies the cause rather than to that portion of the periphery where the symptoms are reflected. Whether the symptoms exist as an almost undetectable subtlety in human communication or in an overwhelming paralysis, this principle must not be violated by those who seek success with the brain-injured patient.

Nothing in this principle had changed by 1957. Nor has it today.

3. What were we *doing*? By 1957 a rather clear program had emerged. This program was taught to the parents by us and carried out at home under our careful supervision. We accepted as inpatients only those children who had not succeeded on a carefully conducted home program.

Whether administered by us or by the parents at home, the program was as follows:

(a) All nonwalking children spent all day on the floor on their stomachs crawling (if they could) or on their hands and knees creeping (if they could).

(b) All children were "patterned," that is to say, they would be given external help in going through the basic motions of, say, crawling if they could not yet crawl well on their own.

(c) Children who demonstrated sensory losses were given specific sensory stimulation.

(d) A program to establish clear-cut cortical hemispheric dominance was established for children who were mixed up as to which side was dominant.

(e) After careful medical examination to be sure that they were candidates for this program, a masking program to improve the vital capacity of the lungs and thus give optimum oxygen to the brain was used on all children.

4. What were the *results*? By the beginning of 1958 it was clear that we were achieving results such as we had never achieved before, and it now seemed time to subject the new methods of treatment to the same kind of testing we had given the old treatment many years earlier.

This testing was made easier by the presence at The Institutes of two French research physicians. Their names were Jean and Elizabeth Zucman and they were man and wife. Dr. Jean Zucman was an orthopedic surgeon who was carrying out a one-year research program for us under the direction of Dr. Edward LeWinn, who had finally joined our staff, at first as a consultant and later as the director of the Research Institute.

Dr. Elizabeth Zucman, like my brother, Bob, was a physiatrist and was fascinated by the children's clinic which, for reasons too lengthy to describe, was held on weekends with the staff donating its time. It was to this weekend clinic that the parents who were treating their children at home returned periodically for consultation. While it may be difficult to credit, it is nonetheless true that this clinic began on Saturday morning at 8:00 A.M. and ran *without stopping* until late Sunday afternoon.

Betty Zucman, who was studying at The Institutes on a Fulbright Scholarship, worked a normal week and was not required to work those incredible weekend hours.

Still she heard rumors of some of the results being achieved with the children under our program, and although she was quite polite she obviously didn't believe them.

Would *"Monsieur Le Directeur"* permit her to attend the weekend children's clinics of which she had heard?

But of course. And so she did. She stayed awake and alert through three weekends from beginning to end. She was deeply impressed.

Would *"Monsieur Le Directeur"* permit her to attend all future clinics and might she—ah—that is—take notes?

But of course.

She took her notes. She drew her conclusions. And she chose her words carefully. The results, she reported, were not as rumored. The results were far greater than rumored. She had been skeptical to begin with, but had come away completely persuaded that something extremely important was going on.

Some severely brain-injured children were markedly improved. Despite the fact that everyone said that such was not possible, some of them were actually walking.

We *must*, she declared, carefully study the results and make a statistical evaluation of them, and we *must* do it immediately. We *must* report our findings in an article and submit that article to the most important medical journal in the United States at once. It *must* be the *Journal of the American Medical Association*. We must. We *must*. She would hear of no objections and she would hear of no delay. It *must* be done.

If it must be done, I had allowed, then she herself could very well begin the statistical evaluation right now since she was a skilled medical researcher.

And so she did in a study of the children we were treating in 1958 and 1959.

The results were highly impressive compared with any other results of treatment of brain-injured children that we could find in the medical literature, and we had searched carefully. In truth, we could find no other report in the medical literature of anyone who had ever reported any positive result in the treatment of brain-injured children.

We wrote our report and argued about every word in it. We spent two whole weeks arguing about the title alone.

When we were satisfied, we submitted it to the *Journal of the A.M.A.* It was accepted, and published on September 17, 1960. That article (reprinted in its entirety in the Appendix) reported on the results achieved in the treatment of 76 severely brain-injured children, none of whom were given much chance of any significant improvement under conventional therapy. Seventy-four of the 76 made measurable progress. Twenty-one, in fact, learned to walk well and easily in full cross pattern, including 3 who had initially been unable to crawl, 6 who initially had been unable to creep, and 12 who initially had walked, but badly. Furthermore, most of the children were, at the time the study was completed, continuing to improve, having been on the program for an average of only 11 months.

Not only did the *Journal of the A.M.A.* publish the article, but they sent an advance news release to major newspapers and magazines in the United States telling them that a very important article about brain-injured children would appear in the next issue of the *Journal.*

We received thousands of requests for reprints and not a word of criticism about the article itself, although some of the establishment thought all that newspaper publicity wasn't seemly. They wished we hadn't notified the newspapers.

However, it was now on record that there was new hope for an effective treatment of the brain-injured.

Clinical research is a stimulating, exhilarating, often intoxicating thing. When years of work and hope finally start paying off in terms of really producing function in severely brain-injured children, it can even be an ecstatic thing. And for us it was.

It is also a provoking, hectic, frustrating, frenetic, infuriating, demoniacal thing.

A clinic is about as far removed from the theoretical, neatly ordered, contemplative, disembodied sort of laboratory research as one can imagine.

In some kinds of pure research I suppose one can routinely stop work at five o'clock and just lock the door and go home.

But I wouldn't know. My own work has been too clinical.

One cannot lock the door at five o'clock on desperately needy children whose needs are no less desperate because they can't voice them. Face to face with a child who may be paralyzed, often gasping for breath, frequently speechless, sometimes vomiting, occasionally convulsing, and always hurt, hurt, hurt, there is little opportunity for scholarly contemplation.

We strove for order and neatness, but in the chaotic circumstances which surrounded our work, we rarely attained it.

Sometimes we worked our way tidily from theory to application. More often, we improvised, then worked back from practice to theory. Most often what ended in a new treatment began as a simple hunch, arrived at by observing a single child and checked out by observing a hundred others. A good hunch would survive scrutiny; a bad one would fall by the wayside. If the hunch was to the effect that certain kinds of children would benefit from more of A, or less of B, we'd look for ways to provide more of A or less of B. Then we'd check periodically to see whether this helped or not. That's the way it is with clinicians. It's sloppy, but you can say in its favor that it never hurts if you're careful and that it often works. In fact, this method of approaching problems accounts for most of human progress since time began.

With us there were occasions when our theory was more advanced than our practice. At other times, and more commonly, it was much the other way around, and this was certainly the case when the fifties ended.

The early years of the sixties were spent in improving methods of treatment, but with the ever-broadening group of extraordinary people who were joining us we were also coming to be able to understand much more clearly why the things we were doing worked.

There was that courageous and brilliant Brazilian surgeon, Raymundo Veras, who had brought his beloved son, José Carlos Veras, to Philadelphia for treatment and found his highly respected, dignified and orderly life torn asunder when he saw what happened to his son. He remained to become a postgraduate student when he was already in his forties. He returned to Brazil to become the founder of the Centro de Reabilitação, Nossa Senhora da Gloria, an almost exact reproduction of The Institutes in Philadelphia, and in the process of doing so his highly respected, dignified, and orderly life disappeared along with his family fortune, which had been substantial. In its place came our seven-day week and twenty-hour day (which is reasonably alien to prominent families in Brazil) and a new kind of respect based not on who he was or what his name was but rather on what he did for children.

As a result of his continuing dedication, thousands of children have been helped, and another center was established in Barbacena by Léa Cascapera.

There was Gretchen Kerr, whom I originally didn't like and wouldn't hire. Gretchen worked for months as a volunteer before I saw my error. In a lifetime during which I had made some superb judgments about people (often against everyone's advice), and some gigantic boners about people (often against everyone's advice) my instant, instinctive, intuitive judgment that I didn't like Gretchen Kerr stands out not merely as the major mistake of my lifetime but perhaps might be the supreme misjudgment of the twentieth century. What I had seen as coldness was monumental calm. What I had seen as complete reserve was constant thoughtfulness. She became the director of the Children's Center.

Three more extraordinary M.D.s had joined the permanent staff. There was Dr. Roselise Wilkinson, a pediatrician. There was Dr. Evan Thomas, the man who had earlier done himself out of a job as one of the world's leading syphilologists by finding the answer. (After his controlled study on the effects of penicillin in the treatment of syphilis, the problem of finding an effective treatment was a problem no longer.)

They would both, in the years to come, accompany us into the most primitive countries in the world in our search for the developmental stages in children that are common to all cultures. These two, like Dr. Leland Green, internist and allergist, contributed mightily toward working out the scientific reasons why some of our methods worked as well as they did.

Two physical therapists also joined us, namely Art Sandler and Peter Moran. Both had come because they could no longer live with themselves in the face of their failures with brain-injured children after having used classical methods of treatment.

For like reasons, Dr. Neil Harvey and Bill Wells came to us from education and human engineering respectively.

Then there was Meg Tyson, a laboratory and X-ray technician who brought us not only her specific skills but also a vast love of children, and Elaine Lee of the prodigious memory who never forgot that every folder or punched card in her files is also an individual she could call by first name.

These new staff members along with the earlier staff members and many others who have not been described threw their knowledge and weight into the battle for the kids' progress and into the understanding of that progress.

17

SPEECH

No privilege is more important to man than the ability called speech. Speech may be defined as the ability to assign a specific sound to symbolize an idea. In English as in most modern languages the sound is almost invariably symbolic, contrived, and abstract, having no relationship to the idea except whatever relationship we assign to it. English is not an onomatopoetic language. Man agrees to visualize a specific idea when another man makes a specific sound.

In the English language we have agreed that if we hear a human being make the noise *pencil*, we will visualize a long thin object containing a lead in its core which is used to write with. There is no innate correspondence between the noise and the object. In French they have agreed that the sound *crayon* will evoke the same thought. In Portuguese they have agreed that the sound *lapis* will signify the same thing. Further sophistication of the same idea has created and refined the approach until very complicated ideas can be communicated.

In no area is man more vulnerable to misunderstanding, criticism, and downright abuse from his fellow man than if he should fail to develop speech or, having gained it, should lose it—for when man loses the ability to express himself by speech he is suspect in the world of having lost, also, the senses by which he arrives at the conclusions which he would express in speech. The world feels, it might be said, that if he can't say his name, it proves that he doesn't know his name. This is as unfair as holding that if a paralyzed man doesn't walk it must necessarily be because he does not know what walking is.

The same brain injury that stops walking also frequently stops talking, as I could easily remember from my stroke cases of a dozen years earlier. Lest you, the reader, if you are young, immediately disqualify yourself from this category, let it be understood that if you are old enough to read this paragraph, you are old enough to have a stroke, for not even children are immune to this devastating problem. We have seen stroke cases at every age level from one year or less to ninety-six years of age. The child who has had a stroke resembles, tragically, in every way, the older person who has suffered a stroke.

Imagine if you can the tragic circumstances that might well occur if you yourself were to suffer a stroke—a so-called "cerebral vascular accident." The tragedy we are about to describe occurs daily all over the world and has since man first existed.

Your stroke might be caused by many circumstances. To name only two:

1. You could suffer cerebral hemorrhage; that is to say, a break in one of the arteries or capillaries or veins which carry the blood to and from the brain. This would release blood into the surrounding tissues, and could drastically interfere with the function of the affected tissues. This could happen because of an injury to the head from an automobile accident, a falling brick, a diving accident, a bullet on the battlefield, weakening brain blood vessels due to advancing age, or any number of additional reasons.

2. You could suffer a stoppage of the blood circulation to a portion of the brain, occasioned by the blocking of one of the passageways of the blood by a blood clot. This would deprive that brain tissue of its normal supply of oxygen and cause damage to that part of the brain. This could happen because you had just undergone surgery in some other part of the body, or because you (if you are female) had recently borne a child, or for a number of other reasons. Clots can form anywhere, and can move freely through the larger arteries, then clog the first smaller channel they attempt to enter.

Let us suppose that your tragedy has taken place and that at some hour of the day or night you have lost consciousness, unaware of what happened to you. After a period of unconsciousness (of which, of course, you are unaware) you might eventually waken to find yourself alone in a hospital bed. Having asked yourself where you are and why you are there, you then might attempt to get out of the bed, only to find yourself completely or partially paralyzed on the side of your body in which your handedness exists; that is to say, if you are a right-handed person you might find yourself paralyzed on the right side.

You might also discover that even the other side of your body did not seem to respond as well as it should, and after unsuccessful attempts to get out of bed you might lie back to ponder what has happened to you. It is not impossible that shortly thereafter a nurse might enter the room and you,

THE
INSTITUTES
DEVELOPMENTAL
PROFILE™

	PREDOMINANT BRAIN STAGE	TIME FRAME		VISUAL COMPETENCE	AUDITORY COMPETENCE	TACTILE COMPETENCE
VII	SOPHISTI-CATED CORTEX	Superior	36 Mon.	Reading with total understanding	Understanding of complete vocabulary and proper sentences	Tactile identification of objects
		Average	72 Mon.			
		Slow	144 Mon.			
VI	PRIMITIVE CORTEX	Superior	18 Mon.	Identification of visual symbols and letters within experience	Understanding of 2000 words and simple sentences	Ability to determine characteristics of objects by tactile means
		Average	36 Mon.			
		Slow	72 Mon.			
V	EARLY CORTEX	Superior	9 Mon.	Differentiation of similar but unlike simple visual symbols	Understanding of 10 to 25 words and two couplets	Tactile differentiation of similar but unlike objects
		Average	18 Mon.			
		Slow	36 Mon.			
IV	INITIAL CORTEX	Superior	6 Mon.	Convergence of vision resulting in simple depth perception	Understanding of two words of speech	Tactile understanding of the third dimension in objects which appear to be flat
		Average	12 Mon.			
		Slow	24 Mon.			
III	MIDBRAIN and SUBCORTI-CAL AREAS	Superior	3.5 Mon.	Appreciation of detail within a configuration	Appreciation of meaningful sounds	Appreciation of gnostic sensation
		Average	7 Mon.			
		Slow	14 Mon.			
II	BRAIN STEM and EARLY SUB-CORTICAL AREAS	Superior	1 Mon.	Outline perception	Vital response to threatening sounds	Perception of vital sensation
		Average	2.5 Mon.			
		Slow	5 Mon.			
I	EARLY BRAIN STEM and CORD	Superior	Birth to .5	Light reflex	Startle reflex	Babinski reflex
		Average	Birth to 1.0			
		Slow	Birth to 2.0			

THE INSTITUTES DEVELOPMENTAL PROFILE™ BY GLENN J. DOMAN	MOBILITY	LANGUAGE	MANUAL COMPETENCE
	Using a leg in a skilled role which is consistent with the dominant hemisphere	Complete vocabulary and proper sentence structure	Using a hand to write which is consistent with the dominant hemisphere
	Walking and running in complete cross pattern	2000 words of language and short sentences	Bimanual function with one hand in a skilled role
	Walking with arms freed from the primary balance role	10 to 25 words of language and two couplets	Cortical opposition bilaterally and simultaneously
	Walking with arms used in a primary balance role most frequently at or above shoulder height	Two words of speech used spontaneously and meaningfully	Conical opposition in either hand
	Creeping on hands and knees, culminating in cross-pattern creeping	Creation of meaningful sounds	Prehensile grasp
	Crawling in the prone position culminating in cross-pattern crawling	Vital crying in response to threats to life	Vital release
THE INSTITUTES FOR THE ACHIEVEMENT OF HUMAN POTENTIAL® 8801 STENTON AVENUE WYNDMOOR, PENNSYLVANIA 19038	Movement of arms and legs without bodily movement	Birth cry and crying	Grasp reflex

much relieved, might say to the nurse, "What am I doing here, where am I, what happened to me?" But you might find, to your horror, that the words emerging from your mouth are, "Dub dub dub dub dub" or "Zuu zuu zuu zuu zuu zuu."

If the nurse then looked upset but quickly recovered to say, "Everything is fine," it would be understandable if you then said, "Everything is *not* fine, I am paralyzed, and I find I am having difficulty in speaking." If what emerged from your mouth was, again, "Dub dub dub dub dub," one might well understand your distress.

Let us suppose that next your family arrived. You might well try to say to your family, "Where am I and what happened to me and thank goodness you're here." If again you heard yourself say, "Dub dub dub," imagine your feelings at this time.

Let us further suppose that the family now stood at the foot of the bed and said across your totally aware body, "Isn't it terrible, he was always such a bright person." If by this time you in your frustration in attempting to make the family understand that while you can't talk you understand those things taking place about you and know very well what you want to say. . . if you pick up a bedpan and throw it at the family, this action, of course, would in no way solve the problem but would be very likely to produce this reaction, "And now not only is he off his rocker but he's becoming violent."

If this example seems impossible or overdrawn, it can only be said that, tragically, it takes place daily. We have seen many patients who, following a stroke and the loss of speech, were dealt with as if they were psychotic and eventually ended up with their bodies in restraint. In such a situation it can well be understood why the patient's anguish might quickly result in another cerebral vascular accident, perhaps the final one.

You can also well imagine the satisfaction many patients felt in their initial interview at The Institutes when the examiner, realizing instantly that the patient was *aphasic* (the proper name for the inability to communicate due to a cortical problem), said, "Mr. Jones, while you can't talk, I know perfectly well that you know what you want to say, but can't say it."

It was a great pleasure, in those days before the children crowded most of the adults out of the doors of The Institutes, to watch the patient sigh a gigantic sigh of relief and say very clearly with his countenance, if not with words, "Thank the good Lord that someone knows I am not off my rocker because I can't say the things I want to say."

Perhaps the reader is saying to himself that what I have described is a terrible thing, and that while such dreadful things may have happened fifty or a hundred years ago they couldn't possibly happen today.

If you are thinking any such thing it would be prudent to disabuse yourself of the notion. It was at this time in history (the beginning of the 1960s) that a very famous man had a stroke and was paralyzed on his right side and unable to speak.

It was also at about this time in history that I was teaching a large class of professional people including physicians, therapists, psychologists, and others. When I discussed this aspect of speech problems I could see disbelief on the faces of several people. This rather annoyed me.

"Very recently," I began, "a very famous man had a stroke and I understand has a speech problem. It is quite conceivable that some therapist is at this moment showing him a picture of a cat and saying, 'Ambassador, this is a *cat*. This is the cat's *head* and this is the cat's *tail*.'

"This particular man," I continued, "has made a half a billion dollars. He has a son who is President of the United States, another son who is Attorney General of the United States, and still another who is a Senator. I am quite confident that Joseph Kennedy knows what a cat is. Still, it is quite conceivable that he is being treated as if he were feeble-minded just because he can't talk."

Two and a half years later I had opportunity to learn that this was almost precisely what had been happening to Joseph Kennedy.

One often wonders what might happen if one day when the door opened to admit the therapist with the pictures of the cat a patient might not in sheer anguished frustration pick up an ash tray and hit the therapist right on the head. If the patient happened to hit the therapist in exactly the right spot on the head (a couple of inches above the ear, on the dominant side of the brain) with exactly the right amount of force (enough to rupture the middle cerebral artery—but not enough to kill), then there would be two people who would know what a cat was but be unable to say "cat."

While I am, in principle, pretty much opposed to anybody hitting anybody on the head, I think that in such a case I would be a good deal more in sympathy with the hitter than the hittee.

A patient who can't talk is not necessarily feeble-minded, insane, or bewitched, but may simply have lost the ability to say words. What has happened to the patient is referred to in medicine as *aphasia*. Although there are many definitions of aphasia, we have chosen to define aphasia as an inability to *communicate* due to an injury in the cortex.

It is important to note that we have not used the term inability to *speak* but instead have used the term inability to *communicate*. The word *communicate* is obviously a much broader term than the term *speak*. The patient who is unable to speak due to aphasia is also unable to communicate in terms of writing, sign language, etc., and he can read only in relationship to his understanding of the spoken word. He can write only to the degree that he can talk, for aphasia is indeed a loss in the whole area of communication and not simply in the area of speech itself.

We have dealt with adults at this length because it is important to compare the problems of adult patients who have lost their powers of speech and communication with the problems of children who may never have gained speech due to brain injury. Let's return to the definition of aphasia itself, *a loss in the ability to communicate due to an injury in the cortex.* Does this description fit the children who also may not speak due to an injured cortex? It does except for one word: loss. It can't be said that a human being has lost something he didn't have in the first place. Since the children who do not speak due to a brain injury—at least those of them who incurred their injury prior to one year of age—have never spoken, it is fair to say that they cannot lose what they have never had.

In these circumstances it would obviously be improper to say that a child who had never spoken had lost his ability to speak. If this were a mere play on words it would not be important, but it is more than that. When comparing the children and the adults it is important to note that each has an advantage over the other.

The child holds over the adult one simple advantage. Let us suppose that a child was originally intended to be a right-handed child. This would mean that his left cortex would be the area responsible for his speech. Now let us suppose that prior to the time that speech had formed in that left hemisphere, the left hemisphere was injured. What would happen here would be a very simple thing. In the vast majority of cases, the child would simply develop speech in his *right* hemisphere instead, and this speech would be developed as well as if he had developed it in the hemisphere originally intended to carry his speech. Obviously then, in this respect the child has a tremendous advantage over the adult whose speech is firmly established in his left hemisphere (if he is right-handed). Only if the child is hurt in both sides of his cortex will he be truly aphasic.

What advantage does the adult have over the child? His advantage is merely this: He has known how to speak before and understands thoroughly what is required of him. The brain-injured child who may have damage in both of his hemispheres and therefore does not develop speech does not enjoy this advantage.

Let us consider now the speech problems of brain-injured children. It is certain that the majority of brain-injured children have a speech problem of one kind or another. Some of them find it difficult even to make sounds. Others can make sounds, but sounds that are without significance. Others make significant sounds but have no words. Others have a free flow of language but the voice does not have meaning. Sometimes the brain-injured child demonstrates no problem except speech.

Nothing is more vital to his wellness than the development of speech.

We had studied first the speech, or, more exactly, the lack of speech of the injured children themselves, many, many years before. We had come from that study thoroughly mystified by what we had found, or, again more precisely, what we had failed to find.

We turned next to what is called in medicine, the literature. Here, in contrast to the lack of information that had existed in relation to a well child's mobility, we found a moderate amount of information on a well child's speech and a large amount of writing on the subject of the brain-injured child's speech. However, we came away from this study even more confused than from the study of the children themselves! The things we read in this area were extremely contradictory.

This despite the fact that scientists and mothers alike had observed the development of speech carefully and recorded it carefully throughout history. There is even disagreement in the literature as to when various stages or levels of speech occur. Some observers, as an example, held that "babbling" occurred in the first month or two of life, others held that babbling began in the second year of life. Very few, if any, had defined babbling. When one turned to the dictionary he found babbling defined as babylike talking, the talking of an idiot, or the sound made by a brook.

Some of the disagreement as to when things occurred was unquestionably due to the fact that the language describing language was highly inexact, and babbling or cooing obviously meant different things to different observers.

Also, as has been noted, much of what had been recorded about the speech of well children appeared to us to be true but not significant. The word *significant* in scientific usage does not mean exactly the same thing as in normal usage. Perhaps this can best be explained with an obvious example of a true but not significant observation.

Suppose one studied a thousand children under one year old and noted that the vast majority of them did not have speech. Suppose one then studied a thousand twenty-year-olds and noted that a thousand of them did have speech. He might then properly observe that those people who have speech are a great deal taller than those people who did not have speech, and while this would be true he would have to be careful not to come to the conclusion that speech was a result of getting taller.

It was our opinion that while babbling, cooing, and various other baby-like sounds occurred along the way in the development of speech, these did not have to be present in themselves for the creation of speech but were merely a method of measuring the development of that speech rather than the reasons for the development of that speech. So again we returned to the well children themselves, and were now not surprised at all to find that there were again four significant stages in the development of speech in a child and that these four stages again paralleled in chronological span and in development the four stages which we had now seen many times.

These four stages are:

Stage 1—The child actually begins life itself with a birth cry, which is reflex in nature and has its developmental utility but is not significant in terms of communication. This cry of the infant denotes nothing more than the presence of life itself, and when mother hears the cry she learns nothing except that the child is alive. This cry carries no message of happiness or unhappiness. The factor to measure at this level is the mere presence or absence of the ability to cry or make other sounds.

Stage 2—The infant can now convey by sound the fact that he is experiencing severe pain which may actually threaten his existence and these sounds are, in essence, a cry for help. Mother recognizes quickly that this cry is imperative, day or night, and responds to it immediately and instinctively.

Stage 3—This is the stage of significant, meaningful sound, short of language but beyond the simple cry for help. In this stage the child can convey pleasure, displeasure, apprehension, anticipation, and other states of happiness or unhappiness. The world recognizes cooing, for instance, as indicating happiness. The significance of this stage lies not so much in the newfound ability to make varying sounds by varying mouth positions and breath control but is instead in the fact that each variation is now meaningful and conveys a clear, although limited, message. The factor to measure here is whether or not these sounds are meaningful to mother even though no words yet exist. This stage is goal-directed, and the child can get many things he wants although he has no words.

Stage 4—At this level the baby actually begins to imitate the sounds he hears and to use them meaningfully. It matters not to the central nervous system whether these words happen to be English, French, Portuguese, or whatever. It is significant only that the nervous system has matured to the point where it can now deal in symbolic sounds. The baby begins to say single words and to establish a vocabulary. His language will continue to improve in scope and meaning until around six years of life at which time the significant brain maturation will be complete. This obviously does not mean that his ability to improve in speech stops at six, but the difference between an adult of few words and an adult with the eloquence of Winston Churchill is not dependent upon simple maturation but rather upon many, many factors which space will not permit us to touch upon.

Now that we felt that we understood the basic stages of speech growth, the next question was: What can we do about the speech problems of the brain-injured child?

We had not been impressed with the results of speech therapy in the brain-injured children. Indeed we did not believe we had ever seen a speechless child due to a brain injury who had learned to speak as a result of the standard methods of speech therapy.

Our belief, which was now very strong, that when an injury existed in the brain, it was the brain you had to treat, seemed to hold true in the case of the absence of speech. We concluded that a child could not have his speech problem solved by dealing with his tongue, mouth, lips, and larynx any more than a child could have his walking problems solved by dealing with his feet, knees, ankles or hips, if the reason for both of these problems existed within the brain. We were then totally unaware that as our new treatment methods progressed we had been developing adequate methods of training the brain-injured child to talk, by treating his brain and then simply giving him opportunity to talk.

18

READING

The parent of a severely brain-injured child who comes to this chapter entitled *Reading* may well be astonished at the thought that a brain-injured child with a problem in talking might be far enough along to have a problem in reading.

The mere fact that such a chapter exists in a book on brain-injured children delights us, and we cannot help but reminisce about the pathway that led us so far in a mere decade or so of time.

At the outset, it had been our goal to make the child with a severe brain-injury move just a little. Later it was our goal to make the child move just a little more. When we had succeeded in doing this with some regularity, it then became our goal to make the child walk. When we began to accomplish this in many children, it became our goal to make him walk normally.

Once it was our limited goal to help the child with a severe brain injury to make meaningful, if limited, sounds. Then it became our goal to make him speak just a little more. And then it was our goal to make him speak normally.

When this had sometimes been accomplished, it became our goal to get the child into a school, any school. Still later, it was our goal to get the child into a school with well children, no matter how far behind he might be. Still later, it was our goal to get him into a school with well children of the proper age, even though he was at the bottom of his class. Finally it became our goal to have him keep up with his peers in every way, in school and out. Let me make haste to point out that we do not mean to imply that this is always *possible* but at least today it is *always* our goal.

I should like to hazard a guess that many of you who are parents of brain-injured children are saying at this point, "I should be so happy if our child could only walk or talk and never mind being able to read."

I cannot help but remember an incident that took place a long, long time ago when I had just finished my schooling and had taken my place as a staff member of a large hospital. I remember very clearly the attractive thirty-year-old woman who was diagnosed as having an incurable illness. This illness not only prevented walking and most other movements but was quite painful since her legs frequently flexed involuntarily, pulling up on her chest and causing great pain.

I remember well the patient's tearful request which began with the explanation that she understood she could never possibly walk, but, she said, "If only the terrible pain would stop." This patient was treated long and arduously and the day did come when the pain stopped. The patient then said, "I know I shall never be able to move, but if only I could wiggle my feet a little bit it would feel so good to know they were mine." And after much work and effort some leg movement was achieved. The patient then said that she knew she could never function or perform, but if only, using her arms, she could put a little weight on her feet, how good it would be to feel herself in the upright position. After more months of work this was accomplished. This time the patient said she knew she could never walk, but if only she could lift one foot and the other as she stood supporting herself with her arms . . . and this too was accomplished. And by this time it began to appear as if indeed the miracle of walking itself was possible. I will not soon forget the day when she was to take her first steps. It was a dramatic moment. Many of the principal members of the hospital staff were present that day in the exercise department when the patient was stood up and told to take her first steps. She walked across an entire room unsupported, and I remember waiting anxiously for the first words she would say after this miraculous accomplishment because I was sure they would be words to cherish forever. It is true that what she said was not soon to be forgotten. Having walked across the room, she turned to the delighted staff and snarled, "Does this mean I'm going to limp?"

Her miraculous recovery was a remarkable example of great good fortune and very bad diagnosis. Each time we hear a parent say, "I would be so pleased if only my child could get to do this, that, or the other thing," I am reminded of that patient so long ago.

The fact is that today brain-injured children only two and three years old regularly learn to read on The Institutes program. It was Tommy Lunski who opened our eyes. It was difficult for us to believe the absurd story that Mr. Lunski told us about Tommy. And this is strange, because when we first saw Tommy at The Institutes we were already aware of all the things we needed to know in order to understand what was happening to Tommy.

Tommy was the fourth child in the Lunski family. The Lunski parents hadn't had much time for formal schooling and had worked very hard to support their three nice, normal children. By the time Tommy was born Mr. Lunski owned a taproom and things were looking up.

However, Tommy was born very severely brain-injured. When he was two years old he was admitted for neurosurgical examination at a fine hospital in New Jersey. The day Tommy was discharged the chief neurosurgeon had a frank talk with Mr. and Mrs. Lunski. The doctor explained that his studies had shown that Tommy was a vegetable-like child who would never walk or talk and should therefore be placed in an institution for life.

All of Mr. Lunski's determined Polish ancestry reinforced his American stubbornness as he stood up to his great height, hitched up his considerable girth and announced, "Doc, you're all mixed up. That's *our* kid."

The Lunskis spent many months searching for someone who would tell them that it didn't necessarily have to be that way. The answers were all the same.

By Tommy's third birthday, however, they had found a competent neurosurgeon.

After carefully making his own neurosurgical studies, he told the parents that while Tommy was indeed severely brain-injured, perhaps something might be done for him at a group of institutions in a suburb of Philadelphia called Chestnut Hill.

Tommy arrived at The Institutes for the Achievement of Human Potential when he was just three years and two weeks old. He could not walk or speak more than a few words.

Tommy's brain injury and his resultant problems were evaluated at The Institutes. A treatment program was prescribed for Tommy. The parents were taught how to carry out this program at home and were told that if they adhered to it consistently, Tommy might be greatly improved.

There was no question but that the Lunskis would follow the strict program. They did so with religious intensity.

By the time they returned for the second visit, Tommy could crawl.

Now the Lunskis attacked the program with energy inspired by success. So determined were they that when their car broke down on the way to Philadelphia for the third visit, they simply bought a used car and continued to their appointment. They could hardly wait to tell us that Tommy could now say his first two words: "Mommy" and "Daddy." Tommy was now three and a half and could creep on hands and knees. Then his mother tried something only a mother would try with a child like Tommy. In much the same manner that a father buys a football for his infant son, Mother bought an alphabet book for her three-and-a-half-year-old, severely brain-injured, two-word-speaking son. Tommy, she announced, was very bright, whether he could walk and talk or not. Anyone who had any sense could see it simply by looking in his eyes!

While our tests for intelligence in brain-injured children during those days were a good deal more involved than Mrs. Lunski's, they were no more accurate than hers. We agreed that Tommy was intelligent all right, but to teach a brain-injured three-and-a-half-year-old to read—well, that was another question.

We therefore paid very little attention when Mrs. Lunski later announced that Tommy, then four years of age, could read all of the words in the alphabet book even more easily than he could read the letters. We were more concerned and pleased with his speech, which was progressing constantly, as was his physical mobility.

By the time Tommy was four years and two months old his father announced that he could read all of a Dr. Seuss book called *Green Eggs and Ham*. We smiled politely and noted how remarkably Tommy's speech and movement were improving.

When Tommy was four years and six months old Mr. Lunski announced that Tommy could read, and had read, *all* of the Dr. Seuss books. We noted on the chart that Tommy was progressing beautifully, as well as the fact that Mr. Lunski "said" Tommy could read.

When Tommy arrived for his eleventh visit he had just had his fifth birthday. Although we were delighted with the superb advances Tommy was making, there was nothing to indicate at the beginning of the visit that this day would be an important one for all children. Nothing, that is, except Mr. Lunski's usual nonsensical report. Tommy, Mr. Lunski announced, could now read anything, including the *Reader's Digest*, and what was more, he could understand it, and what was more than that, he'd started doing it before his fifth birthday.

We were saved from the necessity of having to comment on this by the arrival of one of the kitchen staff with our lunch—tomato juice and a hamburger. Mr. Lunski, noting our lack of response, took a piece of paper from the desk and wrote, "Glenn Doman likes to drink tomato juice and eat hamburger."

Tommy, following his father's instructions, read this easily and with the proper accents and inflections. He did not hesitate as does the seven-year-old, reading each word separately without understanding of the sentence itself.

"Write another sentence," we said slowly. Mr. Lunski wrote, "Tommy's daddy likes to drink beer and whiskey. He has a great big fat belly from drinking beer and whiskey at Tommy's Tavern."

Tommy had read only the first three words aloud when he began to laugh. The funny part about Dad's belly was down on the fourth line since Mr. Lunski was writing in large letters.

This severely brain-injured little child was actually reading much faster than he was reciting the words aloud at his normal speaking rate. Tommy was not only reading, he was speed-reading, and his comprehension was obvious!

The fact that we were thunderstruck was written on our faces. We turned to Mr. Lunski.

"I've been telling you he can read," said Mr. Lunski.

After that day none of us would ever be the same, for this was the last piece of puzzle in a pattern that had been forming for more than twenty years.

Tommy had taught us that a severely brain-injured child can learn to read far earlier than normal children usually do.

Tommy, of course, was immediately subjected to full-scale testing by a group of experts who were brought from Washington for this purpose within a week. Tommy—severely brain-injured and just barely five years old—could read better than the average child twice his age—and with complete comprehension.

By the time Tommy was six he walked, although this was relatively new to him and he was still a little shaky; he read at the sixthgrade level (eleven- to twelve-year-old level). Tommy was not going to spend his life in an institution, but his parents were looking for a "special" school to put Tommy in come the following September. Special *high*, that is, not special low. Fortunately there are schools now for exceptional "gifted" children. Tommy has had the dubious "gift" of severe brain injury and the unquestionable gift of parents who love him very much indeed and who believed that at least one kid wasn't achieving his potential.

Tommy, in the end, was a catalyst for twenty years of study. Maybe it would be more accurate to say he was a fuse for an explosive charge that had been growing in force for twenty years.

The fascinating thing was that Tommy *wanted* very much to read and enjoyed it tremendously.

A revolution was already underway, and the cause of the revolution was television.

The kids didn't know that they would be able to read if the tools were given them, and the adults in the television industry, who finally furnished them, knew neither that the children had the ability nor that television would supply the tools that would bring about the gentle revolution.

It's astonishing really, that the secret had not been discovered by more kids long before this. It's a wonder that they, with all their brightness—because bright they are—didn't catch on.

The only reason some adult had not given the secret away to the two-year-olds is that we adults had not known it either. Of course, if we had known, we would never have allowed it to remain a secret because it's far too important to the kids and to us too.

The trouble is that we have made the print too small.

The trouble is that we have made the print too small.

The trouble is that we have made the print too small.

The trouble is that we have made the print too small.

It is even possible to make the print too small for an adult's sophisti-cated visual pathway—which includes the brain.

It is almost impossible to make the print too big to read.

But it is possible to make it too small, and that's just what we've done.

We have tended to keep type so small that the typical child of preschool age simply fails to notice that words differ one from another. He can see, all right. As any mother knows, he has no trouble "seeing" a pin lying on the floor, or an ant crawling on the ground. He may not, however, have "noticed" that words differ, just as many an adult has never troubled to take notice of the difference between a bee and a wasp.

The secret is simply to make it easy for him to notice that printed words do differ. And television had given away the secret— through the com-mercials.

When the man on television says, *Gulf, Gulf, Gulf,* in a nice, clear, loud voice and the television screen shows the word **GULF** in nice, clear, big letters, the kids all learn to recognize the word—and they don't even know the alphabet.

For the truth is that very young children can read, provided that, in the beginning, you make the print very big.

But isn't it easier for a child to understand a spoken word rather than a written one? Not at all. The child's brain, which is the only organ that has learning capacity, "hears" the clear, loud television words through the ear and interprets them as only the brain can. Simultaneously, the child's brain "sees" the big, clear television words through his eye and interprets them in exactly the same manner.

It makes no difference to the brain whether it "sees" a sight or "hears" a sound. It can understand both equally well. All that is required is that the sounds be loud enough and clear enough for the ear to hear and the words big enough and clear enough for the eye to see so that the brain can interpret them—the former we have done but the latter we have failed to do.

People have probably always talked to children in a louder voice than they use with adults, and we still do so, instinctively realizing that children cannot hear and simultaneously understand normal adult conversational tones.

Nobody would think of talking to one-year-olds in a normal voice —we all virtually shout at them.

Try talking to a two-year-old in a conversational tone and chances are that he will neither hear nor understand you. It is likely that if his back is turned he will not even pay attention to you.

Even a three-year-old, if spoken to in a conversational tone, is unlikely to understand or even heed you if there are conflicting sounds or another conversation in the room.

Everyone talks loudly to children, and the younger the child is the louder we talk.

Suppose, for the sake of argument, that we adults had long ago decided to speak to each other in sounds just soft enough so that no child could hear and understand them. Suppose, however, that these sounds were just loud enough for his auditory pathway to have become sufficiently sophisticated to hear and understand soft sounds when he got to be six years of age.

Under this set of circumstances we would probably give children "hearing readiness" tests at six years of age. If we found that he could "hear" but not understand words (which would certainly be the case, since his auditory pathway could not distinguish soft sounds until now), it is possible that we would now introduce him to the spoken language by saying the letter A to him, and then B, and so on until he had learned the alphabet, before beginning to teach him how words sound.

One is led to conclude that perhaps there would be a great many children with a problem of "hearing" words and sentences, and perhaps instead of Rudolf Flesch's well-known book called *Why Johnny Can't Read*, we would need a book called *Why Johnny Can't Hear*.

The above is precisely what we have done with written language. We have made it too small for the child to "see and understand."

Now let's make another supposition.

If we had spoken in whispers while simultaneously writing words and sentences very large and distinct, very young children would be able to read but would be unable to understand verbal language.

Now suppose that television were introduced with its big written words and accompanying loud spoken words. Naturally all kids could read the words, but there would also be many children who would begin to understand the spoken word at the astonishing age of two or three.

And that, in reverse, is what is happening today in reading!

TV has also shown us several other interesting things about children.

The first is that youngsters watch most "kiddie programs" without paying constant attention; but as everyone knows, when the commercials come on the children run to the television set to *hear* about and *read* about what the products contain and what they are supposed to do.

The point here is not that television commercials are pitched to the two-year-old set, nor is it that gasoline or what it contains has any special fascination for two-year-olds, because it does not. The truth is that the children can *learn* from commercials with the big enough, clear enough, loud enough, repeated message and that all children have a rage to learn.

Children would rather *learn* about something than simply be amused by Mickey Mouse—and that's a fact.

As a result then, the kids ride down the road in the family car and blithely read the Gulf sign, the McDonald's sign, and the Coca-Cola sign as well as many others—and *that's* a fact.

There is no need to ask the question, "*Can* very small children learn to read?" They've answered that, they *can*.

I have already described the method by which children on The Institutes program learn to read in my book *How To Teach Your Baby To Read*, first published in 1964.

1960 to 1970

THE DECADE OF EXPANSION

19

FINDING THE BREAK
IN THE CIRCUIT

As the decade of the 1960s began, a couple of related facts emerged. First: While brain-injured children had a great deal in common, it was obvious that no two brain injuries were precisely alike. It was equally obvious that the differences between the children were a direct reflection of the differences between the location and the degree of their brain injuries. It was obvious that if we could determine in a more precise way exactly what a child could not do of the things he *should* do, we could then prescribe a program tailored *exactly* to his needs.

Second: We had by now measured literally thousands of children (including many hundreds who appeared to be totally well) to find out precisely what they could do. Somewhere within that vast amount of data there had to be a pattern, a vitally important pattern.

For at least five years I had had stronger and stronger feelings that deep within me I already *knew* that pattern, and that if I just sat and thought and thought and thought I would be able to pull that pattern from my knowledge.

There were certain things that I already knew.

I knew that there were six different, important, measurable functions, the lack of which indicated trouble within the cortex. Three of these were receptive (sensory) skills, namely reading, understanding speech, and identifying objects by feel. Three were expressive (motor) skills, namely walking, speaking, and certain manual skills culminating in writing. On the road to mastery of each of these six skills, every individual went through four or more predictable stages.

I knew that what we were searching for was a pattern of growth, the grand plan, the design of how a human being got to be a human being. It was the developmental diagram we were looking for. Not *my* developmental diagram, not our developmental diagram, but Nature's diagram.

I knew that this was a diagram of brain growth rather than physical growth.

I knew that the process ended far before physical maturity and probably before ten years of age.

I even had a name for it (which I had mentioned to no one). I called it the *developmental profile*. It was a profile of how a child's brain matured.

I was confident that we had every piece of the puzzle within our grasp and had had for some time. The question was: Which of hundreds of thousands of pieces of information were the truly significant ones? Which really mattered? Which were rungs in the ladder and which were effects rather than causes? We had a pretty clear idea of that up to one year of age—but not beyond.

It was like having a song right on the edge of my mind to which I couldn't remember either the words or the music. It was maddening. Never entirely out of mind. Most of the time on the edge of my mind. Sometimes occupying most of my mind but occasionally driving everything else from it. But instead of going on for hours it had been going on for years. I had to bring that picture of a normal child into focus.

Then one of the head nurses, Florence Sharp, said something that made things start to fall in place. She was primarily responsible for the inpatient children, and that morning I asked her a question about a specific child (that same question that was driving me mad about all the children).

"How," I had asked, "is Mark doing?"

Sharpie said, "He is *much, much* better."

"Sharpie," I said irritably (and unreasonably), "how much better is *much, much* better? And don't tell me that *much, much better* is better than *much better* but not as good as *much, much, much better.*" I don't really know why I should have given Sharpie a bad time for not knowing the answer to a question that had been driving me mad for years.

"He is better."

It made me want to scream.

If he is better, then everything is peachy keen. But is it?

I had watched kids go down the drain because they were *not* better for twenty years, but I had also watched some kids go down the drain because they *were* better. Remember the kids we had found who were *better* in our original study? More than a third of them were *better*. Remember that Johnny could hold his head up better and that Mary was less spastic. But remember too, that if they had continued to get *better* at the same rate, it would have taken them until they were a hundred years old to begin to walk.

Every time I thought of this dilemma I thought of a close friend of mine and the response he always gave when anyone asked him, "How's your wife?" He would counter with a grave expression on his face and a twinkle in his eye, "Compared to whom?"

That was the heart of the question about the brain-injured child who was *better*. Better compared to whom?

Historically, that question had always been answered by comparing him to himself, which is to say by comparing him to a brain-injured child.

If an automobile that had been smashed in an accident were always compared to an automobile smashed in an accident instead of to an undamaged car, how in the world would you ever hope to fix it?

Thus, if a brain-injured child were compared only with himself and were even a tiny fraction better we might be satisfied—and that satisfaction would destroy him.

And what tools had we used to make even *that* distinction? There were two kinds of tests, but they were equally irrelevant when applied to brain-injured children.

First, there were the physical tests. These were muscle tests in which each of the hundreds of muscles in the body were individually tested by the therapist who assigned a score to each. The score might range from 0 to 10 with 0 representing total paralysis and 10 representing total strength.

In brain-injured children these tests were totally unreliable (which is to say, that five different therapists might give five different scores when testing the same muscle).

In addition, there was no sensible way to add up the results. As an example, if one tested a hundred muscles he ended up with a hundred scores. Did he, then, add them up and divide by 100 to get an average score? Let's suppose that half of the muscles tested at 0 and half tested at 10. That would give us a total of 0 and 500 to add together to come up with a total of 500. If we now divided by 100 to get an average, we would come up with an average of 5. Thus, a child who had half of his muscles totally paralyzed and half of his muscles at full strength would come up with a score of 5, showing that he was precisely in the middle, which would represent a total untruth and would describe no single muscle in his body. If, on the other hand, we regarded each of the hundred muscles individually and on a subsequent visit found thirty of his muscles to be improved by one point each and thirty of his muscles to have weakened by one point, the question would remain, was he better or worse than at the previous visit, and compared to whom?

Finally, there was the fact that the tests were not valid for the simple reason that we were testing the wrong thing. We were not testing his brain function, we were testing his biceps strength.

Testing his intelligence was even harder than testing his muscles.

The tests that are commonly used to test intelligence in the United States are *reasonably* reliable and *reasonably* valid tests of a well child's *abilities*. They are nothing more. There is a great and growing suspicion on the part of almost everyone who uses them that they do not in fact test true intelligence *even* in the well child.

When these tests are used on brain-injured children they are an almost precise test of his *disabilities*. *Disability* is not to be confused with *inability*, which is an inherent lack of ability to perform an action; *disability*, on the other hand, arises from a deprivation or loss of the ability to perform an action.

Now there is nothing wrong with testing abilities, and there is certainly nothing wrong with testing *disabilities*. Providing one gigantic proviso: Providing that when we are testing abilities we *know* we are testing abilities, and providing that when we are testing *disabilities* we *know* we are testing disabilities. But when we test disability and believe we are testing ability, only devastating results can follow, and that is precisely what occurs every single time we apply such tests to a brain-injured child. Yet the tests continue to be given and, worse, the ratings that result are often accepted as a basis for action. Brain-injured children by the hundreds of thousands have been "put away" in institutions for life on such evidence.

We knew this and knew it to be a tragedy. It was not enough, however, to know that these tests should not be relied upon in evaluating brain-injured children. We needed to come up with an acceptable alternative.

It was painfully clear why these so-called intelligence tests did not work. Every one of them depended on one or more of three possibilities.

If a child was over six, he was expected to take a test involving reading the questions and writing answers. If, because he was brain-injured, he was unable to read or write, it would be assumed that he had failed the test because he was not intelligent enough to read and write. That would get him the score of a total idiot if he was totally unable to read or write due to his brain injury or that of a moron or imbecile if he could read or write only a little due to his brain injury.

If a child was under six, or if it was recognized that the reason he couldn't read or write was due to brain injury and not to idiocy, he would be given a verbal test. The examiner would ask verbal questions and expect verbal answers. Now if he was unable to speak, due to brain injury, he would be rated an idiot on the assumption that he was not "intelligent" enough to answer the question. If he could, as a result of a lesser brain injury, answer only partially, due to the speech problem, he would come up with a score of imbecile or moron.

If a child was under three, or if it was recognized that the reason he was unable to carry on a conversation was because he was brain-injured rather than because he was an idiot, then he would be given a test that did not require him to answer the questions but simply to follow directions such as "go close the door." Now if a child was paralyzed due to brain injury and thus was unable to "go close the door," then it would be assumed that he was an idiot because he was not "intelligent" enough to go close the door.

If a very bright and sensitive examiner recognized that the reason he did not close the door was because he was paralyzed and not because he was too stupid, the examiner might fall into the final trap. He might take some function he had seen the child perform and therefore knew that the child could do, let's say rubbing his eyes; he might ask the child to do that to see if he was bright enough to understand the question. Now if the child had an auditory problem due to his brain injury and as a result was unable to interpret the question, even our sensitive examiner might well conclude that he was a complete idiot.

It happens all the time.

I am appalled that in this nation which prides itself on the fact that even a confessed murderer has many courts of appeal before he can be institutionalized for life, a child whose greatest sin is that he is hurt can be institutionalized for life—and in an institution which is almost invariably far worse than any criminal would put up with.

In the early days we knew with horrible certainty what was wrong with measurement. But we didn't know what was right.

The tangle began to unwind for me when Sharpie answered my question. Despite the unreasonable way in which I had asked it, Sharpie answered me softly and with understanding of my frustration.

"What I mean by *much, much better*," she said, "is that when we saw him first a year ago he was four years old but he was behaving like a well six-month-old. Now he is five years old and behaving like a well two-year-old."

"Sharpie, that's about the first sensible thing I've heard anybody say about how a kid's doing."

"Ummmm," she said and smiled. "You always say you want sense from the staff."

"That just might be brilliant, Sharpie."

"You mean I said something brilliant?" asked Sharpie.

"Ummmm," I said and smiled.

I headed north on campus from Clarke Hall where I'd been talking to Sharpie toward the Blackburn Building where we lived. I stopped for a while on a bench in a sun that was warm for March.

I had the feeling once again that I was right on the edge of understanding, and I thought very slowly so as not to lose my place.

If Mark had been four years old acting like a six-month-old, it meant that until we saw him first it had taken him forty-eight months to grow six months' worth, so his total progress had only been $1/8$ of what it should have been.

Now if in the year that we had been seeing him he had gained a year in age but a year and a half in performance that was obviously great! His rate of progress had jumped from $1/8$ of normal to $1 1/2$ times normal.

Normal? What was normal? Was it—could it be—as simple as saying that a five-year-old is normal when he can do what other well five-year-olds can do when they are five years old?

Now my mind was racing and all attempts to make it move slowly went out the window. I literally ran to my house. I ran into the house and to my den and locked the door. I gathered pencils, pen, papers, colored crayons, thumbtacks.

I switched on the light over my drawing board and tacked down a large piece of drawing paper.

At the top I printed:

"THE DEVELOPMENTAL PROFILE"

I didn't print it very well. I was out of breath from running and highly excited and my hand shook.

If I could do what I was beginning to believe I could do, I would have a simple, workable, valid, reliable, and relevant tool for measuring the degree of disability and rate of progress of brain-injured kids. Without the ability to measure there can be no science, and I had been disturbed by our lack of ability to measure our own results for many years. If it worked, we could *measure* our results—both our successes and our failures. It was impossible to say which was the most important.

Good-bye, thank God, to expressions such as "he looks better," which I had listened to in treatment facilities around the world for years. Indeed, any statement to the effect that a child "looks better" had long since been banned at The Institutes. (If somebody slipped and said it, there was a standard answer: "Don't tell me he looks better. I'm not interested in your opinion. What can he *do* that he *couldn't* do before?")

No wonder I had long felt on the edge of it. For years we had been asking each other, "What can he do that he couldn't do before?" That was the key.

Now I believed that might be the key to Nature's grand design. So simple. So clear. It had always been there, right before my eyes.

No wonder I couldn't find it. The obvious is always the most difficult to appreciate.

I got to work.

How had Sharpie known that Mark had been behaving like a six-month-old a year ago?

That was simple. We had measured hundreds of well six-month-olds. A well six-month-old could crawl but not creep. He could make some meaningful sounds but not all of them. He had a grasp reflex and he could let go. He had pretty good vision and could see outlines very well. He could understand a good many meaningful sounds and had pretty good bodily sensations.

How had Sharpie known he was now acting like an eighteen-month-old? That was easy, too. We knew hundreds of well eighteen-month-olds. Eighteen-month-olds could walk, they could say about eighteen words, they could pick up tiny objects between thumb and forefingers. They could do those motor things because they could converge their vision. They could understand many words and they could feel the third dimension.

That's what she had done. That's really all she'd done.

I looked at my drawing board on which I had lettered:

"THE DEVELOPMENTAL PROFILE"

I was ready to begin.

In the past we had talked of children only up to a year of age, and we had talked of four significant stages. We now knew that from one year of age until about six years of age, when all the basic human neurological processes were functioning at full efficiency, there were three additional stages.

So, all together there were seven stages in the life of a child, running

THE DEVELOPMENTAL PROFILE

VII	**72 Months**
VI	**36 Months**
V	**18 Months**
IV	**12 Months**
III	**7 Months**
II	**2.5 Months**
I	**Birth**

FIGURE 11

the full spectrum from birth until all human functions were in place and operating.

Seven stages in the spectrum of brain development just as there were seven colors in the spectrum of visible light.

I drew seven horizontal bands and I lightly sketched in the colors of the spectrum starting at the bottom. Red, orange, yellow, green, blue, indigo, and violet.

I therefore drew seven horizontal bands, and since I knew from our years of observing children of all kinds the approximate ages at which the normal child moved from stage to stage, I sketched them in. (See Figure 11.)

We knew that a child moved upward through these seven stages as succeedingly higher brain stages came into play. Starting at the bottom, I filled them in: early brain stem and cord, brain stem and early subcortical areas, midbrain and subcortical areas, and the four significant stages in the development of the human cortex which we called the initial cortex, the early cortex, the primitive cortex, and the sophisticated cortex. (See Figure 12.)

Now what were the distinctly human capabilities toward which the human brain had evolved?

What were the functions that distinguished the well child from the hurt child? What were the functions in which our brain-injured children were behind?

They were reading, hearing (so as to understand speech), feeling, walking, talking, and writing. I assigned a column to each. (See Figure 13.)

However, the functions of reading, understanding, feeling, walking, talking, and writing weren't really completely functional until six years of age in an average child, and it was necessary to be able to measure a child at *any* age. Fortunately, we had in our data all the significant steps at the seven critical stages of development for every one of those six functions. We could trace every one of them back to birth.

We were not talking simply about the human ability to read, which is present in the average child at six years of age, but about the whole area of human *visual competence*, which begins at birth with a light reflex.

We were not talking simply about the human ability to understand complete sentences through the ear, which is present in the average child by six years of age, but instead of the whole area of human *auditory competence,* which begins at birth with the startle reflex.

We were not talking simply about the human ability to understand what an object was by feel alone, which is present in an average child by six

THE DEVELOPMENTAL PROFILE

VII	72 Mon.	SOPHISTICATED CORTEX
VI	36 Mon.	PRIMITIVE CORTEX
V	18 Mon.	EARLY CORTEX
IV	12 Mon.	INITIAL CORTEX
III	7 Mon.	MIDBRAIN and SUBCORTICAL AREAS
II	2.5 Mon.	BRAIN STEM and EARLY SUBCORTICAL AREAS
I	Birth	EARLY BRAIN STEM and CORD

FIGURE 12

THE DEVELOPMENTAL PROFILE

			READING	HEARING	FEELING	WALKING	TALKING	WRITING
VII	72 Mon.	SOPHISTI-CATED CORTEX						
VI	36 Mon.	PRIMITIVE CORTEX						
V	18 Mon.	EARLY CORTEX						
IV	12 Mon.	INITIAL CORTEX						
III	7 Mon.	MIDBRAIN and SUB-CORTICAL AREAS						
II	2.5 Mon.	BRAIN STEM and EARLY SUBCORTI-CAL AREAS						
I	Birth	EARLY BRAIN STEM and CORD						

FIGURE 13

years of age, but the entire area of human *tactile competence,* which begins at birth with a number of skin reflexes such as the Babinski.

We were, therefore, not talking simply about the cross-pattern walking, which is achieved by six years of age in an average child, but instead about the whole area of human *mobility,* which began at birth with reflex movements of arms and legs.

We were not talking simply about the talking in complete sentences, which is achieved by six years of age in an average child, but instead about the whole of human language, which began at birth with one reflex birth cry.

We were not talking simply about using the hands to write language, which the average child begins by six years of age, but instead about the whole of human *manual competence*, which begins at birth with the grasp reflex.

So I could actually draw the Developmental Profile with six vertical columns from birth to six years of age and give them their larger names. (See Figure 14.)

Now I knew I had what I'd been dreaming about for six years. I finally had my tool. I did not know the precise details, but I saw the pattern with utter and complete clarity.

In my seven layers and six columns I now had forty-two blocks. Each of them was as important as every other because one needed to have every one of them to be neurologically normal.

The seven horizontal bands were for the seven critical ages. The six vertical columns divided three and three. There were three sensory columns, each with its seven squares, and three motor columns, each again divided into the seven critical ages. (See Figures 15 and 16.)

Now I had a picture of a well child's schema of neurological growth. I had forty-two squares each with the age at which the function occurred.

What I had actually come to was a means of determining a child's precise *neurological age* instead of his mere chronological age.

If the ages I had assigned to each of these functions were true, I had my invaluable tool. If the ages I had assigned were not true but only approximations, I had only to dig into the data and refine my approximations.

I'm sure everyone has experienced at least once in life that hugely satisfying feeling of knowing without any shadow of a doubt that he is absolutely right about something even before all the facts are assembled. It isn't something that happens often, but it is such a magnificent feeling that one doesn't need it often. It was the way I felt at that moment. I *knew* and would have staked my life on it.

THE DEVELOPMENTAL PROFILE

			READING	UNDER-STANDING LANGUAGE	IDENTIFYING by FEEL	WALKING	TALKING	WRITING
VII	SOPHISTI-CATED CORTEX	72 Mon.						
VI	PRIMITIVE CORTEX	36 Mon.	↑	↑	↑	↑	↑	↑
V	EARLY CORTEX	18 Mon.	VISUAL COMPETENCE	AUDITORY COMPETENCE	TACTILE COMPETENCE	MOBILITY COMPETENCE	LANGUAGE COMPETENCE	MANUAL COMPETENCE
IV	INITIAL CORTEX	12 Mon.						
III	MIDBRAIN and SUBCORTI-CAL AREAS	7 Mon.						
II	BRAIN STEM and EARLY SUBCORTI-CAL AREAS	2.5 Mon.	↓	↓	↓	↓	↓	↓
I	EARLY BRAIN STEM and CORD	Birth	LIGHT REFLEX	STARTLE REFLEX	BABINSKI REFLEX	REFLEX MOVEMENT	REFLEX BIRTH CRY	GRASP REFLEX

FIGURE 14

THE SENSORY COLUMNS

VISUAL COMPETENCE	AUDITORY COMPETENCE	TACTILE COMPETENCE
Reading with total understanding	Understanding of complete vocabulary and proper sentences	Tactile identification of objects
Identification of visual symbols and letters within experience	Understanding of 2000 words and simple sentences	Ability to determine characteristics of objects by tactile means
Differentiation of similar but unlike simple visual symbols	Understanding of 10 to 25 words and two couplets	Tactile differentiation of similar but unlike objects
Convergence of vision resulting in simple depth perception	Understanding of two words of speech	Tactile understanding of the third dimension in objects which appear to be flat
Appreciation of detail within a configuration	Appreciation of meaningful sounds	Appreciation of gnostic sensation
Outline perception	Vital response to threatening sounds	Perception of vital sensation
Light reflex	Startle reflex	Babinski reflex

FIGURE 15

THE MOTOR COLUMNS

MOBILITY	LANGUAGE	MANUAL COMPETENCE
Using a leg in a skilled role which is consistent with the dominant hemisphere	Complete vocabulary and proper sentence structure	Using a hand to write which is consistent with the dominant hemisphere
Walking and running in complete cross pattern	2000 words of language and short sentences	Bimanual function with one hand in a skilled role
Walking with arms freed from the primary balance role	10 to 25 words of language and two couplets	Cortical opposition bilaterally and simultaneously
Walking with arms used in a primary balance role most frequently at or above shoulder height	Two words of speech used spontaneously and meaningfully	Cortical opposition in either hand
Creeping on hands and knees, culminating in cross-pattern creeping	Creation of meaningful sounds	Prehensile grasp
Crawling in the prone position culminating in cross-pattern crawling	Vital crying in response to threats to life	Vital release
Movement of arms and legs without bodily movement.	Birth cry and crying	Grasp reflex

FIGURE 16

Now instead of merely measuring a child's chronological age we could measure six neurological ages (one in each of the functions), and then we could assign him an overall neurological age. What's more, others could use the same tool with reasonable certainty of getting the same results.

As an example, if we are measuring mobility in a child with a chronological age of two years, we know that he should be able, if he is average, to walk with his arms freed from the primary balance role, as the mobility column shows for an eighteen-month-old, but not yet to be able to walk and run in cross pattern as a thirty-six-month-old is able to do.

Now, let us suppose that in actuality he is only taking his first steps, as the mobility column shows a twelve-month-old to be able to do. Then his neurological age in mobility would be only twelve months, or half of his chronological age.

Or take language. Suppose this same two-year-old had only two words of speech. This being the level of language function of a normal twelve-month-old, we are once again looking at a neurological age of only half his chronological age.

Let us suppose we go on to record his level of achievement in the other four functions, using the other four columns. We might come up with the following rather precise picture of this child.

Chronological Age	Function	Neurological Age
24 months	– visual competence	– 15 months
24 months	– auditory competence	– 18 months
24 months	– tactile competence	– 10 months
24 months	– mobility	– 12 months
24 months	– language	– 12 months
24 months	– manual competence	– 10 months

Chronological age: 24 *months* Aggregate neurological age: *77 months*
Divide by 6
Overall neurological age: *12.8 months*

With this new tool I saw at once that I could do a dozen vital things that I had never been able to do before. Many of the things I could do with the

Developmental Profile did not become clear to me for several more years, but among the things I knew even then were these:

1. Now that we could measure a child's precise neurological age as well as his precise chronological age, we could tell who needed us and who did not. If his neurological age was below his chronological age, he needed us.

2. Closing the gap between his neurological age and his chronological age in each column was our assignment.

3. When his neurological age in each column reached his chronological age in each column, we had done our job.

4. By comparing his initial neurological age with his initial chronological age, we could determine his average rate of growth up to the time he saw us. Take, for example, another child, three years old, but operating at the level of a one-year-old:

Neurological age: *12 months*   = 30% ($^1/_3$ of normal)
Chronological age: *36 months*

5. By comparing his increase in neurological age with his increase in chronological age at any time after treatment began, we could determine whether a child's development was improving significantly. For example, the child cited above might have been measured again after a year on the program with the following results.

Neurological age: *30 months*—increase in neurological age:
18 months
Chronological age: *48 months* —increase in chronological age:
12 months

We could now find his *rate* of change by comparing his growth rate before doing the program with his growth rate after one year of program.

Initial rate of growth: 30% ($^1/_3$ of normal)
Present rate of growth: 150% ($1^1/_2$ faster than normal)
Rate of change: 500%

In other words, after 12 months of the program this child is growing *5 times faster* than he was *before* the program.

In such a case it would be clear that *something* had made a significant improvement in his rate of growth. (Theoretically, the improvement could have been the result of chance or misdiagnosis rather than our programs of treatment, but after our case histories climbed into the hundreds and later into the thousands, we allowed ourselves to credit the programs.)

6. I could now demonstrate that a child who performs (as a result of brain injury) at a far lower level than other children, does so because of disability and not because of low intelligence.

Although I shall not take the space to discuss it here, I could also demonstrate, simply by looking at a Profile with a line drawn across it at a child's chronological age and with six lines drawn across at the child's actual level of performance, whether or not a child was brain-injured; if brain-injured, whether the injury was mild, moderate, severe, profound, or complete; whether it was focal or diffuse; whether it was on one side of the brain or on both and at what level of brain the injury existed.

Although I did not know it at the time we would one day be able to use it to measure intelligence, to demonstrate the reason for that I.Q. and, finally, to demonstrate what to do to raise the intelligence. These areas are covered in other books, including *How To Multiply Your Baby's Intelligence, How To Teach Your Baby To Read, How To Give Your Baby Encyclopedic Knowledge, How To Teach Your Baby Math,* and *How To Teach Your Baby To Be Physically Superb.*

But all this was much in the future, and at that moment at my drawing board so long ago I was sublimely happy. Although it was by then after 10 P.M. I *had* to test my idea and my approximations.

I called in the two people I believed had the most actual detailed knowledge of children. Interestingly, they were both nurses. I called Sharpie and I called my wife, Katie. I was sure they would both still be working, and they were. They came at once.

Since Katie has always known me and my moods and since Sharpie was also an extremely perceptive person, they could see instantly that I was elated.

"You've discovered something and it's something very important," Katie said with absolute certainty.

"It has to do with measurement and it's a product of my brilliance," said Sharpie with equal certainty.

"Each of you take a pad and pencil," I said, "and write the answer to questions that I'm going to ask you."

They had begun to catch my sense of elation and they looked at me expectantly.

"A child is just beginning to take his first steps. Write down how old he is."

"A well child?" asked Katie. "Yep, a well child."

They both wrote.

"Suppose he wasn't well but instead was brain-injured?" I asked.

"Severely brain-injured?" asked Sharpie.

"Yep."

"Then," she allowed, "he would never walk unless we did something about it."

"Suppose he were mildly brain-injured?"

"He might walk between two and three years of age," said Katie.

"What did each of you write on your paper for the well child?"

"Twelve months," said Sharpie.

"One year," said Katie simultaneously.

"Next question: A child is just twelve months old. Write down what he's doing visually."

"A well child?" asked Sharpie.

They both clearly had the picture of what we were doing although they had not yet seen the diagram.

"Yes," I said.

We all wrote that a well one-year-old had: (a) a light reflex, (b) outline perception, (c) the ability to see details, (d) could converge his vision and did.

We played the game for an hour with Sharpie and Katie becoming more and more excited as they began to see the ramifications.

"You're comparing the way a child actually behaves..." Sharpie began.

"That's called neurological age," I interrupted.

"...with the age he actually is," finished Sharpie.

"And that's called actual age," guessed Katie.

"Close but not exactly. It's called chronological age on the Developmental Profile."

"What is a Developmental Profile?" inquired Katie.

I showed it to them, and they both saw its significance immediately.

We tried one more game.

"If a child cannot crawl, use his hands or say a single word, is he normal?"

"He is if he's a newborn," said Sharpie.

"And if he has a chronological age of ninety-six months?"

"Severely brain-injured."

"And if he has a chronological age of twelve months?"

"Moderately brain-injured."

"And if he's got a chronological age of nine months?"

"Mildly brain-injured."

We talked till daylight.

For many months Bob, Carl, and I discussed the Profile at great length. We confirmed and reconfirmed the data.

We spent the next twelve years refining the data as we examined hundreds and hundreds of children.

Up to that time our work had been entirely pragmatic in nature no matter how elaborate the theoretical structure upon which it was based. Of course, we had collected large amounts of empirical data, and no clinician in his right mind would sneer at or in conscience ignore empirical data (especially in large quantities). Nonetheless, it was empirical.

With the development of the Profile we could begin to measure, and as a consequence, we could fairly begin to think of ourselves as scientists as well as clinicians.

The Profile was 75 years in the making, beginning with Dr. Fay and culminating with the founding members of The Institutes staff, who traveled the world to study children and who listened to mothers, the world's leading experts on child development.

The developmental pathways shown on the Profile were not invented by The Institutes staff. Mother Nature and the Good Lord invented them and we wrote them down. The quest to do so arose from our tremendous need to answer the important question "What is well?" This is the primary question that must be answered in order to solve the problems of the brain-injured child

It is a masterpiece of exclusion. Rather than listing the hundreds of activities a child might engage in on the road to neurological maturity, the Profile lists *only* the vital steps in human development. All the other abilities are a *product* of these.

If the Institutes is remembered for anything 200 years from now, it should be for The Institutes Developmental Profile. It has been used to record precise data, to measure, to evaluate, to diagnose, to design treatment, and to re-evaluate thousands of children in the United States and children from 100 nations.

In excess of a quarter of a million evaluations have been done using the Profile in the United States alone. It has been in constant use since 1961, when it was first published.

The Profile has stood the test of time.

Note: The Institutes Developmental Profile was copyrighted in 1962. The current Profile appears in this edition of the book.

20

CLOSING THE BREAK
IN THE CIRCUIT

A s the 1960s began, each child was having an individual program pre-scribed for him, but the factors which those programs had in common were as follows:

1. Each child was being measured carefully in the visual column of the Profile in order to identify the upper limits of his visual development. He was then given active stimulation aimed at breaking through any barrier to function in the visual neural circuits at the next higher level.

2. Each child was being measured carefully against the auditory column of the Profile in order to identify the upper limits of his hearing development. He was then given active stimulation aimed at awakening function in the audio neural circuits at the next higher level.

3. Each child was being measured carefully in the tactile column of the Profile in order to identify the upper limits of his tactile competence. He was then given active stimulation aimed at helping him break through to the next higher level.

4. All children, including the children who walked poorly or who could not run, were encouraged to spend a maximum period of time on the floor except when being treated, fed or loved. That time on the floor was spent in the prone position if at Level I in the mobility column of the Profile. If the child was at a higher level but still unable to crawl properly, he crawled while on the floor. If he was at a higher level but did not creep properly, he crept while on the floor. In addition to crawling and creeping, children who walked poorly or who could not run were given the opportunity to walk and eventually run.

5. All children were patterned in truncal patterning, homolateral patterning, or cross patterning depending on where the gaps existed in the mobility column or in any other column of the Profile.

6. All children were being given oxygen enrichment during each waking hour so that they would build better chests to cut down on respiratory

illnesses and to supply better nutrition to the brain in terms of the oxygen.

7. All children were being given a language-development program. This emphasized unlimited opportunity to perform at the upper limits of their existing competence. We identified the level at which a child was not yet fully proficient, and gave him opportunity to reinforce that function, as well as unlimited opportunity to embark upon the next higher level.

8. All children were receiving a program of manual-competence development. This aimed to provide unlimited opportunity to perform at both the lowest level on the Profile at which they were not yet fully proficient and also at the highest level. (Detailed programs for all levels of manual competence are provided in the book *How To Teach Your Baby To Be Physically Superb,* by Glenn Doman, Douglas Doman, and Bruce Hagy.)

It was more than interesting that in these motor areas (mobility, language, and manual competence) a therapist's role *could not be an active one,* since it was clear beyond question that the motor pathways were one-way paths from the brain out, and thus the therapist could in no way affect the brain by use of them. Only the patient could play an active role. All we could do here was to pinpoint the level in each motor column of the Profile at which the patient's function ceased or slowed, and then provide the patient with enormous *opportunities* to push ahead on his own.

It now dawned on us that whereas there was *no way* the physical therapist, speech therapist, or occupational therapist could reach the brain through the outbound motor pathways of the nervous system, there was an enormously important role for him in reaching them through the inbound sensory pathways.

No wonder therapists had been dejected over the persistent failure of their best efforts. It was as if they had been trying to drive north in the southbound lane of a busy highway. On the other hand, a simple change of lanes—a change to the sensory lanes—might let them progress beyond their fondest hopes. The sensory pathways into the brain through the eyes, ears, and skin of the patient were also entirely one-way—but *in.*

Here was revelation indeed for not only had we traditionally tried to put our message *in* through the outward-bound motor pathways instead of through the inward-bound sensory pathways, but in all of my own education in physical therapy I cannot remember any single suggestion that the sensory pathways *might* be used. Except as a neurophysical fact in neurophysiology, neuroanatomy, and neuropathology, they were scarcely mentioned.

Not only is it true that we never so much as suspected that we had any responsibility for treating a patient's sensory pathways, I am confident that if someone in, let's say 1955, had suggested that therapy could effectively be administered only in sensory areas, he would have been considered as mad as a hatter.

And this is odd, considering that knowledge of the neural pathways is more than a hundred years old.

How then did we locate the "road closed" signs in the neural pathways in order to be able to concentrate our efforts on that stretch of pathway where the trouble really lay?

It is helpful to look once more at a diagram showing how visual stimulation, auditory stimulation, and tactile stimulation enter the brain through the back of the central nervous system to supply the information which the brain needs to supply a motor response, or output, through the front of the central nervous system in terms of mobility, language, or manual response. (See Figure 17.)

While all three sensory pathways supply information to the brain and thus to all of the motor pathways, there is a general correspondence between the three pathways described as separate loops.

If tactile pathways are totally destroyed, mobility will be totally destroyed as will manual competence.

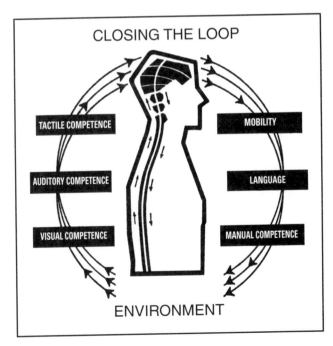

FIGURE 17

If auditory pathways are totally destroyed, language will be virtually destroyed.

If visual pathways are destroyed, manual competence will be greatly interfered with, as will mobility.

If *all* sensory pathways are destroyed entirely, the loop will be broken and the human being will not survive long without extraordinary measures being taken.

If *all* motor pathways are destroyed entirely, the loop will be broken and the human being will not survive long without extraordinary measures being taken.

It is not *possible* to completely destroy all six pathways without destroying the human being.

If these pathways are partially destroyed, there will be partial loss of functions.

Until such a partial or total gap in the loop is found and repaired, there will be a mild, moderate, severe, profound, or total loss in human walking, talking, writing, reading, understanding, or feeling, or in several or in all of these human functions.

On the other hand, the brain is not at all the delicate organ we have for so long fancied it to be. It is a tough organ, one of the hardiest in the body, capable of taking grave insult and yet surviving. It would have to be, or else man would never have survived.

I have three personal friends who each got a bullet through the brain, and each not only survived but survived very nicely. It is worthy of note that none of them are friends of mine as a result of rehabilitation. They are military friends, and I had nothing to do with their rehabilitation. It might be worthwhile to tell the stories of these men.

The first of my friends was an infantry officer commanding a rifle company in combat in Germany very close to where I was doing the same job. He was wounded and unconscious. When he regained consciousness, there was a German soldier standing beside him who asked Bob if he was an American. Upon being told that he was indeed an American, the German soldier removed Bob's helmet, put a pistol to the right side of his head and pulled the trigger—and thus the bullet entered Bob's brain by the right side. A little over twenty years later, Bob had an important job in Washington which he performed in a superior manner. He was as bright as he ever was and was in better physical condition than I was since he had not allowed himself to grow as—well, as stocky as I had.

The second of my friends, also an infantry officer, was wounded in action in Korea by a bullet which went in the back of his skull and emerged in the front. He spent several months in Walter Reed Hospital, primarily, as he pointed out, because nobody could understand why he didn't have more problems than he had. His own explanation was highly beguiling but may be less than scientifically conclusive. He explained that he had a Swedish father and an Irish mother and that this had given him a very thick Swedish skull and a very small Irish brain which allowed the bullet to pass through his head without touching his brain. Be that as it may, he had gotten his Ph.D. since his brain injury and was also in even better physical condition than I was. Both he and Bob worked every day of their lives, and the only co-workers who knew that they were severely brain-injured were the ones they had told.

My third friend was the most hurt of all. George was commanding a rifle company in Belgium during the Battle of the Bulge not far from where I was doing the same thing. He was advancing against the enemy through the sub-zero temperature and deep snow when he was hit through the shoulder by a bullet from a machine gun. As he fell, the next round hit him in the front of his skull on the right side of his forehead and came out through the back of his skull. His company, having seen him hit, advanced to find him lying with a bullet through his brain. Infantry combat does not provide time for mourning even one's best friends. His men shed a tear, swore in bitterness, stuck a rifle in the ground with a helmet on top so that the graves registration people could find the company commander's body in the snow, and continued the attack. *Three days later* the burial party found George's body. As they picked it up to place in the truck to be taken for burial, George moved a little bit, so they took him to the hospital instead. The freezing cold had saved his life in a crude form of human refrigeration or *hypothermia* (which Temple Fay had pioneered so brilliantly five years earlier at Temple University Hospital). Since this was accidental hypothermia, the cold that had saved his life had also frozen him, and so, in the hospital, it was necessary to amputate both of George's legs below the hips and to amputate all the fingers as well as the thumb from his right hand. Starting at the bottom, George had no legs, was partially paralyzed on the left side due to the bullet through the right side of his brain, had no fingers nor thumb on his good hand, had a bullet through his left shoulder and a bullet through the right side of his brain.

In those early days of rehabilitation during World War II, methods were not as good as they are today, and George was pretty badly hurt. George was provided with artificial legs, and during the process of learning how to use them George fell down and broke both hips. Two decades later, George had two artificial legs, two surgically pinned hips, was partially paralyzed on the left side, had no fingers or thumb on his right hand and had bullets through his left shoulder and his right brain. George also walked and worked. The last time I saw George personally was when I met him accidentally in a night club in Paris in 1960. George was all right except for the fact that he was having a little trouble balancing. George doesn't always have trouble balancing, but then he isn't always in a night club in Paris, either. I noticed a good many people were having trouble balancing that night, and some a good deal more trouble than George. George had gotten himself from Boston to Paris without any help and, while I haven't seen him since, I am quite confident that he also got himself home again.

Each of these men had a bullet through the brain, each had his brain severely injured, and each was a fine, effective human being. George, who functioned well but who had several problems which were quite visible, had them because he was frozen rather than because of his brain injury.

As I have said, the brain is a tough organ, but despite the splendid recovery of my three friends, brain injury *can* affect any of the six areas of function mentioned. Let me review the kind of treatment we developed, area by area.

VISUAL COMPETENCE AND BILLY

Billy is thirty-six months old and should therefore be at Level VI on the Developmental Profile if he were an average three-year-old. But as you see from his Profile (Figure 18), Billy is unable to perform even at the level of a normal newborn. He does not even have a good light reflex.

We have, then, located the break in the environment-sensory-brain-motor-loop. Now we must close the loop if we are to expect normal performance.

Our goal is to give Billy a *good* light reflex, which is to say, make his pupils contract sharply and promptly when exposed to light and dilate sharply and promptly when exposed to darkness. Billy's light reflex is presently both slow and late in occurring.

Since this break in the loop is in the sensory pathway, the role of patient

PREDOMINANT BRAIN STAGE		TIME FRAME	VISUAL COMPETENCE
VII	SOPHISTI-CATED CORTEX	Superior 36 Mon. Average 72 Mon. Slow 144 Mon.	Reading with total understanding *O*
VI	PRIMITIVE CORTEX	Superior 18 Mon. Average 36 Mon. Slow 72 Mon.	Identification of visual symbols and letters within experience *O*
V	EARLY CORTEX	Superior 9 Mon. Average 18 Mon. Slow 36 Mon.	Differentiation of similar but unlike simple visual symbols *O*
IV	INITIAL CORTEX	Superior 6 Mon. Average 12 Mon. Slow 24 Mon.	Convergence of vision resulting in simple depth perception *O*
III	MIDBRAIN and SUBCORTI-CAL AREAS	Superior 3.5 Mon. Average 7 Mon. Slow 14 Mon.	Appreciation of detail within a configuration *O*
II	BRAIN STEM and EARLY SUBCORTI-CAL AREAS	Superior 1 Mon. Average 2.5 Mon. Slow 5 Mon.	Outline perception *O*
I	EARLY BRAIN STEM and CORD	Superior Birth to .5 Average Birth to 1.0 Slow Birth to 2.0	Light reflex *functional*

CHRONOLOGICAL AGE __*36*__ months

VISUAL AGE __*0*__ months

FIGURE 18

Billy will be passive and the role of Billy's parents will be active. Billy's parents will simply stimulate his light reflex over and over again. (The "over and over" part is crucial; we shall often speak of the importance of *frequency, intensity, and duration* as basic tactics in our fight to awaken dormant neural pathways.)

Billy gets up at 7:30 a.m. and goes to bed at 9 p.m. He will receive a session of stimulation of the light reflex at least 30 times during the day. Billy's mother takes him into a completely blackened hallway or room. She places Billy on his back on the floor so that he is safe and comfortable and she can see his eyes easily. She uses a simple two-cell flashlight which she shines into Billy's eyes from 8 to 10 inches away.

She shines light into the right eye for 2 seconds. She says, "This is light." She says this in a loud, clear voice. While she is shining the light into the right eye she gently covers the left eye with her other hand. She then turns the light off and she waits 5 seconds (counting to herself one thousand one, two thousand two, three thousand three.) Then she covers the right eye and shines the light into the left eye for 2 seconds.

She alternates back and forth between the right and left eye in this manner for 60 seconds and then she stops. The light reflex will need time to recover so she will wait at least 5 minutes before she does another session. At each session each eye will receive at least 4 stimulations or 120 total stimulations in the entire day.

The chances are very strong that Billy's light reflex will improve greatly. As his light reflex improves, his chances of beginning to see outline are also improved (the second block up on the Profile). Thus, we have found the break in the cybernetic loop and we have moved to close it.

AUDITORY COMPETENCE AND MARY

Now let's find an example in the auditory column (also a sensory column). This time we'll take a gap slightly higher in the circuit.

Mary is ten months old and has very large auditory problems. While Billy was in fact functionally blind, Mary is for all practical purposes deaf, but she is not as deaf as Billy was blind. She is also considerably younger than Billy. Her auditory column on the Profile looks like this. (See Figure 19.)

Here then is Mary who at ten months of age, if she were an average baby, should be about to enter Level IV but who is instead functioning at

PREDOMINANT BRAIN STAGE		TIME FRAME	AUDITORY COMPETENCE
VII	SOPHISTICATED CORTEX	Superior 36 Mon. Average 72 Mon. Slow 144 Mon.	Understanding of complete vocabulary and proper sentences *O*
VI	PRIMITIVE CORTEX	Superior 18 Mon. Average 36 Mon. Slow 72 Mon.	Understanding of 2000 words and simple sentences *O*
V	EARLY CORTEX	Superior 9 Mon. Average 18 Mon. Slow 36 Mon.	Understanding of 10 to 25 words and two couplets *O*
IV	INITIAL CORTEX	Superior 6 Mon. Average 12 Mon. Slow 24 Mon.	Understanding of two words of speech *O*
III	MIDBRAIN and SUBCORTICAL AREAS	Superior 3.5 Mon. Average 7 Mon. Slow 14 Mon.	Appreciation of meaningful sounds *O*
II	BRAIN STEM and EARLY SUBCORTICAL AREAS	Superior 1 Mon. Average 2.5 Mon. Slow 5 Mon.	Vital response to threatening sounds *O*
I	EARLY BRAIN STEM and CORD	Superior Birth to .5 Average Birth to 1.0 Slow Birth to 2.0	Startle reflex *perfect*

CHRONOLOGICAL AGE ___10___ months

AUDITORY AGE ___1___ months

FIGURE 19

Level I—the level of a child one month old.

Auditorily, she has a startle reflex, which is normal to a newborn. This is to say, if a sudden, loud noise occurs (such as a door slamming), she will immediately jump.

She will jump as often as the sudden noise occurs, even if it occurs five times in succession. This is not a product of being afraid, and Mary is not afraid. It is simply a startle reflex and it is normal to a newborn baby. But Mary is not a newborn baby and should be more advanced auditorily. At Mary's age (and at any age beyond four months) her response should be different to a sudden unexpected noise. It should be different in two ways: first, she should jump and *be frightened* since sudden, loud noises may actually pose a threat to her life (house caving in, earthquake, etc.) and, second, she should not jump or be frightened by subsequent repetitions of the noise since she does not, in fact, find herself threatened by those noises. This second level in the auditory pathway is no longer reflex in nature. It is a vital response to threatening sounds.

While Mary has a true startle reflex, she does not have a vital response to threatening sounds; here is the break in the loop in Mary's case. This will virtually destroy the entire auditory-language loop and will cause large problems to the entire environment-sensory-brain-motor-environment loop.

Since this is a sensory pathway rather than a motor pathway, the parents' role will again be active rather than passive while the baby's role will be passive rather than active.

Let's suppose that Mary wakes at 7 a.m. and is put to bed at 7 p.m. Mother will stimulate her auditorily every waking half-hour, which will give her twenty-four sessions a day. Mother will do so by unexpectedly banging two blocks of wood together just behind Mary's head. She does so ten times at three-second intervals in each of the twenty-four sessions. This will give Mary two hundred and forty threatening sounds daily and will require thirty seconds out of each half-hour, twenty-four times a day, for a total of 720 seconds, or twelve minutes.

Since Mary *does* have a startle reflex and does *not* have a vital response to threatening sounds, the result, at first, will be that Mary has two hundred and forty startle reflexes daily. Since this is perhaps one hundred or two hundred or three hundred times as many opportunities for startle reflex as the environment would normally provide, and since moving to each higher brain level of function is the result of brain growth—which is, in turn, a product of the number of times one has the opportunity to use his *present* level of brain function—our hope is that Mary will soon change. Pretty soon we expect that she will *not* jump ten times if the sound is repeated ten times in a row; she will jump perhaps only nine times, and then only eight, and then only seven, and so on. As the number of times Mary startles at repeated noises reduces, Mary will begin not only to startle but also to be afraid and to cry. It is proper to be frightened by a sudden, loud, unexpected noise. Mary has now arrived at Level II on the auditory pathway and should now begin spontaneously to react not only to threatening noises but to other meaningful sounds (such as laughter) as well. If she does not do so spontaneously, she will need stimulation at Level III as well.

Mary's mother has found the break in the cybernetic loop, and she has moved to fill it in.

TACTILE COMPETENCE AND SEAN

The third function to be considered is tactility—the most ignored of all of the sensory functions and one that is vital to movement itself.

Let's consider the case of Sean who is six years old but who is awkward both in walking and in manual competence. We find him to be extremely low in the tactile column of the Profile for a boy who is beginning to read. His tactile column looks like this. (See Figure 20.)

If Sean were an average six-year-old, he should be performing at Level VII. Because Sean is hurt, we find him instead performing successfully at Level I. He has normal superficial reflexes such as the Babinski. He also has normal perception of vital sensation at Level II, which is to say that he is aware of being burned, being frozen, or being physically damaged; however, he has sub-normal ability to feel at the level of Level III. This is the level of a normal five-month-old. We have found the gap in the circuit for Sean.

Level III is the ability to appreciate gnostic sensation. It is the ability to "know" meaningful sensations at a more subtle level than at the mere survival level of knowing that one is being burned to death, frozen to death, or torn to death. Where Level II deals with the crude but vital perception of *cold,* Level III deals with the appreciation of *cool.* Where Level II deals with the crude but vital perception of *hot,* Level III deals with the appreciation of *warm.* Where Level II deals with the crude but vital perception of being cut, crushed, or beaten, Level III deals with the appreciation of being stroked, rubbed, or massaged.

158

PREDOMINANT BRAIN STAGE	TIME FRAME	TACTILE COMPETENCE
VII SOPHISTI-CATED CORTEX	Superior 36 Mon. Average 72 Mon. Slow 144 Mon.	Tactile identification of objects *O*
VI PRIMITIVE CORTEX	Superior 18 Mon. Average 36 Mon. Slow 72 Mon.	Ability to determine characteristics of objects by tactile means *O*
V EARLY CORTEX	Superior 9 Mon. Average 18 Mon. Slow 36 Mon.	Tactile differentiation of similar but unlike objects *O*
IV INITIAL CORTEX	Superior 6 Mon. Average 12 Mon. Slow 24 Mon.	Tactile understanding of the third dimension in objects which appear to be flat *O*
III MIDBRAIN and SUBCORTI-CAL AREAS	Superior 3.5 Mon. Average 7 Mon. Slow 14 Mon.	Appreciation of gnostic sensation *functional*
II BRAIN STEM and EARLY SUBCORTI-CAL AREAS	Superior 1 Mon. Average 2.5 Mon. Slow 5 Mon.	Perception of vital sensation *perfect*
I EARLY BRAIN STEM and CORD	Superior Birth to .5 Average Birth to 1.0 Slow Birth to 2.0	Babinski reflex *perfect*

CHRONOLOGICAL AGE **72** months
TACTILE AGE **5** months

FIGURE 20

Sean deals poorly at Level III and only dimly appreciates warm, cool, and other gnostic sensations in his hands.

Since tactility is a sensory pathway, his mother's role will again be active. Mother will give Sean tactile stimulation.

Since Sean is older than the other two children we have examined, he wakes up at seven o'clock in the morning but doesn't go to bed until ten at night. Sean, therefore, has fifteen waking hours and therefore thirty half hours during which a few minutes can be devoted to tactile stimulation.

Sean's mother makes a list of tactile items: sandpaper, soft brush, cool water, velvet, hard brush, plastic pot scrubber, soft towel, warm water, etc. She then pairs these items for contrast: sandpaper-velvet, soft brush-hard brush, cool water-warm water. She will alternate between these paired items using one pair at each session and cycling through as many pairs as she has. For example in one session Sean's mother gets two pans big enough to hold both of Sean's hands. In one pan she puts warm water and in the other she puts cool water. First she sees that Sean puts his hands in the warm water and holds them there for five seconds while she instructs him to look at his hands and reminds him that the water is warm but not hot. She sees that he then removes his hands from the warm water and plunges them directly into the cool water for five seconds while she again directs that he look at his hands and again she tells him that this water is cool but not cold. After five such cycles requiring a little less than a minute in all, she empties the water from the pan. She then puts fresh warm water in one pan and fresh cool water in the other pan and repeats the dipping process five times, thus using about five minutes of each half hour of his waking day.

Sean is receiving tactile stimulation 600 times daily. In addition, he was patterned four times a day, five minutes each time, seven days a week, using cross pattern. If one depended on the accidents of environment for this experience we would find that he might be exposed to warm and cool or rough and smooth half a dozen times a day. Thus, Sean's mother provides him in each day with the sensory experiences he might normally have in sixty days.

By so doing, she is providing greatly expanded sensory stimulation. With any luck, his sensory pathway of tactility will begin to develop and as it does he will come to appreciate gnostic (knowing) sensation fully. When he does, he will begin to be able to deal with the third dimension in a tactile sense, which is Level IV in the tactile pathway.

Sean's mother has thus found and moved to fill in the break in the loop. By the end of the 1950s we were closing such breaks with a good deal of regularity, and while we understood what we were doing and what was happening to the kids, we were still reasonably inarticulate as to *why* it was happening—although it was clear that what was happening was good. Very good.

In the cases we have discussed so far, mother has taken an active role and the child a passive role. It is possible for mother to feed visual, auditory, and tactile information into her son's brain, even against his will.

She can *not*, on the other hand, walk for him, talk for him, or write for him. These things he must, in the end, do for himself. If we find a break in these three motor pathways, we can only provide every opportunity for the child himself to perform these functions. We must do this with great energy, enthusiasm, patience, and ingenuity.

Strangely, although everyone had always considered that a child who could not walk or talk or use his hands *must* naturally have his injury in motor areas of the brain (after all, walking, talking, and using the hands are motor functions), we found that in the vast majority of brain-injured children this only *appeared* to be the case. In truth we found that the break in the loop is far more commonly on the sensory side of the loop than it is on the motor side of the loop. This did not mean, of course, that his motor skills would test higher than his sensory skills.

When one has time to think about it, it becomes embarrassingly obvious that a child is *never* higher on the motor side of the Profile than he is on the sensory side, and indeed quite the reverse is almost always the case. Almost invariably the child is considerably higher on the sensory side of the Profile than he is on the motor side. Even a little loss of function on the sensory side usually implies more loss of function on the motor side. Indeed, how could it be otherwise? How, for instance, could a child put out normal language on the motor side if he did not take in language on the auditory column on the sensory side of the Profile, which is after all nothing more than the other side of the same coin?

How could a child move his body from place to place (on the mobility column on the motor side of the Profile) if he could not *feel* his body and so did not know where his body was now (in the tactile column on the sensory side of the Profile)?

How could a child write a language (in the manual competence column on the motor side of the Profile) if he could not see what that language looked like (on the visual column on the sensory side of the Profile)?

The sum of the sensory side of the Profile always equals (and in the vast majority of cases it exceeds) the sum of the mobility side of the Profile. For indeed we cannot possibly put out what we have not somehow taken in.

We're ready now to consider what gaps *can* occur in children on the motor side of the Profile and how we may fill them in and thus close the loop.

MOBILITY AND LISA

The first column on the motor side of the Profile is mobility, so let's consider the case of Lisa who at four years old did not speak and had visual problems. She appeared to be bright and intelligent although she had no ways of proving that beyond the brightness of her eyes and the fact that she smiled and frowned and cried at appropriate times.

The mobility column in her Profile looked like this. (See Figure 21.)

If she were average, she should be at Level VI on the mobility column. Instead, Lisa had successfully reached only that level in the Profile (Level I) where we would expect to find an average one-month-old infant.

Lisa's mother was a high school graduate and Dad was a shop foreman. Lisa's parents had been told over and over again that Lisa was a vegetable and an idiot and that she should be "put away before you get to love her." Her dad pointed out that it was already too late since he had already loved her for four years and that her mother had loved her long before she had known whether Lisa was going to be a boy or girl. In any event, by the time she was four years old Lisa's family had discovered The Institutes.

Lisa was given a program of visual, auditory, and tactile stimulation of the brain with increased frequency, intensity, and duration. In between her other periods of stimulation she was to be placed in the prone position on the clean linoleum-covered floor of a warm room so that she might have virtually unlimited opportunity to discover how to move her arms and legs in such a way as to push herself forward and crawl. Thus, Lisa's parents were giving her opportunity to crawl and, thus, to fill in the mobility gap. It is an obviously reasonable approach to mobility, and in a high number of children it works.

After two months of intensive treatment by her parents (nine hours a day, seven days a week), Lisa was a different child, and when she returned to The Institutes for her first re-evaluation her parents were extremely enthusiastic and very grateful. Her understanding of language was now beyond question. She could use her hands for the first time. Her personality had blossomed and

PREDOMINANT BRAIN STAGE		TIME FRAME	MOBILITY
VII	SOPHISTI-CATED CORTEX	Superior 36 Mon. Average 72 Mon. Slow 144 Mon.	Using a leg in a skilled role which is consistent with the dominant hemisphere *O*
VI	PRIMITIVE CORTEX	Superior 18 Mon. Average 36 Mon. Slow 72 Mon.	Walking and running in complete cross pattern *O*
V	EARLY CORTEX	Superior 9 Mon. Average 18 Mon. Slow 36 Mon.	Walking with arms freed from the primary balance role *O*
IV	INITIAL CORTEX	Superior 6 Mon. Average 12 Mon. Slow 24 Mon.	Walking with arms used in a primary balance role most frequently at or above shoulder height *O*
III	MIDBRAIN and SUBCORTI-CAL AREAS	Superior 3.5 Mon. Average 7 Mon. Slow 14 Mon.	Creeping on hands and knees, culminating in cross pattern creeping *O*
II	BRAIN STEM and EARLY SUBCORTI-CAL AREAS	Superior 1 Mon. Average 2.5 Mon. Slow 5 Mon.	Crawling in the prone position culminating in cross pattern crawling *O*
I	EARLY BRAIN STEM and CORD	Superior Birth to .5 Average Birth to 1.0 Slow Birth to 2.0	Movement of arms and legs without bodily movement *perfect*

CHRONOLOGICAL AGE __48__ months

MOBILITY AGE __1__ months

FIGURE 21

she now demonstrated a keen sense of humor. Lisa had done beautifully in her first two months of treatment. There was only one problem. Despite many hours daily on the floor, Lisa still could not move.

A new program was designed for this new little girl. She was assigned even more time on the floor in the prone position to expand her opportunity to learn to crawl.

When, two months later, Lisa returned for her second revisit her parents were absolutely enraptured with her very obvious progress. Lisa was beginning to talk and now had seven words of language, and although she was only a little past four years of age, Lisa could read words. Now the world could see what Mom had always believed, that despite her staggering disabilities, Lisa was a bright little girl. Only one thing marred their joy. Lisa, despite many, many hours of opportunity could not crawl.

When one watched Lisa on the floor straining every muscle in her body to move, it was obvious that she was using as much effort to move as Dad would have used to move a piano single-handed. It was equally obvious that Lisa had not the faintest notion how to go about moving. Giving Lisa the opportunity to crawl had not been enough.

It is enough for a perfectly well infant. When a well infant is put on the floor in the belly-down position, he does not know how to crawl either, but he is tiny and his arms and legs move freely. He has an additional thing going for him. There is built into his ancient genetic memory a command for his arms and legs to move in a propulsive pattern, and when his body is face down, they will do so. Since he weighs almost nothing, these movements will occasionally result in pushing him forward. When this has happened by accident over and over again, the baby discovers which movements have that effect and which do not. He then discovers how the movements that push him forward *feel* as distinguished from how the movements that do not push him forward *feel*. He finally discovers how to *purposely* reproduce those motions that push him forward and how to synchronize them with each other into a pattern. This may be homologous, homolateral, or cross pattern. In any case, he is now crawling; this is the way babies have learned to move since time began for man. And so powerful is that ancient command to move at all costs and at whatever effort, that even the majority of brain-injured children will move to the rhythm of that ancient beat. Just as Robert Ardrey opted to call his book about the development of man *The Territorial Imperative*, I am sure he would call this "The Movement Imperative." It is built-in, basic, and almost omnipresent. For even the severely brain-injured child, the mere opportunity to be on the floor is usually enough.

For some severely brain-injured children, however, mere opportunity is not enough (because of the severity, or the precise location of their brain injury, or because they are no longer tiny and no longer almost weightless). Lisa was one of these children.

It was not merely that trying to move was a prodigious effort for Lisa nor was it merely that moving her arms and legs had not taught Lisa how to move her body forward. What Lisa had learned was far worse than that. Lisa *had* tried to use her arms and legs to push her body forward and she had not succeeded. Lisa had actually learned that arm and leg movement was *not* what caused her body to move forward. Unhappily what she had learned was not true—but from her own experience she had every right to believe it was true.

It was time for Lisa to see and to feel the truth and the inclined floor was the way to demonstrate that truth to her. Although it now seems to me to be as obvious as the nose on my face, it had not seemed obvious to me years earlier and it had taken me until 1945 to develop the idea.

The purpose of the inclined floor, we explained to Lisa's parents, was to give Lisa a chance to learn that there *was* a relationship between her arms, legs, and movement. (The opposite to what her own abnormal experience had taught her.)

First they were to make an inclined floor. (See Figure 22. Instructions on how to build the inclined floor can be found in the Appendix.)

Now if we should put Lisa in that chute with her feet at one open end and with her head toward the far end, and if we should lift one end of that chute up in the air high enough to create a sliding board effect, it is obvious that Lisa would slide down it whether she wanted to or not.

Her parents had to find the precisely perfect elevation point for Lisa. That is, the precise point (generally between three and four feet off the floor at the lifted end) at which Lisa, lying still, will not move at all but where, if she makes the slightest movement of arm or leg, however random, she will slide forward a little bit. At that precise point she will stop and not move forward again until she once again moves an arm or a leg. This will not have to occur too many times before Lisa will discover the clear-cut relationship between movement of arms and legs and getting the body from one place to another. At that moment we shall have accom-

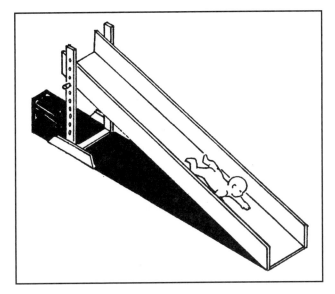

FIGURE 22

plished a very large objective. Lisa will know the secret of crawling. Thus, we will have given Lisa opportunity to move and to close the loop in this area of mobility.

We place Lisa at the top of the inclined floor. Her body needs to be as flat as possible, with her arms in front of her, if possible. Then we do not touch her until she gets to the bottom.

Our role here is passive and the child's role is active, but we have clearly *helped* her to be active.

We also have another objective for Lisa and that is that Lisa should *like* moving and conclude that moving is a good and rewarding thing do. To accomplish this latter objective, we gave Lisa's parents the following instructions:

1. The inclined floor must always be at the angle that makes movement easy and pleasant for Lisa. It can be set lower at those times of the day when the child is moving best and higher at those times when the child is tired. The lower position is set at one or two holes lower than the higher position.

2. Once Lisa is put on the inclined floor she must know that the only way out is at the other end and that this is inevitable and that fussing will not get her out if she happens to feel irritable.

3. If it takes her longer than two minutes to get to the bottom, the board

is too low and should be raised.

4. When she gets to the bottom she is to be instantly picked up and praised honestly and profusely for her great accomplishment. In short, Mommy is to make clear to Lisa the joy she herself feels at watching her daughter move at last. Lisa is to be rewarded with love, with praise, and with lots of hugs and kisses. There should not be the slightest doubt in anybody's mind that this is a special and most wonderful occasion.

5. When Lisa enjoys the inclined floor and crawls down it consistently, parents were taught not to lower it. Otherwise, she has every reason to say to herself, "I was just getting good at this and enjoying it, but now it's difficult." Keep the inclined floor at one height so Lisa gets better and faster and enjoys it.

6. Once she has reached the bottom and has been praised, she is not to be put back in again for at least five minutes lest Lisa decide that the reward for doing the job well was to have to do it again. By dealing in such a way with Lisa we can arrange for her to say to herself, "Every time Mommy puts me in this thing and I move my arms and legs I move myself forward easily and quickly. What's more, when I finish that exciting business the old girl thinks I'm great and I get loved and praised, and I'll be delighted when she puts me back in again because I love to move."

They may not be the exact words that Lisa will use but that will be the right music.

7. Lisa should begin with one to five trips down the inclined floor daily. Slowly and gradually, over several months, parents should increase the number of trips daily, eventually aiming for 30 to 60 trips a day. As always, the joy of movement and success should be paramount.

8. Once Lisa is averaging less than half a minute per trip, her parents must let her crawl off the inclined floor and onto the flat floor. At first, only her head would go onto the flat floor, but eventually she will move further and further off the inclined floor and onto the flat floor.

Lisa's family understood and went home to make her inclined floor. Two days later they called us to announce that Lisa had just come down her inclined floor for the first time. They were excited, to put it mildly. Lisa had taken to it like a duck to water. As her dad put it, "You could see her discovery of her arms and legs on her face. When she realized that every time an arm or leg moved she moved forward a little, you could see the surprise and pleasure on her face. You could see her saying to herself as she looked at her own arms and legs, 'Holy Mackerel! That's what they're for.' It was wonderful to watch her."

Several months later, they called to say that Lisa was crawling down the inclined floor 45 times daily. Before long, Lisa crawled down the board and just continued to crawl across the floor. They had succeeded using our standard program for Stage 1 in mobility. Lisa had learned to crawl. They had filled in the gap in the loop at Stage II and Lisa was a moving child. She was firmly entrenched on the ancient road to walking and all Lisa's mother had done was to give her opportunity, but she had done so with imagination and with love. Lisa's program is for a child who is at Stage I in mobility. Because mobility is such an important subject for brain-injured children, we will look at additional mobility programs for children.

It is important to note that most children receive some type of patterning, depending on their stage of mobility. (See Chapter 11 for a description of how to administer the patterns.) The children are patterned four times a day, five minutes each time, seven days a week, using truncal pattern (if a child cannot move his limbs well), homolateral pattern (if he cannot crawl well) and cross pattern (if he cannot creep well). If he could walk but did it awkwardly, he was given drill in cross-pattern walking.

Children at Stage 0 in Mobility:

The priority for these children is to improve their respiration and sensory functions. The Masking and Sensory Stimulation Programs have precedence over everything else. The Balance Development Program explained in the book *How To Teach Your Baby To Be Physically Superb* can also be beneficial. As soon as the child has consistent movement of the arms or legs, he will be ready for the Stage I program.

Children at Stage II in Mobility:

As is the case for the Stage I Mobility Program, doing the Patterning Program in conjunction with the Mobility Program is an absolute requirement. All of our experience over the last half-century has taught us that doing the maximum number of patterning sessions daily speeds mobility development.

If a child consistently crawls independently and happily at least 20 to 30 yards daily on a flat floor, he no longer needs the inclined floor. Ideally, the child should be on a smooth, hard, flat floor. He should wear a "onesie" or short pants and sleeves, so that his hands, elbows, knees, and feet are bare. This combination reduces the friction between the floor surface and the child's body, thus making crawling easier and faster.

Remember, crawling is an active program. This means that only independent crawling leads to independent movement. Helping the child only convinces him that he is not independent. The child should be allowed to learn to move by himself.

Gradually, day by day, parents encourage the child to increase his crawling distance slightly, so that the average daily distance increases by 5 to 10 yards weekly.

Depending on the age of the child he should build up to a total of 75 to 300 yards of crawling daily. One- to two-year-olds will become independent at transporting themselves when they can crawl 75 to 125 yards daily. Three-year-olds to six-year-olds need to crawl 300 yards consistently in order to be independently mobile. Seven-year-olds to adults crawl between 300 and 800 yards daily before becoming independently mobile.

Once these goals have been achieved, a child should learn to crawl on all kinds of surfaces, including carpeting. He should be taught how to crawl up and down stairs. If he does not get into the quadruped position independently, parents can put him in it so that he can learn to creep.

Children at Stage III in Mobility:

For a child who can creep, the ideal surface is a short-pile carpet. Clothing should consist of long, loose-fitting pants. Hands should be bare. The combination of the carpeted floor and the cloth pants provides secure traction.

Gradually, day by day, parents encourage the child to increase his creeping distance slightly, so that the average daily distance increases by 5 to 10 yards weekly.

The goal is to achieve 600 to 1600 yards of creeping day in and day out. When two- to three-year-olds consistently creep 600 to 800 yards daily, they begin to experiment with holding on to furniture to stand. Five-year-olds to six-year-olds need to creep 800 to 1000 yards daily in order to begin experimenting with standing or cruising (walking while holding on to furniture). Seven-year-olds to adults will creep as much as 1600 to 2400 yards daily in order to achieve the next higher level of mobility.

Children Who Can Walk:

Brain-injured children who can walk need the opportunity to crawl and creep as well. To make crawling as easy as possible, it should always be done on a smooth surface, such as linoleum, smooth hardwood floors, or smooth tile. Hands, elbows, knees, and feet should be bare in order to provide the best traction for crawling. A short-pile carpet is the best surface for creeping, and some children prefer to creep outside on grass when possible. Loose-fitting, long pants help protect the knees during creeping. Creeping and crawling goals for walking children are below.

Parents should always start with the easiest program in order to create success. They should never exceed the nonstop distances below, even if they are too easy. It takes months for the skin on the hands, knees, and feet to become tough. This tough skin is good and makes movement easier and faster.

In most cases, one- to three-year-old brain-injured children have not had the same opportunity to walk as well children of the same age have had. Before beginning a crawling and creeping program, a child should gradually build up to at least 1000 yards of walking spread throughout the day. After this goal is achieved, he should gradually increase his nonstop walking, beginning with five minutes nonstop, then ten minutes, until he reaches 30 minutes of nonstop walking daily. Finally, he works to increase the speed of his walking until he can walk 1000 yards in 30 minutes.

Three- to five-year-old children who can walk should begin with crawling and creeping short and easy distances. A child should start with one session of 5 yards of crawling and one session of 10 yards of creeping. Parents then gradually increase the number of sessions done throughout the day, working towards 20 to 40 sessions a day.

Parents should use the same procedure for creeping, gradually increasing the number of 10-yard sessions to 30 sessions or more a day.

During the above process, a parent will find that her child can easily crawl 10 yards or more nonstop. At this point she can gradually decrease the number of sessions while she increases the nonstop crawling distance. For example, throughout the day the child might do 10 to 20 sessions of 10 yards of crawling. The goal for crawling is at least 100 to 200 yards daily.

The same applies to creeping. The parent should increase the distance of nonstop creeping to 50 yards and decrease the number of sessions to 12 to 20 a day. The final goal is to reach 600 to 1000 yards of creeping daily.

For five- to eight-year-olds, parents should begin with the same distances of 5 yards of crawling and 10 yards of creeping, then gradually increase those distances. The goal for these children is to slowly increase crawling to a total of 150 to 400 yards daily and to slowly increase creeping to a total of 1200 to 1600 yards daily. This is achieved by gradually increasing the nonstop crawling distance from 15 yards to 40 yards, done ten times daily. Likewise, parents can gradually increase the child's non-stop creeping distance from 120 to 160 yards, done ten times daily.

Nine-year-olds to adults should follow the same procedure described above. Their goal for crawling is to build up to 400 to 800 yards daily. This is eventually accomplished in ten sessions of 40 to 80 yards of non-stop crawling.

Their goal for creeping is to build up to 1600 to 2400 yards a day. This is eventually accomplished in ten sessions of 160 to 240 yards of nonstop crawling.

As the child becomes physically bigger and heavier, he may require kneepads for creeping. Usually, this is not needed until age ten or above. Kneepads made for wrestling are form-fitted to the knee and make creeping more comfortable. A child should never creep on a hard concrete surface.

When beginning to crawl, some teenagers and adults may need to wear both elbowpads and kneepads in order to make crawling more comfortable.

The key for success for all children is to make crawling and creeping into a game.

Parents need to be creative and always introduce some new fun activity into the game. Our best advice is for a parent to get down on the floor, crawling and creeping alongside her child. The book *How To Teach Your Baby To Be Physically Superb* is strongly recommended. It provides many examples of how to do the program with a child and how to involve brothers and sisters.

LANGUAGE COMPETENCE AND CHRIS

Chris was four years and two months old and as bright as a button, but Chris couldn't say one word of English even though he clearly understood all that anyone said to him (and, for that matter, what the grownups said to each other). He had been paralyzed when we had seen him originally at three, but he had learned to crawl and now he could creep on hands and knees. He was on his way to walking, but for all of that, as I have said, he couldn't speak one word of English and the language column on his Profile looked like this. (See Figure 23.)

Chris, who was fifty months old, should, if he were an average four-plus child, be at Level VI in language.

Instead Chris was at Level III. At birth he'd had the reflex birth cry

PREDOMINANT BRAIN STAGE		TIME FRAME	LANGUAGE
VII	SOPHISTI-CATED CORTEX	Superior 36 Mon. Average 72 Mon. Slow 144 Mon.	Complete vocabulary and proper sentence structure *O*
VI	PRIMITIVE CORTEX	Superior 18 Mon. Average 36 Mon. Slow 72 Mon.	2000 words of language and short sentences *O*
V	EARLY CORTEX	Superior 9 Mon. Average 18 Mon. Slow 36 Mon.	10 to 25 words of language and two couplets *O*
IV	INITIAL CORTEX	Superior 6 Mon. Average 12 Mon. Slow 24 Mon.	Two words of speech used spontaneously and meaningfully *O*
III	MIDBRAIN and SUBCORTI-CAL AREAS	Superior 3.5 Mon. Average 7 Mon. Slow 14 Mon.	Creation of meaningful sounds *perfect*
II	BRAIN STEM and EARLY SUBCORTI-CAL AREAS	Superior 1 Mon. Average 2.5 Mon. Slow 5 Mon.	Vital crying in response to threats to life *perfect*
I	EARLY BRAIN STEM and CORD	Superior Birth to .5 Average Birth to 1.0 Slow Birth to 2.0	Birth cry and crying *perfect*

CHRONOLOGICAL AGE __*50*__ months

LANGUAGE AGE __*7*__ months

FIGURE 23

(Level I). He then learned to cry in such a way that his mother would come (and come running) if he cried in such a way as to indicate that he was in great pain. This was Level II.

He was now operating at Level III, meaning that he could make all sorts of meaningful sounds and mother could tell whether he was happy, bored, excited, hungry, content, irritated and a number of other things just by listening to the sounds he made even when she was in another room from him and couldn't see him. He was, however, fifty months old, and should have been able to do all this at seven months.

There was absolutely no question that Chris could hear and understood all he heard. If you didn't want him to understand you had to spell and some words it wasn't even safe to spell, like *bed* and *bath*, both of which he hated.

Still Chris had no word of English, and only two sounds that were wordlike. He said something that sounded like "may" and something that sounded like "uhh." It was decided to use these two sounds to establish two words—*Mom* and *up*.

Chris woke up at 7:30 a.m. and went to bed at 9 p.m., which gave him thirteen and a half waking hours or twenty-seven half-hour periods.

Chris and his mother would have twenty-seven five-minute language-opportunity periods during the day.

They went to the most comfortable arm chair in the house, away from all commotion. Mother began by explaining to Chris that she knew that he was a very smart boy but she also knew that he had trouble talking.

She then explained that they were going to take the sound "may," and in order to make that *Mom*—herself—anytime he ever said "may" she would respond as if he had said "Mom." She also explained that they would take the sound "uhh," which he could already say, and use that to mean "up," so that anytime he said "uhh" she would come and pick him up. She also explained that this was really the exact way that everyone else had learned to talk and that almost everywhere in the world mothers were called "Mom" or "Ma." (This is no coincidence but is a result of the fact that the "M" sound is one of the first sounds a baby can make and that mothers the world over have always said, "You bet, that's me.")

Then mother and Chris would spend the rest of the five minutes trying. Every time Chris said "may" or anything like it, mother would say, "Yes, Chris, what is it?" Any time Chris said "uhh," mother would say, "Yes, Chris," and then she would pick him up.

Chris enjoyed the game and tried very hard. Chris's mother never said,

"No, Chris, that doesn't sound like 'Mom,' say it again." Instead she always responded every time Chris said any "m" sound or any "u" sound. Sometimes Chris forgot and said "may" when he didn't mean "Mom," but his mother always responded any time during the day when he said "may" as if Chris had called her. This made them both laugh. She also picked him up every time he said "uhh."

Within a month Chris came to use the "may" sound only to mean mother and the "uhh" sound only when he wanted to be picked up. In another month the "may" sound had begun to sound a lot like "Mom" and the "uhh" sound a lot like "up." He had also developed some new sounds. Thanks to the other aspects of the program his chest got better (from increased mobility) and his brain functioned better (from the increased oxygen supply to the brain). Chris had progressed to Level IV in the language column of the Profile and was headed for Level V.

His mother had found the break in the loop and she had wisely given Chris the opportunity to complete the loop.

MANUAL COMPETENCE AND SUZIE

Suzie was two and a half years old and had staggering problems. She had been a perfectly healthy baby up until eleven months of age at which time she had had a very high temperature for twenty-four hours and a severe encephalitis. The encephalitis had left Suzie with an almost total lack of function.

Her manual competence column looked like this. (See Figure 24.)

Suzie, who was thirty months old should, if she were average, have been performing at Level V.

In fact, because she was a very brain-injured little girl as the result of her encephalitis, she could operate only at Level I in manual competence, which is to say that she had a grasp reflex. This meant that if you put something inside Suzie's clenched fist it would remain clenched in her fist until in moving her arms it would eventually be knocked out.

It wasn't that Suzie could *hold* on to an object as a newborn baby can. It was that, exactly like a newborn baby, she couldn't *let go*. This was Level I, grasp reflex.

Suzie could *not* perform at Level II in the manual-competence column. Level II occurs at 2.5 months of age in an average baby, and it is the function of being able to let go. This stage first occurs in a normal baby as an

PREDOMINANT BRAIN STAGE		TIME FRAME	MANUAL COMPETENCE
VII	SOPHISTI-CATED CORTEX	Superior 36 Mon. Average 72 Mon. Slow 144 Mon.	Using a hand to write which is consistent with the dominant hemisphere
VI	PRIMITIVE CORTEX	Superior 18 Mon. Average 36 Mon. Slow 72 Mon.	Bimanual function with one hand in a skilled role
V	EARLY CORTEX	Superior 9 Mon. Average 18 Mon. Slow 36 Mon.	Cortical opposition bilaterally and simultaneously
IV	INITIAL CORTEX	Superior 6 Mon. Average 12 Mon. Slow 24 Mon.	Cortical opposition in either hand
III	MIDBRAIN and SUBCORTI-CAL AREAS	Superior 3.5 Mon. Average 7 Mon. Slow 14 Mon.	Prehensile grasp
II	BRAIN STEM and EARLY SUBCORTI-CAL AREAS	Superior 1 Mon. Average 2.5 Mon. Slow 5 Mon.	Vital release
I	EARLY BRAIN STEM and CORD	Superior Birth to .5 Average Birth to 1.0 Slow Birth to 2.0	Grasp reflex

perfect

CHRONOLOGICAL AGE __30__ months

MANUAL AGE __1__ month

FIGURE 24

NEUROLOGICAL
ORGANIZATION

NEUROLOGICAL ORGANIZATION

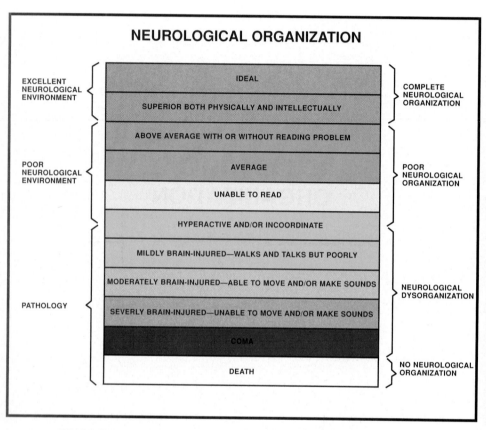

EXCELLENT NEUROLOGICAL ENVIRONMENT

POOR NEUROLOGICAL ENVIRONMENT

PATHOLOGY

IDEAL

SUPERIOR BOTH PHYSICALLY AND INTELLECTUALLY

ABOVE AVERAGE WITH OR WITHOUT READING PROBLEM

AVERAGE

UNABLE TO READ

HYPERACTIVE AND/OR INCOORDINATE

MILDLY BRAIN-INJURED—WALKS AND TALKS BUT POORLY

MODERATELY BRAIN-INJURED—ABLE TO MOVE AND/OR MAKE SOUNDS

SEVERLY BRAIN-INJURED—UNABLE TO MOVE AND/OR MAKE SOUNDS

COMA

DEATH

COMPLETE NEUROLOGICAL ORGANIZATION

POOR NEUROLOGICAL ORGANIZATION

NEUROLOGICAL DYSORGANIZATION

NO NEUROLOGICAL ORGANIZATION

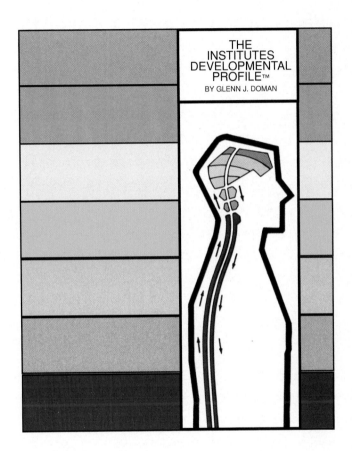

THE
INSTITUTES
DEVELOPMENTAL
PROFILE™
BY GLENN J. DOMAN

accident. However, each time the baby happens to let go of something by accident he is (also accidentally) getting the feel of what it is like to let go.

The baby comes finally to feel precisely what all those accidents had in common and learns how to "reproduce the accident" as it were. This is called vital release.

Now it was Suzie's mother's job to give Suzie the opportunity to let go. Nowhere is the example of supplying opportunity more clear than it is in this example of vital release. If you want someone to let go of an object, it is obvious that you have only to put it in his hand until he lets go of it and then to put it back in his hand again.

It is possible that this happens to a one-month-old baby eight or ten times a day since the baby can only let go of an object that some adult has put in his hand.

Suzie's mother had her job cut out for her. She had to supply Suzie in one day with as many opportunities to let go as a well infant gets in fifty or sixty days. She got two half-inch wooden rods (dowels) two inches long which fit snugly, one in each of Suzie's hands, and every time Suzie lost one of the dowels, her mother put it back in her hand again.

There are more exciting jobs in the world than putting a dowel in a child's hand several hundred times a day, but perhaps there are not many more exciting jobs if a mother sees her paralyzed daughter's hands begin to function as Suzie's hands began to do as a product of performing the function over and over and over again. For it is function that creates structure and even in the end the structure of the brain, just as in the evolutionary process man's brain was structured by its functions.

So Suzie's mom had found the break in the loop and had moved to close the circuit. Suzie advanced.

We have looked at one example in each of the six columns of the Profile.

All one does, then, is to check out a child in each of the six columns of the Profile and identify the squares above which the child does not perform normally.

You then start at whatever point the child is below-normal in his skills and try to give him vastly more opportunities to learn what it is like to perform at the next level.

If the breaks are in any of the three sensory columns, mother simply starts at the lowest break and gives huge amounts of *stimulation* in each area where the child is falling short.

If the breaks are in any of the three motor columns, mother simply starts at the lowest break and gives the child huge amounts of *opportunity* to perform at the next level.

So it was with Billy, Mary, Sean, Lisa, Chris, and Suzie. Each mother had devoted five or so minutes out of each waking half-hour to filling in the particular break in the circuit which has been described. Does it seem like a terribly large amount of time to give, considering the possible pay-off?

Of course as one reflects about it, he remembers that each of the children was probably also being patterned for five minutes at least four times a day, seven days a week.

Come to think of it, you may say, don't they also get oxygen enrichment every hour? Now the time is beginning to add up.

And are you suddenly struck with the fact that few kids are brain-injured in such a way as to be involved in only one column, and most kids are involved in all six columns?

If you multiplied what you do in one column by six columns and then you added . . .

If it occurs to you that if you added it all up there is little time left for performing little tasks like cleaning, cooking, shopping, ironing, and other little things, I can only say that we never promised anyone a bed of roses, or for all of that, any bed at all.

A light schedule for a child who has only a reading problem may involve as little as an hour a day. That however would be an exception, and a more typical program would involve eight hours a day. A program might, in point of fact, extend up to thirteen or even more hours a day. Before we have a look at what such a program might be like, let's consider a cardinal point that may not, at first glance, meet the eye. Parents rarely ask for an easier program. When occasionally we think parents need a rest and insist that parents take a break of two months or so, we almost invariably meet the only serious resistance we ever encounter with parents. When a child's entire life is at stake and heroic efforts must be made in a child's behalf, it is not parents who complain about the prodigious efforts that must be made. Rather, it is everyone else who complains on behalf of the parents, whether the parents want such championing or not.

Parents have spent every waking second considering the monumental size of the problem they face. A typical parent comment when faced with a program which would stagger any human being other than a parent is, "What am I going to do if I *don't* do the program?" It isn't that the much maligned parents are so much smarter than anyone else, it is simply that no one else has spent as much time considering the alternatives as they have, and it is also true that no one else loves their child as much as they do.

I am sure that there must, in the world, be parents who do not love their children all that much. It is, I guess, just that those parents don't go to the trouble and difficulty of bringing their children to The Institutes. Philadelphia is, after all, very far from all the places in the world that are very far from Philadelphia. Just how far, far is, is highly related to just how important problems seem to each of us.

Parents are in many ways like the staff of The Institutes, and one of these ways is that they spend every waking hour thinking about the problem. They, like we, have often considered the obvious. In this case, the obvious is that while we are not yet smart enough to know *a priori* which kid will win and which kid will lose, it is clear that each kid who is going to win will have to do the things that will help him to function normally "X" number of times. While we have no way of knowing whether "X" is 5,692 times or 56,920 times, it is clear that we can spread "X" out over a lifetime by doing it one time a day for twenty years or by doing it ten times a day for two years.

The parents' choice about which of these to do is very clear. I remember a mother to whom I had just given a program that would stagger a marathon runner. "And now," she said, "I hope that while we're home doing this until midnight that all of you will spend whatever spare hours you can find to discover new methods that might make my child better more quickly so that the next time we see you, you can add them to this program."

Bright gal—that's what we do.

It is natural that parents reading this book wish to have some clear action they can take to help their brain-injured child as soon as possible. However, the treatment of brain-injured children, especially severely and profoundly brain-injured children, does not lend itself to simple recipes or solutions.

At The Institutes a neurological program is designed for each child only after a careful functional neurological evaluation and a medical examination are completed. Many mothers and fathers who plan to attend courses for parents given at The Institutes wish to begin some program while they are waiting to attend. When they attend their first course these families already have the experience of doing a program everyday and often their children have made significant improvement in their condition. These two factors help our parents to understand the information presented during the course at a higher level. For this reason, we have included two examples of beginning programs for two very different children.

BENJAMIN'S PROGRAM

Benjamin is six years old. He is able to walk but not yet run. He understands the everyday activities in his home but he is not yet at his age level
intellectually. He has a few words of speech. He is hypersensitive to
sounds and tactile stimulation.

Benjamin's Goals:
Intellectual Growth
Physical Growth
Physiological Growth

Benjamin's Programs:
Reading
Primary Human Development
Patterning

Benjamin's Techniques:
Auditory Stimulation
Tactile Stimulation

Benjamin's Health:
Nutrition
Liquid Balance

Benjamin's Beginning Program

Time	*Activity*
7:00 a.m.	Wake up and dress
7:30 a.m.	Nutritious breakfast
8:00 a.m.	Tactile Stimulation
	Patterning
	Crawling 25 meters
	Reading*
	Auditory Stimulation
	Creeping 100 meters
	Reward: Reading session
	Help Mom clean house

10:00 a.m. Tactile Stimulation
Patterning
Reading*
Crawling 25 meters
Auditory Stimulation
Creeping 100 meters
Reward: Reading session
Help Mom prepare lunch

Noon   Nutritious lunch
Walk in neighborhood

1:30 p.m. Tactile Stimulation
Patterning
Creeping 100 meters
Reading*
Auditory Stimulation
Crawling 25 meters
Reward: Reading session
Greet brother and sister when they come
home from school

3:30 p.m. Tactile Stimulation
Patterning
Creeping 100 meters
Reading*
Auditory Stimulation
Crawling 25 meters
Reward: Reading session
Help Mom prepare dinner

5:30 p.m. Nutritious dinner
Outdoor activity with brother and sister

7:00 p.m.   Tactile Stimulation
            Patterning
            Reading*
            Auditory Stimulation
            Tactile Stimulation
            Patterning

8:00 p.m.   Bath
            Story at bedtime

Benjamin's reading program: This should be done at happy, relaxed moments throughout the day. These sessions should not be scheduled but rather should occur when mother and Benjamin are well fed, well rested, and ready to learn together.

Benjamin has gradually worked up to 400 meters of creeping, 100 meters of crawling, 6 patterns, reading, auditory, and tactile stimulation. He is off to a very good start.

NAN'S PROGRAM

Nan is three years old. She is not yet able to see or crawl. She can hear but not yet identify all the sounds around her. She has a delayed reaction to pain.

Nan's Goals:
Physical Growth
Intellectual Growth
Physiological Growth

Nan's Program:
Sensory Stimulation
The Floor as a Way of Life
Patterning

Nan's Health:
Nutrition
Liquid Balance

Nan's Beginning Program:

Sensory Stimulation: 15 minutes every waking hour of the day

The Inclined Floor: 3 times every waking hour

Patterning: 5 minutes every hour

Sensory Stimulation
Vision: 1. Stimulation of the light reflex
            2. Locating light
            3. Seeing black-and-white shapes on slides

Auditory: 1. Appreciation of meaningful sounds

Tactile: 1. Stimulation of vital sensation
          2. Stimulation of gnostic sensation

This is a good start for Nan. If all goes well, she should outgrow this program in 3 to 12 months, depending on the frequency, intensity, and consistency of the program that she receives.

Parents, then, are perfectly capable of carrying out such staggering programs, and with the help of the entire family they manage to do so sometimes for years on end.

Then how about the child? Can a twisted, paralyzed, bright-eyed little thing hold up for years of such regimentation? Such a tiny, such a hurt little thing? Of course she does. As a matter of fact, it's quite good for her despite all that might be said by all those who insist that the very best thing we can do for such children's own sake is to expect nothing from them and to pop them forever into a latter-day Bedlam, which would give the Devil nightmares. Those who think it wouldn't, might like to have a glance at a truthful and courageous photo essay called *Christmas in Purgatory* by Burton Blatt and Fred Kaplan (Human Policy Press). It doesn't attempt to soften the fact, and it couldn't exaggerate it.

It's the people *doing* the patterning who are getting the workout. Most of the things that require the child's cooperation are by and large the things that are in themselves pleasurable and even joyful. Like reading. No one enjoys reading more or takes greater pride in the accomplishment than a little child, especially a little hurt child who doesn't have the outdoors competing with reading.

Still, all the things are not as joyful as reading, and the ingenuity of mother and all of her family will be taxed to make them happy functions. The chapter on reading and the chapter on motivation will help in that regard. Still, it's a hard job and cannot always be accomplished by all families. Strangely, it is not so much what the child is like, but instead what the family is like that determines the degree of positive motivation that can be achieved. Basically, family opinion falls into two groups among those who seek the help of The Institutes.

The first group of dedicated families is by far the larger group. They are the families who see the hurt child as an extremely positive factor in family life. These are the families who say, "Everybody adores Joanne. She's the star of our family. We would give anything in the world to fix Joanne, and we are going to fix her, but fixed or unfixed we *want* her. She is an addition to the family, and we don't know what we would do without her." These families see the child as the most marvelous of opportunities and are thrilled to have her.

Hank Viscardi, that determined and marvelous man of stature, who is in a sense one of the founders of rehabilitation, once told me this story.

He once said to his mother, "Mother, why was our family given such a problem as to have me, born with no legs?" His mother said, "Son, when it's time for a crippled child to be born, God has a meeting with all of his advisors and says, 'Where is there a family good enough to be made better by a hurt child?'"

Hank's extraordinary career is not so difficult to explain when one knows that about his mother.

Generally, such families seem able to make even drudgery seem worthwhile for hurt little kids.

The other sort of family we see is equally courageous but less likely to be able to make the program joyous. These families also love the hurt child and are willing also to make tremendous sacrifices for the child. These families, however, are much more likely to see the child as a challenge to the family, perhaps as a cross that the family must bear. Both families love the child; both families are prepared to make heroic sacrifices for him, but these latter are much less likely to be able to motivate him in a positive way.

What then?

Well, eagerly or not eagerly, joyous or not joyous, motivated or not motivated, happily or unhappily, he must be treated if he is to have his chance as a well human being.

There are many things in life all human beings have to do which are, in truth, *not* joyous. Some of them, in fact, are downright drudgery or even painful. But drudgery or painful, they must be done, whether adult or child.

The process that gets such things done is the opposite side of the coin called "motivation." For want of a better name, let's call it "discipline." The best kind of discipline, quite obviously, is the kind called "self-discipline" and self-discipline in a child is every bit as possible as in an adult. In either case, what is needed to achieve self-discipline is an understanding of the goal, and this is often easier to explain to an adult than to a child. It is hard, as an example, to explain to a three-year-old precisely why patterning is a good thing. In any event, one must try even with a hurt three-year-old. The easiest way to explain why patterning is a good thing to a tiny hurt child is to demonstrate to him clearly how happy it makes his family (joyousness), and if this works, it is the best way of all.

If, however, it does not work, it is clear that it must be done. Patterning in a sense is a sort of closed brain surgery, and it is clear that if a child needed brain surgery, or any other kind, no family would dream of leaving the decision to the child. So whatever happens he must be treated if we are to succeed, and we must first try self-discipline. If that works, it is the very best way.

If it does not, we must still see that he is treated, and we must, if necessary, impose discipline.

All human beings require discipline and given an opportunity they will impose it on themselves. Both children and adults are constantly searching to find what the rules are, to find where the edges are which one may not go beyond. We find the need to live within a structure that we know and understand.

I'm confident that if I found myself washed up alone on the shore of a desert island, the first thing I would do after I collected myself would be to say, "Now just what are the rules around here?" And finding none, I should have to make rules of my own lest in the absence of rules of self-discipline I should slide into being less than human. The formalized version of those rules I would impose on myself is called The Law. When we adults find ourselves in the absence of law or structure, we create it. When we find ourselves newly introduced into a situation where rules exist, we seek to find where the edges are—how far we can go.

So too do children. They seek desperately to do so. When Mother puts a child to bed seventeen times and he gets back up eighteen times and is finally walloped, it is not that he has made a mistake. He was trying to find where the edges were. In this case he found out. It took eighteen times to find how far he could go.

He was demanding to know where the edges were. In this case he found out. It took eighteen times to find out how far he could go.

A child needs discipline the same way that he needs good food and love and fresh air.

The simplest and the most direct way is the best way: "I want you to do this because it is good for you."

If that works, it is the best way.

If that does not work, then mother has the right and the duty to point out to the child, "I am the mother around here and I make the laws. I decide what we do and what we do not do. When you are a mother or a father then you will get to make the laws."

This is a critical piece of information for the child because every family has to have clear leadership. Mother and father are, in fact, the benign dictators. They must be in order to have a civilized and sane household. This has nothing to do with having a brain-injured child. This is true of every child. It is a grave mistake to assume that because a child is brain-injured that he is not a child. He is, and he will demand the same clear, consistent treatment that all well children demand.

Children want to know who is the mother and who is the father? Who is running the show? If this is not made clear from the very beginning, the child will simply start running the show himself.

We all know what it is like to be in a household where the children are running the house. Nothing gets done in the way it should. In such an environment no one is happy—most especially the children.

A smart mother makes a clear list of what needs to be done every day. This is written in large print and posted on the wall where the child can see it often. If she is clever she has a list of good things that her child can earn from getting his job done. This is also published and posted on the wall. Should the job not get done or be done incompletely, these treats are not available.

On a good day everything goes beautifully, his job is accomplished, and he earns many things that he likes.

On a less good day when he may stop or even refuse to do something Mother does not debate or discuss or negotiate the point with him. Instead she provides brief but very predictable periods of "time out". He learns that it is more fun to get the job done than to not get the job done.

It is as simple as that.

While this process is simple to describe, it is considerably less simple to get up every day and be the consistent and sane parent that we all wish to be (as every parent knows).

By the way, we never resort to corporal punishment. Never. We could discuss at length here the relative merit to this position intellectually, emotionally, or psychologically, but let's not. The reason we do not use corporal punishment (and we recommend strongly that you do not) is simple:

It does not work.

You do not have time to do things that do not work.

Establishing a clear, sane law of the household is critical. Where mother and father are running the household the child will have his fighting chance to do the program and, hopefully, experience remarkable gains.

In households where mother and father are not running the show, there is no chance that a program of this magnitude could be accomplished.

If a child fails to get well, it is of very little importance whether the reason is that he has overwhelming pathology, or whether parents are unwilling or unable to establish the laws of the household.

The Institutes program is an entirely unreasonable program beyond any question.

I know of a dozen or more entirely reasonable programs for brain-injured children. The only problem is that they don't work.

The Institutes program frequently does work.

I have an idea that a reasonable course of action that does not work is unreasonable.

I also have an idea that an unreasonable program that does often work for brain-injured kids—is reasonable.

The Institutes program for parents to treat their children is a terrible program, and it gobbles up the lives of everyone concerned with it. It is surely the world's most difficult program.

Of course, every time I think of that I also think about Nan's father who said to me, "There is only one thing in the whole world that is worse than this darn program, and that is having a little girl whom you love who can't do what other kids do. I must say that the worst day on The Institutes program is better than the best day we had before we began this darn program."

21

SO WHAT'S GOING ON IN THE BODY? FUNCTION DETERMINES STRUCTURE

There is a law in nature that is of vital importance to all children and of overwhelming importance to brain-injured children. We have known this law for many years but we have managed somehow to ignore its staggering implications.

At The Institutes it was what we were seeing happening daily to our brain-injured children that forced us to consider this law and what it meant to them.

We were seeing severely brain-injured children arrive with bodies that were almost invariably tiny and sometimes twisted, with shoulders, eyes, mouths, and feet that were frequently extremely abnormal, with heads so tiny as to be microcephalic, and chests so shallow as to barely supply a breathing apparatus.

When we failed those children, their bodies remained tiny or twisted and so did their backs, hips, eyes, mouths, and heads.

But when we succeeded, their bodies became in every way normal.

What is the law that explains this staggering fact? That law states simply that "function determines structure." That law explains why life on earth developed as it did from single-celled life in the primordial tide pools, to fishes, amphibians, mammals, and man (phylogeny). That law also explains how human life develops from embryo, to fetus, to newborn (ontogeny).

It is the law that states that weight lifters have huge muscles because they lift weights. It is not that they lift weights because they have big muscles. Function determines structure.

Architects, for example, must first know what a building is to be used for before they can draw plans for it because its function will determine the structure.

A baby who is raised for the first year of life in near darkness (as is the case with certain beautiful but pre-Stone Age Xingu tribes with whom we have lived in the interior of Brazil's Mato Grosso) will not develop visually and will retain the visual pathways and competence of a newborn until brought out of the dark hut into light. His lack of visual function will have prevented earlier maturation of his visual pathway.

A child chained since infancy to a bedpost in an isolated attic by a psychotic adult will not develop normal hip sockets since no child is born with true hip sockets but instead actually cuts hip sockets by wearing them into the bone as a result of crawling, creeping and walking. It is not that we walk because we have hip sockets (as we once insisted on believing) but rather that we have hip sockets because we crawl, creep, and walk. It is *not* that structure determines function but rather that function (moving) creates structure (hip sockets).

The brain-injured child who cannot move (due to his brain injury) does not develop hip sockets either. Sooner or later someone who does not believe that brain injury is in the brain but instead believes that brain injury is in the legs will send him for hip X-rays and will find that he does not have normal hip sockets. The child will then have orthopedic surgery to create artificial hip sockets. This of course will not work since the child will still not walk for the precise same reason that he did not walk in the first place (brain injury). Not only is it true that function determines structure, but it is equally true that lack of function results in an immature or abnormal structure.

The vast majority of severely brain-injured children are quite tiny in physical size when they are first seen at The Institutes. That is to say, in height, in chest, in head size, in weight, they are, in about 75 percent of the cases, significantly below average, and 50 percent are below the smallest 10 percent of the population, sometimes far, far below. Yet at birth (except for the premature ones) they tended to be at or very near average size. As they get older they become smaller and smaller as compared to children their own age since the lack of physical functioning results in a lack of physical structure. This is exactly the opposite of what happens to the weight lifter. Yet once we start such a child on a program of neurological organization, his rate of growth will change, and often change dramatically. Quite often, in fact, a child who had been growing far slower than normal will suddenly start to grow far faster than normal for his age.

When we last did a study of our children 78% were below the 50th percentile in their growth. This was not surprising. However, 51 percent of our children were below the 10th percentile. More than half of our children were in the group of the smallest children. It is not unusual to see a child who has been in that 10th percentile all his life experience chest growth that is two, three, or four times faster than his well peers.

While this phenomenon appears to be virtually unknown to those who deal with brain-injured children, it is well known to anthropologists and even has a name.

It is called the *catch-up phenomenon.*

This rule says that if a child is seriously ill for any reason, his physical growth will slow down or virtually stop, depending on the illness and its severity. The rule further states that if the child becomes normal, he will then grow faster than his peers to catch up. This, of course, is why it is called the *catch-up phenomenon.*

We see this occurring every day of our lives at The Institutes.

We see also, and it is hardly surprising, that there seems to be a high correspondence between the rate of success and the rate of growth as well as between the ultimate degree of growth and the ultimate degree of success.

That is to say, children who fail to make progress also fail to change in growth rate, children who succeed markedly but not completely, grow markedly but not completely, and children who succeed entirely, grow entirely. While this rule, like all other rules I know, is not invariable, it is almost always so.

This is simply another way of saying that lack of function creates an immature or abnormal structure and that function determines structure.

At The Institutes in Philadelphia, all brain-injured children, except those who are blind, are started on a program of reading, using extra-large letters that can be discerned by the immature visual pathways of all except children who are blind or who are unable to discern outlines. (With blind children, reading is delayed until they are able to see some detail, which is Level III in Visual Competence.) As a result of this exposure to reading, two things happen.

First: There are many hundreds of brain-injured children who are two, three, or four years old and can read with total understanding. Their ability ranges from a few words for some to many, many books for others. I know a few three-year-olds who can read in several languages with complete understanding. The size of the words is reduced as they progress.

Second: Although the world at large believes that children under five are unable to read because their visual pathways are too immature and because their brains are not sufficiently developed, there are thousands of two-, three-, and four-year-olds who are *in fact* reading. What is more, they are brain-injured and what is more, their visual pathways are now *more* highly developed than are the visual pathways of *older* children who are *not* brain-injured and who do not read. How can this possibly be explained?

It certainly can *not* be explained on the basis of age, since they are younger, not older, than those children who do not read (average five-year-olds).

It certainly can *not* be explained on the grounds of some natural superiority. Far from being superior, these children are brain-injured and have often previously been diagnosed as being "mentally retarded." I don't know anyone who believes it is an advantage to be brain-injured.

It can only be explained on the grounds that these children have simply had an *opportunity* to learn to read that other children have not had. That opportunity permitted function, and function in turn created more mature visual pathways since function determines structure.

Very few facts are more important in the treatment of brain-injured children.

The lack of this realization is what has been wrong with the world of brain-injured children in the past. The awareness that function determines structure is one of the important things that is right about the world of brain-injured children today.

22

SO WHAT'S GOING ON IN THE BRAIN?
FUNCTION DETERMINES
STRUCTURE

Nobody in the world knows with absolute certainty what is actually going on in the brain and neither do we at The Institutes, but we've got some pretty strong suspicions.

No one in all of history has watched an entire human brain function in a microscopic cellular sense. However recent advances in science and brain imaging have given us some insight into the brain's amazing abilities. We are learning more and more about the brain's growth and development. We also are beginning to understand how the brain can change and adapt. This is what scientists and doctors call "neuroplasticity."

Brain function is not only beyond knowing, but is conceivably beyond understanding even if we knew.

But it is not beyond reasonable surmise or reasonable deduction, and surmise we must in order to explain to the best of our ability those things we see occurring in brain-injured children and in average children as well.

If there is much we do not know about that most incredible of organs, the brain, there is also much that we do know about animal brains in general and human brains in particular.

We know, first of all, that an inflexible rule of nature which has guided medicine, psychology, engineering, architecture, and a host of other arts and sciences, is at work no less in the brain than in other mechanisms. That law says that "function determines structure."

It does so no less in the brain than in the body.

Before we look at the neurophysiological evidence that proves this—and proves it beyond the shadow of a reasonable doubt—let's consider those changes we've just discussed which take place in the bodies of children who are being programmed here at The Institutes in Philadelphia.

Let's consider just two of the changes: first, changes in head size among the brain-injured children.

Why, we must ask, do brain-injured children's heads go from growing much slower than average children's heads before treatment begins, to growing two or even three times faster than well children's heads after treatment commences?

It has been a moot question up to now as to whether skulls grow to accommodate the brain or whether the brain was simply restricted to the size that the skull permitted it to be. With the exception of a very, very small group of children who have a premature closing of the fontanels (which are the soft spots on top of infant heads), it would now appear that it is the skull which is forced to grow to accommodate the brain.

We are now seeing skulls growing not only far beyond the rate at which they are supposed to grow, but far beyond the time when they are supposed to have stopped growing.

In fact, one analysis of 278 case histories of consecutively admitted children from our files shows (for further details see chapter 30) that whereas 82.2 percent were below normal in head size at the start of treatment, *all but 37 of the children moved to an above-average rate of growth* in head size over the fourteen-month period covered by the survey, and in fact the average rate of growth during treatment was 254 percent of normal for that age.

We must consider also the fact that the visual maturation that is occurring in the tiny brain-injured children who are reading exceeds that of well children who cannot deal visually with the small print as the hurt children do.

It must be remembered that visual maturation is a *brain* process since the visual pathways, along with the auditory, tactile, olfactory, and gustatory pathways, actually make up virtually all of the back of the central nervous system itself.

To say that one is maturing or growing the visual pathways is quite literally to say that one is maturing or growing the brain.

To say that one is growing the auditory or tactile pathways is also to say that one is growing the brain itself.

It must be remembered that many children have come to The Institutes cortically blind, and ended up reading. (Cortical blindness is due to an injury to the visual areas of the brain rather than an injury to the eye or optic nerve.) It must be remembered that many children have come to The Institutes cortically deaf, and ended up hearing and some ended up talking. (Cortical deafness is due to an injury to the auditory areas of the brain rather than an injury to the ear or auditory nerve.) It must be remembered that many children have come to The Institutes without feeling of any kind, and ended up able to distinguish between very small objects by feel alone.

These sensory pathways make up the back or sensory half of the central nervous system.

As regards the motor pathways, it must be remembered that many children have come to The Institutes completely paralyzed and have ended up walking. It must be remembered that many children have come to The Institutes unable to move a finger, hand, or arm, and have ended up writing. It must be remembered that many children have come to The Institutes unable to make a sound, and have ended up talking.

These motor pathways make up the front or motor half of the central nervous system.

The motor and sensory pathways taken together with their interconnections *are* the brain.

I must hasten to add that there are also children who have come to The Institutes blind or deaf or insensate or paralyzed or speechless who remain so, and these children are our failures.

These facts and others would tend to make us believe that in these children the brain can be made to grow just as the body can be made to grow since function determines structure in the brain as well as in the body.

There is a tremendous amount of evidence to support this view among the world's leading neurophysiologists. Two outstanding examples will illustrate this.

First, there is the work of that brilliant Russian neurosurgeon and neurophysiologist Boris Klosovskii, who was Chief of Neurosurgery at the Academy of Medical Sciences of the USSR in Moscow.

So important did we believe Professor Klosovskii's work to be that at the height of the Cold War in the 1960s we traveled to Moscow to see it and to talk to Klosovskii.

Here is what he had done. He had taken newborn litters of kittens and puppies and had divided them into two exactly equal groups, one as the experimental group and the other as the control group. Into the experimental group he had placed a female kitten and into the control group he had placed a sister from the same litter. He then did the same thing with each of the male kittens from each litter. He also divided the puppies in the same fashion until he had two perfectly matched groups, each containing kittens and puppies from each of the litters.

The kittens and puppies in the control group were then permitted to grow in the usual way in which kittens and puppies normally grow. The experimental animals, however, were simply placed on a slowly revolving turntable and lived there throughout the experiment.

The only difference, then, in what had happened to each of the groups was that the experimental group saw a *moving* world while the control group saw only as much as newborn kittens and puppies normally see.

When the animals were ten days old, Klosovskii began to sacrifice matched pairs of the kittens and puppies and to study their brains. He had sacrificed the last of them by the twenty-first day of life.

What Klosovskii found in the brains of his experimental animals should be required reading for every parent of a small child.

The experimental animals had from 22.8 to 35.0 percent more growth in vestibular areas of the brain than did the control animals.

To state the same thing in clearer language, in ten to twenty-one days of seeing a moving world, the experimental kittens and puppies had almost one-third more brain growth in balance areas of the brain than did their brothers and sisters who had not seen a moving world.

This is the more astonishing when one considers that a ten-day-old kitten or puppy or even a nineteen-day-old kitten or puppy is not yet much of a creature; yet the animals that saw a moving world had actually almost one-third more brain growth (and some of them more than one-third more). Just what does more growth mean? Did Klosovskii see one-third larger number of brain cells in his microscope? Not at all; he saw the same number of brain cells but one-third larger and one-third more mature.

When I consider the control animals, I think of average three-and four-year-old children, and when I think of the experimental kittens and puppies with one-third more brain growth, I think of our hurt kids who are reading. Then I cannot help wondering what would have happened if Klosovskii had taken a third group of kittens and puppies and put them in darkness. Would they have had one-third less brain growth and would they have reminded me of those little Xingu babies who live in dark huts?

But Klosovskii did not have a third group of animals, and thus we cannot know how it would have been.

Perhaps, however, we can conclude what might have happened had Klosovskii had a third group by going to the opposite end of the world to meet that genius David Krech, whose brilliant work at Berkeley supplies me with my second example.

Dr. Krech was not only a scientist whose impeccable conclusions were beyond question; he was more than that, perhaps much more than that, since in addition to great scientific knowledge he also had great wisdom. This is a wonderful combination because science is not always wise, nor is all wisdom always scientific. How I wish that gentle, witty David Krech could be heard by all parents rather than only by those who read scientific journals.

Dr. Krech spent an important portion of his life repeating an experiment with slight modifications each time. He began by raising two sets of infant rats. One set lived in an environment of sensory deprivation; that is to say, an environment in which there was little to see, hear, or feel. The other rats were raised in an environment of sensory enrichment; that is to say, one in which there was a great deal to see, and hear, and feel.

He then tested the intelligence of the rats by such tests as putting food in mazes. The deprived rats either could not find the food or found it with great difficulty. The rats raised in the enriched environment found the food easily and quickly.

He then sacrificed the rats and examined their brains.

"Rats which had been raised in sensory deprivation," he noted, "had small, stupid, undeveloped brains, while rats which had been raised in sensory enrichment had large, intelligent, highly developed brains."

He then stated his scientific conclusion which, befitting a world-famous neurophysiologist, was scientifically immaculate.

"It would be scientifically unjustifiable," says Dr. Krech, "to conclude that because this is true in rats that it is also true in people."

Then he added great wisdom.

"And it would be socially criminal to conclude that it is not true in people."

The last time I had the opportunity to see Dr. Krech I asked him if he envisioned doing anything about people.

His eyes twinkled as he replied, "I have not devoted my life to this for the purpose of creating more intelligent rats."

Amen.

David Krech had a problem. He could not turn his rats into people and thus prove conclusively that human brains also grow by sensory stimulation.

We, too, have a problem. For years we have been giving human children sensory stimulation and seeing them progress, sometimes extraordinarily. However, we cannot make our children into rats and sacrifice them to examine their brains, although there are those who insist that we do.

I remember a good example of this many years ago.

I was having the privilege of addressing a group of graduate physicians at the Medical School of the University of São Paulo, Brazil. Although Dr. Veras was with me, the dean of the Medical School was translating for me since my Portuguese did not extend very far beyond that necessary for good manners.

After the speech there were a good many highly intelligent questions and an extremely good-humored exchange of comments. There seems, however, to be one in almost every audience; the dean nodded to a man in the first row with his hand raised who turned out to be a neurologist.

He aroused my suspicions first by turning around to face the audience while he asked me his question. Then he spoke for twenty minutes. Now there are no twenty-minute questions. There are twenty-minute speeches, but no twenty-minute questions. As he continued to talk, some of the doctors began to mutter. *"Stupido,"* several of them were saying, and even with my limited Portuguese I could make out what that meant.

When at long last he had finished his question, the dean boiled down the twenty-minute harangue. "The doctor," the dean said, a little apologetically, "wants to know how you know a child is well if you succeed in making him well."

"Our standards are simple, sir. If a child acts in every way like other children his age, and if we can't tell him from his peers, and his parents can't, and if his doctor can't, and if his teacher can't, and if his playmates can't, we call that well."

There were friendly smiles around the room as the dean translated.

The doctor was not to be silenced by the dean or by his colleagues and again he turned his back and made another twenty-minute speech. This time there were less polite protests, and he was obviously being invited to sit down.

This time the dean was clearly embarrassed. "It is a ridiculous question," he said, "and there is no need to answer it. He wants to know if when you have successfully treated a child you then examine his brain physically to see if it is now well."

I responded to the dean's embarrassment. "If I may answer him in the same spirit in which he asked the question I'd be glad to."

The dean smiled and answered me with an Americanism, "Be my guest."

"In the United States we have some quaint customs and even some rigidly enforced taboos. One of them is that if we succeed in bringing a hurt child to total function, his parents don't want us to then operate on his brain to see what it looks like inside. It is also a tribal taboo, since even the government would be opposed to our doing so. I've noticed that these same customs seem to exist here in Brazil, too. However, the doctor does not seem to share these customs and concerns, so perhaps we could have a look at his own brain to see precisely what happens to it before and after treatment."

The dean smiled and translated, and on that cheery note the meeting broke up.

When people do not choose to be reasonable, they are not restrained by the bands of reason.

One of my great personal heroes, Dr. Jonas Salk, once said to me, "Now go on, don't stop to prove over and over again what you've already proven. The bright people will understand it the first time you say it. Those who don't want to understand, won't understand it if you say it five thousand times."

David Krech could not make his rats into people.

We can't make our children into rats.

I don't suppose we'll be able to actually watch human brains operate for a long time to come, except indirectly with brain scans or EEGs.

But there is a moment in history when the circumstantial evidence to support a view mounts to the point where to ignore the evidence and continue to do nothing while children's future lives are at stake becomes in every way as criminal as to introduce dangerous techniques without sufficient evidence to support them.

The brain, it would appear, grows through use exactly as a biceps does.

The problem in the brain-injured child is precisely that the brain injury acts as a barrier to the reception of incoming sensory stimulation over the visual, auditory, and tactile pathways, just as it may act as a barrier to outgoing motor response.

How to penetrate this barrier? This was the question on which all treatment of the brain-injured child must rest.

How do you get a stimulus into the brain through a barrier? Again I can hear so clearly the words of my neurology professor years ago.

"There are three ways of insuring the transmission of central nervous system stimuli. You must increase the stimuli in frequency, intensity, and duration."

Frequency, Intensity, Duration.

These three words become the most important words in the life of the brain-injured child—along with two others, family and love. Taken together, these five words are the five that offer a brain-injured child a chance to become a first-class, functioning human being. Family and love are well understood in relation to children. Frequency, intensity, and duration are far less understood. What do they mean?

If a message sent to the brain through visual, auditory, or tactile pathways does not arrive either because it was not strong enough or because a barrier in the form of a brain injury exists (or for any other reason), there are three ways to help the message get through; namely an increase in its frequency, intensity, or duration.

Let's suppose that a pressure on the skin of the arm is the message we wish to transmit to the brain. We have gently squeezed the arm and the message is not received. As an example, we might have my wife squeezing my arm to let me know that it is time to go home so that our hosts can go to bed. But I am deeply involved in a conversation with another guest. She squeezes my arm gently but the message does not arrive and I do not notice. Being a first-class rehabilitationist, she knows precisely how to reach my brain. (I must admit that as a wife she always seems to have known it.)

First she tries increasing the frequency of the stimulus. Instead of squeezing my arm every five minutes, she squeezes it ten times in a row. She knows that frequency facilitates transmission.

If that doesn't work, she tries increasing the duration. She doesn't only squeeze my arm but she keeps it squeezed. She knows that duration facilitates transmission of tactile messages to the brain.

If that doesn't work, she resorts to the last way to facilitate transmission to the brain. She increases the stimulus in intensity. Instead of squeezing my arm, she pinches my arm, and she pinches harder and harder until, however deeply I am engaged in conversation, I get the message.

"Do you think we should be going, dear?"

She smiles sweetly.

I have an idea that other wives who aren't even experts on neurophysiology know this instinctively.

If you are perhaps saying to yourself that of course it would work on you or on me because we aren't brain-injured, I would urge you to wait until you've read the chapter concerning who is brain-injured and who isn't. Then decide how firm a stand you can safely take on whether you or I aren't brain-injured.

However, because you haven't yet read that chapter, let's take a look at how frequency, intensity, and duration facilitate brain transmission in an auditory sense in a human being who is very clearly brain-injured.

Years ago we were having dinner with some friends whose father is ninety years old and who remains active and intelligent. He is, however, paying the price of advancing age. The death of cells in his auditory pathways is preceding the death of cells in other areas of the brain.

Grandfather had enjoyed a cocktail with us in the living room.

"Is everybody ready for dinner?" said our hostess.

"Ready for what?" asked her father.

"Ready for dinner, ready for dinner," repeated his daughter (frequency).

"What?" shouted her father.

"Dinner, dinner, dinner, dinner, dinner," said the daughter smiling (duration).

"What did you say?" yelled her father.

"DINNER," screamed his daughter (intensity).

"Stop yelling at me and let's go eat," said the old man with great dignity.

Let's consider visual facilitation with a child who is so severely brain-injured at six years of age that he is unable to distinguish outlines and has only the light reflex of a newborn infant, which is to say that from a functional standpoint he is totally blind and does not even bother to keep his eyes open.

Here again we will use frequency, intensity, and duration to ensure that the visual message of light actually reaches his brain.

We open his eyes with our fingers and flash light in his eyes as many as one hundred times in five minutes (frequency).

We use a strong light (intensity).

We continue to do so for many weeks if it is necessary (duration).

So frequency, intensity, and duration are words that have overwhelming importance in the homes of all children on the program of The Institutes.

Although all three of these words have the greatest importance for all children, there are varying times in some children's lives when one or another of these words is of overwhelming importance.

An excellent example of this is the brain-injured child who is in a profound coma. This state is as near the state of actual death as it is possible for a human being to get. A very large number of human beings in a profound coma do, in fact, die.

Coma frequently follows a severe brain injury; after the injury, the brain is swollen in a state called edema, which in itself can contribute to coma. In the days following the injury, that swelling tends to reduce and, as it does, many children regain total consciousness. However, most brain edema should be gone at the end of eight to ten days. By thirty days this swelling should be over and the child should have regained consciousness.

Unfortunate indeed has been the child who has not by then regained consciousness, since the chances are high that without aggressive treatment, he will now, sooner or later, develop an infection and die.

We have seen children who have been in coma for six months or a year or two years or four years. A number of years ago I was asked by the Brazilian Government to see a girl who had been in coma for eighteen years. At eight years old she had been hit by a bus and now she was twenty-six years old.

There are two ways that we can deal with a child in coma following a brain injury. We can either patiently maintain him until he one day crosses that line, or we can give him a highly organized and carefully planned program of neurological organization aimed at reaching his brain through the frequency, intensity, and duration with which we put visual, auditory, and tactile stimulation into his brain.

At The Institutes we have employed the highly organized approach for brain-injured children since the early 1960s. We now employ a coma kit and a coma team of physician, a nurse, and a therapist to carry out this program. We put visual, auditory, tactile, and even olfactory and gustatory stimulation into the child's brain for hours on end using frequency, intensity, and duration.

These three.

But the greatest of these is intensity.

At least for the child in coma.

We shine into his eyes a powerful light

In his ears we make a very loud noise.

We pinch his skin strongly.

We put aromatic spirits of ammonia under his nose.

We put a pinch of horseradish on his tongue.

For with this child, to penetrate the barrier of brain injury which has made him functionally blind, functionally deaf, and functionally insensate, over all else we require intensity.

Through every pathway that goes into his brain we are pounding in a message, and that message is:

Child, you are not allowed to resign from the human race. Come back! Come back! Come back!

I wish I could report that every time our coma team has engaged in our coma program the child has promptly come back. That would not be true.

Of the children who were in a state of coma of one month or more after a head injury, 95 percent have come back to consciousness and are ready for intense developmental programs aimed at regaining language and motor functions. Over 50 percent of these children have returned to independent function and activities.

In coma, frequency, intensity, and duration are all of staggering importance. But the most important is intensity.

To a highly alert but paralyzed and speechless brain-injured child, frequency, intensity, and duration are all of great importance, but the most important is frequency.

To a conscious but extensively brain-injured child, frequency, intensity, and duration are all of great importance, but the most important of these is duration.

It is in these three ways that we penetrate the barrier of brain injury.

I can best conclude this chapter as to what is going on in the brain by summarizing in a single paragraph all we have learned about the human brain and then summarizing all we do at The Institutes in another single paragraph.

Here in essence is what we have learned.

The world has regarded brain growth and development as if it were predetermined and unalterable. Instead, brain growth and development is a dynamic and ever-changing process. It is a process that can be stopped (as it is by severe brain injury). This is a process that can be slowed (as it is by moderate brain injury), but, most significantly, it is a process that can be speeded (and were it not so, the far-behind brain-injured child could never catch up).

It is a paragraph that says a great deal. It is a paragraph that is easily proven by the simple comparison of a severely brain-injured child's neurological age (let's say 2 months) with his chronological age (let's say 130 months). For this child, brain growth and development have stopped at 2 months but time has continued for 130 months.

It is proven by the comparison of a moderately brain-injured child's neurological age (let's say 24 months) with his chronological age (let's say 48 months). For this child brain growth and development have slowed to exactly half of normal.

The final sentence is proven by the severely brain-injured child (neurological age 2 months—chronological age 130 months) who now begins a program of neurological organization. A year later he has a neurological age of 26 months and a chronological age of 142 months. In one year of elapsed time he has grown two years' worth. For him the process has been speeded.

The remaining paragraph is the one that tells all we do at The Institutes.

In recognition of the fact that function determines structure, and that in order for function to take place in a brain-injured child, we must facilitate the transmission of brain messages by increasing the stimuli, therefore:

All we do at The Institutes for the Achievement of Human Potential is to give a child visual, auditory, and tactile stimulation with increased frequency, intensity, and duration as well as unlimited opportunity to function in full recognition of the orderly way in which the brain grows.

That, as I have said, is all we do. It is fair to add that in doing so we employ five principles, dozens of methods, and hundreds of techniques. Nonetheless, they all fit into the above paragraph.

This chapter explains what at this moment in history we believe is probably going on in the brain and is probably the explanation for the results we are presently achieving with brain-injured children.

Perhaps on one future day, in light of whatever advances have been made by then, we shall believe a different thing to be the reason for what is happening.

But today all of this seems to us at The Institutes to be the most reasonable and logical possibility.

23

THE DEATH OF TEMPLE FAY

I t had been six years since Dr. Fay had left The Institutes, and I had missed him very much. I had seen him only once since then. That had been in 1960 when I had met him unexpectedly in an international meeting in Detroit where we were both speakers. He had been extremely cordial and kindly and had charmed me as easily as ever.

But I had not seen him since and now it was 1963 and I found myself worrying about him with increasing frequency. I had heard rumors that he was not well and I dreaded that I might one day waken to read in a headline that Fay was dead. Despite our separation I still considered him in every way my mentor and preceptor and I his devoted student and disciple.

When the news came, it was worse than I wanted and not as bad as I feared. Fay was not dead but he had had a stroke.

Bob and I had a talk. I wanted to go immediately to Fay and offer him the full facilities of The Institutes. If anyone in the world deserved the best treatment available for strokes, it was Temple Fay who had contributed so much to the knowledge of what to do about them.

Bob went immediately to see Dr. Fay and offer him the full facilities of The Institutes.

While Bob was gone, I sat in my office and thought. What in the world would that giant of a man with the towering intellect do with a stroke? Would he be paralyzed and speechless, and if he was, could he possibly exist in that way or would he die of sheer agonized frustration?

I remember how often Temple Fay had stepped to a blackboard and, with skilled ease, drawn a brain in profile and said, "Right precisely here is where his lesion must be," as he discussed some brain-injured person.

He would mark the spot with an X. So great was his love of the human brain that he was unable to discuss it without obvious relish. Many who listened to him mistook his delight in the human brain for delight in brain

FIGURE 25

injury and considered him cruel and inhuman when he drew the brain and placed his X to locate the pathology.

Three hours later my brother returned and his face wore a happy grin which relieved me vastly.

Bob couldn't help giggling as he told me his story. Fay, despite a severe stroke, hadn't changed a bit.

After greeting Bob, the first thing Fay had done was to take a large piece of paper; on it, with easy skill, he had drawn a human brain in profile.

FIGURE 26

"Now my lesion," Fay had said to Bob with great relish, "has to be precisely here," making an X.

Bob had brought the paper back with him since Fay had been sure I would want to see it. As I said earlier, Fay could no more resist teaching than he could resist breathing, and his brain, like everybody else's, was teaching material.

Fay, Bob reported, had been partially paralyzed initially but had been unwilling to put up with that for more than a few weeks. He had, in fact, only one remaining problem. Fay had a transcortical aphasia.

Transcortical aphasia is perhaps the lightest of all speech problems, but it is perhaps the most frustrating of all speech problems.

The patient with transcortical aphasia has no problem in speaking and can, in fact, speak easily and fluently and accurately—except for one little thing. He cannot manage the specific names of people or things. This can be maddening.

If you hold up a pencil and say to a person with transcortical aphasia, "What is this?" it is quite likely that he'll respond something like this:

"Oh, that's a . . . You know what it is, it's a . . . You know, you write with it . . . What the devil do you call it . . . It's not a pen, it's a . . . You know, it has lead and it's wood . . ."

If you then hold up a pen and say, "What's this?" it is quite possible that he'll say:

"Oh, of course, it's not a pencil . . . It's . . . You know, ink. It's Waterman's, Schaeffer's . . . You know, you write with it."

If the reader is presently feeling a mild discomfort, then I hasten to point out that all normal people experience this exact same thing for brief periods of time.

Have you ever walked down the street with your mother and met your best friend and had trouble introducing them? "I'd like you to meet. . .that is, she is . . . ah, she's . . . "

Well, she's your mother, that's who she is, but just for the moment it escapes you. You know how awful it is. Well that's how it is with the transcortical aphasic all the time.

And Fay had transcortical aphasia.

Bob offered Fay all the facilities of The Institutes to use as he wished for as long as he wished.

It was then that we saw Fay at his most magnificent.

Speaking carefully and groping for the words he wanted to use, and coping with the staggering frustration of having a transcortical aphasia, Fay said what only Fay in all the world could say.

Fay had told Bob to thank us for our kind offer and to say he found himself with a little spare time. He told Bob to tell me that if I would send the chief of the speech pathology department down to his house every day, *he would be glad to teach her about transcortical aphasia.* I laughed until my sides hurt and so did Bob. I stopped worrying about Temple Fay.

A few months thereafter The International Forum for Rehabilitation voted to give its highest honor, the Statuette With Pedestal, to Temple Fay. I was deeply honored to be asked to make the presentation at the Annual Dinner. I also was chosen to put the bell on the cat. I had to be sure he attended the meeting, which is an extremely elegant affair and which was to be held that year in the stately Lincoln Room of the Union League.

The meeting was only two weeks off when I decided I could delay no longer. Since the recipient is never announced in advance, I decided to enlist Mrs. Fay's help.

I called her during the day and found her beside herself. Dr. Fay was in the hospital, gravely ill with an extremely dangerous chest condition in addition to his stroke. He could have no visitors, and it seemed clear they did not believe he would survive. I mumbled my sympathy, explained the situation and, extremely ill at ease, I asked Mrs. Fay if she might put in an appearance and accept the award for Dr. Fay if his condition permitted her to do so. Mrs. Fay's attention was obviously distracted and she proposed that I call back the following week.

I was disconsolate since it did not seem that Fay would survive long enough to receive the honor which I was sure he would truly treasure. How unfair and ironic it seemed to me that this heroic man, who had been the target of a thousand invidious attacks by lesser men, should die without even knowing of this major tribute.

With heavy heart I phoned Mrs. Fay the following Monday, just five days before the presentation.

When Mrs. Fay answered the phone she was talking in a very subdued voice and I immediately feared the worst, but the worst had not happened. There was a different reason altogether for her quietness.

As I asked her if she could come to the dinner, I heard the click of someone picking up an extension and a tiny, tiny voice, but nonetheless Fay's voice, said, "Glenn, now just what is that all about?"

Fay had decided not to die for a while yet, probably out of precisely the same curiosity that had caused him to be willing to see me that very first day in his office almost a quarter of a century earlier.

It was obvious that Mrs. Fay had told him about the award.

His voice was so tiny I could barely hear him and he still had some trace of his transcortical aphasia. It was obvious that he was having great trouble breathing.

He obviously wanted to hear me tell him about the award, and so I explained it to him again. I ended up by saying that I knew he had been ill and wasn't quite himself yet, but that if he could spare Mrs. Fay just long enough for us to make the presentation to her, we would send a car for her and have her driven right back home again.

It was not what Fay had in mind.

I strained to hear.

"Will it be black tie?" asked Fay.

I could hardly believe my ears. I told him it would be.

Could he come in a wheelchair? asked the faint voice.

Of course he could.

Could he bring his oxygen?

Of course he could.

Could he bring an attendant, asked the voice I could barely hear.

Of course, and we would send a car for him and Mrs. Fay and his daughter, Marion. They could arrive any time they pleased and we would stop wherever we were in the dinner and make the presentation and he could then leave immediately.

His voice was just a little stronger when he asked me the final question. "How long," he inquired, "do you think I should make my speech?"

After I hung up, I sat and looked at the telephone for a long time.

Fay was late for the dinner and I remember looking at the candlelight reflecting off the elegant silverware and the burnished paneled walls of the Lincoln Room and praying that he had survived and would survive this night.

Then the great paneled doors, twice as high as a man, opened and there was Fay, faultlessly attired in his tuxedo, sitting in his wheelchair as if it were the throne of old Rome itself and he, the Emperor. With Mrs. Fay on one side of his chair and Marion on the other, he swept into the room.

Every person in the room rose to his feet and found himself applauding as Dr. Fay, with wheelchair, oxygen tank, and attendant, was rolled into place beside my chair.

"Never before," said Fay in my ear, "has there been so funereal an entrance into this august body."

I dared to disagree. "I believe, sir, it is much more like Louis Pasteur coming before the French Academy."

We finished dinner, although Fay barely touched his food. His conversation was cheerful and he asked the name of every person in the room he didn't know personally.

I presented the Statuette.

Fay made his speech from his wheelchair in a voice that could barely be heard across the room, stopping frequently to take oxygen.

He spoke for thirty-five minutes, and there was not a sound except that tiny voice filling that great room.

He allowed himself just five minutes to cover all of past glory. He spoke briefly of his discovery of human refrigeration saying neither how he had been attacked for it nor that it was now used in every modern hospital in the world. Five minutes altogether.

Then for thirty minutes he talked about tomorrow and what must yet be done, and what he said was prophetic. He spoke much of us at The Institutes and he spoke of us with respect and with deep affection and with humor.

Fay was in every sense a physician, and Fay knew that his moments were numbered, but this he did not say. But I knew that he knew, and he knew that I knew. In that thirty-five minutes, with joy and with happiness and with humor, he passed the torch.

He also handed us a rich heritage both publicly and privately. That night will live in my heart and mind as long as I live. There was not a soul present who did not know that this was the most momentous of evenings.

The party lasted until after midnight and Fay was the last one out the door except for John Tini who was pushing his wheelchair.

I was afraid to call Mrs. Fay the following morning for fear the excitement had been too much for Dr. Fay.

"He hasn't looked so well in years," Mrs. Fay reported. "He told me to ask you if the press was there last night."

Fay operated on Fay's terms.

A few weeks later it suited Dr. Temple Fay to die, and so he did.

When he died most people thought he was a hundred years old. This was because they had known him to be a famous professor thirty years earlier and assumed he had been seventy then. But in truth he had been thirty-eight then.

Fay was sixty-eight when he died.

"The first condition for immortality is death."

By 1963 Dr. Temple Fay had met all the conditions for immortality.

24

PARENTS ARE NOT THE PROBLEM: PARENTS ARE THE ANSWER

When we human beings get a myth firmly planted in our minds, it becomes almost impossible to get it out. Such a myth can make us know what we're going to see before we see it. Then, no matter what actually happens, we see what we *thought* we were going to see.

To put it differently, so much of what we "see" doesn't start with the image sent by the eye to the brain, as it should, but starts instead within the brain. In the same way, so much of what we "hear" isn't what was sent by our ears to our brain, but is instead what we expected to hear.

Professional people are by no means immune to such myths, and the greatest of all these professional myths is the one that maintains that, if it weren't for parents, everything would be absolutely great in the world of children.

This myth so dearly loved by educators, special educators, psychologists, librarians, pediatricians, therapists, and a host of others who deal with parents and children, just isn't so.

Parents are not the problem: Parents are the answer! The greater the number of problems a child has, and the more serious the problems, the more important this basic fact becomes.

Parents are not the problem with children: Parents are the answer.

I see this with crystal clarity at The Institutes in relation to fathers, whom I take as an example because I am a male.

During the first visit which both parents and child spend with us at The Institutes, we teach every father to do a complex program for his child and we make him *reasonably* competent. He will never do the program as competently as I do it for the simple reason that in all his life he will never do the program one tenth as much as I've done it.

But that doesn't mean that I can treat his daughter Mary better than he can. He is her father and I am not. The combination of being reasonably competent *and* her father (which he is) is much more powerful than being highly competent and *not* her father (which I am not). I can make him reasonably competent, but he can't make me her father, even a little bit.

What is true of her father is even more true of her mother.

And oh, what myths there are about mothers. Oh, what sly innuendos and what outright lies, and what outrageous ones. The myths about mothers are so outrageous that they would be absolutely hilarious—if the consequences weren't so tragic and disastrous.

The unspoken law holds that all mothers are idiots and they have no truth in them. The tragic consequence of this is that almost no professional people talk to mothers, and God knows that almost nobody listens to them. What makes this so especially sad is that mothers know more about their own children than anyone else in the world.

The myth says that the trouble with mothers is that they are too emotionally involved with their children. Now surely that suggests that somehow things would be better if mothers were *not* emotionally involved with their children. Have you ever thought what the world would be like if mothers were not emotionally involved with their children?

Every time I think of that, it occurs to me that I'm sure mother alligators are less emotionally involved with baby alligators than mother people are with baby people. But I wonder if that's better for the baby alligators. Or is that maybe why they are baby alligators instead of baby people, because their mothers are not emotionally involved with them? The myth goes on to say that *because* mothers are emotionally involved with their children, they can't be objective about them. I suppose if a mother has got a well kid she can afford her little myth that this kid is going to be President or the First Lady, Pope or whatever. Why not? I suppose somebody is going to be, and who's got a right to deny that this may be the one? If a mother has got a hurt kid, she can't afford any myths, and nobody in the world knows it better than a mother does. Nobody in all of the world. But professionals insist that mothers don't want to know if the children are hurt.

Let me tell you a story. Again, this would be highly amusing if it weren't so tragic. In every hospital in the world, the instant a child is born, a struggle begins between the staff and the mother, with mother making every effort to get her baby and the staff making every effort to prevent her from getting her baby. All mother wants is to get her hands on the baby, get the staff out of the room, strip the baby down to the buff, and start counting. Five toes on this foot, five toes on this foot, two eyes, two ears, one nose.

Now if mother doesn't want to know, what the devil is the inventory for? Why has she taken it if the truth is that she doesn't want to know? When we get smarter, the first thing we'll do when a baby is born is give the baby to the mother and say, "Here's a check sheet. Please check off whether he's got everything or not." Did any reader who is a mother fail to take an inventory of her child as early as possible? Well now, if you didn't want to know whether something was wrong, why were you counting?

Now consider the next step. The Institutes for the Achievement of Human Potential have the most sophisticated records of brain-injured children in the world, the largest number of brain-injured children that were ever treated by a single system in history. Those records are very thorough. In the histories we take from the parents, among the hundreds of questions we ask are these three: (A) Who first decided this child had a problem, (B) When? (C) Why? If you go into our archives and take out a thousand charts and look up that question, in more than nine hundred out of a thousand charts it was *Mother* who first decided the child had a problem, and generally she had a *hell* of a time convincing anybody else.

Here's a typical case history of a severely brain-injured child, who was severely brain-injured from birth. (By the way, if it's a moderately brain-injured child, same story; it just takes longer—three years. If it's mildly brain-injured, it takes still longer—six years. Same story always.)

At three months of age, Mother says, "Doctor, there's something wrong with my baby." And the doctor says, *"All* mothers think that." At six months of age, Mother says, "Doctor, there's something *wrong* with my baby." And he says, "Don't compare one baby to another; they're all different from each other." At nine months of age, Mother's voice is going up. It has a slight edge of hysteria, not because she *knows* she's got a hurt child, but because nobody will listen to her. And she says, "Doctor, there's something wrong with my baby!" And he says, "He's a little slow, but he'll grow out of it." At eighteen months of age, Mother says (she's very calm now, she's made up her mind), "Doctor, are *you* going to do something about my baby or am I going to get another doctor?" And that's the day the doctor discovers severely brain-injured children. That very day. And then an astonishing thing happens. He says, "Not only is something wrong with your baby, but he's hopeless."

Now the question is, what changed that day? Did the baby actually go from being totally normal to totally hopeless in one day? Did Mother change? That's what she's been saying all along. Only one thing changed that day—the professional mind. And then these "emotionally involved," allegedly foolish mothers say an interesting thing; they say, "Doctor, for eighteen months I've been telling you something was wrong and you've been saying it wasn't, and you were wrong. Now you're saying he's hopeless—and you're wrong again."

The myth goes on to say that the problem with mothers is that they're not objective about their children, that they're unrealistic. And then it goes on to describe this unrealistic mother. I have learned that mothers of brain-injured children are so realistic they scare me. They've been laughed at by professionals so long that they're afraid to say anything hopeful about the child for fear they'll be laughed at again, and the consequence of that is that every once in a while I see a little three-year-old kid and I say, "Does he understand the word 'Mommy'?" And Mother says, "Well now I can't prove it . . ." and I say, "Now look, Mom, he's not taking college board entrance requirements, I just want to know if *you* think he understands 'Mommy' or not." There's nobody more realistic than mothers of brain-injured children.

That unrealistic mother—I do see her every once in a while. It isn't that she doesn't exist, she exists all right. And when I see her she's exactly as painted. She brings in a little three-year-old profoundly hurt child and puts him on my floor. He can't move, he can't make sounds, and she tells me about how he can walk and talk. And I have found my unrealistic mother. The only thing is, I've been led to believe that she's unrealistic *because* she's got a brain-injured child. When I find this gal—she's unrealistic about *everything*. She's simply an unrealistic human being who happens to be the mother of a brain-injured child.

I mean, there's nothing about being unrealistic that keeps you from being pregnant, is there? Indeed, there may be some things about being unrealistic that lead to pregnancy. It's quite possible for unrealistic people to become mothers and so, when I find her, she's just exactly as painted. What is lied about is not what she's like; it's her frequency. Because I'm told she's everybody. And I see her regularly . . . every three years. She's one in a thousand mothers.

As I said earlier: *Parents are not the problem with children: Parents are the answer.*

All over the world today, a sad, sad drama is being acted out. All over the world parents are taking their brain-injured children to institutions for what is solemnly called "Evaluation and Diagnosis."

Such evaluations are generally extremely expensive and require the child to be an inpatient for ten days or two weeks. At the end of this period of time it is quite possible for the parents (if they are unlucky) to get back the child and a large bill without anybody even saying good-bye to them. This approach suggests that children exist for the purpose of being evaluated. It is a quaint view of life.

If the parents are luckier, at the end of the child's hospitalization, in addition to receiving the child and the large bill, somebody says good-bye to them, which generally means that someone sits down with them and explains that they have done this test and this test and this test. The conversation then goes like this:

PARENTS: "Yes?"

PRO: "As a consequence of all these tests we have diagnosed your child as *Severely Mentally Retarded.*"

PARENTS: "Yes?"

PRO: "Well that's it. Your child is severely mentally retarded."

PARENTS: "But what does that *mean?*"

PRO: "Why that means your son can't *do* what other children his age can do."

Dad: (After long silence) "You're pulling my leg. You have to be. You wouldn't *dare* bring my child in here and keep him ten days and do painful things to him and then give us a large bill and dare to tell us that he can't do the things that other kids his age can do. Why that's exactly what *we* told *you* when we brought him here. We don't need to pay anybody to tell us what he can't do. His mother here is the world's leading authority on what he can't do—and what he can do. That's all we've talked about every night for the last four years. You're joking, and it's a damned bad joke."

PRO: "No, I'm not joking. I've been in this field for five years and I'm telling you your son is severely mentally retarded and you better face up to it."

PARENT: "We didn't bring our son here to be told what he can't do, and we didn't bring him here to have you put a name on not being able to do what other kids his age do. "We brought him here to find out two things. First: *Why* he can't do what other kids do, and Second: What we're going to *do* about it. If you can't tell us the answer to these questions, we'll look until we find somebody who can."

And, as usual with parents, they are the two exactly proper questions that must be answered if we're going to solve the problems of brain-injured children.

As I think I mentioned before,

Parents are not the problem with children: Parents are the answer.

It took me a very long time to learn this in the face of all the myths I lived with, but I finally learned it.

Most people think that the reason we teach parents to program their children instead of doing it ourselves is because it is so much cheaper for parents.

Certainly it is true that it would cost huge sums of money if we were going to actually treat the kids seven days a week for eight, ten, or twelve hours a day as the parents do. But that's not why we have the parents treat the children.

The reason is that we know without question that if parents are taught thoroughly what is going on and why we do what we do and precisely how to do it, then the simple fact is that parents can do it *better* than we can do it. *Better* than Glenn Doman. *Better* than Katie Doman. *Better* than Suzy Aisen. *Better* than Ann Ball. *Better* than Coralee Thompson.

The reason that parents can treat kids better than we can, if they know what they're doing, is very simple.

Much as everyone on the staff loves brain-injured children, and love them they do, each individual kid is loved even more by his individual parents.

Parents are not the problem with brain-injured children: Parents are the answer.

25

ON MOTIVATION

It's surprising, really, how few mothers ask me about motivation when you consider how much everybody else talks about it.

I suppose the reason why my particular mothers rarely ask me about motivation is that they are already experienced; being the mothers of brain-injured children who are sometimes so severely injured that they must be encouraged to breathe, my mothers are among the world's leading experts on motivating children.

Not being a mother of a brain-injured child, nor even a female, I was not equipped by nature to understand motivation instinctively, nor were the professionals who were my teachers able to enlighten me. I learned about motivation by experience, observation, and thought. Not being able to handle it by instinct, it was necessary for me to define it in words. It is frequently advantageous to be able to put words to instinctive reactions. I am now able to talk about motivation and dare to do so to some of the best motivating mothers in the whole world. Frequently, the mothers who are the best instinctive motivators are the most grateful for being able to evaluate their own actions in words.

When on occasion one of my mothers does raise the question of motivation, she almost invariably puts the question properly: "How," she asks, "can I motivate my child?" The very way she asks the question indicates that she knows the most important part of the answer. She does not ask why her child wasn't born motivated. Her question makes it clear that she believes that the problem of motivation lies within herself rather than being inborn with the child. She already knows the big secret.

For too long we have considered motivation to be a moral value, and an inherited moral value at that. This makes for convenient, quick analysis of a host of problems. If motivation is a product of morality and morality is inbred, then one can quickly understand how it is that highly motivated, highly competitive, well-off achievers beget highly motivated, highly competitive, young, well-off achievers with an occasional unmotivated underachiever exception to prove the rule. It also explains why the unmotivated, unemployed, poor tend to beget unmotivated, unemployed, poor with an occasional highly motivated achiever exception to prove the rule.

Thus, we are shown how morality begets morality, motivation begets motivation, and achievement begets achievement. Thus, we are shown how immorality reproduces immorality, lack of motivation reproduces lack of motivation, and crime reproduces crime.

Motivation is familial and inbred. It's a convenient thought. It's an easy thought. It would explain a lot. The only problem for me is that I don't believe it. I've lived in too many huts in too many jungles and too many deserts to believe it. It conflicts with all I see. It conflicts with all I know. It conflicts, I think, with the facts.

It is *not* that motivation begets success and that *lack* of motivation begets failure. It is quite the other way round. Success *creates* motivation. Failure *destroys* motivation.

There are a couple of similar words which have much to do with motivation. The words are *reward* and *punishment*. Success leads to reward which leads to motivation. Failure leads to punishment which leads to lack of motivation.

I have watched the fascinating process by which the brain-injured child pounds his way to function as a salmon beats his way up impossible waterfalls against enormous odds. For more than a half-century I have been a privileged observer of the brain-injured child trying to crawl across a room on his belly, moving against paralysis, against uncontrollable and unwanted movements, with incomplete vision, incomplete hearing, incomplete sensation, using his fingernails, his toenails, his teeth, using even the uncontrolled and unwanted movement if this chaotic flopping happens to push him forward and struggling onward against it when it pushes him backward.

Although I have watched this Olympian struggle on the part of a tiny child thousands of times, I am at once overwhelmed and totally involved as I sit silently watching. My knuckles whiten, my nails dig deep into my palms, I bite my lip, I am drenched in perspiration. I strain forward in my chair trying to push this heroic little child forward by my will if not by my prayer. Ten minutes pass and the struggle to crawl twenty feet continues and the tension increases as the child, against overwhelming odds, approaches the wall which is his goal. In my heart I cheer for him. I am not religious, but I pray for him. By God, I ask myself, why does he continue to try to gain so little at such cost in superhuman effort? But, by God, how I do admire this endlessly determined, incredibly tough, and heroic hurt child.

His hand flies out and touches the wall and the room explodes in wild applause. My office is filled with joy; parents, graduate students, physicians, staff are on their feet applauding, laughing, congratulating, and I find my own eyes wet with emotion for this little child. Not for a moment do I feel pity, which is a cheap and plentiful emotion; it is admiration which moves me to tears and, more than that, it is respect which courses down my cheek. No ballerina, no concert pianist, no Shakespearean actor in all of history ever received a more spontaneous or sincere ovation than this little hero now receives—and deserves.

I have, as I have said, experienced this drama thousands of times, and today I feel it not less but more than the first time I beheld this miracle of sorts, more than fifty years ago. I suppose I *appreciate* it more.

I have been privileged to behold miracles of motivation, and I have watched those superb motivators, the mothers, countless times. And I have learned much.

I have learned that such monumental motivation has simple enough beginnings, simple not only in the children but in me, for in many ways I am child-like.

Motivation begins, clearly, with those ancient movers *punishment* and *reward*.

Punishment is so hard for the brain-injured child to comprehend that it certainly isn't the answer.

He can do so little that punishing him for a sin of commission is almost impossible. This leaves punishing him for a sin of omission as the only way to teach him the ancient law. Shall we punish him for not walking, not crawling, not creeping? Shall we punish him for not talking? Shall we punish him for not being able to do these things because he is brain-injured?

If we cannot punish him for the transgressions he is unable to commit and if we cannot punish him for what he cannot do, how then shall he learn the ancient law of punishment?

If it is fear of punishment that prevents the child and me from doing those things we should *not* do, it is surely reward that causes the child and me to do the things we should do.

Again, it is easier for me to learn than it is for the child. As I work with my parents, my kids, my team members, and my students, I am a much rewarded man. When I am wise enough and knowledgeable enough to design an individual program that brings about walking, talking, reading, and writing in a child who was motionless, speechless, or blind, I am rewarded far more than just being paid a salary. There are few rewards to compare. And when I am so rewarded, I am inspired to even greater efforts so that I may be so rewarded soon again and more often.

But what of the brain-injured child? What can he do to earn his reward? He is paralyzed and speechless and can neither do nor say the things that will earn his true reward. If this is so, how can we sincerely reward him? Should we then reward him for no accomplishment at all? To do so would be to teach him that in this hard world one is rewarded for nothing at all. To do so would be teaching him a lie. This would be understandable but very unwise.

It becomes clear that it is more difficult to teach a brain-injured child about punishment or reward than it is to teach a well child, and so where are we left?

Let's move back a bit to those predecessors of punishment and reward—*success* and *failure*.

Again let's consider me, for I am in most ways an uncomplicated person and child-like. Strange fellow that I am (as compared with you), I find myself with an extremely clear-cut view about success and failure. I find myself carefully avoiding doing those things at which I fail and repeating over and over again those things which I do well.

I *know* I should not. I *know* I should work hard at those things at which I fail so as to accomplish them and to avoid spending time at those things at which I invariably succeed since I am already accomplished at them. I *know* I would be a better person and that I would become more rounded if I did it the other way around.

Still, it occurs to me that I am round enough, and so I continue to avoid those things at which I fail and to return again and again to those things at which I succeed. I am sure that you do not behave in such an *undetermined* way. But I do.

I have never learned to play tennis nor can I carry a tune, and, despite all the insistence of my friends who play tennis beautifully or who sing superbly that I could easily learn, no one during my entire life has succeeded in getting me onto a tennis court or to sing publicly, at least not since Miss Jeffries, my first grade teacher, blew her pitch pipe to give us *do* and then looked pained—and in my direction. I know I could learn if I wanted to. I just don't want to. I note with interest that all my friends who want to get me onto a tennis court play tennis beautifully and those who would head me for the concert stage sing beautifully.

I continue to avoid the things at which I fail. It's a weakness which I intend to keep.

On the other hand there are some things I do well and a few things that I do extremely well, and I know it. Try as I may to avoid it, I find myself doing those things over and over and over again. It goes like this. I do whatever it is that I do well. Since I know I do it well, I do it completely and confidently. It is almost always a pleasure to see something done well, and so when I am done you say, "Golly, but you did that well."

"Yes, I did do that rather well, didn't I?" I say. "Would you like to see me do that again?"

And so it goes.

In my weakness I am just like the kids whether they are overtly brain-injured or whether they are not. They also tend to avoid that at which they fail while repeating over and over again that at which they succeed.

By the very nature of the severely brain-injured child's brain injury, he is a born loser. He can frequently do absolutely nothing except breathe, and he almost always does that rather badly. Failure is the story of his life until help comes.

Now let us suppose that for some reason it would be a good idea to have a little brain-injured girl wrap her hands around a ³/₄" bar and hang feet down supporting her weight from her hands. (This is, in fact, a first-rate idea for brain-injured children of all sizes and shapes and is a highly sophisticated idea which the staff of The Institutes for the Achievement of Human Potential in Philadelphia spent many years developing). Suppose, in fact, that your child, a four-year-old, let's say, is a patient at The Institutes in Philadelphia and that we have instructed you on the importance of her learning to hang by her hands for one minute even though she is unable to move and unable to speak.

Being a first-rate set of parents, you are most anxious to give your tiny paralyzed daughter every opportunity to be a whole functioning human being. Indeed, you would give anything in the world to bring that about.

Now you build a bar in a doorway a few inches higher than her total height with arms outstretched. You say a little prayer, "Please Lord, let her win just this once!" You are ready to begin.

"Now, honey, I am going to put your hands around this bar and you must hold on for one minute the way all your friends in Philadelphia want you to do. Once you get a grip, I'll let go of you, and it will be just as if you are standing up all by yourself for the first time in your life only your feet won't be touching the floor. Don't worry, honey, because when you can't hold on any longer, I'll catch you, so you don't have to worry. Here we go, honey!"

With your heart in your mouth and a prayer on your lips, you, Mother, open her little hands while your husband supports her weight and you wrap them around the bar.

Now you let go and Mary hangs for exactly one-half second before falling into her father's outstretched arms.

"Oh no, honey," you protest, "that was only one-half a second, and you've got to hang one whole minute. It's so important." To her father, you say, "What are we going to *do*? She *must* hang more than a hundred times that long. How will we ever motivate her to do it?"

Now let's look at that perfectly natural episode from Mary's standpoint. Mary is four years old. Being severely brain-injured, she is very small, as brain-injured children are inclined to be, so she only weighs twenty-six pounds. She has never crawled, crept, hung, stood, or walked in her life. She has just tried to hang for the first time in her life and succeeded for only half a second.

"Well," says tiny Mary to herself (being unable to talk), "that's failure six-thousand-four-hundred and ninety-two. I failed again! That's the story of my life."

Mary, being very hurt, may not be able to articulate it quite that clearly, but that is precisely what she'll feel. What else could she *possibly* think under that set of circumstances?

Now suppose we ask ourselves a question. Just how long *should* a paralyzed, speechless, brain-injured four-year-old child with the body of a two-year-old be able to hang from a bar the first time she tries it? How long should *any* little four-year-old girl hang, for that matter?

Well it is obvious that you don't know and neither do I. If we don't know how long she should be able to hang, it is pretty obvious that *she* doesn't. While I don't know that answer in advance for any one little girl, I know without question that for some little girls the first time out one-half second is a very long time to hang.

Now let's suppose that instead of the "Gosh, honey, that just isn't good enough" approach, you had used a different approach.

Suppose at the end of that one-half second when Mary dropped into Dad's arms, you had taken her into your arms and said, "Wow!"

Suppose you had hugged her and kissed her and said, "Who would have *dreamed* that a tiny little girl like you could have hung on to that bar for a whole half-second?"

Suppose you had told her she was a most extraordinary little girl. Suppose you had told her that she was without question the most remarkable child in the whole city, probably the most magnificent child in the entire state, and possibly the best little girl in the whole *world*.

Suppose you had told her with love and with respect.

Suppose also that you *meant* it. Do you know any other little four-year-old girl who can't move and can't talk who ever even *tried* to hang by her hands?

Let's not play games with whether a speechless four-year-old girl understands what it means to be the most remarkable child in all the city. *She'll* understand the real message. When you squeeze her to your breast you'll feel nice and warm and soft and she'll get the message. When she sees the love and the respect on your face for her superb accomplishment, she'll get that message. When she hears the love and respect in your voice, she'll get that message, and she does not need to understand a word of English to do so.

We adults make the mistake of listening to each other's words to some degree, and we are thus misled when some other adult chooses to mislead us. But nobody really fools kids because when they are listening for important messages (rather than mere information), they don't really listen to the words. They listen to the music.

Considering the two possible approaches, it's immediately obvious that in *either* case she hung for one-half second. We have no way of knowing whether that's good or bad, really, but we do know this. You may look at what she did from two very different vantage points.

If, in your anxiety to get it right for her own good, you insist on looking at the difference between the way she is the first time she tries this new and important treatment and the way you *want* her to be, then you can only bemoan the fact that it is not good enough.

If such is the case, then you must not be surprised when Mary says to herself, "Yep, that's my six-thousand-four-hundred and ninety-second failure, and now the big ones are going to keep at me with this new damned business at which I will now fail as many times a day as they make me do it. It's the story of my life."

And she will.

That's what *I* do.

Now if, on the other hand, what you want is for her to do it again and again and to attack it with enthusiasm and to want to do it again and again, then you might be wise to look at it from the vantage point of where she *was* yesterday and where she *is* today.

Yesterday nobody would have dreamed of asking this immobile and speechless little girl to hang by her hands at all. Today she can support her own weight by hanging from her hands for a full half-second. When *you* appreciate the miracle that has happened and show your respect for that accomplishment, then surely Mary will glow with the pleasure of accomplishment and of Mommy's praise and then she will say with or without words:

"Yes, I did do that well, didn't I? Would you like to see me do it again?"

And she will.

That's what *I* do.

And if you *do* want her to do it again so that every day she gets better, until it's time for her revisit to The Institutes, she can hang for sixty seconds, then I strongly recommend that you appreciate what she *can* do. That's motivation with a capital "M"

It is you, Mother, who *decides* what success or failure is.

If you want to win in making your child well, then look at the difference between where she is and where you want her to be, which is to say the difference between the way she is (hurt) and the way you want her to be (well), but *don't* pound the child's ear about that. That is *your* problem and *mine*. Pointing out how far the child has yet to go makes it sound as if it is her fault.

Thus, we have the formula: failure which leads to punishment which leads to lack of motivation which leads to her stubbornly refusing to try. Or as Mary puts it, "That's the story of my life."

If, on the other hand you want to motivate Mary to try and try and try again until she can hang on a bar for a minute or walk or talk or read or write, then it behooves you to look at where she is today versus where she was before you started such an intensive program, which is to say the difference between the way she is and the way she was, and you must be grateful and enthusiastic and respectful and joyous.

Thus we have the formula: success which leads to rewards which leads to motivation which leads to her actually wanting to do it again and looking forward to doing it again. Or, as Mary puts it, "Yes, I did do that well, didn't I? Would you like to see me do it again?"

If you would like to see her do whatever it is again, try rewarding her with your love and praise.

But of course, being a parent, you always knew all of that in your heart and I'm sure that you've almost always practiced it, but I just thought I ought to mention it.

26

WHO IS BRAIN-INJURED?
WHO IS NOT?

If everyone could simply agree on what is meant by the various terms used to describe brain-injured children, we'd be a long way along the road to solving such problems.

The American psychiatrist Dr. Menninger, of the Menninger Clinic, once told me that when man encounters a mysterious illness he is inclined to label it, to hang tags on it, because he feels that by doing so he has somehow achieved a degree of mastery over it. Dr. Menninger pointed out that this rarely adds to the clarity but instead adds to the confusion.

Confusion of terminology is certainly a problem in the world of the brain-injured child. That's why this book is entitled *What To Do About Your Brain-Injured Child, or Your Brain-damaged, Mentally Retarded, Mentally Deficient, Cerebral-palsied, Epileptic, Autistic, Athetoid, Hyperactive, Attention Deficit Disordered, Developmentally Delayed, Down's Child.* Now that, admittedly, is a terrible name for a book, and all you can say is, "What the devil does that mean?"

That is exactly what I'd hope you'd say because that's exactly the question that needs asking. What the devil do all those words mean?

If you are the parent of a brain-injured child, you have surely heard all of these words. It is quite possible that different specialists have given your child most or even all of these names. We see tiny children who have been diagnosed as every one of those things, each in a different institution, and when I look at a tiny two-year-old child I wonder if it is really possible for one little girl to have so many terrible diseases—if diseases they are.

Just what do these terms mean? Are brain-damaged children the same as *mentally retarded* children? Are all such children *emotionally disturbed*, or is that a different problem? What of children with *cerebral palsy?* Is this one kind of condition when the child is bright, and something else when he is mentally retarded? Are all cerebral palsy children *spastic, flaccid, rigid, or all three?* Always? Sometimes?

Just what do these terms mean? Do they mean what they say? If they don't mean what they say, then what do they mean?

Let's take the term *emotionally disturbed.* Many brain-injured children are diagnosed as being *emotionally disturbed.* What does this term mean? Is it intended to replace *brain injury* as a diagnosis; that is to say, is this child *emotionally disturbed* rather than *brain-injured?* Or is he suffering from two different diseases simultaneously? Just what disease is *emotionally disturbed,* or is it, in fact, a disease at all? What does the term mean? If it means what it says—emotionally disturbed—then I can say that I, one of the most fortunate of men, find myself emotionally disturbed twenty or thirty times a day about one thing or another. I have a sneaky suspicion that you do, too. I don't believe that anyone in his right mind could read the front page of any large metropolitan newspaper without being emotionally disturbed over virtually every front-page story. At least he should be emotionally disturbed if *emotionally disturbed* means what it says. On the other hand, if the term *emotionally disturbed* as used to diagnose brain-injured children does not mean what it says, then the overriding question which remains is: What does it mean?

Or let's take what is probably the best-known term: *Cerebral Palsy.* *Cerebral* means *brain* and *palsy* means *paralysis.* To some people *palsy* means *to shake.* Since the brain can neither shake nor be paralyzed, the term *cerebral palsy* clearly does not mean what it says. The question then is—what does it mean?

One great authority on the subject of cerebral palsy has said that cerebral palsy means *a highly specific set of symptoms produced by a highly specific and specifically located type of brain injury.* Fair enough, and that would do for a term and a diagnosis were it not for the fact that another great authority has said that cerebral palsy means a very different thing. He has said that *cerebral palsy is anything that happens to a child from the neck up.* Also fair enough, if it were not for the first authority. Unhappily this disagreement does not end with these two authorities. There are virtually as many different meanings as there are authorities in the field, and there are many authorities.

Nor does refinement of terms necessarily help.

The term cerebral palsy can be broken down into several different subcategories, one of which is *athetoid cerebral palsy.* In some classifications this term is then broken down further into sub-terms describing ten or twelve types of athetoids. Dr. Fay, who had personally authored or co-authored several classification methods in an early attempt to bring some order out of chaos, used to say rather ruefully that there were actually only two types of athetoids. The two types, Dr. Fay used to say, were "them as had it and them as didn't." That reduced the types of athetoids rather considerably. We come, in the end, to agree with Menninger that "refining the terminology" added to the confusion rather than to the clarification.

The trouble with almost all of the names we have discussed and the many others that exist is every time we use them we are compounding the easy error of mistaking the symptom for the disease.

A good example is the very popular term *mental retardation.* An American adult would have to be not only televisionless and radioless, but deaf and blind as well, not to have heard this term over and over again. *"Mental retardation can strike any home."* "Every two minutes a child is born afflictedwith *mental retardation."* "Fight *mental retardation."* "Give money for research into the cause of *mental retardation."* "This child is a victim of *mental retardation."*

Doesn't all this leave the impression that there is a disease called *mental retardation?* There is no such disease. Mental retardation is a symptom and, like most other symptoms, is a symptom of many very different diseases. One can have the symptom, mental retardation, because his mother and father have incompatible Rh factors. One can have the symptom, mental retardation, because he got hit by an automobile. One can have the symptom, mental retardation, because he was born with the umbilical cord wrapped tightly around his neck. One can show the symptom, mental retardation, because he had measles, which resulted in encephalitis, and so on through a hundred very different diseases and injuries that can result in the symptom of severe, moderate, or mild mental retardation.

To talk about mental retardation as if it were a disease is not only unscientific but, what is more important, seriously delays the finding of rational answers to problems. Because this point is so important, I must risk belaboring it to be sure I have made myself clear. Let's take a clear and fairly precise analogy.

Let's suppose that today someone should announce that he has discovered that seven million Americans have a Fever and that this condition can be as serious as it is mysterious. Suppose that he should announce that this mysterious illness of elevated temperature, or Fever, ranged in effect from a mild inconvenience at one end of the spectrum to actual death at the other and that this very day hundreds of Americans would die afflicted with Fever. Suppose he announced that every eight seconds an

American was born who would someday be afflicted with Fever. Suppose finally he announced that he had just found out that there was no American Fever Society and that he was going to raise millions of dollars to organize such a society for the purpose of combating the killer, Fever.

If that should happen, it is to be hoped that someone would say to this man, "Each of the things you have said is true. You are obviously motivated by the highest and most selfless intentions, *but you must not do this.* While each of the things you have said is true, the conclusion you have drawn is untrue. Fever is not a *disease* but is instead a *symptom* of many different and unlike diseases or injuries. If you form such a society you will convince many people, and even some professionals, that there is actually such a disease. This will hide the truth and, in the end, be a disservice to mankind."

This is what has actually happened as a result of the popularization of that very imprecise term, *mental retardation.*

Mental retardation is no more and no less a symptom than is fever; neither symptom is a disease. If one successfully attacks the disease of which fever is a symptom, the fever will disappear spontaneously, as is the case with the symptoms in other diseases. By the same token, if one successfully attacks the brain injury of which mental retardation can be a symptom, the mental retardation will also disappear spontaneously.

How did this term arise and what does it actually mean?

Most people use the term, mental retardation, to describe children who do not learn as quickly or are not able to learn as much as average children. The symptom of mental retardation can be present in a child because of the combination of genetic factors. This is true in only a fraction of the children who have the symptom.

The term mental retardation was coined in an effort at kindliness. So many human problems begin with someone saving someone else from something he hasn't asked to be saved from. Before the term mental retardation was coined as a subterfuge to protect parents from what was considered to be too harsh a truth (harsh it was, truth it was not), we measured intelligence that fell below average (100 being average or normal) and, having done so, we classified sub-normal children into groups according to their scores, and such groups were called morons, idiots, or imbeciles.

Since it seemed very harsh to tell a parent that her child was a moron, idiot, or imbecile, society invented a euphemism, "mental retardation". This term, in a literal sense, was a splendid choice, which labeled the problem quite well. It is what was eventually done with this good, but symptomatic, term which was the problem. It did not take parents long to come to the conclusion that it was not a compliment to be told that their child was mentally retarded and that what this term really meant was that their child was a moron, idiot, or imbecile.

The parents were not fooled, but now professionals had at least two diseases, idiocy and mental retardation.

It took several years for those who dealt with the parents to come to the conclusion that *mental retardation* meant *idiot* to most parents, and so an even newer term was coined which was an even greater euphemism. This new term to describe children with below-average intelligence was *exceptional*. To call a child with a low I.Q. exceptional was again literally true, but what a splendid euphemism it was. To say that such children were exceptional children rather implied that such children were somehow *better* than other children.

Again the parents were neither flattered nor deceived by such terms. Parents know precisely what their children can and cannot do. Parents very quickly decided that it was not good to be told that their children were exceptional. They decided that what that *really* meant was mentally retarded and what *that* really meant was moron, idiot, or imbecile.

Again parents were neither deceived nor mollified, but now we professionals had at least three diseases—idiot children, mentally retarded children, and exceptional children.

Mental retardation is not a disease, it is a symptom. *Idiot, emotionally disturbed, flaccid, spastic, quadriplegic, paraplegic, hemiplegic, diplegic,* and a host of other terms by which brain-injured children are called, are all symptoms and none of them are diseases.

We do not believe that it is helpful to say that there are hundreds of different categories of children whose problems exist within the brain. We have learned how to help those children who are brain-injured. We do not know how to help children who are not brain-injured. Perhaps, one day we will have answers for all children.

We believe that all the children we see can be placed in three simple categories:

A. Children with peripheral problems
B. Children with psychological problems
C. Children with brain injury

A. Children with Peripheral Problems
It is important to recognize that the nervous system consists of two main

parts—the central nervous system (CNS) and the peripheral nervous system (PNS). The central nervous system consists of the brain and spinal cord.

Some individuals have problems due to disorders that are outside the central nervous system or brain. These disorders may include conditions affecting the peripheral nerves, neuromuscular junction, or muscle. These people may have motor or sensory problems, but the cause is not in the central nervous system or brain itself. An example of such a condition is peripheral neuropathy, which may present itself with motor or sensory symptoms. Some individuals have a neuromuscular junction disorder. They can also have weakness, but the weakness is due to a problem at the junction between the nerve and muscle, *not* due to a brain injury. Some individuals have a muscular dystrophy, or muscle disease. These people may also have weakness, but in this case the weakness is due to the muscle, *not* the brain. Sometimes central nervous system and peripheral nervous system problems co-exist.

The Institutes program is intended for individuals with central nervous system disorders. It is *not* intended for individuals with problems exclusively due to peripheral nervous system disorders, neruomuscular junction diseases, or muscle diseases. In most cases, these problems have been identified beforehand.

B. Children with Psychological Problems

In some cases, a previously well child with no past history of a structural brain injury will develop psychological, emotional, or behavioral problems. Scientists and doctors are trying to understand the complex biological or chemical changes that may occur in the brain, accompanying some of these conditions. Some of these children may benefit from programs emphasizing good nutrition, elimination of allergies and detoxification. Programs focusing on a good physiological environment and programs for social, physical, and intellectual excellence may also be of helpful.

Many children with brain injury have what society has called "psychological", "emotional", or "behavioral" problems. Some of these children may even be said to be "psychotic". The brain runs everything in the body. Some children who have been diagnosed as "psychotic" are not psychotic at all but brain-injured. When this is the case as the brain responds to neurological treatment, these behavioral problems resolve.

C. Children with Brain Injury

When we at The Institutes for the Achievement of Human Potential speak of a brain-injured child, we mean any child who has had something happen to hurt the brain. That something may occur at any time. It may occur at conception, or a minute, an hour, a day, a week, a month, or nine months after conception. It may occur during birth or a minute, an hour, a day, a week, a month, a year, or ten years after birth. It may also happen seventy years after birth, only then he is called a brain-injured adult.

If you could look at the injured brain in the operating room, you might even be able to see the injury which could consist of highly visible harm confined to a small area, or of harm essentially invisible to the naked eye and spread over a broader area. In some cases, the problem may only be seen under a microscope. In some cases the disorder is at the level of cellular function and may not be able to be seen at all with current technology. In some cases, brain studies, brain imaging, electroencephalograms (EEGs), evoked potentials, or other tests may be abnormal. In other cases, these studies may be unremarkable. The brain may be severely hurt or it may be mildly hurt. It may be hurt in a way that limits walking or talking or hearing or seeing or feeling, or a combination of these.

Sometimes different injuries have occurred to a child at different times. Sometimes the child will have a clear-cut cause for the brain injury, such as a major trauma or infection. Sometimes no clear cause for the brain injury will be found. When this book speaks of the brain-injured child, it means a child who has a hurt brain from one of, or some of, any number of causes. Although sometimes the causes may be similar, each case is unique because it affects a unique individual —a child with his own unique potential.

1. The Acutely Brain-Injured Child: Some children have brain injuries due to causes that require immediate or emergency medical or surgical treatment. These injuries may be due to an infection, hemorrhage, tumor, trauma, progressing hydrocephalus, or one of a number of conditions that need to be acutely addressed to insure the survival of the child and to limit the harm done to the brain. This care is usually given in an emergency or hospital setting. After this acute stage, the child may be left with residual brain injury. The brain-injured child may have various degrees of problems in walking, talking, hearing, seeing, or feeling. When left untreated, these problems may become chronic or permanent. We see the brain-injured child after the acute and life-threatening problems have been managed and stabilized. It is important that this child receives treatment as soon as possible to help speed recovery. However, even those who have been brain-injured for many years can benefit from treatment.

2. The "Mentally Deficient" Brain-Injured Child: Formerly called "mentally deficient," this child is one in which there is a malformation or abnormality of the brain. This may be on the basis of a genetic disorder such as Down Syndrome, or due to any number of problems that can affect the development of a child's brain before birth. There may be malformations of other organs or other body features as well. At one time it was thought that children with brain malformations or genetic problems would not benefit from treatment. Many were confined to mental institutions for life. We have had many brain-injured children on our program who have had CT or MRI scans that show abnormalities of brain development. These malformations can include gyri (convolutions) that are too big or too small, or lobes of the brain or other structures that are malformed or missing. We have also seen children with abnormalities of gray or white matter development, sometimes referred to as *heterotopias* or *migrational* disorders. We now know that although the brain may *appear* structurally different, it will respond to stimulation and treatment. These children *are* candidates for a neurological treatment program.

3. The Brain-Injured Child with Neurodegenerative Disorders: Children with neurodegenerative disorders may have diseases or conditions that cause the progressive destruction of the brain and nervous system. In some cases, a metabolic factor or some other problem can be found which may be modified by nutrition, or by altering the physiological environment of the brain. This allows us the opportunity to treat the residual brain injury. In other cases, a disorder may be causing rapid relentless destruction of the brain and nervous system. Fortunately, such cases are rare. In such cases, we may not be able to make a significant impact with our program.

Brain injury can occur at any time. Brain injury can be due to any of a number of causes. Sometimes the cause of the brain injury is not fully understood. Sometimes, brain-injured children will be given labels by medical professionals, educators or society. Those labels are *not* diseases but *symptoms* of one problem—brain injury.

There are literally millions of brain-injured children. I might paraphrase Abraham Lincoln, and I am sure he would not mind in the least, if I said that "God must have loved the brain-injured children because he made so many of them."

These brain-injured children are wonderful kids, they need and deserve our help. We now know that a program of neurological organization will yield results in most brain-injured children. In the future, perhaps there will be answers for all brain-injured children.

27

HOW MANY BRAIN-INJURED
CHILDREN ARE THERE?

The question of how many brain-injured children there may be in this country and abroad may seem of little importance to the parent who already has a brain-injured child. One such child is quite enough for a parent to handle, and knowing how many more there may be in the world may appear to do the parent little good.

However, since many of the Dark Age ideas about the brain-injured child still persist, it may be important for the parent to realize that, in terms of the number of brain-injured children who are actually recognized as being brain-injured, his child is far from alone. If we add the number of brain-injured children, who are not called brain-injured but who are called by any of the several dozen non-specific symptomatic classifications that have been mentioned, then the number becomes very large indeed, and the brain-injured child becomes almost commonplace. If, finally, we should add the number of people who in the technical and scientific sense are brain-injured, that is to say the number of people who have some dead brain cells, we will now find that there are a great many more brain-injured people in the world than there are people who are not brain-injured.

When we at The Institutes meet people who are familiar to some small degree with our work, it is common for them to laugh (a little nervously) and say, "Hey, you know, I'm sure that I must be brain-injured." They are joking, albeit somewhat nervously. The chances are that, in a technical and specific sense, they are right. A top-flight neurophysiologist, McCann, indicates that from thirty-five years of age onward, with each passing day, each of us suffers the death of about one hundred thousand brain cells.

Just how many of us human beings are brain-injured? Due to the almost incredible hodgepodge of terms existing in the jungle of the brain-injured child, it is impossible to know with anything resembling accuracy, but let's take those things we know.

Dr. William Sharpe, the late and prominent New York neurosurgeon, conducted a careful scientific study of five hundred consecutively born newborn children. Within forty-eight hours of their birth, he performed spinal punctures on these children for the purpose of examining their cerebrospinal fluid. (Cerebrospinal fluid is the fluid in which the brain floats. It acts, among other things, to cushion the brain against injury. The cerebrospinal fluid is normally clear and colorless like water.) Dr. Sharpe found that the cerebrospinal fluid taken from 9 *percent* of these presumably normal children contained enough blood to be visible to the naked eye. Dr. Sharpe demonstrated that this was not blood that had been introduced by the puncture of his needle, but instead was blood that was in the cerebrospinal fluid prior to his puncture.

What does this mean? There are many ways to injure the brain which do not put blood in the cerebrospinal fluid, but there is no way to get blood into the cerebrospinal fluid without some break in the internal covering of the central nervous system, in other words an injury.

If Dr. Sharpe's findings of 1924 could be taken as representative of all newborn children, then we would be forced to the surprising conclusion that a minimum of 9 percent of all children are demonstrably brain-injured at birth or at least by the time they are two days old.

What has more recent research had to say about such figures? Dr. Sharpe's studies have been repeated many times since, in many different places, and his findings have been confirmed and, what is more, considerably amplified. In later studies, the cerebrospinal fluid was also subjected to microscopic examination. Such studies reveal that from 70 to 80 percent of newborn children have some blood cells in the cerebrospinal fluid. Dr. Lewis Jacobs, a New York pediatrician who devoted a good deal of time to research in brain-injured children, told me that, as a young resident a good many years earlier, he had observed such a series of tests done and that, in this particular series, blood was found in the cerebrospinal fluid of 85 percent of the newborn babies examined. If we can accept such positive findings as being indicative of some very minor injury in 70 percent of all newborn babies, and of fairly substantial injury (up to and including death itself) in 9 percent of all children born in the United States, the parent of the brain-injured child can readily see that his strange, brain-injured, different child is not at all strange or different from most other children except in degree.

There is also much research to indicate that the process that ends in senility, namely, the gradual death of individual brain cells, *begins* during childhood and continues at a constantly increasing rate throughout life.

It would be difficult to know how one might define brain injury except as that state in which some portion of the brain's cells are dead. From that point on we are only discussing the number of dead cells. In short, having established the presence of one or more dead brain cells, we are thereafter discussing the *degree* of brain injury rather than whether or not brain injury exists. Under such a definition, it is extremely likely that we can count every human being as brain-injured, at least imperceptibly.

It might seem reasonable to include in a definition of brain-injured only those whose dead brain cells were sufficient in number or location to create recognizable problems, but it is possible that by so doing we shall lose sight of a greater and more important truth.

If you want to see brain-injured people in the truest sense of the word, you need only look around you. If you happen to be alone, you might try looking in a mirror, or, failing that, at my photograph on this book.

28

WHAT CAUSES BRAIN INJURY?

Brain injury is due to forces from outside the brain itself rather than to any inherent, preconceptual, built-in deficiency. We know of at least a hundred factors that can hurt a good brain subsequent to that instant of conception. There may be a thousand.

In point of fact, it is not terribly important *how* a brain got injured—what counts is how badly and where it has been injured. Nevertheless, a brain can get hurt in so many ways that it may be worthwhile to review some of them, if only to show that it can happen to anybody.

Among the thousands of brain-injured children who come to The Institutes, we see, for example, the child whose mother and father have an incompatible Rh factor which sets up a blood incompatibility between mother and child. This hurts a good brain.

We see the child whose mother had German measles or some other such contagious disease during the first three months of her pregnancy, or even later in pregnancy. This can hurt a good brain.

We see the child whose mother, during her pregnancy, goes through periods when she doesn't get enough oxygen to supply her needs *and* the baby's.

When I went to school, in the 1940s, we were taught that if during pregnancy there was not enough of something to supply the needs of both mother and child, it would be mother rather than child who would suffer. Today we know that it is baby who will get too little. This hurts a good brain.

We see the baby who is born prematurely and who is simply not "done" yet when he is ejected into the world. Of all the factors that may be associated with brain injury, this factor of prematurity comes up most often in our case histories, in fact about three times as often as you would expect purely on the basis of chance. This does not, of course, mean that a premature baby will necessarily be brain-injured, beyond the point that most of us are brain-injured.

We also see more than our share of postmature babies. Apparently these babies are "too done" as it were, though again (as with most such conditions) the question of what is cause and what is effect is not easy to answer. It is possible that in some of these circumstances it is the brain injury that causes the postmaturity or the prematurity and not the other way round. Nonetheless, we very commonly see these factors associated with hurt children.

We see also the baby whose mother had large amounts of X-ray during pregnancy; even small amounts during the early days can apparently be harmful. Most radiography departments are reluctant to X-ray mothers during pregnancy, particularly during the early days of pregnancy, but this sometimes occurs when the mother is unaware that she is pregnant.

We see also more than our share of children who are born of a precipitous labor, by which we mean a labor lasting less than two hours, or of a protracted labor, by which we mean a labor lasting more than eighteen hours. If either factor is cause rather than effect, then possibly the baby needs a certain time in which to make the violent transition from womb to world—enough time but not too much.

Perhaps because the birth process itself is important, our share of children delivered by Caesarean section is about three times normal. Again there is the possibility that the child may have had to be delivered by Caesarean section *because* he was brain-injured rather than the other way around.

We see, tragically, the baby who is about to be born and whose birth is purposely delayed because the mother has not yet reached the doctor or the doctor has not yet reached the mother. Birth, in these cases we have seen, is generally delayed by having the mother sit up or cross her legs to prevent the baby being born. We have seen so many of these babies that we are completely persuaded that delaying the birth of a baby is a very bad idea. We are persuaded that any nurse, or perhaps even any father, can do a better job of delivering a baby than may result if the birth process is purposely delayed. A friend of ours, was forced to stop en route to the hospital long enough to deliver his own wife of a fine baby in broad daylight in the crowded parking lot of a supermarket. Mother and baby did beautifully although the father remained somewhat shaken for a few days, it being his first delivery. We are persuaded that baby had a better chance of being the fine child it is than would have been the case if the birth had been significantly delayed.

We see also the baby who had obstetrical difficulties due to *placenta previa, placenta abruptio,* and other problems which create difficulties during the birth process. The baby may have been in a position which made his delivery either difficult or even impossible. In such cases, the baby must be manipulated before he can be delivered. In these cases also it is debatable whether the brain injury led to the problem or the problem led to the brain injury.

Long ago, when I went to school, we were given the impression that a high number of brain-injured children were a result of poor obstetrical practices. We have come to believe, however, that this is rare, and that only a very small number of brain-injured children are a result of bad obstetrics. Pre-existing factors in the child frequently make the delivery difficult, thus giving the impression of an unnecessarily long delivery.

The brain can also be injured after birth.

We see the infant who at two months of age falls out of a crib or bassinette, causing blood clots on the brain (which are called *subdural hematomas*), and this hurts a good brain.

We see the one-year-old who inhales certain insecticides, which can cause death or very severe brain injury. One of the most severely brain-injured children we have ever seen, who incidentally was one of our relatively small number of *complete* failures, had been a totally normal child until one year of age at which time he inhaled such an insecticide. We have seen other children, brain-injured as a result of poisoning, who have done very well.

We see the four-year-old who falls in a swimming pool and dies of drowning, but who is then revived and who, during the short period of death, was not getting oxygen to his brain and who is brain-injured as a result.

We see the six-year-old who suffers measles or some other infectious disease or who has encephalitis with a very high temperature and who, as a result, is brain-injured.

We see the nine-year-old who, during surgery for tonsilitis or some other problem, sustains a cardiac arrest and dies on the operating table and is revived by open chest surgery and heart massage or some other technique but who during the time when his heart was not beating, like the child who drowned, did not get enough oxygen to the brain and who, as a result, had his good brain injured.

We see the twenty-year-old girl, who in the hours following the birth of her own baby, has a blood vessel rupture in her own brain giving mother, rather than baby, a stroke. If you have an idea that only old people have strokes, we can tell you that the youngest stroke case we ever saw at The Institutes was two months old and that the oldest stroke case we ever saw was 97 years old.

I should not like to leave the impression that young mothers often have strokes following birth. This is not common, but neither is it rare, and it is another way to hurt a good brain—in this case, Mother's.

We see the twenty-year-old who, on the battlefield, gets a bullet through his brain—but I have already told you of my three friends who each got a bullet through the brain. I have also told you how well they did with millions of brain cells not only dead but gone—blown all over the battlefields of Germany, Belgium, and Korea. Still it is not a good idea to get a bullet through the brain, and that's another way to hurt a good brain.

We see the thirty-year-old who goes through the windshield in an automobile accident, and that's another way to hurt a good brain.

We see the forty-year-old who has a brain tumor, and that's another way to hurt a good brain.

We see the fifty-year-old who is assaulted with a blackjack in a robbery, and that's another way to hurt a good brain.

We see the sixty-year-old who gets Parkinson's disease, and that also hurts the brain.

We see the ninety-year-old who has literally billions, not merely millions, of cells dead for no better reason than the fact that he's getting pretty old.

All the people described above, and many more, are truly brain-injured people, which is no more than to say that they have a good-quality brain which has a great many dead cells.

But so, on the other hand, do I. It is just that at this moment in history I do not have as many.

29

THE PAST, PRESENT, AND FUTURE
OF THE BRAIN-INJURED CHILD

When the final chapter in the long history of brain-injured children is someday written, there will have been four eras in the story.

THE FIRST ERA—DESPAIR

The first era is happily dead and forever gone. It extended from the earliest beginning of man almost to the beginning of the twentieth century. It was the era of despair. It was marked by cruelty, insanity, and what is perhaps worst of all, secrecy.

The first era had no heroes—except the kids themselves, always tough, always brave.

Certainly we do not have to go far back in man's history to find a time when brain-injured children were simply put to death. We can still see this happening today in the heart of Brazil's Mato Grosso among the Xingu Indians who we civilized people consider "primitive". However, even today "civilized" hospitals all over the world sometimes withhold food or medical care from brain-injured infants believing it is "a kindness" to let them die. Consider the modern use of amniocentesis in pregnant women to discover if the baby is brain-injured or "deficient". When a hurt child is discovered in utero it is commonplace for a mother to be advised to terminate the pregnancy. Terrible and primitive and unthinkable as such solutions may be, it might be considered to be a kindness compared with some of the other solutions that occurred during the longest and the most awful era in the story of the brain-injured child. There have been periods—extending up to the eve of the twentieth century—when such hurt children have been tortured for the amusement of unhurt adults. In other periods they have been imprisoned under the most cruel circumstances. They have been starved and they have been beaten.

Under the very best of circumstances, they have been considered a vengeance visited on parents by the Lord as retribution for the sins— either real or fancied—of the parents.

As such, the brain-injured child was a source of shame to his parents and was hidden away in an institution, a back room or an attic so that no one might see their shame, yet throughout the first and most terrible of the four eras of the brain-injured child this was the most benign and kindly of attitudes. Nor did such an attitude disappear entirely with the coming of the second era.

I can remember as a child during the late 1920s that there was, in the neighborhood where I lived, a severely brain-injured child of about ten. I know now that this girl had the type of brain injury that is today called "athetoid cerebral palsy" and that she was very severely involved indeed. I know this today, but I did not, of course, know it then. This child was the daughter of the local pharmacist and this man had the extraordinary courage to put her outside in a carriage daily so that she might have some sunshine and fresh air, as she lay totally paralyzed and twisted in her oversized baby carriage. He had the courage to do so, but he paid the price for his courage.

I remember that the children accepted her quite naturally as she lay in her carriage, as much a part of her surroundings as the drugstore itself. I am sure the children would have paid her no attention at all and would have come to the conclusion that such a child was a natural part of every drugstore in the land, in much the same way that a red-and-white barber pole stood outside every barber shop, had it not been for the adults in the neighborhood.

It is frequently said that children are cruel, like animals, and savage, like, well, like savages, toward other children and especially toward hurt children. If there is any truth at all in this idea, it is only true after adults have taught them to be cruel. Children are not born full of fears, preju- dices, and superstitions. They are taught those things, and we adults are the teachers. Children are born with total acceptance of the way things are. Skies are blue, some kids have red hair, some kids have green eyes, some kids can run fast, and some kids can't move. They learn to question why these things are so as quickly as they learn to talk, but they accept as total truth whatever answers adults give them. They also learn without asking questions, by simply listening to what adults say to each other, and what most of the adults said about our neighborhood brain-injured child was cruel, untrue and ignorant in its content and worse in its implications. The child, it was said, was a monster and anyone would think that "they" would have enough decency not to let the sight of her offend the eyes of decent people. The least they could do was to "put her (or it) away." It was implied that such monsters were no accident, and normal, healthy families did not produce such children. What kind of diseased or twisted mind or heritage would parents have to have to produce such an offense to the community? Such a disease would have to be a dirty disease which must have its roots in sex and, moreover, run in the family.

One occasionally still hears such talk today, but today, thanks to the heroes of the second era, such filthy superstition is the exception rather than the rule. When I was a boy in the 1920s it was the rule rather than the exception, and I was raised in a "nice middle-class neighborhood." My neighborhood was not exceptional and people are little different today than they were then. What happened in my neighborhood was simply a reflection of the pathetic ignorance of the time in relation to brain-injured children. That was only the 1920s.

THE SECOND ERA—DISCOVERY

The second era in the story of the brain-injured child was the era of discovery. It was a happier era, and if it did little to solve the disabilities of the brain-injured child, and if it made a great many mistakes as to treatment, it did many things of inestimable value, among which were the vital accomplishments of bringing the brain-injured child into the blessed light of day, making it respectable to discuss his problems. The second era is still very much alive today.

The second era had a handful of very great heroes as well as thousands of less-heroic and less-brilliant followers. While many of these courageous leaders are now gone and have taken their proper place in the history of those who have contributed to man's progress, others of them remain alive today to receive the homage due them.

These great men and women were innovators. They had come to make changes in the way things were, and man has never taken kindly to great changes or to the innovators who insist on such changes. Perhaps it is well that this is so. New ideas, however logical or however true, must ever be exposed to the harsh light of scientific question in the continuous quest for truth so that what is dishonest, untrue, specious, or spurious may be weeded out. In the end, the truth will defend itself.

However, the light of scientific question is hard on what is false and what is true alike. This harsh light falls not only on the innovation but also, and more particularly, on the innovator, be he charlatan or genius. Not all innovators have had the courage to withstand the harsh but necessary treatment which all innovators receive, and many who have espoused important truths have wilted and run from such investigations when their courage did not match the value of the truths they offered. When such has been the case, such truths have been reburied to await rediscovery by people whose brilliance in unearthing truth was matched by the strength and courage needed to defend it.

These heroes of the second era had courage to match their beliefs. Their way was not easy. The battle that these men and women fought was not against an organized and ruthless foe who defended a different view. They had no such easy task. Such an enemy is visible and, however formidable he may be, he can be seen, identified and therefore attacked. The giants who introduced the second era had a much more subtle, difficult, and elusive enemy. This enemy was superstition, folklore, and indifference. The goal of the leaders of the second era was clear and simple. They wanted to make the world aware that brain-injured children are just that, children who are brain-injured. Not monsters, not objects of shame or ridicule, but children pure and simple. Children who are like many other children, hurt, but hurt in the brain rather than with broken arms or appendicitis. Today this may seem pathetically clear and simple. Today it may seem obvious, but it wasn't then. Remember my druggist.

The enemies—superstition, folklore, and indifference—were everywhere but they were also nowhere. How does one fight an enemy he can neither identify nor see? There are few more infuriating, frustrating, and difficult battles to be fought than those whose enemy is almost total apathy. One must first find his enemy; he must then make his enemy aware that he is the enemy (for who admits superstition, indifference, or belief in folklore, even to himself?); and then he must make the enemy defend himself. Only then can he begin an honest fight. All these were the problems faced by the heroes of the second era. They fought these problems and they fought them well and in the end, although it took nearly half a century, they won. Fifty years may seem a very long time to win such a clear and simple point—unless you consider the hundreds of thousands of years of ignorance that preceded it.

Although there were a very few others prior to the turn of the century, perhaps we can begin the second era, the Era of Discovery, with a physician named William John Little, 1810-1894. Dr. Little was a British surgeon who described the *congenital spastic diplegic,* paralyzed in both legs.

While Dr. Little's work with the brain-injured child served to make physicians aware that such children should at least be diagnosed, and provided physicians with a name by which to call such children (they were now called Little's Disease), his work did little or nothing to bring such children to the attention of the general public.

By the 1930s and the early 1940s, the names of the more successful heroes of the second era, the ones who made it stick, began to be heard and known to many physicians and to many parents. Those names were Winthrop Phelps, Temple Fay, Meyer Pearlstein, Maria Montessori, and a dozen others in the United States, England, and elsewhere.

These men and women had fought a noble and courageous battle against difficult odds to make the public aware that the brain-injured child was hurt and needed and deserved help. They fought and they won.

In their wake came public awareness, physician interest, the formation of professional groups to study the problem of brain-injured children, as well as lay groups which collected funds for treatment and research and for public education. All these were huge steps in the right direction. All of them made both scientists and lay people aware that this problem existed and that something should and must be done about it.

As a result of these societies and of increased public awareness, treatment centers followed in their wake. By the time of World War II, a very few treatment centers were in existence, such as Dr. Phelps' Institute for Brain-Injured Children in Maryland and Dr. Fay's Neurophysical Rehabilitation Center in Philadelphia. By the year 1950, there were a few more inpatient institutes for treatment of brain-injured children in this nation, and outpatient treatment centers had sprung up in almost every state. By 1960 there were hundreds.

All this was a very necessary step in the right direction and was made possible by the few courageous pioneers who had arisen to meet this problem.

The names of Phelps and Fay are justifiably famous. Without such people there would not be the rest of us or the work this book describes. They are our personal heroes.

Those of the original pioneers who are still alive, are honored teachers, professors, and practitioners. Having survived their own days as innovators and pioneers they remained to reap the rewards of honor and respect they so justly earned. Students flock to their doors from all over the world to learn and pay homage. This is exactly as it should be. These innovators earned their place in history, a history which those of us who followed will write and are even now writing.

As is natural and proper, these pioneers are also today the arbiters of *what* is right and wrong and *who* is right and wrong in their world of the brain-injured child. The circle has come around. The former pioneers, radicals, and innovators grew respectable and deeply respected since the truths that they espoused were made obvious and, therefore, respectable.

However, during the second era, when so many, many things had to be accomplished and so many things remained undone, it was inevitable that some of the answers which came into being should be partial answers, incomplete answers, or even sometimes no answers at all. This was true of the second era in terms of treatment itself. The second era did not propose that the goal of treatment was or should be to make the brain-injured child *well*. Such a goal was considered to be not only highly improbable but more than that, impossible. To talk of making a brain-injured child well was considered to be not only dangerous and highly irresponsible but, what was worse, downright silly. There were few if any of the second era who would have been willing to accept such talk even as a future and some-day goal. To make a brain-injured child well seemed clearly, to almost everyone, to be a contradiction in terms. However, such talk was seldom a problem in the heyday of the second era of the brain-injured child since, if there were none of the leaders who would listen to such wild talk, there were very few who would dare to have such thoughts and virtually none who dared to voice such radical ideas.

Human beings frequently do not succeed in attaining the objectives they set for themselves—and they very rarely attain *higher* objectives than those they seek. Since making brain-injured children well was not even a goal of the second era, it was not accomplished, and brain-injured children did not get well.

If wellness was not the goal of treatment during the second era, it is reasonable to ask what the goals were.

The goals were actually three in number. The first was to prevent the child's symptoms from becoming worse and, where possible, to lessen such symptoms as spasticity, tightening of heel cords, or the deformity of joints. The treatment that had been pioneered by the leaders of the second era frequently succeeded in preventing the worsening of these symptoms, and it sometimes, although not too often, succeeded in the reduction of such symptoms.

The second goal of treatment was to fit the child into his world better by altering his environment so that he could live more easily or more successfully as a cripple. As an example, if a child could not walk due to his brain injury, he might be able to achieve some degree of independence in a wheelchair if he could manipulate such a wheelchair with his hands and if his home could be altered to replace steps with ramps. While the example I have used is simple, such methods were frequently ingenious and highly engineered.

The third goal of treatment was to teach the brain-injured child anything he seemed capable of learning within the limitations imposed by his brain injury. Thus, the brain-injured child who could not function might be taught to feed himself with spoons twisted into unusual shapes to counteract his deformities, or with a spoon strapped onto his hand. If the child was able to learn to count, to recite poetry, to read, or to write, he was provided with teaching so that he might improve, to the highest point possible, whatever skills he had.

It is quite clear that the second era offered the brain-injured child and his parents circumstances far superior to those of the first era. It was so obviously better for the brain-injured child to have his symptoms lessened rather than increased. It was better for him to be able to move around in a wheelchair than not to be able to move around at all. It was better for a child to be able to feed himself with a special spoon strapped on his hand than not to be able to feed himself at all. There is no question that the second era offered the brain-injured child a life far superior to the tortures of the first era. The new life fell far, far short of normality, however, and almost as far short of happiness or usefulness. It in no way solved the parents' problem of what, in the end, was going to happen to their child.

The whole treatment concept of the second era was based on the assumption that to attack his symptoms was the best thing to do since there would be no way of attacking the problem where it actually existed, in the brain itself. That basic assumption remained unchallenged through many years of the second era, and brain-injured children did not get well.

It was astonishing that the basic assumption that nothing could be done about the brain itself should remain unchallenged for almost half a century of modern times and modern medicine. It was inevitable that it would one day be challenged, and I believe it was our group who first seriously challenged this notion.

Interestingly enough, it was Temple Fay himself, one of the great leaders of the second era, who was becoming daily more disenchanted with the lack of positive results, who laid the groundwork for the ultimate destruction of the second era and planted the seeds for the establishment of the third era. Fay, who had been a cofounder of the Academy of Cerebral Palsy, and who, with Phelps, had been largely responsible for the successes of the second era, had two serious complaints about what was happening. First, he complained that what was happening was helpful but, to a large degree, unmedical. He pointed out repeatedly that the traditional role of medicine was to seek out and attack the damaged or diseased part itself and to seek to repair it rather than to teach people how best to live with a disability. He strongly questioned whether teaching people how to live with a disability was the role of modern medicine or at the least whether this should remain the primary objective.

Fay complained, secondly, that although brain-injured children clearly had neurological problems, the treatment they were receiving was almost entirely orthopedic. He pointed out that we could not hope to solve a neurological problem by orthopedic treatment. Fay also conceded that this was due in large part to the fact that in the early 1940s very few neurologists or neurosurgeons demonstrated much real interest in the problems of brain-injured children. Since Fay himself was both a neurologist and a neurosurgeon who had earned an international reputation in those fields, he was eminently qualified to voice such an opinion.

Fay's genius, indeed Fay's mere presence on our team, could not help but draw our attention away from the brain-injured child's symptoms which existed everywhere in the child's body from his toes to his eye, and to direct our attention to the brain itself where the child's real problem actually existed. It is simultaneously ironic and highly proper that Dr. Fay, a pioneer of the second era, should also have been the inspiration, if not the prime mover, for its eventual destruction.

It is difficult to know when the third era began. Certainly the seeds were planted by 1941, as we, Fay's students, began to ponder the implications of his emphasis on the relation of brain injury and bodily dysfunction.

Certainly his presence on the team and the role of leadership he played from 1945 until 1957 were vital. Fay's vast knowledge of how the brain functioned, as well as his many theories as to how we might approach treatment were invaluable in bringing about the third era, although at the time we were unable to achieve much in the way of practical results.

I do not know just when the third era began. Perhaps it began in our minds in 1941, without our awareness that it existed. Its theories were surely evolving in our awareness by 1950. By 1955 we were quite aware of the necessity for the third era. By 1960 we had announced the third era to those colleagues who chose to listen, and by 1965, although the second era was still very much alive, the third era was definitely in being and obviously here to stay.

THE THIRD ERA—RATIONAL TREATMENT

While the second era attacked the symptoms of the brain-injured child and had as its goal the prevention of deformity, the lessening of symptoms, and the adroit fitting of the child into his environment, the third era is the era of rational and successful *treatment* of the brain-injured child. The third era attacks the brain itself where the problem lies and the objective of such treatment is not to make the child a happy or successful cripple but instead to make him a non-cripple, in both physical and intellectual terms.

I wish that I could now report that we are presently able to do this successfully with all children who seek treatment. This, of course, is not the case, but it *is* the case that we are making *some* brain-injured children completely well and even some severely brain-injured ones completely well. The majority of brain-injured children we are seeing today are markedly and measurably improved.

It is hardly astonishing that we should sometimes fail to make brain-injured children well in a world which by and large still believes that such an objective is an impossibility. It should be surprising that we sometimes succeed.

By the beginning of the third era, the innovators, radicals, and pioneers of the second era had become the respected leaders of the world of brain-injured children as well as its guardians and arbiters, and a new group of radicals, innovators, and pioneers had come forth to demand to be heard and to add their new knowledge, ideas, and energy to the war on brain injury.

Who were these new dissidents? Fay was certainly one of them as was the team of younger men and women Fay had inspired and led.

However, if I have given, up to now, the impression that we were the only ones who were dissatisfied with the results being obtained, I must hasten to correct this view, for such is not the case. While those who were looking for better methods of treatment did not necessarily agree with each other, they did have one thing in common. They were all looking away from limbs and orthopedics and toward the nervous system and neurology. Most of these innovators had stopped talking of "musculoskeletal disorders" and now spoke of "neuromuscular disorders." Such a view, if it did not entirely abandon the symptoms and the muscles, had at least made a distinct move toward the human central nervous system and thus the cause.

While Deaver and Phelps still clung to muscles and bracing as the answer, others such as Knott, Kabat, Rood, Ayers, and Semans were advocating either various neuromuscular techniques or the use of neurological reflexes, which Fay had urged as early as the late 1930s and which we had used in 1941 and advocated in the immediate post-war years.

Others had gone even farther from the musculoskeletal symptoms and were actually looking to the brain itself for answers. These people included the Bobaths, Brunnstrom, Wind, and others, both in this country and abroad.

It is quite difficult to know how to deal fairly with the third era and its cast of characters since this was a highly transitional time.

While most of the world continues to *treat* the brain-injured child by the symptom attack of the second era, a majority of the world is dissatisfied with the old techniques and at least half of the world is presently seeking to learn about the new methods so that they can begin to utilize them. Greater numbers are daily looking in the direction of the new methods. However, at this time there remain the advocates of the old methods (some are passionate in their advocacy) and there are the advocates of the new methods (some also passionate in their advocacy). This presents a real problem in reporting the coming of the third era, with due recognition to those responsible for its coming.

If I should assume that we at The Institutes for the Achievement of Human Potential are solely responsible for the coming of the third era, I shall surely be criticized by many advocates of the third era for taking undue credit.

If, on the other hand, I give due credit to the others who have purposely or even unconsciously played an important role in bringing about the third era, I shall unquestionably be criticized by some advocates of the second era for trying to spread the blame for something which they consider to be radical, controversial, and perhaps, in their opinions, even full of dangerous new ideas. So, unquestionably, in some quarters I shall be damned if I do and damned if I don't. These are invariably the problems of all people who have something new to say that runs contrary to the ideas the present day cherishes. In addition to the people who line up clearly on either side of an issue, there are always a great number who stand in the middle, who cannot make up their minds, and who want the comfort of both while denying the responsibility for either. Their argument generally runs that the new ideas are new, dangerous, silly, and unproven and, besides all that, these ideas are not new and they have always done them that way anyhow. Such fence straddlers always remind me of the Army recruit who writes home that Army food isn't fit for pigs, in addition to which you get such small servings.

I shall solve my dilemma by reporting the third era and its people exactly as it and they appear to me, and in so doing assume the role of a reporter who, while much involved in his subject, is doing his level best to report the happenings as they appear to him.

To do so, I herewith absolve completely from blame for our ideas anyone who wishes to disassociate himself from such ideas, while simultaneously acknowledging the complete contributions of anyone who has contributed, whether I am aware or unaware of his contribution, as well as welcoming to their place in the third era all those who choose to be associated with it whether they have contributed much, little, or nothing except their own accord to its existence. I do all of the above while remaining completely responsible for our own contributions, ideas, and work.

While my group does not claim complete credit (or blame) for the third era, it is safe to say that we have been an important part of it from its earliest beginnings.

Where does the third era now stand? Most children in the world are still being treated by the methods of the second era, although today many thousands of other children in dozens of nations on all continents are being treated by the methods developed by The Institutes, while thousands more are being treated by the neurological methods espoused by the Bobaths, by Brunnstrom, Rood, Knott, and others who are, in our opinion, an important part of the third era.

Many of the leaders of the second era have become convinced that the new methods have something of value to offer the brain-injured child and are using the new methods in part or in full. Others hold tightly to the old method, but the tide is swinging, and swinging rapidly.

Students and postgraduate practitioners from all of the fields concerned in the treatment of the brain-injured child still flock to the respected leaders of the second era, as they properly should and as we ourselves had done, although there is some feeling that such journeys today are compounded less out of the need to learn than out of the desire to pay homage to some of medicine's greats.

Of the students still going in large numbers to learn from and pay homage to the leaders of the second era, many are going as well to those who advocate the new methods of the third era.

Time was when mention of The Institutes raised only eyebrows in some circles. Today, such mention, as like as not, draws enthusiastic comment from individuals who have actually been patterners. Thousands of physicians have referred children for treatment. Hundreds have put their own brain-injured children on the program. Scientific seminars now rarely discuss the old techniques but are almost entirely devoted to the methods and the proponents of the new third era.

In sum, the third era and its people are respectable. We are becoming a little more conservative. It is to be hoped that we do not too quickly become too conservative because complete conservativeness almost always brings with it a closing of the mind to new ideas.

It now seems certain that the ideas of the third era will replace the second entirely, and when they do, its advocates will assume their new positions of complete respectability, and eventually reverence, and will themselves become the arbiters of what is right and what is wrong and, as such, the sole custodians of the truth as they see the truth. It is probable that we of The Institutes will be numbered among these people. If that day comes, I am sure that we, like the others before us, will completely enjoy such veneration and prominence, and the third era will have fulfilled its promise. When that day comes when we are considered right instead of always wrong, it is likely that we will then be held to be *always* right, even when we're wrong.

Then one day, the fourth, final, and best era of the brain-injured child will begin.

THE FOURTH ERA—PREVENTION

It will probably begin with a new and unheard of group of angry young men and women in Upper Tomahawk, Kansas, or San José, Brazil, who will probably say, with fine disregard for proper reverence, "Those old jugheads in Philadelphia (and elsewhere) have not had a new idea about brain-injured children in twenty years." They will probably go on to say, "Those old gents were fine in their day, but they are wrong in their basic assumption that the best thing to do about brain-injured children is to make them well; it was all right years ago but it's no good today." Then they are surely going to say, "The real answer to brain-injured children is not to cure them but to prevent them" (and they won't mean using amniocentesis to discover and destroy them).

Those young people, of course, will be absolutely right. They will not only be right in what they say (many people, including us, are already saying it), but what is much more important, they'll know how to do it. Probably at first they will not know how to prevent all brain-injured children but only some of them, but as they continue, the numbers they will be able to prevent will continue to grow.

Those young pioneers will probably say of us, "We love and respect those old innovators in Philadelphia and we are for giving them parades, medals, professorships, awards, and the place they have earned in history." They will also add ominously, "But we are not in favor of sacrificing a single child to them." In this, too, they will be absolutely right.

We sometimes find a few minutes (generally at two or three A.M.) to think about that future day and discuss it. We know it will come and pray for its coming, for it will be a glorious day for the world. We like to think that when that day does come we will say, "Listen to these youngsters because they are unquestionably right." We like to believe that when that day comes we will not only agree with them but will rally whatever influence or prestige we may then have behind them. We like to believe that by joining them, we, like Fay, will have the golden opportunity to be part of two eras in the history of the brain-injured child. If we do, they will welcome us with open arms and learn from us, as we welcomed and learned from the truly great Dr. Temple Fay.

We like to believe all that, but we are also students of history and realists to boot. The odds are against us doing so, and we know it. Unhappily, history and the odds indicate that when those new pioneers arrive on the scene we will say, "It is young people like these, full of wild impossible ideas and given to overstatement, who cause all the trouble in the world," and thus proceed to condemn them for threatening all the ideas we fought so long and so hard to establish.

We vow we shall *not* do this, but history testifies that we will. We often talk about putting a letter in the safe addressed to ourselves to be reopened and reread on the first of every new year. This letter will say, "Are there any young people around who are giving us a particularly bad time who just might be right?" We often talk about writing such a letter, but it seems more than a little interesting that we have not yet done so. I wonder if that means anything?

In the off chance that we never do get around to writing that letter, then let this book serve as my accolade to and full acceptance of that future group of young men and young women.

1970 to The Present

THE FUTURE

30

THE END OF THE BEGINNING

I date the end of the beginning from that day in May of 1971, when a letter came from Dr. Samarão Brandão, Presidente, da Associação Brasileiro de Paralisia Cerebral.

Dr. Brandão most cordially invited me to be the principal speaker and the guest of honor of the Fourth Brazilian Congress of Cerebral Palsy of which he was the *presidente* and Dr. Raymundo Araujo Leitão was the *secretario*. Dr. Brandão was a leading orthopedic surgeon of Brazil as well as a physiatrist, while Dr. Leitão was professor of neurological physiatry at the Neurological Institute of the University of Brazil. He was also the author of the leading Brazilian textbook on cerebral palsy.

The Association was the most distinguished medical body in Brazil and was composed primarily of physiatrists, pediatricians, neurologists, orthopedic surgeons, and neurosurgeons. The paramedical services were also represented.

The invitation meant a great many things. Many of the people within the Congress represented other groups who had opposed Dr. Veras' doing our work in Brazil. The fact that I was to be the principal speaker could have indicated only that Brazilian professionals wanted to know firsthand what I had to say about the work we had carried on for more than thirty years. However, the fact that I was the guest of honor meant far, far more. If the invitation did not mean that the philosophy, concepts, methods, and techniques of The Institutes were the *only* ones accepted by Brazilian medical and professional people, it did at least mean that our work was fully recognized in Brazil and was one of the principal methods with full acceptance in that nation.

I wished desperately that Mae Blackburn could have been around to enjoy this breakthrough in professional acceptance of our methods—she and Jay Cooke and General White and Dr. Sigmund LeWinn and Mr. Henshaw and General Kemp and A. Vinton Clarke and Eleanor Borden and Betty

Marsh and all the others who had shared the dream and fought the fight and stood fast in the face of failure, adversity, and criticism and who had never, up to the moment of their deaths, wavered in their determination to find better worlds for brain-injured kids, and I thought of terms that suited:

"We few, we happy few, we band of brothers..."

I thought of others:

"Theirs was a royal brotherhood of death..."

And more:

"Here was a man, take him all in all,
We shall not see his like again."

But mostly I thought of Temple Fay and how he would have relished this day of recognition in Rio de Janeiro.

The Congress itself, which took place the second week of November 1971 at the Copacabana Hotel in Rio de Janeiro, strongly increased my feeling that our philosophy was widely accepted and widely used throughout Brazil.

During the sixties the techniques pioneered by The Institutes were used to some extent, whether well or badly, in a majority of treatment facilities in the United States, but often on a bootlegged basis. That is to say, our techniques were being used to one degree or another virtually everywhere in the United States, though many a user was afraid to acknowledge this, and often our techniques were used improperly since those using them had never been trained to do so. (The department head used them but did not admit so to the chief of physical medicine, and so on.)

What a switch Brazil turned out to be! More than five hundred people registered to take the course in The Institutes work. Attending were doctors from Brazil, Ecuador, Venezuela, Argentina, Spain, Peru, the United States, and other countries.

Quite literally, hundreds of people sought me out to tell me privately as well as publicly that in their institutions they used only the techniques of The Institutes. I was immensely thrilled and flattered, but as more and more people told me this I began to be at first slightly uneasy and then completely suspicious. Was it possible that everyone in all of Latin America used only our techniques? It seemed unlikely. So I began to inquire more deeply.

It was clear that a great many people and institutions had come around to our way of thinking under the influence of those who had studied with us, notably Drs. Raymundo Veras, José Carlos Veras, Ivan Porto, Raymundo Arauja Leitão, Raymundo Fontes-Lima, and others in Brazil. It was also abundantly clear that Dr. Eduardo Sequeiros in Argentina and Dr. Antonio Silva in Peru, after being trained by Dr. Raymundo Veras in Brazil, had taught many others in their own nations and other nations. Our philosophy was clearly widely known and widely practiced in Latin America, but it was equally clear that there were many others who said that they used our methods but who had insufficient knowledge to do so.

How political times do change and how the sands of professional opinion do shift with favorable winds! Whereas before many people had used our techniques while swearing that they did not, now there were some who swore that they did while in truth they did not.

The Institutes had long enjoyed the love and respect and the trust of parents, and this The Institutes had always sought to have and to deserve.

Now The Institutes had the respect and admiration of the professional people of a continent and this it had many years earlier stopped seeking since the earlier price of professional acceptance had been for us to abandon our work.

We were in.

An additional report made at this Congress strengthened our position even further. I had heard vaguely about the report a couple of years earlier.

Toward the end of 1969 the *presidente* (Señora Martinez) of an Argentinian foundation (Da Fundacao Obrigado) had approached Dr. Eduardo Sequeiros, the medical director of The Institutes for the Achievement of Human Potential in Buenos Aires, with a proposal. There was in the city of Córdoba in Argentina a large rehabilitation institute that used classical methods in treating a large number of children. The staff of this institute were convinced that they were achieving no results with their most severe cases, and questionable results with less severe cases. They had heard about The Institutes program and wanted to do a study using The Institutes methods to see if better results might be obtained. This institute was also supported by APANE (Parents Association of Exceptional Children).

Dr. Sequeiros had consulted Dr. Veras in Brazil and they agreed to such a study, imposing two conditions.

1. All staff members of the Córdoba Institute who would work with the children to be tested would be thoroughly trained by Dr. Sequeiros in Buenos Aires and would treat the children in the test group under the direct supervision of Dr. Eduardo Castellani, the medical director of the Córdoba Institute. Dr. Castellani himself would be trained personally by Dr. Sequeiros. Therefore, the children under treatment by The Institutes

method would be treated *only* by the physicians, psychologists, physical therapists, speech therapists, social workers, etc., of the Córdoba unit with none of the personnel of The Institutes for the Achievement of Human Potential involved.

2. The treatment group would consist only of children who had been on conventional methods of treatment for a substantial period of time *and who had failed to show any improvement whatsoever.*

Dr. Castellani decided to make his report to the Congress in the form of a motion picture showing what had occurred to the children after one year of treatment. There was, however, a large problem. Everyone at the institution in Córdoba who had been involved in the experiment wanted to come to Rio with him. The modest budget could not cover thirty-five international plane fares.

A happy solution was achieved. Señora Martinez, the foundation *presidente,* is a wealthy woman, loved and admired by all for her incredible energy and total devotion to brain-injured children. She rented a bus, and thirty-five staff members, Señora Martinez herself, and Dr. Castellani drove three days and three nights to attend the Congress.

Their film report was fascinating. Their objective in the study had been simple: to see if any child in a group of fifty who had failed to show *any* improvement on a protracted program of conventional treatment would show any improvement on the program of The Institutes for the Achievement of Human Potential.

They considered the results to be little short of astonishing. *Every* child on the program had shown some improvement. Many had shown extremely important improvement, and some had shown astonishing improvement.

I had used my first three teaching days to cover:

1. Measurement of the brain-injured child
2. Philosophy of treatment of the brain-injured child
3. Treatment techniques

On the last day I had determined to present precisely what had happened to a group of children on the program of The Institutes in Philadelphia.

I had heard Dr. Leitão, professor of physical medicine of the Neurological Institute of the University of Brazil, beginning his final introduction of me.

". . . The people of The Institutes for the Achievement of Human Potential who have endured the criticism and sometimes outright hostility of those of us who are their colleagues, claim to have developed a system of treatment by neurological organization. But we are aware that this is not true. The truth is that these people have pioneered the entire field of neurological rehabilitation and are alone responsible for having told us first in all the world that brain injury is in the brain and that if we are to treat brain-injured people with any hope of success it is the brain itself that we shall have to treat. They have shown us over and over again that this is possible and how it is possible."

It was fortunate that I knew what I was going to say initially, because my eyes were too misted to follow my notes. The essentials of the report I presented to that Congress constitutes the remainder of this chapter. I began:

"MEOS CAROS AMIGOS E COLEGOES: We have all of us come through a most trying and difficult number of years. For myself it is more than thirty years. It was, I suppose, inevitable that those years should be marked not only by search, by discovery, and by reward, but also by quarrels, by recriminations, by attacks, and by defenses since man has always been fearful of change. Yet it must be equally obvious to all of us that the mighty problems which face the children of the world and consequently all of us, do not allow even a moment for family quarrels. The past has clearly failed the brain-injured child and his parents. Let us today bury the past with its recriminations forever. Surely we are no longer helpless.

"During this week you have heard from the two Maggies. Margaret Rood is my friend, and she speaks to you of neurology. It must be clear to you that she has something of value for the children of the world. For the children's sake let us *use* it and bury a non-productive past.

"During this week you have also heard from Margaret Knott. She is my friend, and she speaks to you of neurology. It must be clear to you that she has something of value for the children of the world. For the parents' sake let us *use* it and bury a past in which there was little of which to be proud.

"During this week we have not heard from the Bobaths, but we all know of their work. The Bobaths are my friends, and they speak to you of neurology. It must be clear to all of you that they have something of value for the children of the world. For God's sake let us *use* it and bury forever the quarrels of the past.

"Let us get on with the job.

"It seems more than likely to me that my own job in South America is now drawing to a close.

"It is obvious that what bitter quarrels you once had, the volume of which prevented you from listening to each other, will now be replaced with honest minor disagreement and laudable discussion.

"I salute you as professional men and women of good will and I now leave you to your own highly capable leaders in South America, Drs. Veras, Brandão, Leitão, Fontes-Lima, Silva, Sequeiros, Brandt, Crespo, Porto, and the rest.

"I shall look to you now to teach us in the future as we have been privileged to teach you in the past. I believe that the brilliant work of Drs. Raymundo and José Carlos Veras in the treatment of Down Syndrome is simply the first in a long line of breakthroughs where the students will become the teachers.

"As for us, we must now turn our eyes to our own North America where the battles, quarrels, and recriminations have raged longest and most intensely and to Europe where they are just beginning. We must work and hope and indeed pray that those of us responsible for the brain-injured child will find ourselves so busily engaged in finding new or better answers for these kids that there will remain ample time for discussion but no time at all for destructive and demeaning attacks on each other.

"It seems time now to put aside the endless theoretical discussions we have sometimes enjoyed and sometimes hated in the past three decades and examine some clear hard facts for, as interesting as theories are and as important as they may sometimes be, the fact remains that a theory which produces no result is worthless. Conversely, it is equally true that if a system produces real results, it may be reasonably argued that a theory to support it might not even be necessary.

"For a long time a great many of you have talked to me and written to me to tell me of your complete dissatisfaction with what has been happening to brain-injured children as a product of classical treatment and have asked me to tell you precisely what had been happening to the children we have been treating in Philadelphia using our program of neurological organization.

"It is a fair question which cries out for answering, but all of you who are involved in treatment and in statistical procedures appreciate just how difficult it is to answer that question.

"Ideally, such a report of results should be that arising from a rigorously controlled study, and the people of The Institutes have been unremitting in their efforts to obtain such a study. Many of you are personally aware of a good many of these efforts.

"Neither parents nor those physicians and other professional people faced with the present reality of brain-injured children can wait for years to find the scientifically immaculate results of such studies.

"Indeed, even the organizations that saw fit to publish in 1968 a statement casting doubt on the work of The Institutes said in that statement, 'Advice to parents and professional workers cannot wait for conclusive results of controlled studies of all aspects of the method.'

"My own Institutes in Philadelphia heartily concur with that statement, and we feel that it is incumbent upon us to make known precisely what is happening to children under treatment. We, of course, feel that it is incumbent upon all other groups treating brain-injured children by classical methods or any other method to do the same thing.

"It seems obvious that until controlled studies can be done, it is necessary that the advocates of all treatment methods, whether classical or not, make available some careful factual reports of what is actually happening to the children under treatment by that particular method. By so doing, it will be possible for parents and professionals alike to draw their own conclusions about significance and results of various methods until more scientific evidence is available."

I then went on to present the findings from two studies we had made, as follows:

"One study dealt with easily measurable physical factors. As previously mentioned, some remarkable physical changes are taking place in the severely brain-injured children being treated at The Institutes in Philadelphia. As already pointed out, a very high percentage of brain-injured children are extremely small in physical size when compared to their chronological peers, but begin to grow at remarkably fast rates of speed when treatment is commenced.

"These observations of startling growth were first reported by Roselise Wilkinson, M.D., and Evan Thomas, M.D., both of The Institutes staff, at a meeting of the American Academy of General Practice, Ohio Chapter, in August 1970.

"The particular study which I wish to summarize was done by Edward LeWinn, M.D., the medical director of the Research Institute of The Institutes for the Achievement of Human Potential in Philadelphia.

"In a study of 278 consecutively accepted brain-injured children under treatment at The Institutes in Philadelphia, he found that at onset of treatment 81.9 percent of the children had chests smaller than the 50th percentile (i.e., were below average for their age), and 54.7 percent of the children had chests below the 10th percentile (smallest 10 percent of children).

"At the end of the study (after fourteen months of treatment) only 64.4 percent of the children were now below average, and only 24.8 percent remained in the lowest tenth. During the fourteen months of treatment their chests had grown at a rate which averaged 286 percent of normal, and growth was continuing.

"In the course of treatment, 243 of the 278 children moved to a rate of chest growth that was above normal for their age, as follows:

Number growing at less than 100% of normal				35
"	"	from	100% to 199% of normal	58
"	"	"	200% to 299% of normal	69
"	"	"	300% to 399% of normal	67
"	"	"	400% to 499% of normal	34
"	"	"	500% and over	15

"The story was much the same in terms of head growth. At the start of treatment 82.2 percent of the 278 children had a head circumference below the 50th percentile. At the end of the study (fourteen months later) only 70.1 percent were below average for their age.

"The average rate of growth in head circumference during the fourteen months of the study was 254 percent of normal. At the end of the study the children were still under treatment and still continuing to grow in head size.

"In the course of treatment, 241 of the 278 children moved to a rate of growth in head circumference that was above normal for their age, as follows:

Number growing at less than 100% of normal				37
"	"	"	a rate between 100% and 199%	81
"	"	"	a rate between 200% and 299%	82
"	"	"	a rate between 300% and 399%	38
"	"	"	a rate between 400% and 499%	18
"	"	"	a rate of 500% and over	22

"Since these children ranged in age from 75 months to 198 months at the onset of treatment, and since each child was being compared in growth to his own exact chronological peers, it would appear that this remarkable change in growth rate had to be a product of the program of neurological organization.

"If these figures were being studied by workers in some field other than the human sciences, as for example by leaders in the Space Program, which is more pragmatic and more result-oriented than is our own, I believe that these results might be considered as constituting in themselves reasonable evidence that the program of neurological organization is substantially and favorably altering severely brain-injured children. As Thoreau has observed, 'Some circumstantial evidence is very strong, as when you find a trout in the milk.'

"I should now like to present another group of case histories, as follows:

"Two hundred and ninety brain-injured children applied for and were accepted for treatment during the year 1968 at The Institutes for the Achievement of Human Potential in Philadelphia, Pennsylvania. The children were actually treated daily at home by their parents. Parents and child returned no more often than every two months (and frequently less often) for re-evaluation of the child and revision of his program.

"Eliminated from the 290 children were ninety-five children who were under treatment for less than a year, since such children would have had, at the most, five visits and, at the least, no revisits at all; the staff is persuaded that five or less visits are seldom enough to give The Institutes method a truly fair trial. It is, however, interesting that in those children eliminated, two had been discharged as functioning normally, while only one had been discharged as a failure. Also eliminated were twenty-five children under three years of age to remove the possibility that these children were simply "slow starters" who might yet have walked and talked without treatment.

"There were 170 children who met both the requirements of a year or more of programming and the age limit. They ranged from mildly brain-injured children who walked and talked, but badly, to profoundly brain-injured children who were unable to move or make sounds. Some of these were functionally completely blind or deaf. They ranged in age from thirty-six months to seventeen and one half years. The median age was 104 months. The mean age was 105.4 months.

See
AGE DISTRIBUTION CHART
(next page)

AGE DISTRIBUTION CHART

Age	Number of Children
3 years	13
4 years	18
5 years	16
6 years	14
7 years	11
8 years	21
9 years	13
10 years	19
11 years	10
12 years	12
13 years	9
14 years	5
15 years	4
16 years or over	5

"Let me show you now the results we achieved with just one of these 170 children in terms of the following facts:

"First: *Initial Chronological Age.* This is simply the child's age in months, when we first saw him. In my example this was forty-three months.

"Second: *Initial Neurological Age.* This is determined through use of the The Institutes Developmental Profile. In my example this was fifteen months.

"Third: *Initial Rate of Progress.* This is the ratio of initial neurological age to initial chronological age. In my example it is 15/43 or 36 percent.

"Fourth: *Present Chronological Age.* In my example this is seventy-one months. In other words, he remained on program for twenty-eight months since he first came to us at age forty-three months.

"Fifth: *Present Neurological Age.* In my example this is thirty-four months. In other words, he gained nineteen months in neurological age since he came to us with an initial neurological age of fifteen months.

"Sixth: *Present Rate of Progress.* In my example this is 67.5 percent, a figure derived from the ratio of his gain in neurological age while on program (nineteen months) to his gain in chronological age (twenty-eight months) while on program.

"Seventh: *Comparison of New Growth Rate with Old Growth Rate.* In my example this is 190 percent, a figure derived from the ratio of his new growth rate (67.5) to his former growth rate (36).

"Eighth: *Estimated Time to Neurological Maturity at Normal Rate of Growth.* This is arrived at by taking this child's present neurological age (thirty-four months) and subtracting it from the seventy-two months that is assumed in the Profile to represent neurological maturity.

"Ninth: *Estimated Time to Neurological Maturity for this Child.* In my example this is given as fifty-six months—based on dividing the thirty-eight months that would be required at normal rate of growth by the child's present rate of progress (67.5 percent of normal). In other words, *if he continues to progress at 67.5 percent of normal*—he will net thirty-eight months of progress over the next fifty-six months of chronological time.

"We have on file the detailed results for the 170 children, [which we considered too much data for the average reader of this book]. Each example is summed up in a Comment. In my example we rate the outlook as Good inasmuch as this six-year-old, if he continues his present rate of progress, may well reach full neurological maturity by the time he is eleven years old. By contrast, we rate the next case in our file as Poor inasmuch as it would take that particular six-year-old nearly sixteen years to reach neurological maturity at his present rate.

"Other cases, depending on the indicated outlook, are rated Superb, Splendid, Excellent, Good, Fair, Poor, or Impossible. These ratings don't necessarily reflect how well or poorly The Institutes program has done for the child, but rather the probable chance of success, *assuming* continuing progress at the rate established during a year or more on the program.

"It must be stressed that the goal is seventy-two months of neurological age, i.e., competence to see, hear, feel, walk, talk, and do manual tasks as well as a fully normal six-year-old. When an individual reaches that level he may still be behind his peer group in terms of education and experience, but he will now be able to push ahead on these fronts as well as any normal individual—and will be able to catch up if we give him education and experience at an accelerated rate. We have found over and over again that a child at home with mother can learn as much in an hour as the average child learns in a day at school; as much in a day as the average child learns in a week at school.

"Overall, these 170 children had been on the program at the timeof the study for a minimum of twelve months and a maximum of thirty-five months. The average time on program was twenty-four months. The outlook at the time of this study (i.e., after one to three years on program) was as shown in Fig. 27.

NUMBER OF CHIL- DREN	PER- CENTAGE OF ENTIRE GROUP	TIME REQUIRED FOR CHILD TO REACH NEUROLOGICAL MATURITY ASSUMING THE CONTINUATION OF PRESENT RATE OF GROWTH	OUTLOOK
61	35.9%	One month to 23 months	SUPERB
22	12.9%	24 months to 35 months	SPLENDID
13	7.6%	36 months to 47 months	EXCELLENT
5	2.9%	48 months to 59 months	GOOD
24	14.1%	60 months to 119 months	FAIR
17	10.0%	120 months to 191 months	POOR
28	16.5%	192 months and upward	PRESENTLY IMPOSSIBLE
170			

FIGURE 27

"Among these 170 children, 146 highly important gains were made during the period of treatment. These gains were highly important by anyone's standards, even our own. These gains were:

5 children who could not walk were now walking.

17 children who could not talk were now talking.

3 children who were blind could now see.
(Two of them could read, and I mean with their eyes.)

60 children who could not read could now read.

2 children who could not pick up objects with their hands could now do so.

35 children who could not write could now do so.

5 children who were deaf could now hear.

4 children who had seizures or convulsions no longer had them.

"Are such results good or bad?

"It depends, I believe, on whose standards you are using at which moment in history.

"This determination of how long it will take a child to reach normality is a critically important factor, because how long the parents can maintain their strength and determination is strongly related to how quickly a child is winning and how much longer treatment will take.

"It must be remembered that this determination is based on the *assumption* that this child will continue to grow at this rate. What we have done can be charted (Fig. 28), comparing him to normal.

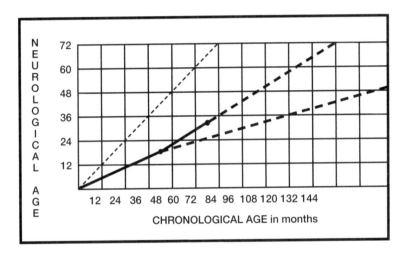

FIGURE 28

"The dotted line represents the average well child in his progress to neurological normality within the normal chronological time span.

"The solid line to the first dot at forty-three months of chronological age (and fifteen months of neurological age) represents the brain-injured child's growth (in my example) to the time we first saw him.

"The solid line to the second dot at seventy-one months of chronological age (and thirty-four months of neurological age) represents what has happened in the twenty-eight months he has been on program. By projecting the new line we can see that he will reach normalcy in about four and one half more years, *assuming* he continues this rate of growth.

"However, children seldom, if ever, grow at even rates of speed, which seems to invalidate such measurements as a means of making judgments. However, we actually see the child every two months and replot the child each visit so that we know precisely where we are. Sometimes the rate of growth increases. Sometimes it slows.

"In life a child's chart often looks like Figure 29, each of the dots representing a visit:

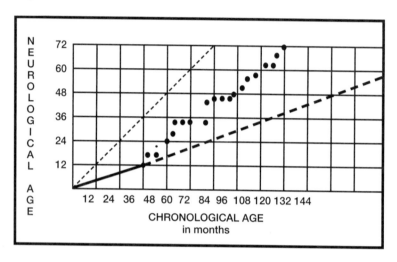

FIGURE 29

"Now we know:

1. Where the child was at the initial visit (prior to treatment).
2. How long it took him to get there.
3. His rate of progress prior to treatment.
4. Precisely where he is now, compared to himself prior to treatment.
5. How long it took him to get there.
6. His present rate of speed compared to his previous rate of speed.
7. His present rate of speed compared to an average well child.
8. How far he has yet to go to be functioning normally.
9. How long it will take him to get there with re-evaluations of that position every two months.

"That is a great deal to know as compared to the classical methods of measurement which generally tell us either nothing or, worse, something that isn't true. At best, they boil down to the less than scientific question, *How do you think he looks today?"*

31

WHERE DO WE GO FROM HERE?

As I approach the end of writing this book, I realize that I have left much unsaid. Some of what I have left unsaid remains unsaid because you have to stop somewhere if a book is ever to be done, since clinical research is an ongoing thing and new discoveries happen every day. For that reason we have talked not at all about brachiation, which is a discovery of 1968, but you have to stop somewhere. (Brachiation is explained in detail in the book *How To Teach Your Baby To Be Physically Superb.*)

There are also things of great importance which we understand and use but do not yet understand well enough to be able to explain them in all their complexities in a book. Included among these things are the full oxygen availability program, the spatial relations program, and others.

Still, we have covered much, and the parents of the brain-injured child who wish to begin him on a program certainly have enough important information to make a substantial difference in their child if they wish to do so—and that, I think, is a good thing.

Now I must ask myself where we are now. What of the past, what of the present, and what of the future?

When the most senior members of our group began our work together more than 60 years ago we had never seen or heard of a single brain-injured child who had ever gotten well.

Things are a lot better than that now and along the long, long road that has run from then to now many, many kids have gotten well—more even than I remember. Instead of comparing our work with everyone else's, I much prefer to simply compare our own results of today with our own results back in the old days when we were using what are called, with a good deal too much dignity, "Classical Methods" of treatment. I must say that comparing us with us there is no comparison—for in those days nobody ever got well or even significantly better, and today many get well and a substantial majority get significantly better, and between no results and substantial results there is simply *no* comparison.

So, I must ask myself, how do I feel about it all these many years later? How do we all feel about it? Well, I think that the staff and all the people of The Institutes feel substantially overworked and substantially under-paid—in money that is, but it's equally clear that you couldn't get rid of them with wild horses. I don't know anyone with whom they'd trade jobs. The truth is that the staff feels just a little sorry for everybody else.

I personally alternate between exultation and despair depending on which way I'm looking. When I remember those old days when no child ever made it and when it was considered immoral even to hope and when I compare that with the children who make it today, I am in sheer exulta-tion and to look at the children who make it is little short of glorious.

But I cannot for the life of me exult too long because ever intruding on my thoughts are the kids who fail, even today, and they are far too many and there remain a few who are actually not changed at all, and when I think of these kids and their parents, who are often marvelous people, my exultation dissolves and I am left with the bleakest of despair because for these children, it is much as it was in the darkest days of centuries past.

So is today superb, or is it tragic? It is both, and which it is for each sin-gle child is a product of our knowledge or of our ignorance. Seldom, indeed, is the failure a product of the parents, who by and large are mag-nificent and who vary from each other only in the incredible amounts of strength they can muster to do routinely the difficult-to-do, frequently the unbelievable, and to do more often than occasionally—the impossible. Whoever said the impossible takes a little longer must have been speaking of parents. Sometimes it takes a *lot* longer.

So it is today and new discoveries not only continue to happen but indeed they are happening faster than ever they did before and at a break-neck pace as compared to the way they had happened to us in the begin-ning, and these new discoveries are daily changing the way things are for brain-injured kids. Today's results are unquestionably better than even the results we have reported in this book because they report on kids who started the program decades ago and we know about new worlds since then. Today's kid unquestionably has a better chance than did the kid of decades ago. I would be more than surprised if tomorrow's child does not do better—far better than the boy or girl who starts today. Were it not better, I should stand not surprised but in open-mouthed astonishment.

Through the years, since kids first began to go all the way, each year has been better. Each year the number of successes has increased and the number of failures has declined, and so I believe it will continue to be in the future. Treatment will, I believe, become simpler and perhaps not so terribly demanding as it is today. So demanding is the program today that I know of only one thing in all the world that is more difficult—that is to have a child whom you love who can't do what other kids do. That is more difficult, and parents feel that the *worst* day on The Institutes program is better than the *best* day when they have no answer. Still I think that our continuing discoveries will make things not quite so impossible as they sometimes seem to be today.

Surely one day we shall see the end in brain injury either because we shall have learned to solve it always or we shall see the end because we shall learn a better thing—how to prevent it. That will be a splendid day for kids and parents alike as it will be a great day for the staff of The Institutes for the Achievement of Human Potential in Philadelphia, in Brazil, in Italy, in Mexico, and in Japan. But will it then be the end of all the long years of work with children? I think not. It is impossible to watch day by day as profoundly brain-injured children struggle their way upward to wellness, without coming over and over again to a most startling conclusion. Consider it.

I offer you Child A (the average child). He is eight years of age and he performs at an average level, which is to say, he performs exactly in the middle of the group of children his own age.

Now I offer you Child B (the brain-injured child). When he was born he was severely brain-injured and had millions—indeed billions, of dead brain cells. We have taught his parents and they have treated him for five long years and today he is eight years of age and performs exactly as Child A, the average child, *yet Child B still has suffered the death of billions of brain cells.*

This we have seen over and over again. How long can we look at that without asking, What in the devil is wrong with *Child A* (not Child B).

Surely if Child B with billions of brain cells dead and gone can perform and function in every way as well as the average unhurt child, then there must be something wrong with Child A.

For many years we have made this inescapable observation.

Now we present Child C (Child C has had a hemispherectomy). When

Child C was born he appeared to be perfectly normal but some time subsequent to his birth he suffered a blood clot on one side of his brain. By three years of age he was completely paralyzed on the right side of his body, his behavior was wild indeed and he was having overwhelming *grand mal* convulsions. His condition was rapidly worsening and it was clear that unless something was done he was not going to survive. Something was done. Our neurosurgeon had surgically removed the left half of his brain. It was not only the cortex which was removed but half his brain; everything, in fact, except two ancient sections called the thalamus and the head and tail of the caudate nucleus. Now Child C was eight years old and Child C could do everything that *Child A* could do.

How long could the brain surgeon look at that without saying to himself, What in the devil is wrong with *Child A?* Why can Child A with a whole brain not perform better than Child C who has half his brain in his head and half his brain in a jar?

For many years the neurosurgeon had made the same observation.

Why indeed should two children, B and C, with demonstrably profoundly injured brains be able to perform as well as Child A with a relatively uninjured brain.

When one has observed this and pondered this for many years he is led inescapably to a simple and clear conclusion. *The average child is not functioning half as well as he ought to be,* and everybody who has thought about it knows it. How else can we explain that phenomenon known as the P.T.A.?

Where else do we see lay people telling the professionals how to do it. Everyone knows that something is wrong but nobody knows what. One father says that the school needs a swimming pool. A mother believes that the school day is too long—or too short. And so it goes. Everyone agrees only that something is wrong.

All over the world we have had opportunity to talk to groups of mothers and over and over again I have had opportunity to ask this question. "Will every mother in the room who thinks her child is doing as well as he or she could be, please put up your hand." The world over, no hand has been raised. Perhaps, I have said to myself, these are bashful mothers and so I have reversed the question. "Will every mother in the room who feels her child is *not* doing as well as he or she could be, please put up your hand." All hands go up.

Is it possible that mothers the world over are right in believing that well children are not doing as well as they should be doing?

Is it possible that average kids could be a great deal more effective than they are?

Is it possible that we have somehow vastly underestimated our children?

Is there any evidence that children could accomplish a great deal more than they are accomplishing?

There is indeed, and what is more they are considerably happier kids.

In Australia there are a couple of Olympic swimmers named Mr. and Mrs. Tim Timmermans, who teach infant babies to swim. Dr. Fay had long ago observed that if you put a one-day-old baby on his belly in a few inches of water he will hold his breath when his face is in the water and breathe when he lifts his head. Why not? He has been swimming, as it were, for the previous nine months. The Timmermans have *done* something about Fay's observation. In the early 1970s we had the opportunity to visit the Timmermans in Melbourne to watch.

It was a joyous and beautiful thing to watch as a dozen lovely pink-skinned, bikini-clad mothers splashed in the pool with as many pink-and-cream, two- and three-month-old infants. I shall not soon forget the lovely sight they made together as they individually bobbed their babies up and down in the very warm water of the large pool. Soon each mother was dropping her baby into the water while the child, with obvious enjoyment would swim to the surface to be caught up in mother's arms. They swam with gusto.

We photographed Claire Timmermans' three-year-old daughter, who had earned a Red Cross Life Saving Badge, tow her mother the length of the pool with ease and pride.

Her two-year-old son insisted over and over again that I throw him into the deep end of the pool from which he would clamber and demand again that I throw him in until I and not he was too tired to continue the game.

Australia lies surrounded by seas and as her name implies they are Southern seas. Is there then some genetic code deeply written into Australian children, some aquatic imperative that perforce makes them swim? But these children were not aborigines five generations earlier; their parents had trod England's green and pleasant land, and the Timmermans are Holland-born. To one not initiated to the potential of children it would appear strange.

I remember my friend John Eaglebull of Army days. John was a Sioux and a Chief at that. He was a college graduate as befitted a Sioux Chief, and since his name began with an E and mine a D we slept beside each other through Infantry Officer Candidate School. I remember the day that Eaglebull with great pride, showed me a snapshot of his two-year-old son. Looking at it made me nervous. Here was this tiny two-year-old boy sitting unassisted and alone on the back of a full-grown horse, with reins in hand.

I complained to Eaglebull that it was a dangerous thing to do.

"What is dangerous," demanded Eaglebull, "about taking a snapshot?"

"Suppose," I said, "the horse had moved."

"It would have spoiled the snapshot," Eaglebull said.

"But nobody is holding your son. He could have fallen off and fractured his skull," I explained.

"For Pete's sake, that's his horse," said Eaglebull patiently as if he were explaining to a child. "I don't know anybody at home who can remember when he couldn't ride a horse any more than you know anyone who can remember when he couldn't walk."

That superb teller of Indian-Cavalry stories and historian of the post-Civil War days, James Warner Bellah, once described the Sioux as "Five thousand of the world's finest light cavalry." And why not? Like my friend John Eaglebull and his son, they were born on horses.

Is this superb horsemanship not some equestrian imperative written on every plains Indian in some immutable genetic code over the hundreds of thousands of years that such codes take? It would seem so, for surely the Indians were superb horsemen—until one remembers that until the coming of the Spaniards, less than five hundred years ago, no American Indian had ever seen a horse.

In the early 1960s I learned of a man in Japan, Dr. Shinichi Suzuki, who was supposed to have taught hundreds of two-, three-, and four-year-old children to have played the violin. I am a musical incompetent and have never been able to so much as carry a tune, but I have friends who are first-rate musicians, and they tell me that the violin is among the most difficult of instruments to master. The man who told me about the Japanese children playing the violin did not believe the story and was sure it was not possible for any three-year-old child to play the violin. I believed the story instantly since all my findings of the previous twenty years had led me to the conclusion that any tiny child can learn to do anything at all that an adult can present to him in a reasonable way. I was also persuaded that tiny children learned the most involved things imaginable (such as language) without the slightest effort.

Everything I knew had led me to the conclusion that when it comes to taking in raw data without the slightest effort, no adult could hold a candle to any two-year-old. I had, in fact, written Doman's First Law of Human Dynamics which stated that "All adults are hopelessly mentally retarded compared to any two-year-old."

Everything about the story fitted my own knowledge and my own biases. Naturally, I believed it. The man who told me the story and who did not believe it became visibly upset when I, who had never heard it before except from him, did believe it.

It was ten years before Katie and I got to Matsumoto, Japan, to meet that genial genius, Dr. Suzuki. Dr. Suzuki had been kind enough to arrange a concert for us, and I must say that in a lifetime which has been most fortunately graced with lovely sights, few could compare with the sight of fifty tiny Japanese girls and boys of three to six years playing a two-hour concert not of "Old MacDonald Had a Farm" but instead of Bach, Mozart, Beethoven, and Liszt. There remains in my memory of that moving afternoon at Talent Education a little four-year-old girl whose training was so advanced that she played the entire concert. She was on the front row of the stage and she played with great poise, enthusiasm, and beauty. In the midst of a lovely concerto she stopped and quietly stooped to place her violin on the floor, at which time her mother came forward and they left the auditorium together. In a few minutes and before the concerto had ended she returned quietly to the stage and resumed playing.

It is the only time in my life I recall seeing a virtuoso leave the concert stage to go to the bathroom with her mother because while she played the violin superbly, she did not yet take care of herself in the bathroom alone.

Even now as I write my eyes grow blurred as I remember that day and thrill to the beauty of those superb and superbly happy children who glory in their enjoyment of playing.

The Japanese, of course, are an ancient people and as everyone knows extremely clever with their hands and with their brains and one thinks that surely there is written in some ancient genetic code a musical imperative that gives Japanese children a special license to play Beethoven on the violin—until one remembers that it is only slightly over a hundred years ago that the first Japanese ever set ear to Beethoven or eye to a violin.

Dr. Suzuki taught many thousands of little children to play the violin.

Thousands of especially gifted children? Yes. Gifted only with a mother who brought each child to have the opportunity.

I have already spoken of how that brilliant man, Dr. Raymundo Veras, in Brazil taught a one-year-old girl to begin reading in three languages so that by the time she was three she could read entire books in Portuguese, English, and German. You will remember that she was diagnosed as having Down Syndrome. He has taught dozens of children with Down Syndrome to read before they are four years old. Around The Institutes those terms "Mongoloid" or "Down Syndrome" have been replaced. We call these children "Veras kids."

Much has been said about genetics in relation to those kids diagnosed as having Down Syndrome, but I never met anyone in the world who believed they had a genetic advantage. Neither do I.

I used to love to ski, but since I learned to do so as an adult I was quite naturally a poor skier. I tried to make up for my lack of ability with first-rate equipment and first-rate instructors, but it availed me little. I stood on the top of a slope and pretended to be admiring the scenery while in truth I was getting up my nerve. I stood with my expensive cap and my expensive Head skis, and if the truth be known I am sore afraid until behind me some five- or six-year-old yells, "Out of the way, Mister," and down the slope he tears with his barrel staves and rubber bands shusshing and slaloming. He can't pronounce them but can he do them!

Is it genetic to Vermont children? Easy as duck soup but not genetic. When I was a boy only the rich skied and that in Switzerland. Vermont made magnificent maple sugar.

In 1971 my book, *How To Teach Your Baby To Read,* was published in the twelfth language, Japanese, and a new world opened to me.

In Japan I found whole groups of true geniuses when I was invited by E.D.A. (Early Development Association) and the Japanese *Reader's Digest* to lecture in that beautiful land.

E.D.A. itself was a superb organization doing what I have long dreamed of seeing. It was a product of the fertile brains of brilliant Dr. Masaaki Honda, a pediatrician, Mr. Toshiyuki Miyamoto, a splendid editor, Mr. Masaru Ibuka, a genius whose brain recognized no horizons. Not content with being the founder of the Sony Corporation and the chairman of the board, he wrote the most charming book I have ever read. It is called, *Kindergarten Is Too Late,* and is a must for all parents-to-be or parents of tiny children. Finally, there was Mr. Akira Tago, a first-rate educator.

Vividly in my mind's eye do I remember my first visit to E.D.A. in Tokyo where for the first time I met my colleague, Professor Isao Ishii with whom I had long corresponded. Appropriately enough my first sight of that astonishing man was a view of him surrounded by a semicircle of two-, three-, and four-year-old Japanese children who sat with their eyes riveted on his face. Although we had long awaited this moment, neither he nor I acknowledged each other in the slightest way lest the spell between him and the little kids be broken.

In Japan there are a few written forms. One is Kanji, which consists of Chinese characters. There are thousands of them that can represent words by themselves. The other form is Kana, and there are two types, each consisting of 90 syllables. One is a phonetic alphabet, which was developed in Japan. First-graders begin by learning these Kana and then gradually learn Kanji. The higher they advance in education, the more Kanji they learn.

Professor Ishii had begun as a university professor and had quite properly worked his way upward to being a kindergarten teacher. He had quite properly learned that children could learn Kanji quite as easily as they learned Kana and a good deal easier than adults. Having read my book he had experimented with teaching tiny children and older "mentally retarded" children Kanji. He was delighted to find that the smaller the children were, the easier it was to read Kanji.

Now at last I was face to face with him. At the level of his forehead he held a series of cards about ten inches square and on each of them was printed a Kanji character. All eyes watched intently. Suddenly he exposed a card for a split second. So briefly was it seen that I had no clear mental picture of this complex Chinese character. "Monkey" shouted the tiny children in unison. "bird," "automobile," "hand," "foot," "mother," "father," "strawberry," and so it went through thirty or forty characters shown at random. Not only were these tiny children reading and reading easily and joyously, but they were reading the complex Kanji and not the phonetic Kana.

In another room we watched the tiny children paint under the direction of a great Japanese illustrator. They painted joyfully and splendidly. They painted not with their fingers but with brushes, and they painted in oils.

In still another room we saw a semicircle of two-, three-, and four-year-olds surrounding an attractive young American girl whose virtue was that she spoke no Japanese but only English. Katie and I watched with rapture while she and the children carried on an English conversation.

Here was in reality a dream we had long dreamed. Our hearts pounded and our spirits soared.

E.D.A. was doing much that we had so long known was possible. Had not we long ago taught tiny children to read, even severely brain-injured ones? Had not we taught tiny children to do a fascinating instant mathematics that no staff member could match?

Did not I have a precious possession in the form of hundreds of letters from mothers the world over reporting to me what had happened to their little boys and girls after they had taught them to read?

Is it not true that when the world begins to bother me I go to my office and lock the door and read the letters my mothers have written me about their children, both well and brain-injured?

Do not those letters restore my soul in their unselfishness and their singleness of purpose in giving their children a better tomorrow?

Is it not obvious that Australian children have no corner on swimming, nor Sioux children on horses, Vermont kids on skiing, Philadelphia kids on reading, Japanese children on violins, and so on and so on and so on the world over?

Is it not obvious that all children can be all things, and that giving them the opportunity to develop their brains is a joyous process for mother and child alike?

It's hard to imagine what the world will be like tomorrow when everyone knows the truth about little kids and every child has his or her opportunity to know all the magnificent things there are to know and is able to do all the great things there are to do.

What we have to do to bring about that lovely day—but there I go trying to say all there is to say in a single book and finding it impossible. The problem is that this book is about how to make brain-injured children well. From doing that we've learned how to make well children weller—but that's really another story, isn't it?

32

THE FAMILY IS THE ANSWER

For as long as there have been brain-injured children, the world has essentially divided into two distinct camps. Those two camps still exist today.

In one camp are those who believe that brain-injured children are hopeless and that they should be medicated, warehoused, and forgotten. The people who hold this view often refer to themselves as "realists". They are very worried about what they call "false hope".

In the other camp are those who believe that brain-injured children are not hopeless. They believe that there are many possibilities for the brain-injured child to be better, much better, even to be completely well. The people who hold this view are often called "dreamers" by the people who call themselves "realists". The "dreamers" do not understand the term "false hope".

How can hope ever be false, they wonder? Are people not permitted to hope that there will be peace in the world some day? In the face of thousands of years of death and destruction on earth is this a false hope? Are parents not to be permitted to hope that a little child who is blind, deaf, and paralyzed might have a chance? As civilized people who love children, isn't it our job to give our brain-injured children a fighting chance to be well?

The "dreamers" ask a lot of troublesome questions like this. They are worried about the dangers of what they call "false despair".

We have been accused of being dreamers and so have our parents. In some ways, it is true that we are dreamers. In fact, we are proud of our dreams. We dream of our blind, deaf, and hurt children being well. Those are proper dreams to have. But we are also hard-nosed realists and, what is even more important, pragmatists.

We are interested in *results* and not another darn thing. We live in the *real* world at The Institutes and so do our families. We live night and day with five hundred initially paralyzed, speechless, sometimes vomiting, convulsing kids—hardly a dream world. If there is a dream world it is on the other side of our stone wall. It's those who say to desperate parents, "Stop worrying so much, bring your child back in six months, and we'll see if he is any better." Dream on—he will be six months further behind.

Our families know that their beloved children have huge problems. They leave no stone unturned to find a solution. They have the dream that their beloved child will be well. It's human and it's natural. It is not a bad thing to dream this dream, it is a good thing. But they follow their dreams with action—real, practical, and effective action.

We at The Institutes live every day nose-to-nose with our successes and with our failures. We do not run away and we do not give up.

No brain-injured child in history was ever fixed by putting him in a warehouse, sedating him, and forgetting him. No brain-injured child will ever be helped by so doing. This is the *reality* of what happens to hurt children who fall into the hands of "realists".

Then there are the other kind of realists. The ones who roll up their sleeves and set about making their dreams come true through determination and hard work.

We are dreamers *and* realists and so are our parents.

It is sad but commonplace for parents of a brain-injured child to be told that they ought to get rid of their hurt child. They are told that the kindest thing to do is to put their brain-injured child in an institution "to save the rest of the family". The argument is that parents must divide their time *evenly*. The notion is that if parents gave brain-injured Billy more time than they gave his well sister Mary, then Mary would grow up to despise him and mother and father too—because Mary did not have the same amount of time that Billy had. So parents must make sure that well Mary gets as much time as very hurt Billy.

This idea must surely be based upon the assumption that parents don't have enough love and affection to cover *both* a hurt child and a well child and so there must be a kind of rationing of what little love there is to go around. Perhaps for the inventors of this repulsive notion, love *is* in short supply. However, for the great majority of parents, love is *not* in short supply when it comes to their children hurt or well.

We human beings are social creatures. We like to bunch. And since time has begun, we have bunched. First and foremost we have bunched into a small gang called the family. We have bunched into bigger gangs called the tribe, the city, the state, the federal government, etc. We tend to bunch together because we're social creatures. Governments have come and governments have gone, and states have come and states have gone, and empires have come and empires have gone. The Roman Empire is no more. The German state that was going to live for a thousand years is no more. But the one thing that has never gone is the family. We have gathered into families since time began. And thank God for that. It is what keeps us sane and decent.

Now, why should the family survive when other groups did not? Why do we have families? I would like to propose that we have families so we can divide our time *unevenly* and give that time to the member of the family who needs it the most. We are family people and that's what we do. The family has survived throughout history and the reason it survives is so that we can divide our time unevenly.

In my lifetime, I've had three families. My first family is the Doman family and that's a true family in every sense of the word. We divide our time unevenly. We're a very, very, very fortunate family. We've enjoyed superb health and happiness. We have never lost a family member to anything but happy and fulfilled old age. Every once in a while I get tired or frustrated or, most likely of all, enraged. This happens when the difference between the way things *are* and the way things *should be* for hurt kids weighs heavy on me. On these occasions my wife, Katie, gets my kids together and says, "You know, the old boy's having a bad time. Maybe we ought to make his life a little easier right now. What do you think?" And each member of the family divides their time unevenly so that I get more time and more attention. It always works. My frustration dissolves in the face of love and support and I am back in fighting form.

Sometimes, Katie, when she was the mother of three young children *and* a head nurse with thirty elderly stroke patients, would get a bit tired. Then I would get the kids together and say, "Kids how about we make a secret plot. Let's agree to make the house cleaner and neater and more peaceful for your mother. Let's help her in every way we can. But nobody squeals." The kids came up with wonderful ways of helping their mother. Their secret: they divide their time unevenly, they give more time to Mom.

And, sometimes, one of the kids is having a rough time so we divide our time unevenly and give it to the one who needs it. That's what we do in the Doman family.

I'll bet that's what you do in your family, too.

My second family is The Institutes family and it's very much a family. We feel the same way about each other as we feel about the members of our own families. The staff love each other, and, if there is a staff member in need we divide our time unevenly to give that staff member whatever it is that he or she may need. That's a given. Nobody even mentions it. That's what we do, and I'll bet that every other group that is fighting for a better world does the same thing.

My third family was my infantry rifle company. That was a true family. In infantry rifle combat, the only people in front of you are the bad guys. They are shooting at you and trying to kill you. You are shooting at them and trying to kill them too. Under these circumstances you make very dear friends very—very, very quickly. More things happen to you in five minutes than might happen normally in a lifetime. Sometimes you stop shooting long enough to crawl out in the field where a lot of shooting is going on in order to grab a wounded soldier by the leg and pull him in. That's dividing your time unevenly. Everybody's in favor of that and it does amazing things to you.

I enlisted on Pearl Harbor Day and they put me in the medics. But it wasn't what I thought I ought to be doing, so I asked to be transferred to infantry. They sent me to Infantry Officer Candidate School. This was a superb experience. They had ninety days to make everybody into West Point graduates. There was not one second wasted. It was the finest school I ever attended, including my university. The things that I was taught at Officer Candidate School were extraordinary.

One of the most important principles I learned there was a law of the infantry. The law is *you never leave the wounded behind.* Officers in the infantry never leave the wounded behind. Most casualties take place in the infantry so it is vital that you never leave the wounded behind. As an officer-in-training you think that you understand it. Then you're in combat and the kid next to you gets a bullet through his chest. And down he goes. It doesn't occur to you for one second to leave him behind. Not because it's a principle you have been taught but because *he is you.* If the wind had been four miles an hour more from the east, you'd be lying on the ground with a bullet through *your* chest. All things being equal, you might well be the one lying on the ground three minutes from now.

You don't leave the wounded behind because that wounded soldier beside you *is* you. That is why you never, never, never leave the wounded behind.

Madison Avenue campaigns for starving children do not move me, not at all. Does that mean I don't care about little children starving in Africa? Of course I do. I just do not believe that those glossy, full-page, color ads have anything to do with little children starving in Africa. They have a lot to do with campaigns to raise money, very little of which will ever find its way to that starving child.

The only ad campaign that moves me is a very famous one, you may remember it. It is an illustration of a twelve-year-old kid with a little boy on his back, and underneath it says, "He ain't heavy, Mister, he's my brother."

That picture touches me.

It gets to me every time.

No Madison Avenue executive wrote that line. Only a kid could say that. "Brother" is not the opposite of heavy, "light" is. "He ain't heavy, Mister, he's my brother."

No one had to teach that twelve-year-old boy that you never leave the wounded behind. Kids just know that, don't they.

The reason we have families is so that we can divide our time unevenly and give the time to the person who needs it most, because the one who needs it most is not heavy, he's our brother, and we never, ever leave him behind.

Let us return briefly to Billy and Mary. If Billy has the chicken pox, doesn't Billy get more time than Mary gets because he's got the chicken pox? I wonder if anybody thinks brain injury is less important than the chicken pox.

Suppose you've got well Mary who's eight and brain-injured Billy who's four. You decide that Billy cannot have any extra time because you are going to divide your time evenly. Billy will be in trouble because he cannot hope to make it without extra time, attention, stimulation, and opportunity. There's no question about it. But you are convinced that it's the only fair thing to do for Mary. Isn't it bad enough that Billy's got a problem without Mary having a problem too? So you divide your time evenly.

Years go by and Mary is twenty-one years old, Billy is seventeen. Billy is now in a wheelchair. You take Mary out to dinner for her twenty-first birthday and tell her how much you love her. You say to her, "Honey, do you want to know how much we love you? Because we love you so much we always made certain that you got just as much time as Billy."

You know what I think Mary would say if she's got any brains and a heart?

I think she would say, "You mean you left my brother in that wheelchair as a favor to me? My brother is in a wheelchair because you wanted to give me *equal* time? You have underestimated me. He's not heavy he's my brother!"

And suppose you said, "Well, we certainly didn't think you'd take it this way. We brought you out for this party to tell you how much we love you. And oh, by the way, Dad and I are getting old now, we're not as young as we used to be, and here's your brother Billy in a wheelchair and we've got a birthday present for you: Billy."

She just might think you haven't done her a favor by dividing your time so evenly.

And she'd be right.

Our parents and their wonderful well kids roll up their sleeves every day and do battle to save their wounded one. Every day they divide their time unevenly. Every night they sleep the sleep of honest fatigue and a job well done.

Sometimes (very, very rarely these days) we lose a child. When a hurt child dies the pain and loss is beyond any words I can muster to describe it. But our families know, beyond any shadow of a doubt, that they have given their full measure to save their child. Each member of the family shares equally in the comfort of knowing that their wounded one got the very best from each of them.

Sometimes, if we are very smart and the family works very hard, we win. Everyone in the family from the youngest to the oldest shares equally in the victory so precious and so hard won.

We find that our families are the happiest people we know. They know what matters and they know what does not matter. They know that in the world of the brain-injured child only one thing matters—*results.*

Whether a family decides to do our program or some other program, all that matters is *results.*

Our advice to you is simply this: If your child is improving, keep doing whatever you are doing and don't let anyone talk you out of it. If your child is not improving, stop doing what you are doing and find a better program for your child because all that matters is results.

And finally, when it comes to your brain-injured child, remember that you are the answer, not the problem.

33

RESULTS—
THE ONLY THING THAT MATTERS

E ach time a child comes to The Institutes, the child is carefully evaluated on The Institutes Developmental Profile to determine the results of treatment. The purpose of The Institutes Developmental Profile is to reduce the thousands of accomplishments that a child enjoys to those achievements that are actually causes rather than mere results of other functions. There are forty-two of them. Any improvement on the Profile is cause for rejoicing, but some accomplishments are more important than others.

In 1973, The Institutes decided that it was important to begin to report on the most important changes we were seeing in the children under treatment. It was decided that results would be published every three months and made available to our parents and anyone else who was interested in what happens when a brain-injured child is actually treated. Since that time, these results have been published every three months in our journal, The IN-REPORT.

We report on crawling, creeping, walking, running, seeing, hearing, understanding, reading, writing, talking, health, detoxification, and graduation. Academic accomplishments such as entering regular school and progressing to above-average levels in intellectual, physical, and social pursuits are all recorded in our archives.

In the summary that follows, we reviewed the results of 1,241 children ranging from 7 months old to 28 years old during a five-year period. The majority of these children were severely or profoundly brain-injured. Some children had been on the program for as little as six months, others for more than five years.

As you read these results it should be noted, and noted strongly, that each and every one of these changes was achieved at home by mother, father, and the child, *not* at The Institutes for the Achieve-ment of Human Potential, but *at home*.

In some ways, this fact is as remarkable as the achievements themselves.

CRAWLING

Of the 436 children who were unable to move, 176 (40%) crawled for the first time in their lives. In short, they went from being paralyzed to being able to crawl across a room without help.

CREEPING

Of the 218 children who were unable to creep, 136 (62%) began to do so. This is to say that they defied gravity to move to the third dimension and are able to move around the house on hands and knees.

WALKING

Of the 223 children who were unable to walk, 109 (49%) began to walk without help for the first time.

RUNNING

Of the 241 children able to walk, but not run, 141 (54%) learned to run for the first time.

SEEING

Of 123 children who were blind, 105 (85%) saw for the first time in their lives and 84 of those children learned to read.

HEARING

Of 55 children who were deaf, 49 children (89%) heard for the first time in their lives.

UNDERSTANDING

Of 453 children whose comprehension was not yet equal to that of the average three-year-old, 408 children (90%) were able to understand at least as well as a three-year-old for the first time in their lives.

READING

Of 585 children who were unable to read, 574 children (98%) read for the first time.

TALKING

Of the 509 children who could not speak, 247 (49%) spoke for the first time.

WRITING

Of the 324 children unable to write, 68 (21%) wrote for the first time.

HEALTH

Of 801 children, 232 (29%) achieved perfect health for at least 12 consecutive months. Of these, 100 had no illness for more than 24 months, and one has had no illness for more than five years.

DETOXIFICATION

Of 256 children who were on antiepileptic drugs, tranquilizers, antidepressants, amphetamines, or any other psychoactive medications, 185 (72%) were completely and successfully detoxified.

GRADUATION TO LIFE

The road to graduation is often a long one. Sometimes, along the way, a child achieves true excellence in one or two areas (which is to say he is clearly above his peers), while he has not yet attained total wellness in one area.

When this occurs one of two possibilities exists: such a child continues on the program until the final area is perfect and then graduates, or the staff and the family agree that the child should join his well peers while continuing to do a neurological program that will solve the remaining problems.

In this second case, the everyday demands of life itself, combined with the continued neurological program, are sufficient to eventually solve the child's remaining problems. This is called "graduation to life."

If all goes well after a child "graduates to life," the remaining problem is totally solved. When this occurs, the child returns for a final evaluation and formally becomes a full graduate.

If the parents do not see the desired progress and changes occurring in life, they contact The Institutes and the child returns to a full program.

GRADUATION TO LIFE BY PARENTS

Sixteen children were graduated to life by their parents. They ranged in age from 2 years 6 months old to 21 years old.

GRADUATION TO LIFE

Twenty-one children were graduated to life by The Institutes staff. They ranged in age from 12 months old to 28 years 3 months old.

GRADUATION

Four children were graduated from the program. They ranged in age from 6 years 3 months old to 11 years 2 months old.

In Conclusion

These results must surely be among the most compelling evidence in existence that the brain *does* grow by use and that mother, father, sister, brother, grandmother, and grandfather make the best therapy team in the world for the brain-injured child.

These results are, to our knowledge, the only figures being published in the world on what actually happened to a group of brain-injured children under treatment. If this is not so, we would be delighted to know about it so that those results could be published to provide a standard of comparison.

For every child that The Institutes for the Achievement of Human Potential accepts, there are hundreds of thousands of children just like them that The Institutes cannot accept. These results are of vital importance to those children, their parents, and the professionals who seek to help them.

The results that the parents and the children at The Institutes are achieving do not represent the way things *are* in the world (except for the tiny number of children being seen at The Institutes), but they do represent the way things *might* be for millions of brain-injured children the world over.

When we review our results we are struck by two very strong but very conflicting emotions. The first is the joy of knowing that our children *are* getting better. The vast majority of children who we see experience major change in at least two important areas of function. Indeed, it is rare that a child does not improve at all. The second equally strong emotion is frustration for the children who are not making progress as fast as we want them to do so.

This is the world in which we live and will continue to live until we have found the shortest pathway to make all brain-injured children well. This is our objective and until we reach it we will never give up.

The IN-REPORT

The Institutes for the Achievement of Human Potential reports the Victories achieved by brain-injured children in its quarterly journal, The IN-REPORT.

For each child that earns a Victory, The IN-REPORT provides his or her specific name, age, country of residence, and ability prior to beginning the program.

Subscriptions to The IN-REPORT are available through:
The Institutes Finance Office
Phone: (215) 233-2050, ext. 1263
Fax: (215) 233-3117
E-mail: accrecv@iahp.org
    or
The Institutes Website
http://www.iahp.org

DO YOU NEED HELP?

•**DESIGN** a home program for your child based upon what you have learned.

•**START** your program.

•**BE CONSISTENT** in whatever you do.

•**KEEP A SIMPLE DIARY** of the changes you observe and the questions you have.

•**LEARN MORE** about how you can help your child.

TO LEARN MORE PLEASE:

CALL the *What To Do About Your Brain-Injured Child* Registrar
Phone: 215-233-2050
Toll-Free: 800-736-4663
Fax: 215-233-9646

VISIT the website of The Institutes for the Achievement of Human Potential:
www.iahp.org (in English, Italian, Japanese, Spanish)

WRITE to the *What To Do* Registrar:
The Institutes for the Achievement of Human Potential
8801 Stenton Avenue
Wyndmoor, PA 19038 USA

READ other books in The Institutes Gentle Revolution Series
published by:
The Gentle Revolution Press
Toll-free:1-866-250-BABY
Website: www.gentlerevolution.com

APPENDIX A

DETOXIFICATION FROM ANTICONVULSANTS
25 YEARS OF EXPERIENCE
WITH BRAIN-INJURED CHILDREN

In 1971, The Institutes for the Achievement of Human Potential presented to The World Organization for Human Potential a cautionary note to the
medical world and to the parents of brain-injured children regarding the
widespread and sometimes indiscriminate use of anticonvulsant drugs.
Since that time, we have regularly and successfully removed such drugs
from many children and young adults. This practice has become an inte-
gral part of our treatment of brain injury.

In addition to our desire to avoid adverse effects of the drugs, our
rationale is also based on our strong belief that seizures serve a physiological function, as do the many other defense mechanisms of the body.
Coughing, vomiting, diarrhea, fainting, and fever could also be viewed as
dysfunctions, but we know that they are designed to protect the organism.
So also are seizures. A seizure is an activity of great metabolic activity of
the brain, and during its presence cerebral blood flow increases, providing
more oxygen and glucose and increasing excitatory amino acids necessary
for establishing the neuronal wiring and function.

A mature and well-organized central nervous system has less need for
seizure activity since other options are more available to provide its needs.
The seizure control we seek is to develop a more mature cortex and to provide for the physiological needs that have produced the seizure state. This
is a more rational and more successful approach than the use of drugs,
which dull the senses, inhibit motor activity, and interfere with growth
and metabolism.

Our comprehensive treatment of brain-injured children is a very intensive
program applied by the parents at home, after careful teaching by the staff
during the course of five days every six months. Close telephone and mail
contacts are maintained. This contact is also vital to the successful manage-
ment of a detoxification program, as it provides great reassurance for parents

who have been made terrified of seizures by the medical profession.

Medication is tapered very gradually at a rate appropriate for each child and his or her seizure situation. It is not unusual for the process to take one to two years to accomplish withdrawal. There are times when it must be suspended or a temporary return to medication may be indicated, but this is rare. Generally, status epilepticus must be interrupted because of prolonged marked motor activity in order to avoid acidosis, hyperthermia, and hypoxia. It is important, at all times, to seek the precipitating cause of the seizure and to correct adverse internal or external environmental factors.

Great attention must be paid to supporting the body's physiological processes if detoxification is to be successful. Most important is the overall improvement of brain function. Therefore, the total neurological program designed to gain for each child normal function in all areas is of paramount importance. A mature, well-organized cortex reduces the need for seizures.

Additional measures are:

I. Optimize respiratory function to increase oxygen availability.

II. Masking—a procedure of rebreathing for short periods to gain CO_2 enrichment resulting in a favorable acid base balance and to increase cerebral circulation. This technique is useful to shorten individual seizures as well.

III. Restriction of sodium and liquids to prevent fluid retention and increased intracranial pressure.

IV. Excellent nutrition to maintain good health and structures and to provide for energy and all needed vitamins, minerals, and neurotransmitter precursors.

V. Magnesium and calcium supplements to promote central nervous system membrane stability.

VI. Pyridoxine to support GABA and to increase the efficient use of oxygen by the brain.

VII. Control the environment: Pollution, toxins, hyperthermia, reduced oxygen availability.

VIII. Maintain excellent health—avoidance of infections, etc.

We have kept very careful records of the results of medication reduction and elimination and have reported overall statistics periodically. The figures are remarkably stable from 1971 through 1996. Included are the specifics for a typical year, 1993.

Detoxification Results: 1993

Total Children on The Institutes Intensive Treatment Program: .629

Children with positive seizure history: 332 (52.78%)

Children with seizures current to first visit: 233 (37.04%)

Children taking anticonvulsants at first visit: 197 (31.32%)

Children who completed detoxification: 132 (67.00%)

Of the 132 children who completed detoxification,
the following seizure activity was recorded:

No seizures for at least 6 months post-detoxification: 63 (47.72%)

Fewer seizures for at least 6 months post-detoxification: .45 (34.09%)

Same number of seizures as before detoxification: 1 (0.76%)

More seizures than before detoxification: 13 (9.85%)

Replaced on medication before the study was completed: 5 (3.79%)

Contact lost during the follow-up: 5 (3.79%)

Conclusion: .
Of the children from whom all medication was gradually eliminated, 81.81% had an improved seizure picture while receiving a program of neurological organization and intensive physiological support.

—ROSELISE H. WILKINSON, M.D
MEDICAL DIRECTOR EMERITUS

Dr. Wilkinson was the medical director of The Institutes for the Achievement of Human Potential from 1964 to 1998. At this writing she has more experience in the detoxification of the brain-injured child than of any physician living or deceased.

APPENDIX B

CHILDREN WITH SEVERE BRAIN INJURIES
Neurological Organization in Terms of Mobility

Robert J. Doman, M.D., Eugene B. Spitz, M.D., Philadelphia, Elizabeth Zucman, M.D., Paris, Carl H. Delacato, Ed.D., and Glenn Doman, P.T., Philadelphia

A new system has been developed for the treatment of children with severe brain injuries. This concept, based on neurological organization, is aimed at the injured central nervous system rather than at the resultant peripheral symptoms. The authors devised a developmental mobility scale which described 13 levels of normal development as the criteria of progress during a two-year study of 76 children. The program consisted of permitting the child normal developmental opportunities in areas where the responsible brain level was undamaged, externally imposing the bodily patterns of activity which were the responsibility of damaged brain levels, establishment of hemispheric dominance and early unilaterality, respiratory improvement as measured by vital capacity, and sensory stimulation to improve bodily awareness and position sense. The results of this study are significantly better than those achieved by the authors with previous methods.

The large number of conferences, seminars, and publications regarding the brain-injured child indicates not so much the volume of new information available but rather the intensity of the search for new information.

We had long been dissatisfied with the results of our own methods of treatment and believed that the time requirements in treating children with severe brain injuries could scarcely be justified in light of the low percentage of marked successes as compared with children who were essentially without treatment.

During 1956 and 1957 we developed a new approach to such cases, the goal of which was to establish in brain-injured children the developmental stages observed in normal children. The program, which aimed at both normal and damaged brain levels, consisted of: (a) permitting the child normal developmental opportunities in areas in which the responsible brain level was undamaged; (b) externally imposing the bodily patterns of activity which were the responsibility of damaged brain levels; and (c) utilizing additional factors to enhance neurological organization.

The team used consisted of a physiatrist, a neurosurgeon, an orthopedic surgeon, a nurse, a physical therapist, and a psychologist. In 1958, a two-year outpatient study was begun which used these developmental stages in the treatment of 76 brain-injured children. Each patient was seen bimonthly.

MATERIAL

Subjects—This study of 76 children includes every child seen in the Children's Clinic during the study period who met the following criteria: 1. The existence of brain injury. (For the purpose of this study, brain-injured children are defined as those children whose lesion lies in the brain. The definition includes both traumatic and nontraumatic lesions but excludes children who are genetically defective.) 2. A minimum of six months' treatment. 3. No child was eliminated because of the severity of his involvement.

Diagnosis of Brain Pathology—The diagnosis was made after neurological examination and, in most patients, after an EEG (36), air study (42), and subdural tap (22) had been done. The group of 76 was composed of children who had spasms, athetosis, ataxia, rigidities, tremors, and mixed symptoms; 24 of these children had clinical seizures.

Classification of Brain Pathology—The brain pathology was classified as to type, location, and degree in the following manner.

1. Type: (a) unilateral brain damage: This group contained 15 children with either subdural hematoma (all operated on), vascular malformation, or hemiatrophy of nonspecific causation. Of these 15 children, 4 had hemispherectomies performed by us; (b) bilateral brain damage: This group contained 61 children with conditions such as hydrocephalus, subdural hematoma (all operated on), kernicterus, postencephalitic damage,

dysgenesis of corpus callosum, dysgenesis of cerebellum, dysgenesis of cortex, porencephaly, or diffuse conical atrophy of nonspecific causation. We performed 14 ventriculojugular and 2 ventriculoperitoneal shunts on the 16 hydrocephalic patients. The therapeutic program was instituted no sooner than 10 months after surgery.

2. Location: Upon air study, 30 children demonstrated dilation of the lateral ventricles, and 12 demonstrated dilation of the entire ventricular system, thus indicating the presence of subcortical as well as cortical damage. Locating these lesions in terms of the Phelps-Fay classification, there were 61 cerebral lesions (spastic patients), 12 midbrain lesions (athetoid patients), three basal ganglion lesions (two patients with tremor, one with rigidity), and 10 cerebellar lesions (ataxic patients).

TABLE 1.

Stage	Level	Mobility	No. of Children
Movement	0	None. 20	
	1	Rolling over. 17	
	2	Circling or going backward.	2
	3	Moving forward flat on abdomen without pattern.	5
Crawling	4	Homologously.	4
	5	Homolaterally.	3
	6	Cross pattern. 2	
	7	Without pattern	1
	8	Homologously. 2	
Creeping	9	Homolaterally. 0	
	10	Cross pattern 0	
Walking	11	Pulling up to erect position holding on to furniture & standing, holding on to furniture.	0
	12	Walking without help, without pattern. 20	
	13	Walking, cross pattern. 0	

FIGURE 30

3. Degree: Both clinical examination and neurosurgical diagnostic procedures indicated that the degree of brain damage ranged from mild to severe. No child was eliminated from this study due to severity of either clinical symptoms or degree of brain pathology.

Age at Beginning of Study—The ages ranged from 12 months to nine years, with a median age of 26 months and a mean age of 30 months. The children were separated into three age groups of developmental significance: 0—18 months, 16 children; 18—36 months, 41 children; and over 36 months, 19 children.

Level and Stages of Movement at Beginning of Therapy—The level of movement was defined according to a modification of the developmental patterns of Gesell and co-workers[2-3] and Fay,[4-5] and these were numerically designated for reference purposes. The stages described are: (a) moving arms and legs without forward movements, (b) crawling, (c) creeping, and (d) walking (Table 1). In our experience, each stage described was dependent on the successful completion of the previous stage.

IQ, Affect, and Speech—No child was eliminated because of severity of deficiency in these areas.

Duration of Treatment—The duration of treatment ranged from 6 to 20 months, with a mean of 11 months.

METHOD

After thorough neurological studies, the children were evaluated to determine their disabilities in functional terms. An outpatient program of neurological organization was then prescribed and taught to the parents. The parents were required to carry out the program exactly as prescribed. The children's course was reviewed by the team on an average of every two months, and treatment changes were made to correspond to new developmental levels of accomplishment. The treatment consisted of two types.

Treatment Type I—All nonwalking children (56) were required to spend all day on the floor in the prone position and were encouraged to crawl (prone method) or creep (hand-knee method) when that level of accomplishment was possible. The only permissible exceptions were to feed, love, and treat the child. This increased the opportunity for the reproduction of the normal functional-positional situation of a healthy child during the first 13 months of life.

Treatment Type II—In each case, at that level of accomplishment at which pathology precluded the child's advancement to the next developmental stage, a specific pattern of activity was prescribed which passively imposed on the central nervous system the functional activity which was normally the responsibility of that damaged brain level. Initially these patterns were in some cases partially, and in other cases completely, those which had been described by Fay.4 As time passed, our team discontinued some of these, modified others, and added those which it believed to be useful. Each of these patterns had its counterpart in the normal developmental growth of a healthy child so well described by Gesell and Amatruda.2 The children were patterned for five minutes, four times daily, seven days a week without exception. The patterns were administered by three adults. One adult turned the head, another moved the right arm and leg, and the third moved the left arm and leg. The patterns were to be performed smoothly and rhythmically at all levels.

Activity Pattern I (Homolateral): Children who could not crawl (44) and

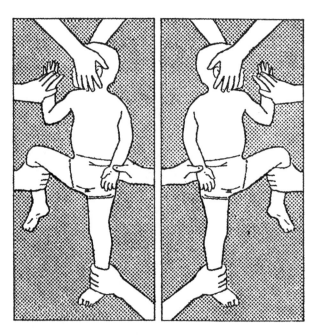

Homolateral Patterning: demonstration of pattern of activity in treatment of children with severe brain injuries who cannot crawl.

FIGURE 31

those who crawled below cross-pattern level (7) were patterned in the homolateral pattern, which was accomplished by one adult turning the head while the adult on the side to which the head was turned flexed the arm and leg. The adult on the opposite side extended both limbs. As the head was turned, the flexed limbs extended while the extended limbs flexed (Fig. 31).

Activity Pattern II (Cross Pattern): Children who could crawl in cross pattern or who could creep (5) were patterned in cross pattern, which was accomplished by one adult turning the head, while the adult on the side toward which the head was turned flexed the arm and extended the leg. The adult on the opposite side extended the arm and flexed the leg. When the head was turned, the position of the limbs was reversed (Fig. 32).

Activity Pattern III (Cross Pattern): Children who walked but poorly (20) were also patterned at the cross-pattern level.

Treatment for Neurological Organization—To enhance neurological

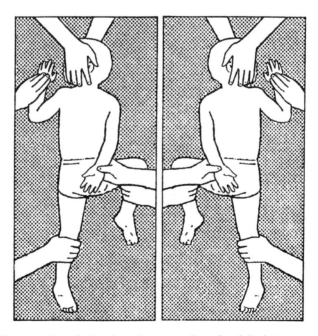

Cross-pattern Patterning: demonstration of activity in treatment of children who can crawl or creep, or walk but poorly.

FIGURE 32

organization, the children were evaluated in the light of the functions described below, and a treatment program was devised. The program included the following stages: 1. When tests showed sensory losses or when results of tests were indefinite due to communication problems, the children were placed on a program of sensory stimulation which included application of heat and cold, brushing, pinching, and establishment of body image appreciation by letting the child experience the relationship between his hand and his face, his hand and his mother's face, and similar relationships. 2. As each child reached the point where laterality influenced neurological organization, a program to establish dominance was instituted. 3. A breathing program to improve vital capacity was prescribed. All other therapy and use of mechanical aids were discontinued, except for anticonvulsant medication when indicated.

TABLE 2.

Level	Children at Beginning of Study		Children at End of Study	
	No.	%	No.	%
0	20	26.3	0	0.0
1	17	22.4	0	0.0
2	2	2.6	6	7.9
3	5	6.6	9	11.8
4	4	5.3	4	5.3
5	3	3.9	5	6.6
6	2	2.6	5	6.6
7	1	1.4	3	3.9
8	2	.6	0	0.0
9	0	0.0	1	1.3
10	0	0.0	8	10.5
11	0	0.0	4	5.3
12	20	26.3	7	9.2
13	0	0.0	24	31.6
Total	76	100.0	76	100.0

FIGURE 33

RESULTS

The results were evaluated according to the following categories: (1) global results, (2) results in the light of chronological age, (3) results in the light of the individual disposition of each patient, and (4) results in the light of the functional level at the onset of the program.

Global Results—The mean improvement of mobility was 4.2 levels. The mean level of mobility was 4.4 at the beginning of the program and 8.6 at the end of the program. The range of improvement was 0 to 13 levels. If we consider perfect walking the potential for every child, the group achieved 51% of this goal (Table 2 and Fig. 33).

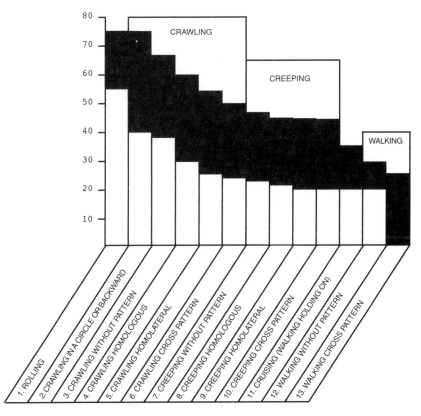

Graphic presentation of results, in terms of mobility levels, of treatment of children with severe brain injuries.

FIGURE 34

The following findings are of interest: Of the 20 children unable to move and the 17 unable to walk, none remained at these stages. Twelve children were ready to walk at the end of the study. Eight were creeping cross pattern (level 10), and four were holding onto objects (level 11).

Eight of the group who could walk initially improved significantly in their walking but did not become perfect and, therefore, could not be considered as having increased their functional competence by one level. All but two of the other children improved by one or more levels.

Eleven children learned to walk completely independently. All but two of these had begun treatment at, or before, two years of age, and all achieved completely independent walking in less than 12 months of treatment. The functional level of this group at the beginning of the study was virtually the same as the level of the other 65 children. The entire group mean level at the outset was 4.4, compared with a mean of 4.1 for this group of 11 who learned to walk independently.

Only six children were discharged, all of whom had learned to walk perfectly; three of these had been walking poorly and three had been unable to walk at the beginning of the program. The other 8 who had learned to walk and the other 17 who had improved in walking were not discharged because of residual problems in speech or behavior.

Results in Light of Chronological Age—The children were separated into three age groups of developmental significance for purposes of evaluation. There was no significant difference of mean improvement among the three different age groups (Table 3).

Individual Results in Light of Functional Level at Beginning of Study—An analysis of the original level-ultimate level disposition of each case indicates an over-all improvement of 4.1 levels within the study. The improvement in individual patients is shown in Table 4.

Rate of Improvement in Light of Functional Level at Beginning of Study—The levels of improvement were evaluated by analysis of 13 levels in terms of functional components (Table 5).

COMMENT

We found significant improvement when we compared the results of the classic procedures we had previously followed with the results of the procedures described above. It is our opinion that the significance of the difference tends to corroborate the validity of the hypothesis set up as the theoretical basis of the program.

TABLE 3.*

Improvement

No.	Age, Mo.	In Stages, Mean	Maximum Possible	% of Potential Achieved
16 .... Under 18		5.0	10.8	46
41 .... 18 to 36		4.1	8.2	50
19 .... Over 36		3.2	6.7	47

*Numerical representations correspond to 13 levels of development described above.

FIGURE 35

These procedures are based on the premise that certain brain levels, i.e., pons, midbrain, and cortex, have separate, consecutive responsibilities in terms of mobility. The goal of these procedures (neurological organization) is to create a climate in which a brain-injured child may develop and utilize those brain levels which are uninjured as they are developed in the normal child concurrent with myelinization during the first 18 months of life.[6]

We have observed that the opportunities to crawl and creep are rarely accorded to the brain-injured child. Great emphasis should be placed on permitting the brain-injured child to remain on the floor, which Gesell and co-workers have described as the normal child's "athletic field," thus giving the child an opportunity to utilize and exploit uninjured brain levels and achieve the functions for which such brain levels are responsible.

After neurological examination and testing had established the level of brain injury, we imposed on the child's central nervous system patterns of activity which have as their goal the reproduction of normal activities which would have been the product of the injured brain level had it not been injured. The pattern aspect of the procedure was achieved after a study and modification of Fay's work with the brain-injured child and Gesell's work with the normal child and was then integrated into the procedure developed by us.

It is our opinion that to be successful in such a program, the procedure must be carried out "wholistically." While we placed varying emphasis upon the importance of different areas within the program, it was our

TABLE 4.

Developmental Level															
No. of Children in Each at		Level at End of Study													
No.	Beginning	0	1	2	3	4	5	6	7	8	9	10	11	12	13
0	20	..	..	5	4	3	2	..	1	..	1	1	..	1	2
1	17	..	..	2	1	1	2	4	1	..	..	4	2	..	..
2	2	..	..	..	1	..	..	..	..	..	..	1	..	..	..
3	5	..	..	..	2	..	1	1	..	..	..	1	..	..	..
4	4	..	..	..	..	..	..	..	..	..	..	..	2	2	..
5	3	..	..	..	..	..	..	..	1	..	..	..	..	1	1
6	2	..	..	..	..	..	..	..	..	..	..	..	..	2	..
7	1	..	..	..	..	..	..	..	..	..	..	1	..	..	..
8	2	..	..	..	..	..	..	..	..	..	..	..	..	..	2
9		..	..	..	..	..	..	..	..	..	..	..	..	..	..
10		..	..	..	..	..	..	..	..	..	..	..	..	..	..
11		..	..	..	..	..	..	..	..	..	..	..	..	..	..
12	20	..	..	..	..	..	..	..	..	..	..	..	..	8	12
13		..	..	..	..	..	..	..	..	..	..	..	..	..	..
Totals	76	..	..	7	8	4	5	5	3	..	1	8	4	14	17

FIGURE 36

experience that success could not be achieved by using the components of the program in isolation.

We believe that the program must include: (*a*) the opportunity for the brain-injured child to spend prolonged periods on the floor in the prone or quadruped position, so that he may crawl or creep in order to utilize uninjured brain areas in physiological development. Given this opportunity, the brain-injured child may advance several developmental levels unaided; (*b*) the utilization of patterns of activity administered passively to a child which reproduce the mobility functions for which injured brain levels are responsible; (*c*) a program of sensory stimulation to make the child body-conscious in terms of position sense and proprioception. We believe that sensory reception is a prerequisite to motor expression; (*d*) a program of establishing cortical hemispheric dominance through the development of

TABLE 5*

Functional Level	Improvement		
	In Levels, Mean	Maximum Possible	**% of** Potential Achievement
No mobility	5.8	13.0	43
Rolling	5.7	12.0	47
Circling	4.5	11.0	45
Moving straight without pattern	2.4	10.0	24
Crawling	6.5	8.0	80
Creeping	4.3	5.3	80
Walking	0.8	1.0	80

*Numerical representations correspond to 13 stages of development described above.

FIGURE 37

unilateral handedness, footedness, and "eyedness." This was instituted when a lack of neurological organization at this level so indicated;7 and (e) the institution of a breathing program to achieve the maximal vital capacity, since, in our experience, we had observed the restricted vital capacity and the recurrence of respiratory difficulties in many brain-injured children.

While we think that this program resulted in benefits to the children studied in the areas of language and affect, we confined this report to results achieved in terms of mobility. A later report will deal with the results achieved in other areas by this program of neurological organization.

We wish to stress the fact that no child was eliminated from the study due to initial lack of affect or mobility. It can be observed from the facts presented that many of the children, when initially evaluated, showed little affect and no mobility, and that a large number of them made significant progress. It should also be stressed that during the study all other programs of therapy or habilitation were discontinued and that no mechanical aids, such as braces or crutches, were used.

We place emphasis upon the fact that the children studied were evaluated and treated with reference to the central neurological lesion rather than upon the symptomatic results of the central lesion.

It is our opinion that the results of this study, when compared with the results of our previous work, are sufficiently encouraging to warrant an expanded and continued study of these procedures.

We do not believe that all the techniques which would be useful in achieving neurological organization have been developed by this study. We think that many additional techniques may be developed which could speed the process of habilitation of children with severe brain injuries and perhaps increase the number of types of brain injuries which can be treated. Later reports will deal with the results of studies being conducted at the time of writing.

SUMMARY

A two-year study was conducted on 76 brain-injured children. Its goal was to determine whether a program aimed at neurological organization would be productive of greater results in terms of mobility than we had previously achieved by more classic therapy.

The children studied were both evaluated and treated in light of their central neurological lesions in a program which we had devised to utilize undamaged brain levels to achieve the physiological functions for which such levels are responsible and to assist children at damaged brain levels in achieving function, as far as possible, by means of a program designed to reproduce normal activity. The preliminary results of this study are encouraging. Further studies of these procedures will be undertaken.

8801 Stenton Ave. (18) (Dr. R. J. Doman).

Thanks are due to Lieut. Col. Anthony R. Flores (MSC), Rosemary Warnock, R.N., and Lindley C. Boyer, staff members of the Children's Clinic, whose work and technical assistance made this study possible. Mr. Lloyd P. Wells, staff photographer, made all photographs necessary to this study.

Reprinted from the *Journal of The American Medical Association,*
September 17, 1960, Vol. 174, pp. 257-62,

REFERENCES

1. Abbott, M. *Syllabus of Cerebral Palsy Treatment Techniques.* New York: College of Physicians and Surgeons, Columbia University, May 1953, p. 10.

2. Gesell, A. L., and Amatruda, C. S. *Developmental Diagnosis: Normal and Abnormal Child Development,* Ed. 2. New York: Harper & Brothers, 1947, Chap. 11.

3. Gesell, A. L., and others. *Infant and Child in Culture of Today: Guidance of Development in Home and Nursery School.* New York: Harper & Brothers, 1943.

4. Fay, T. "Neurophysical Aspects of Therapy in Cerebral Palsy," *Archives of Physical Medicine.* 29:327-34 (June) 1948.

5. Fay, T. "Origin of Human Movement," *American Journal of Psychiatry,* III: 644-52 (March) 1955.

6. Thomas, A., and Dargassies, S. A. *Etudes neurologiques sur le nouveau-né et le jeune nourrisson.* Paris: Masson, 1952.

7. Delacato, C. H. *Treatment and Prevention of Reading Problems: (Neuro-Psychological Approach).* Springfield, Ill.: Charles C. Thomas, Publisher, 1959.

THE INCLINED FLOOR
INSTRUCTIONS

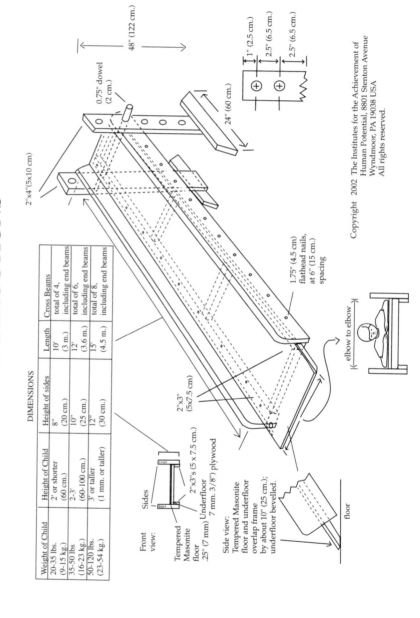

DIMENSIONS

Weight of Child	Height of Child	Height of sides	Length	Cross Beams
20-35 lbs. (9-15 kg.)	2' or shorter (60 cm.)	8" (20 cm.)	10' (3 m.)	total of 4, including end beams
35-50 lbs (16-23 kg.)	2-3' (60-100 cm.)	10" (25 cm.)	12' (3.6 m.)	total of 6, including end beams
50-120 lbs. (23-54 kg.)	3' or taller (1 mm. or taller)	12" (30 cm.)	15' (4.5 m.)	total of 8, including end beams

2"x4"(5x10 cm)

0.75" dowel (2 cm.)

48" (122 cm.)

24" (60 cm.)

1" (2.5 cm.)
2.5" (6.5 cm.)
2.5" (6.5 cm.)

1.75" (4.5 cm) flathead nails, at 6' (15 cm.) spacing

Front view:

Sides

Tempered Masonite floor
.25" (7 mm)

2"x3"s (5 x 7.5 cm.)
Underfloor
7 mm. 3/8") plywood

Side view:
Tempered Masonite floor and underfloor overlap frame by about 10" (25 cm.); underfloor bevelled.

2"x3" (5x7.5 cm)

elbow to elbow

floor

CREDITS

1940-1950

Mae Blackburn
Glenn Doman
Katie Doman
Robert Doman, M.D.
Temple Fay, M.D.

1950-1960

Eleanor Borden
Lindley C. Boyer
Rosemary Boyle
Claude Cheek
Daniel Cianchetta
Hugh Clarke
Mr. A. Vinton Clarke
Mrs. A. Vinton Clarke
Jay Cooke
Carl H. Delacato
Greta Erdtmann
Anthony R. Flores
Elizabeth Galbraith
George Leader
Alice Letchworth
Edward B. LeWinn
Sigmund LeWinn
Betty Marsh
Frank D. McCormick
Martin Palmer
Jean Peters
Howard Peters
Charles Peterson
Florence Sharp
John Tini

José Carlos Lobo Veras
Lourdes Lobo Veras
Raymundo Veras, M.D.
Chatham R. Wheat, III
Thomas R. White

1960 to 1970

Ferris Alger
J. Michael Armentrout
Sandra Brown
Walter Burke
Frank Cliffe
Patrick Coyne
Marjorie Dart
Raymond Dart, M.D.
Janet Doman
Maria Drea
Connie Ellopoulos
Fred Erdtmann
Mr. Rogers Follansbee
Mrs. Rogers Follansbee
Rosalie Gabriel
Dave Garroway
Margaret George
Claire Gold
Leland Green, M.D.
Harry Guenther
Neil Harvey
Dr. and Mrs. Tohru Higashi
Max Karpin, M.D.
Gretchen Kerr
David Krech
Elaine Lee

Pearl LeWinn
William MacNutt
Robert Magee
Doris Magee
Mr. and Mrs. Wm. McMillan
Peter Moran
Robert Morris
Selma O'Hara
Nathan Rachmel
Richard Ransom
Harriet Richman
Cathy Ruhling
Arthur Sandler
Jacqueline Schweighauser
Eduardo Sequeiros, M.D.
Evan Thomas, M.D.
Vicki Thornber
Meg Tyson
Lloyd Wells
William Wells
Bertha White
Roselise Wilkinson, M.D.
James Wolf

1970 to 1980

Susan Aisen
Ann Ball
Barbara Barstow
Frank Caputo
Janet Caputo
Beatriz Carrancedo
Leá Cascapera
Rose Craddock

Adelle Davis
Helen Derr
Robert Derr
Douglas Doman
Rosalind Klein Doman
Joseph Gay
Bruce Hagy
Stanley Holt
Masaru Ibuka
Vanessa Ingram
Fumikatsu Inoue
Prof. Isao Ishii
James Kaliss
Walter Krogman
William Lavorgna
Grace Luft
Claire Mapow
Kaname Matsuzawa
Harold McCuen
James McGeehan
Liza Minnelli
Daniel Melcher
Margaret Melcher
Sam Metzger
Miki Nakayachi
Mitsue Noguchi
Lourdinha Veras Norton
Ralph Pelligra
Dawn Price
Judy Reif
Leia Coelho Reilly
Gloria Rittenhouse
Marilyn Rogers
Susumu Samoto
Jerry Schwartz
Dorothy Spady
Prof. Shinichi Suzuki
Teruki Uemura
Conceicão Veras
Herbert Vykukal

1980 to Present

Donald Barnhouse
Jill Bell

Jeffrey Bland
Pio Bonvicini
Connie Breyer
Kathleen Brown
Tammy Cadden
Susan Cameron
Jennifer Myers-Canepa
Polo Canepa
Gratziano Ceccanti
Lucia Cellucci
Cynthia Cobucci
Zelda Coleman
Dot Coulston
Barbara Cutts
Monchita de Cosio
Mihai Dimancescu, M.D.
Rumiko Ion Doman
Philomena Fishbourne
Gisela Fitzner
Janet Gauger
Guido Giuntini
Stewart Graham
Elisa Guerra de Rodriguez
Nigel Hawthorne
Atsushi Higa, M.D.
Sherman Hines
Hachiro Hirose
Eliane Hollanda
Shirley Hollis
Nest Holvey
Milan Hurtak
Masako Ichikawa
William Johntz
Yukie Kamino
Vanita Khandpur
Futami Kitagawa
Richard Klich
Kathryn Knell
Teruko Koide
Hiroshi Kojima
Yoshiki Kumagai
Pearl Lynch
Philip Maffetone
Linda Maletta

Denise Malkowicz, M.D.
Rogelio Marty
Wayne Matson
Gisela Melignano-Blanco
Julian Meyer
James Miller
Janet Mills
Aline Miranda, M.D.
Bertino Miranda, M.D.
Jerold Morantz
Naoko Mori
Yuko Mori
William Mueller
Alison Myers
Chip Myers
Ginette Myers
Katharine Myers
Nati Tenacio Myers
Richard Norton
Lori O'Connor
Olivia Fernandes Pelligra
Diane Phillips
Philip Phillips
Harriet Pinsker
Juanita Richards
Luzia Rodriguez
Darlene Ross
Colleen Brown Rumpf
Walter Schmitt
Marcella Serafin
Masato Shibuya, M.D.
Margaret Shields
Dolores Simonetta
Regina Sogno
Allan Sosin, M.D.
Mary Standley
Regina Texeira
Coralee Thompson, M.D.
Ernesto Vasquez, M.D.
Marsha Walsh
Li Wang
Christopher Weidig
Noriko Yamada
Jill Zimmerman

BIBLIOGRAPHY

Dart, Raymond, M.D.: *Adventures with the Missing Link* (Philadelphia, PA.: The Better Baby Press, 1982; Great Britain: Hamish Hamilton, Ltd., 1959.)

Diamond, Marian Cleeves, Ph.D.: *Enriching Heredity, The Impact of the Environment on the Anatomy of the Brain* (New York, NY: The Free Press, 1988.)

Doman, Glenn, C.B.D., et al.: *The Non-Surgical, Central Approach to the Problem,* Part I (The first in a series of papers presented before the Eastern Pennsylvania Group of the American Physical Therapy Association at Lankenau Hospital, Philadelphia, PA, Winter, 1957.)

Doman, Glenn, C.B.D., et al.: *The Non-Surgical, Central Approach to the Problem,* Part II, *Reflex Therapy* (The second in a series of papers presented before the Eastern Pennsylvania Group of APTA at Lankenau Hospital, Philadelphia, PA., Winter, 1957.)

Doman, Glenn, C.B.D.: *How To Teach Your Baby To Read* (New York, NY, Philadelphia, PA: The Better Baby Press, 1986; Avery Publishing Group, 1993; The Gentle Revolution Press, 2002.)

Doman, Glenn, C.B.D., et al.: *Neurological Organization, The Basis for Learning* (Helmuth J., Learning Disorders, Seattle Special Child Publications, 1966.)

Doman, Glenn, C.B.D.: *How To Teach Your Baby Math* (New York, NY: Simon & Schuster, 1979, Avery Publishing Group, 1993; The Gentle Revolution Press, 2001.)

Doman, Glenn, C.B.D.; Armentrout, Michael: *The Universal Multiplication of Intelligence* (Philadelphia, PA: The Better Baby Press, 1980.)

Doman, Glenn, C.B.D., et al.: *The Encyclopedia of Human Intelligence* (Philadelphia, PA: The Better Baby Press, 1985.)

Doman, Glenn, C.B.D.: *The Philosophy of the Treatment of Brain-Injured Children Utilizing Principles of Neurological Organization* (Helmuth J., Learning Disorders, Seattle Special Child Publications, 1966.)

Doman, Glenn, C.B.D.: *What To Do About Your Brain-Injured Child* (New York, NY: Doubleday, 1974; Philadelphia, PA.: The Better Baby Press, 1989; Avery Publishing Group, 1993; The Gentle Revolution Press, 2003.)

*Doman, Glenn, C.B.D., et al.: *Temple Fay Revisited: The Other Side of a Fit* (The In-Report, Vol. V, No. 6, November/December, 1977.)

Doman, Glenn, C.B.D.: *How To Multiply Your Baby's Intelligence* (New York, NY: Doubleday, 1984; Avery Publishing Group, 1993; The Gentle Revolution Press, 2001.)

*Doman, Glenn, I.A.C.B.D.; Wilkinson, Roselise H., M.D.; Pelligra, Ralph, M.D.: *The Non-Surgical, Centrally Directed Approach to the Treatment of Profoundly and Severely Brain-Injured Children* (A paper presented to the Japanese Society for Pediatric Neurosurgery, Kurume, Japan, May 11, 1988.)

Doman, Glenn, I.A.C.B.D.; Doman, Douglas M.; Hagy, Bruce: *How To Teach Your Baby To Be Physically Superb* (Philadelphia, PA: The Better Baby Press, 1988.)

*Doman, Glenn, I.A.C.B.D.; Wilkinson, Roselise H., M.D.; Pelligra, Ralph, M.D.: *Child Brain Development from the Pre-Stone Age Children of Brazil's Xingu to the Renaissance Children of the Twenty-First Century* (A paper presented to The Instituto Piaget, Lisboa, Portugal, 1989.)

Doman, Glenn, C.B.D.: *How To Give Your Baby Encyclopedic Knowledge* (Philadelphia, PA: The Better Baby Press, 1984; Avery Publishing

Group, 1993; The Gentle Revolution Press, 2001.)

*Doman, Glenn, I.A.C.B.D.: *Reading and Writing as a Function of the Brain* (A presentation to the symposium on The Future of Writing and Multi-Lingualism, Lausanne, Switzerland, June 1991.)

*Doman, Glenn, I.A.C.B.D.: *The Gentle Revolution* (A paper presented to The International Congress for Early Education, Vitoria, Spain, December 1991.)

Doman, Glenn, I.A.C.B.D.; Wilkinson, Roselise H., M.D.; Dimancescu, Mihai, M.D.; Pelligra, Ralph, M.D.: *The Effect of Intense Multi-sensory Stimulation on Coma Arousal and Recovery* (Neuropsychological Rehabilitation, 1993, 3 (2) 203-212.)

*Doman, Glenn, I.A.C.B.D.: *Is It Good To Be Brain-Injured or Are Well Children as Well as They Are Able to Be? And Should Be?* (A lecture at The University of California at Berkeley to the Second Annual Symposium on the Human Brain; Implications of Breakthroughs for Teachers and Parents, October 7-8, 1995.)

Doman, Glenn, I.A.C.B.D.; LeWinn, Edward, M.D.; Dimancescu, Mihai, M.D.; Wilkinson, Roselise, M.D.: *The Developmental Profile: A Quantitative Measure of Neurologic Development in Brain-Injured and Normal Children* (Clinical Practice of Alternative Medicine, Spring 2000).

Doman, Robert J., M.D.; Doman, Glenn, C.D.B.: *A Useful Aid in Early Paraplegia Training* (The Physical Therapy Review, Vol. 36, No. 9, September 1956.)

Doman, Robert J., M.D., et al.: *Children with Severe Brain Injuries; Neurological Organization in Terms of Mobility* (Journal of the American Medical Association, 174: 257-262, 1960.)

Fay, Temple: *Neurophysical Aspects of Therapy in Cerebral Palsy, The Outcome of 177 Patients, 74 Totally Untreated* (Pediatrics, 29: 605, 1962.)

*Green, Leland J., M.D.: *An Ill Wind...* (A discussion on air ionization and its effect on our environment; Proceedings, 12th Annual Meeting, World Organization for Human Potential, Philadelphia, PA, May 10, 1979.)

Gunby, Phil, C.B.D.: *NASA Research Fosters Rehabilitative Device* (The Journal of The American Medical Association, Vol. 246, No. 16, October 16, 1981.)

Harvey, Neil, Ph.D., C.B.D.: *The Relationship Between Stanford-Binet Test Scores and The Institutes Developmental Profile Scores Achieved by Brain-Injured Children* (A master's thesis on file at the University of Pennsylvania, Philadelphia, PA, 1965.)

Harvey, Neil, Ph.D., C.B.D.: *Kids Who Start Ahead Stay Ahead* (New York, NY: Avery Publishing Group, 1994.)

*Harvey, Neil, Ph.D., C.B.D.: *Needed for the Eighties: A Mandate for Higher Order Literacy* (The In-Report, Vol. IX, No. 3, May/June 1981.)

*Lee, Elaine, C.B.D.; Doman, Glenn, C.B.D.; Kerr, Gretchen, C.B.D.: *The Practical Results of a Program of Neurological Organization of The Institutes for the Achievement of Human Potential* (A report of the results obtained with 170 children; Proceedings, 4th Annual Meeting, World Organization for Human Potential, Appendix K, May 1971.)

*LeWinn, Edward B., M.D.: *Report of Effect of Treatment Based on Principles of Neurological Organization on Certain Physical Measurements in Brain-Injured Children* (Proceedings, 4th Annual Meeting, World Organization for Human Potential, Appendix K, May 1971.)

LeWinn, Edward B., M.D.: *Effect of Environment Influence on Human Behavorial Development* (New York State Journal of Medicine, December 15, 1967.)

LeWinn, Edward B., M.D.; Dimancescu, Mihai D., M.D.: *Environmental Deprivation and Enrichment in Coma* (The Lancet, July 15, 1978.)

LeWinn, Edward B., M.D.: *The Coma Arousal Team: Procedures for the Patient's Professional Attendants and for His Family* (Royal Society of Health Journal, February 1980.)

LeWinn, Edward B., M.D.: *The Measurement of Neurological Development*

(International Journal of Neuropsychiatry, Vol. 3, No. 2, 1967.)

LeWinn, Edward B., M.D.: *Human Neurological Organization* (Springfield, IL: Charles C. Thomas, 1969.)

*LeWinn, Edward B., M.D.; Thomas, W., M.D.: *Some Physical Characteristics of Brain-Injured Children—Chest Circumference* (A report on a population of 278 brain-injured children; Human Potential, Vol. 3, 1970.)

LeWinn, Edward B., M.D.: *The Accident Process* (Spectator, November 1975.)

*LeWinn, Edward B., M.D.: *The Young Patient in Coma: A Statement to Our Parents* (The In-Report, Vol. IV, No. 4, September/October, 1976.)

*LeWinn, Edward B., M.D.: *A Bill of Particulars on Seizures and on Discontinuing Anticonvulsant Drugs* (The In-Report, Vol. V, No. 4, July/August 1977.)

LeWinn, Edward B., M.D.: *Physiological Factors in Childhood Epilepsy* (Epilepsia 21: 425-432, 1980.)

LeWinn, Edward B., M.D.: *Coma Arousal* (New York, NY: Doubleday, 1982.)

Morrow, James, Ph.D.: *Mind Meets Brain, The Developmental Theories of Piaget and Doman* (Harvard University, 1970.)

Pelligra, Ralph, M.D.; Matson, Wayne R., Ph.D.; Norton, Richard D.; Wilkinson, Roselise H., M.D.: *Rett's Syndrome: Stimulation of Endogenous Biogenic Amines* (Neuropediatrics 23: 131-137, 1992).

Perlish, Harvey N., Ph.D.: *An Investigation of the Effectiveness of a Television Reading Program, Along with Parental Home Assistance, In Helping Three-Year-Old Children Learn to Read* (A study based upon the work of Glenn Doman of The Institutes for the Achievement of Human Potential, Philadelphia: A Doctoral Dissertation, Frederick B. Davis,

Ed.D., Dissertation Supervisor; Philadelphia, PA, University of Pennsylvania, 1968. Microfiche—Ann Arbor, MI, 1968.

Taylor, Raymond G., Jr., Ed.D.: *Statistical Research at The Institutes for the Achievement of Human Potential: Measurement of Neurological Development* (Human Potential, Vol. I, No. 2, pp. 75-84, 1968.)

Thomas, Evan W., M.D.: *Public Health and the Brain-Injured* (Congressional Record, Subcommittee on Labor, Health and Education, Welfare, United States Senate, Washington, D.C., pp. 2394-2399, 1965.)

Thomas, Evan W., M.D.: *Doman-Delacato Therapeutic Programme* (Medical World, Vol. 105, No. 1, January 1967.)

Thomas, Evan W., M.D.: *Brain-Injured Children* (Springfield, IL: Charles C. Thomas, 1969.)

Veras, Raymundo, M.D.: *Children of Dreams, Children of Hope* (Chicago, IL: Henry Regnery Company, 1975.)

*Wilkinson, Roselise H., M.D.: *Results of Anticonvulsant Medication Elimination in 71 Children* (Proceedings, 12th Annual Meeting, World Organization for Human Potential, May 1971.)

*Wilkinson, Roselise H., M.D.: *Study of the Use of Megadose Vitamins in Affecting Behavior and Performance: Results in 170 Children* (Proceedings, 4th Annual Meeting, World Organization for Human Potential, Appendix J, May 4, 1971.)

Wolf, James M., Ed.D.: *Temple Fay, M.D., Progenitor of the Doman-Delacato Treatment Procedures* (Springfield, IL: Charles C. Thomas, 1968.)

Wolf, James M., Ed.D.; Anderson, Robert M., Ed.D.: *The Multiple-Handicapped Child* (Springfield, IL: Charles C. Thomas, 1970.)

Wolf, James M., Ed.D.: *The Results of Treatment in Cerebral Palsy* (Springfield, IL: Charles C. Thomas, 1970).

* *Available from The Institutes for the Achievement of Human Potential*

INDEX

Examining Issues Through POLITICAL CARTOONS

Terrorism

Examining Issues Through
POLITICAL CARTOONS

Terrorism

Titles in the Examining Issues Through Political Cartoons series include:

EXAMINING ISSUES THROUGH
POLITICAL CARTOONS

Terrorism

Edited by William Dudley

Daniel Leone, *President*
Bonnie Szumski, *Publisher*
Scott Barbour, *Managing Editor*

**GREENHAVEN
PRESS®**

THOMSON
—————★—————™
GALE

San Diego • Detroit • New York • San Francisco • Cleveland
New Haven, Conn. • Waterville, Maine • London • Munich

LIBRARY OF CONGRESS CATALOGING-IN-PUBLICATION DATA

Terrorism / William Dudley, book editor.
    p. cm. — (Examining issues through political cartoons)
Includes bibliographical references and index.
ISBN 0-7377-1322-4 (lib. : alk. paper) — ISBN 0-7377-1323-2 (pbk. : alk. paper)
    1. September 11 terrorist attacks, 2001—Caricatures and cartoons. 2. War on terrorism, 2001—Caricatures and cartoons. 3. Terrorism—Caricatures and cartoons.
I. Dudley, William, 1964–   . II. Series.

HV6432 .T443 2003
973.931'022'2—dc21

                       2002024580

Contents

Foreword

Political cartoons, also called editorial cartoons, are drawings that do what editorials do with words—express an opinion about a newsworthy event or person. They typically appear in the opinion pages of newspapers, sometimes in support of that day's written editorial, but more often making their own comment on the day's events. Political cartoons first gained widespread popularity in Great Britain and the United States in the 1800s when engravings and other drawings skewering political figures were fashionable in illustrated newspapers and comic magazines. By the beginning of the 1900s, editorial cartoons were an established feature of daily newspapers. Today, they can be found throughout the globe in newspapers, magazines, and online publications and the Internet.

Art Wood, both a cartoonist and a collector of cartoons, writes in his book *Great Cartoonists and Their Art:*

> Day in and day out the cartoonist mirrors history; he reduces complex facts into understandable and artistic terminology. He is a political commentator and at the same time an artist.

The distillation of ideas into images is what makes political cartoons a valuable resource for studying social and historical topics. Editorial cartoons have a point to express. Analyzing them involves determining both what the cartoon's point is and how it was made.

Sometimes, the point made by the cartoon may be one that the reader disagrees with, or considers offensive. Such cartoons expose readers to new ideas and thereby challenge them to analyze and question their own opinions and assumptions. In some extreme cases, cartoons provide vivid examples of the thoughts that lie behind heinous acts; for example, the cartoons created by the Nazis illustrate the anti-Semitism that led to the mass persecution of Jews.

Examining controversial ideas is but one way the study of political cartoons can enhance and develop critical thinking skills. Another aspect to cartoons is that they can use symbols to make their point quickly. For example, in a cartoon in *Euthanasia*, Chuck Asay depicts supporters of a legal "right to die" by assisted suicide as vultures. Vultures are birds that eat dead and dying animals and are often a symbol of repulsive and cowardly predators who take advantage of those who have met misfortune or are vulnerable. The reader can infer that Asay is expressing his opposition to physician-assisted suicide by suggesting that its supporters are just as loathsome as vultures. Asay thus makes his point through a quick symbolic association.

An important part of critical thinking is examining ideas and arguments in their historical context. Political cartoonists (reasonably) assume that the typical reader of a newspaper's editorial page already has a basic knowledge of current issues and newsworthy people. Understanding and appreciating political cartoons often requires such knowledge, as well as a familiarity with common icons and symbolic figures (such as Uncle Sam's representing the United States). The need for contextual information becomes especially apparent in historical cartoons. For example, although most people know who Adolf Hitler is, a lack of familiarity with other German political figures of the 1930s may create difficulty in fully understanding cartoons about Nazi Germany made in that era.

Providing such contextual information is one important way that Greenhaven's Examining Issues Through Political Cartoons series seeks to make this unique and revealing resource conveniently accessible to students. Each volume presents a representative and diverse collection of political cartoons focusing on a particular current or historical topic. An introductory essay provides a general overview of the subject matter. Each cartoon is then presented with accompanying information including facts about the cartoonist and information and commentary on the cartoon itself. Finally, each volume contains additional informational resources, including listings of books, articles, and websites; an index; and (for historical topics) a chronology of events. Taken together, the contents of each anthology constitute an amusing and informative resource for students of historical and social topics.

Introduction

The events and images of September 11, 2001, will not be soon forgotten by those who witnessed them. On that day, two jet passenger planes were hijacked by terrorists and flown into the Twin Towers of the World Trade Center (WTC) in New York City. The planes, laden with jet fuel, created huge fires that led to the collapse of the towers less than two hours later. Another hijacked plane crashed into the Pentagon in Washington, D.C., causing a section of that building to collapse. A fourth plane crashed in rural Pennsylvania. Shocked television viewers in America and other nations watched both live and recorded images of planes crashing into the WTC, people jumping out of the buildings, the collapse of the skyscrapers, and the burning Pentagon. The two towers, 110 stories tall, were the highest structures in New York City and the workplace for fifty thousand people. The Pentagon, a massive landmark in its own right, is the headquarters for America's military establishment. The targeted buildings were widely recognized symbols of U.S. political and economic power.

While the first aircraft crash could possibly have been seen as a freak accident, it was clear when the second plane crashed that America was under a deliberate attack. The national landscape changed. Wall Street ceased operations. Planes were grounded and air travel suspended, stranding thousands of travelers. Previous domestic political debates and news stories were swept aside as President George W. Bush pledged to a stunned citizenry to wipe out terrorism in "the first war of the twenty-first century." Volunteers rushed to help rescue workers in New York and Washington. People grieved over those killed, the precise number of which would not be known for months.

The feelings and reactions Americans shared in the hours, days, weeks, and months following September 11, 2001, were deep and visceral. It was a time of great fear and anxiety over whether another attack was coming, a fear that increased in the month of October when several letters containing deadly anthrax powder were mailed to public and media figures. It was a time of deep anger directed at the anonymous suicidal terrorists—and at government and airline officials who failed to stop them. It was a time of heartfelt sorrow for the victims and their families. It was a time of pride celebrating the heroism and compassion of the police officers, rescue workers, and citizens who responded to the calamities (and the air passengers in the fourth flight in Pennsylvania who had apparently foiled the hijackers' plans). For many, it was also a time of a reawakened or strengthened sense of patriotism and community.

It was also a time of grappling anew with the problem of terrorism. Previously considered by many to be a worrisome but distant problem that mostly affected people overseas, terrorism was now seen as a direct and immediate threat to American security and well-being.

Defining Terrorism

The words "terrorist" and "terrorism" were first applied to leaders of the French Revolution in the 1790s who arrested and summarily executed thousands of people in order to maintain their political power by weeding out "traitors" and creating an atmosphere of fear in order to maintain their political power. The term has since been used to describe the actions of those who engage in violence or threats of violence in an attempt to instill fear in a community and to thus achieve political goals. Terrorist actions could include the assassination of public figures, the kidnapping of diplomats and other foreigners, bombings that kill civilians, airplane hijackings, and other atrocities that are designed to create a climate of fear. Terrorist goals can be political (overthrowing a government, achieving political independence of a region or people), religious (the removal or extermination of "infidels"), or a combination of both (the replacement of a secular government with a religious one). The development of more lethal weapons and explosives as well as the rise of the mass media made terrorism a large and recurring problem in past decades.

The Federal Bureau of Investigation (FBI) has defined terrorism as "the unlawful use of force or violence against persons or property . . . in furtherance of political or social objectives." E.S. Heyman defines terrorism as "the use or threat of extraordinary political violence to induce fear, anxiety or alarm in a target audience wider than the immediate symbolic victims." Paul Pillar, a terrorist expert who at one time was deputy head of the CIA's Counterterrorist Center, has proposed four key elements that make terrorism different both from war and from other forms of violent crime:

1. It is premeditated—planned in advance, rather than an impulsive act of rage.

2. It is political—not criminal, like the violence that groups such as the mafia use to get money, but designed to change the existing political order.

3. It is aimed at civilians—not at military targets or combat-ready troops.

4. It is carried out by subnational groups—not by the army of a country.

In recent decades, the Middle East has been the site of much of the world's terrorism. The region is home to a number of fundamentalist Islamic groups fiercely opposed to what they believe are corrupting Western influences in the region and to the existence and actions of Israel, a Jewish state closely allied with the United States. Various Islamic and Palestinian groups, such as Hamas, have carried out suicide bombings and other terrorist attacks against Israel. Countries in the region on the U.S. State Department's official list of states that have sponsored terrorism include Libya, Iran, Iraq, Sudan, and Syria.

America's Experiences with Terrorism Prior to September 11

Americans have in recent decades been frequently targeted by terrorists. The U.S. State Department has stated that 47 percent of terrorist incidents it cataloged in 2000 involved American victims or American property. But most past incidents of terrorism against the United States have occurred outside its borders. Notable past examples include the seizing of 52 American hostages in Iran in

1979, two 1983 suicide car-bomber attacks against the U.S. embassy and marine barracks in Beirut, Lebanon, that killed a total of 258 Americans, and a planted bomb that destroyed Pan Am Flight 103 over Lockerbie, Scotland, in 1988, which was later traced back to agents from Libya. More recently, the U.S. embassies in Kenya and Tanzania, Africa, were bombed by terrorists in 1998, killing 224 people. In 2000 a U.S. Navy destroyer refueling in Yemen, the USS *Cole,* was damaged by terrorists using a bomb-laden boat, killing 17.

The September 11 attacks, however, were not the first time terrorists had struck within America. On February 26, 1993, a van packed with one thousand pounds of explosives was parked in an underground parking garage beneath one of the World Trade Center towers and then detonated. The attack resulted in six fatalities and more than a thousand injuries (most of them smoke inhalation). Within a month, four foreign individuals were arrested for the bombing. Following a six-month trial in federal court, they were each sentenced in 1994 to 240 years in prison. The person believed to be the leader in the attack, Ramzi Yousef, had fled the country, but a few years later he was apprehended in Pakistan and extradited back to the United States, convicted in a federal court, and sentenced to 240 years. The people accused and convicted of the attack were all extremist believers in Islamic fundamentalism. Investigations before and after their trials revealed the existence of a shady network of international terrorist groups that provided logistical and financial support for each other.

Another attack on U.S. soil occurred on April 19, 1995, when a truck bomb exploded outside the Alfred P. Murrah Federal Building in Oklahoma City, ripping an enormous hole in the front half of the building. Many Americans initially wondered whether this, like the attack on the WTC, was carried out by Muslim extremists. In this case, however, the attack, which killed 168 and injured more than 500, could not be blamed on foreign enemies. Two days later, police arrested a young American named Timothy McVeigh, a former soldier who had fought in the Persian Gulf War and had turned to extreme right-wing views. McVeigh and another American were eventually tried and convicted of terrorism; McVeigh was executed in June 2001. In interviews, McVeigh confessed to the bombing and argued that the act was necessary to promote his message that the federal government was the enemy of the American people and that it should be overthrown. "In his mind, it was a military action," one of his lawyers stated on the day McVeigh was executed.

In both 1993 and 1995, Americans reacted with shock, grief, and anger. They debated the foreign and domestic sources of terrorism and how best to prevent it from happening again. Congress did indeed pass several laws designed to improve America's security against terrorism. However, when terrorism burst back onto the scene on September 11, 2001, some expressed disappointment that America had failed to truly learn its lessons from the prior incidents.

The September 11 attacks were unprecedented in their scale and the amount of human life that was lost. Approximately three thousand people, including airline passengers, office workers, and rescue personnel, perished on September 11. The attacks illustrated a trend in terrorism that was evident as the twenty-first century opened—that even as the number of terrorist attacks worldwide was declining, the number of fatalities per attack was rising. This was due both to the use of increasingly larger weapons, such as bombs, and the willingness of some terrorists to sacrifice their own lives.

Who Was Behind September 11?

James F. Hoge and Gideon Rose, editors of *Foreign Affairs*, write in their book *How Did This Happen?* that Americans had entered a new era following September 11:

> The nation awoke that morning to find itself at war. But it was a strange kind of war, one without front lines or massed troops, fought in the shadows against an elusive enemy, without a clear sense of where it would lead or how it would end.

In subsequent weeks, Americans learned some facts about the "elusive enemy" that had attacked them. Many experts suspected that, Oklahoma City notwithstanding, the terrorists were probably foreign in origin. Cell phone calls made by passengers on the fatal flights described the hijackers as being of Middle Eastern appearance. Investigators for the FBI pursued thousands of leads in attempting to find out who was behind the attacks and whether more were planned. Within days, they were able to identify the nineteen passengers that had hijacked the four planes. All were from Middle Eastern countries and had entered the United States illegally or on tourist or student visas. Many had apparently lived in the United States for several years. Suspicion quickly fell on one particular group as having what one reporter described as "the will, wallet, or gall to attack the U.S." That was al-Qaeda (the base), a loose global network of terrorists led by Osama bin Laden.

Bin Laden, like those involved in the 1993 WTC attack, was an adherent of a fundamentalist strain of Islam. He had long been opposed to American soldiers stationed in Saudi Arabia and to American presence and influence in Islamic nations in general. In 1996 bin Laden declared a jihad or holy war, to drive all Americans and other non-Muslim "infidels" from Saudi Arabia and other Islamic countries.

To carry out his aims, bin Laden made use of both his multimillion-dollar personal fortune and his military experience in fighting Soviet Union troops in Afghanistan in the 1980s to create a global terrorist network. Based first in Sudan and then in Afghanistan, al-Qaeda has been blamed for several previous terrorist attacks, including the 1998 African embassy bombings and the attack on the USS *Cole*. In Afghanistan bin Laden forged a close relationship with the nation's fundamentalist Muslim regime—the Taliban. Bin Laden and others espoused the creation of similar Islamic regimes in other nations.

Following September 11, bin Laden at first neither denied nor confirmed involvement with the attacks, although he did express satisfaction with their results. However, months later the American media broadcast a privately shot videotape in which he took credit for planning the September 11 attacks and noted that the total collapse of the towers was an unexpected success in the operation.

The revelations regarding al-Qaeda's involvement in September 11 sparked a national debate over the role the religion of Islam played in inspiring the hijackers to kill so many, including themselves. Some commentators, such as scholar Daniel Pipes, declared that September 11 was the logical culmination of what he called a rising "militant Islam" that "seeks to destroy the United States . . . as presently constituted." Others contend that Islam as practiced by most Muslims is a religion of humanitarianism; they insist that pronouncements by bin Laden and others for war against Western nations do not represent the religion. "The [September 11] attacks had nothing to do with Islam," according to Zahid Bukhari, a fellow at Georgetown University's Center for Muslim-Christian Understanding. President

15

Bush was among those who warned Americans against targeting Muslim Americans for suspicion or vigilante violence.

The American Government Responds

Incidents of vigilante violence against suspected Muslims—and condemnation of such acts by the American government—were just part of the response of the American people and the American government to the attacks. President Bush pledged that the government would find and punish anyone involved in perpetrating the September 11 attacks. Law enforcement officials arrested more than seventeen hundred people possibly connected to al-Qaeda or other terrorist groups and interviewed thousands of recent immigrants from the Middle East. In an address to Congress on September 20, Bush argued that the evidence pointed to al-Qaeda and called for a "war on terror" that "will not end until every terrorist group of global reach has been found, stopped, and defeated." Congress passed a resolution authorizing Bush to use military force. The United States issued a series of demands to the Taliban regime in Afghanistan, including the surrender of bin Laden and his lieutenants, the cessation of all support of terrorism, and the release of foreign aid workers. On October 7, 2001, the United States, with the help of Great Britain and other allies, launched a military campaign against Afghanistan. Within a few months the Taliban regime was toppled and a U.S.-supported interim government was installed. Thousands of al-Qaeda operatives were captured and sent to a military prisoner camp in Guantanamo Bay, Cuba, although bin Laden himself remained at large.

In addition to going after the terrorists, the U.S. government (and people) grappled with the problem of preventing future attacks. Within hours of the September 11 attacks, lawmakers and others were calling for the passage of new laws to give the federal government greater powers to fight terrorism. Within two months, President George W. Bush signed legislation crafted by Congress that gave federal law enforcement agencies greater powers in electronic surveillance and wiretapping of suspected terrorists as well as increased authority to search suspect's residences, detain noncitizens, and track the movement of money. Bush also authorized the creation of secret military tribunals to try suspected terrorists and established a federal Office of Homeland Security to coordinate and direct the federal government's counterterrorism efforts; in June 2002 Bush went further and proposed that the office be raised to a Cabinet-level Department of Homeland Security. Civil libertarians worried that giving the federal government too many powers to investigate and detain people threatened Americans' civil liberties. But polls showed that as many as four in five Americans would be willing to give up some freedoms in exchange for greater security from terrorist attack.

A concern expressed by many both in and out of government was whether terrorists would strike again in even worse ways, such as by using poisonous chemicals, deadly germs, or nuclear or radiological weapons. Whether or not al-Qaeda or other terrorist groups possess the ability to use chemical or biological weapons against the United States has became a matter of dispute. "I'm not trying to be alarmist," stated presidential assistant Andrew J. Card to the *Washington Post*, "but we know that these terrorist organizations . . . have probably found the means to use biological or chemical warfare." But terrorism expert Amy Smithson argues that such fears are misplaced and that waging chemical and biological warfare would "require an infrastructure and scientific knowledge that groups like al-Qaeda just don't possess." The fact that such horrific possibilities were even being discussed added to the anxiety many people felt after September 11.

Political Cartoonists and the American People

American people generally rallied around their leadership following the September 11 attacks. President George W. Bush's approval ratings soared to over 80 percent following September 11. Polls also reflected high satisfaction with both Republicans and Democrats in Congress, as well as support for the subsequent military campaign in Afghanistan. Stores ran out of American flags as many Americans sought to buy and display them, including those who did not gravitate to such patriotic displays before September 11. "I'm a child of the sixties—marching against the war in Vietnam, sit-ins at the Capitol, everything," one woman said. "I used to equate flags with the conservatives, with the politicians. But boy, all that's changed. I've got flags in our house, a flag on the car. I can't believe this is me."

Many Americans also expressed the urge to help others and strengthen a sense of community. Volunteers rushed to the World

Trade Center site, dubbed Ground Zero, to help rescue and cleanup work, or to give blood or charitable donations. "It was clear," columnist Nancy Gibbs wrote soon after the attacks, "that people ached to live bigger lives, to find some way to be a brave and generous part of what most of us were consigned to watch only on television."

Political cartoonists shared all these responses with their fellow human beings, including the urge to help out or do something. They also had a unique platform with which to express their reactions. "On the morning of September 11, millions of people turned away from their jobs as they reacted to the terrorist attacks on the World Trade Center and the Pentagon," observed cartoonist V. Cullum Roberts. "But for editorial cartoonists, reacting to those attacks *was* their job." Political cartoons, often vehicles for lighthearted humor or the ridicule of public figures, became somber reflections on the tragic events of September 11 as well as patriotic affirmations of America. David Horsey, cartoonist for the *Seattle Post-Intelligencer*, argued that September 11 was the "moment that American editorial cartoonists remembered why they have the privilege of appearing in the nation's newspapers: not to tell jokes, but to express ideas and create riveting images. Editorial cartooning is serious business and serious times bring out the best in us." The following collection of cartoons on terrorism concentrates on the period following September 11, 2001, when terrorism was the number one concern of virtually all Americans. It provides a concise and diverse sampling of reactions to the acts of terrorism on that fateful day.

Chapter 1

A Day of Terror and Sorrow

Preface

September 11, 2001, began as a typical workday for most Americans, including the thousands of people employed in the offices of the enormous World Trade Center in New York City. The leading political concern in Washington, D.C., was the shrinking federal budget surplus. The leading news story involved the expected announcement that star basketball player Michael Jordan would end his retirement and return to the NBA. Political cartoons published that morning or the day before featured a wide array of topics, including Democrats and Republicans arguing over spending priorities, the decline in U.S. auto sales, the standoff between Israeli and Palestinian leaders in the Middle East, and Little League baseball players found to be too old to legally compete.

Within a few hours any semblance of normality had vanished. At 8:45 A.M., a jet airplane struck one of the Twin Towers of the World Trade Center, causing a giant fire. Eighteen minutes later, a second plane flew into the other Twin Tower, dispelling any idea that the first crash was some sort of accident. The United States was apparently under attack. The Federal Aviation Administration (FAA) halted all airplanes from taking off and ordered those flying to be grounded nationwide. A few minutes after the FAA issued its order, a third plane, which appeared to be headed toward the White House, veered suddenly and instead crashed into the Pentagon. Shortly after that, one of the Twin Towers, weakened by fire, collapsed, filling up the streets of New York with debris and dust. Within the next hour, a fourth plane crashed in Somerset County in Pennsylvania, the UN buildings in New York and all federal buildings in Washington, D.C., were evacuated, and the second Twin Tower collapsed.

By the end of the day, this much was known: The United States had suffered the worst terrorist attack in its history. New York City looked like a war zone. Airports remained closed. President George W. Bush had placed the U.S. military on highest alert and stated: "Make no mistake, the United States will hunt down and punish those responsible for these cowardly acts." When asked about the number of people killed, New York mayor Rudolph Giuliani replied that "it will be more than any of us can bear."

Suddenly, the nation's political cartoonist had only one topic to respond to. Many of them were irresistibly drawn to variations on the same image: the Statue of Liberty. Like the destroyed Twin Towers, the Statue of Liberty was a New York City landmark instantly recognized by most Americans. It was an iconic symbol of American values, and one that was in close proximity to the New York attacks. Some observers later criticized the cartoonists for their lack of creativity. Steve Benson, an editorial cartoonist with the *Arizona Republic,* responded to such criticism by arguing that the point of many cartoons was not to "offer . . . brilliantly innovative commentary" but to "underscore our emotional connection with our fellow Americans during these particularly trying times." The Statue of Liberty cartoons "represent a gut, emotional reaction in terms of horror and rage" and thus "express the feelings of many of our fellow citizens." The cartoons in this chapter offer a sampling of cartoons made in immediate response to the September 11 terrorist attacks on America.

Examining Cartoon 1:
"Declarations of War"

About the Cartoon

Many of the editorial cartoons following the September 11, 2001, terrorist attacks utilized similar or even identical themes. Cartoonist Bill Day makes use of several widely used motifs in this cartoon dated September 12. Each of the three overlapping panels represent different "Declarations of War." The first panel, "Pearl Harbor," depicts the famous scene of Japan's December 7, 1941, attack in Hawaii. Many Americans believe that the Pearl Harbor attack, which was also a surprise assault that resulted in a large number of American casualties, is one of the few events that is comparable with September 11. The second panel, "The Pentagon," is one of the relatively few cartoons that pictured the terrorist attack on the huge Washington, D.C., building that serves as national headquarters for America's military. The third panel, "New York City," is a scene that was drawn by many cartoonists following September 11—New York's famous Statue of Liberty grieving over the smoky destruction of the World Trade Center. Day posits in his cartoon that the planes crashing into the Pentagon and the World Trade Center amount to a declaration of war against America, just as Japan's Pearl Harbor attack had ushered in a state of war between America and Japan in 1941.

About the Cartoonist

Bill Day is a cartoonist for the *Commercial Appeal* newspaper in Memphis, Tennessee.

Examining Cartoon 2:
"Reality TV"

About the Cartoon

Prior to September 11, 2001, "reality TV" referred to shows that presented footage of police pursuits, accidents, and game shows that placed contestants in challenging circumstances. However, as this Kirk Walters cartoon suggests, the term gained a chilling new meaning on September 11, 2001. The September 15 cartoon depicts an ordinary American television viewer who is aghast while watching a live television news shot of the burning World Trade Center skyscrapers. On that day, millions of Americans were glued to their TV sets as they watched both live and repeated scenes of the planes crashing into the Twin Towers and the buildings' subsequent burning and collapse.

About the Cartoonist

Kirk Walters has been a cartoonist for the *Toledo Blade* since 1985. His work is syndicated to approximately 160 newspapers nationwide. He also does a weekly comic strip on local issues called "Maumee Dearest."

Examining Cartoon 3

About the Cartoon

The September 11, 2001, terrorist attacks against the United States elicited numerous responses of sympathy from other nations. Editorial cartoonists worldwide responded to the attacks. This stark drawing by a Chilean cartoonist makes effective use of New York City's nickname—the "Big Apple." It shows a jet airliner that has crashed into a giant apple and the pool of blood that has resulted.

About the Cartoonist

Hervi is an architect and cartoonist who resides in Santiago, Chile. In addition to being published in local magazines and journals, his work has been published in magazines and newspapers in Europe and in North and South America.

Examining Cartoon 4:
"Still Standing"

About the Cartoon

This September 12 cartoon, like many published in the immediate aftermath of the September 11 terrorist incidents, seeks to both capture the horror of the attacks and express confidence in America's ability and resolve to overcome them. The Twin Towers of the World Trade Center have been destroyed, but the United States as a nation, as symbolized by Uncle Sam, still stands tall, his clenched fist implying a determination not to be defeated. This cartoon was later blown up into poster size and displayed in one of the buildings close to Ground Zero—the area of rubble created by the attacks.

About the Cartoonist

Mike Ritter is the editorial cartoonist for the Tribune Newspapers, a regional Arizona newspaper chain. His work has also appeared on ABC's *Good Morning America* and in *USA Today*. His awards include three citations as best cartoonist by the Arizona Press Club.

Chapter 2

Heroes of 9/11

Preface

Richard Gephardt, the ranking Democrat in the House of Representatives, stated in a September 22, 2001, radio address that the terrorists who struck the United States on September 11 "felt Americans were weak and spoiled, and thought we would fold." And indeed, Americans both in the vicinity of the attacks and watching on television were initially stunned and bewildered by the horrific events. "But then," Gephardt went on, "something extraordinary happened. Person by person, confusion gave way to courage. Everywhere, in acts large and small, people rallied to help."

This theme of American heroism under fire and caring for others permeated much commentary and reaction to the events of September 11. Stories circulated about how people carried others down scores of flights of stairs at the World Trade Center, how Pentagon workers risked their lives to find and rescue people trapped in that burning building, how the passengers on United Airlines Flight 93 had apparently resisted the hijackers and caused that plane to crash in the Pennsylvania countryside, killing those on the plane but no others. Much attention focused on the actions of New York's firefighters and rescue workers, many of whom rushed into the World Trade Center buildings after the two planes hit, only to perish when the buildings collapsed. Whole units of firefighters were lost. The casualties at the World Trade Center included 343 firefighters and paramedics, 23 New York police officers, and 37 Port Authority police officers.

In the days and weeks following September 11, Americans throughout the nation sought to honor those killed and to contribute in various ways. Entertainers held telethons and other fundraising events. People gave blood, bought and displayed American flags, and contributed to charities. Many gathered and prayed together at places of worship and at candlelight vigils. In such actions, Gephardt pronounced, "we saw the heart of America"—a spirit that the terrorists tried but could not destroy. The cartoons in this chapter examine the various ways in which Americans responded to the terrorist attacks of September 11.

Examining Cartoon 1

About the Cartoon

Among the casualties of the September 11 attacks were hundreds of members of the New York City's fire and police departments, many of whom fearlessly entered the World Trade Center buildings following the attacks and were subsequently killed when the buildings collapsed. September 11 also featured stories of heroism from everyday Americans who helped others evacuate the World Trade Center and assisted in rescue and cleanup efforts. This cartoon by Robert Ariail was one of several published immediately after September 11 that honored such heroes by using a famous World War II photograph as its model. On February 23, 1945, Joe Rosenthal photographed five U.S. Marines planting the American flag on a mountaintop on the island of Iwo Jima during a bitter and ultimately victorious struggle to take the island from the Japanese.

It became the most reproduced photograph in history. On September 11, 2001, American casualties were not soldiers in a distant battleground, but civilians, including fire and police workers, in the heart of New York. Ariail replicates the photograph with ordinary American workers, including a policeman and a fireman, standing in for the marines and a pile of rubble instead of a mountaintop.

About the Cartoonist

Robert Ariail is the editorial cartoonist for the *State*, a newspaper published in Columbia, South Carolina.

Examining Cartoon 2:
"The New York Spirit"

The New York Spirit

About the Cartoon

New York, America's most populous and in many ways most cosmopolitan city, suffered the brunt of the terrorist attacks of September 11, 2001. Following the attacks, most Americans greatly sympathized with New Yorkers and cheered the way they carried on through the tragedy. Negative stereotypes of New Yorkers as being rude and obnoxious were replaced by positive images of energy and pluck. This cartoon by Jeff Danziger, himself a transplanted New Yorker, encapsulates the "New York Spirit" by showing a person still intent on doing his work even as he is being carried by stretcher from the remains of the World Trade Center.

About the Cartoonist

Jeff Danziger, cartoonist for the *Christian Science Monitor* from 1986 to 1997, is an independent nationally syndicated cartoonist. He is a resident of Manhattan, New York, and was there when the terrorist attacks occurred.

Examining Cartoon 3

About the Cartoon

George W. Bush became president in January 2001, following a historically close and disputed election. Prior to September 11, 2001, Bush was frequently depicted in editorial cartoons as a callow and even bumbling politician. However, his public image and popularity both soared after the attack as the nation rallied behind the president. Even former critics and political opponents were generally supportive of his decisions and actions. On September 20, he addressed Congress in a special session and delivered, by most accounts, an effective and moving speech that declared a "war on terror" that "will not stop until every terrorist group of global reach has been found, stopped, and defeated." This cartoon, first published three days later, shows an assured Bush at a speaker's podium. Behind him stand the ghostly images of two famous heroes of World War II: British prime minister Winston Churchill, flashing his famous V for Victory sign, and an applauding U.S. president Franklin D. Roosevelt. The cartoonist implies that these past heroes, much like the American public, are lending their support to Bush's actions as president in these troubled times.

About the Cartoonist

Kevin Siers began his career drawing community newspaper cartoons between shifts mining iron ore in Minnesota. Now the editorial cartoonist for the *Charlotte (North Carolina) Observer,* his work has also appeared in the *New York Times* and *Newsweek.*

Examining Cartoon 4:

"A Special Message from the War Information Council"

About the Cartoon

In the weeks following the September 11 attacks, America lionized numerous heroes, including rescue workers, police and firefighters, soldiers fighting in Afghanistan, and political leaders including New

York mayor Rudolph Giuliani and President George W. Bush. In addition, many of the tributes and patriotic events were tinged with religiosity: People sang "God Bless America" and pledged allegiance to the flag of "one nation under God." This cartoon, part of the weekly satirical *This Modern World* by Tom Tomorrow, presents a skewed and tongue-in-cheek perspective on both these post 9/11 trends. Presented as a public service message from a fictional "War Information Council," it features a stern Uncle Sam who implores Americans to stand up for basic American values. But instead of such traditional patriotic values as fidelity and courage, the cartoon calls attention to the values of dissent, criticism, and diversity. Uncle Sam notes that these values are anathema to terrorist leader Osama bin Laden and Islamic fundamentalists including the Taliban regime in Afghanistan, but they are also often disparaged by many of the most fervent and self-proclaimed "real Americans" at the forefront of the country's patriotic celebration. While many such Americans may equate patriotism with supporting President Bush, true patriotism, in the cartoonist's view, includes the duty to proclaim that "George Bush still seems like a doofus." The cartoon also singles out (and perhaps satirizes) feminists, gays, and atheists as those who have special patriotic duties to perform by proclaiming their beliefs.

About the Cartoonist

Tom Tomorrow (a pseudonymn for Dan Perkins) is a satirist and the creator of *This Modern World*, a weekly cartoon on politics and culture that appears in numerous magazines, newspapers, and alternative weeklies. His work has been collected in five books, including *When Penguins Attack*.

Chapter 3

The Terrorists

Preface

M ost Americans felt anger as well as shock following the terrorist attacks of September 11, 2001, but did not know where to direct their anger. It was clear that the attack was a major operation requiring much planning and preparation, but the identity and motivation of the attackers was, at first, a mystery.

The largest terrorist incident in America prior to September 11, the 1995 Oklahoma City bombing, proved to be a case of domestic terrorism in which the bomber and his accomplices were disaffected Americans. However, investigators of the September 11 attacks soon determined that the nineteen suspected terrorists on the four affected planes were all from foreign countries, most from the Middle East. Suspicion quickly settled on Osama bin Laden, a fundamentalist Islamic leader, and his organization, al-Qaeda. Bin Laden was already well known in foreign policy circles and among terrorism experts. He soon became a household name among all Americans, and his gaunt bearded face was soon featured in many news photographs and editorial cartoons.

Bin Laden, a native of Yemen who was raised in Saudi Arabia (where his father became a wealthy construction magnate), came to embrace a fundamentalist version of Islam. In 1979 he moved to Afghanistan to support that nation's successful guerrilla war against the Soviet Union. He later resided in Sudan before moving back to Afghanistan in 1996. He established al-Qaeda in 1987, an organization that has been described as a "Ford Foundation" of terrorism that gives financial support to other terrorist groups. Al-Qaeda is believed to have maintained cells in sixty nations and to have trained thousands of individuals in camps in Afghanistan. Upset at American influence in the Middle East, bin Laden issued official pronouncements called fatwas in 1996 and again in 1998 urging all Muslims to kill Americans wherever they can.

Osama bin Laden's proclamations of a holy Islamic war against Americans has led to debate on the role of Islam itself as a cause of terrorism. President George W. Bush has repeatedly stated that America's war on terrorism was not a war on Islam, a centuries-old religion with more than a billion adherents worldwide. Bush and others have maintained that terrorism had no place or justification in mainstream Islam, an opinion seconded by some Islamic scholars such as Zahid Bukhari at Georgetown University, who asserted that "the [September 11] attacks had nothing to do with Islam." The cartoons in this chapter address this debate as well as present various depictions of Osama bin Laden.

Examining Cartoon 1:

"Objects in Hindsight Are Much Larger than They Appeared"

About the Cartoon

Rats—animals seen as both vile and threatening—have often been used by editorial cartoonists to represent terrorists. This cartoon makes the point that the threat of terrorism seems much larger to Americans after September 11 than it did before the attacks—and perhaps should have been taken more seriously in the past. The rat is holding a knife, which may or may not refer to the fact that September 11 terrorists are believed to have used knives or box cutters in their hijackings.

About the Cartoonist

Jimmy Margulies is the editorial cartoonist for the *Bergen Record*, a New Jersey newspaper. Previously he was the cartoonist for the *Houston Post.*

Examining Cartoon 2:
"Attack!"

About the Cartoon

An important question after the September 11 terrorist attacks was whether Islam was a cause of terrorism. Investigators quickly found that the individuals behind the airplane hijackings were from the Middle East and were presumably part of an Islamic terrorist movement. In many countries Islamic fundamentalist leaders had long condemned the United States; some called for jihad, or holy war, against America. However, many people, President Bush among them, asserted that the terrorists were not acting in the true spirit of the religion and that Americans should not view the campaign against terrorists as a campaign against Islam. Such an opinion is also expressed in this cartoon, which shows a bearded and turbaned figure calling for attack. However, his sword instead cuts through the Koran, Islam's holy book—implying that Islamic terrorists are opposed to and indeed destructive of Islam's tenets.

About the Cartoonist

Kevin Kallaugher, who signs his work KAL, is an editorial cartoonist for the *Baltimore Sun* and the *Economist* magazine of London. He worked ten years in London as a cartoonist before moving back to the United States in 1988.

Examining Cartoon 3

About the Cartoon

Osama bin Laden, a fundamentalist Islamic leader and Saudi Arabian exile, was already a wanted terrorist prior to September 11, 2001. However, it was not until after the events of that day that the name of his organization, al-Qaeda, became a household word and he became America's public enemy number one as the prime suspect behind the attacks. The above cartoon was made shortly before Halloween in 2001. Since October 7 of that year the United States had waged a bombing campaign against Afghanistan, where bin Laden and his followers had resided since 1996 as guests of that country's Taliban regime. However, during the initial weeks there seemed to be little progress made in toppling the regime or capturing bin Laden. Meanwhile, Americans faced a new fear: anthrax. Several Americans died from the disease in October, and Congress had closed down after several members received letters containing deadly anthrax spores. In this cartoon, Patrick Oliphant draws children going trick-or-treating, but what is normally a fun-filled Halloween scene is chilled by the specter of Osama bin Laden hovering ominously above them. The cartoon hauntingly captures the mood of many Americans during this time when fear of terrorism lurked everywhere.

About the Cartoonist

Patrick Oliphant is a native of Australia who moved to the United States in 1964 to become editorial cartoonist for the *Denver Post*. He moved to the *Washington Star* in 1975, then became an independent syndicated cartoonist; his work appears in five hundred newspapers in the United States and other countries. He has won several awards, including a 1967 Pulitzer Prize.

Examining Cartoon 4:
"World Terrorist Mastermind!!"

About the Cartoon

This Walt Handelsman cartoon was created on November 19, 2001. It presents a much different picture of Osama bin Laden than the preceding Oliphant cartoon, drawn a few weeks earlier. During that interval the U.S.-led military campaign in Afghanistan, which some observers feared was in danger of turning into a quagmire, had scored some important successes. Several important cities in Afghanistan, including its capital Kabul, were captured by the U.S.-supported Northern Alliance (a coalition of armed Afghan opposition groups). In addition, U.S. air strikes killed Mohammad Atef, a key al-Qaeda deputy. Osama bin Laden himself was believed at this time to be on the run and hiding somewhere in a cave in the mountains of Afghanistan. This cartoon suggests that bin Laden's reputation as a terrorist mastermind and threat to America may have been overinflated following the September 11 attacks.

About the Cartoonist

Walt Handelsman joined *Newsday* as its editorial cartoonist in 2001. He previously worked for the *Times-Picayune* in New Orleans, where he won a Pulitzer Prize in 1997.

Chapter 4

Americans Respond

EXAMINING ISSUES THROUGH
POLITICAL CARTOONS

Preface

In remarks delivered on September 11, 2001, President George W. Bush asserted that, in addition to helping the injured, America had two top priorities. One was "to take every precaution to protect our citizens at home and around the world from further attacks." The other was to bring those responsible for the terrorist attacks to justice. Bush added that "we will make no distinction between the terrorists who committed these acts and those who harbor them."

Since then the U.S. government has taken actions on both these priorities. To prevent future attacks, Bush established the executive Office of Homeland Security to coordinate efforts to detect and thwart terrorist activities. In addition, Congress passed and Bush signed several pieces of legislation designed to protect Americans from terrorism, including reforms of airport security practices and laws granting police agencies greater investigative powers. To respond to the terrorists, Congress passed a resolution authorizing the president to "use all necessary and appropriate force against those . . . [who] planned, authorized, committed, or aided the terrorist attacks . . . or harbored such organizations or persons." Under Bush, the United States has taken a range of diplomatic and military actions against terrorist groups. The response that attracted the most attention was Bush's authorization on October 7, 2001, of military strikes against Afghanistan, the country harboring the man believed responsible for the attacks of September 11, Osama bin Laden. Within a few months that country's regime had been toppled and thousands of suspected terrorists were killed or captured.

Although most Americans have remained strikingly united on the importance of improving homeland security and responding to the terrorists, some differences have emerged on exactly how to accomplish these goals and whether other important American values will be sacrificed in the process. Some critics questioned whether the civil liberties of America's people were being compromised by the rush of legislation giving law enforcement new tools and powers. Others opposed America's military campaign in Afghanistan, arguing that diplomatic options were not given enough of a chance before the U.S. military campaign began, and that innocent Afghanistan civilians were being killed. The cartoons in this chapter address some of these issues surrounding America's responses to September 11.

Examining Cartoon 1

About the Cartoon

For many Americans, the initial reaction of grief to the September 11 attacks was closely followed by anger. Steve Breen's September 12 cartoon was a grieving Statue of Liberty. His September 13 one is featured here. It depicts a bald eagle—America's national bird and symbol—quietly sharpening its claws. The action, as well as the expression on the eagle's face, symbolizes American resolve to take action against the terrorists who inflicted such trauma on the nation —something felt by many Americans in the days and weeks following September 11.

About the Cartoonist

Steve Breen became the staff political cartoonist for the *San Diego Union-Tribune* in 2001, having previously held the same position for the *Ashbury Park Press* in New Jersey. He won a Pulitzer Prize for editorial cartooning in 1998.

Examining Cartoon 2:
"United We Stand"

UNITED WE STAND

About the Cartoon

Like the preceding cartoon, this one also features America's national bird, the bald eagle. Instead of American anger, however, its theme is American unity. Its title—"United We Stand"—is a slogan that appeared everywhere in America following September 11, 2001. The eagle is comprised of a collage of American people of different colors and ethnic backgrounds. It represents Americans coming together in a spirit of patriotism in the days and weeks following the attacks.

About the Cartoonist

Marshall Ramsey began his cartooning career while a student at the University of Tennessee. He won the John Locher Memorial Award, the top American prize for collegiate cartoonists, in 1993. He is the staff cartoonist for the *Clarion-Ledger* in Jackson, Mississippi.

Examining Cartoon 3:
"Big Brother"

About the Cartoon

In his classic dystopian novel *1984*, George Orwell described a society ruled by a totalitarian government whose leader was known as "Big Brother." The ruling party could watch all the people through two-way television screens; posters announced that "Big Brother Is Watching You." Following September 11, many commentators wondered whether, in the quest for security and the prevention of future terrorist attacks, the United States would create a "Big Brother" of its own in the form of an intrusive and oppressive government apparatus. Cartoonist Jim Borgman posts this question in this cartoon published several weeks after the September 11 attacks. A shell-shocked and infantilized American clings to his "Big Brother"—a behemoth composed of cameras, retinal scans, listening devices, and other technological gadgets that can snoop into people's lives. Borgman raises the question of whether Americans are allowing their fear of terrorism to make them timid, dependent, and too willing to trade their civil liberties for security.

About the Cartoonist

Since 1976, Jim Borgman has been the editorial cartoonist for the *Cincinnati Enquirer*. He won a Pulitzer Prize in 1991. He is also the coauthor of the comic strip *Zits*.

Examining Cartoon 4:
"Mr. President, We've Secured Bin Laden"

About the Cartoon

While the September 11 terrorist attacks elicited an outpouring of sympathy from around the world, many people outside the United States worried about how America would respond. The above cartoon is by a native of Pakistan, a country that borders Afghanistan, where terrorist leader Osama bin Laden was believed to have been residing. It depicts a globe being destroyed by bomb blasts, while the U.S. president celebrates the capture of bin Laden before pointedly asking whether there have been any *American* deaths— as if the deaths of non-Americans did not matter. Shahid Mahmood, the cartoonist, has stated that this cartoon is "dedicated to all the people who died on September 11; and all the people who will die in the future as a consequence." Less than three weeks after this cartoon was created, the United States did begin to bomb Afghanistan. The military operation received some criticism for killing innocent people in Afghanistan, but U.S. officials claimed that the United States was doing what it could to minimize civilian casualties.

About the Cartoonist

Shahid Mahmood grew up in Pakistan and was the editorial cartoonist for *Dawn*, the national newspaper, and *Newsline*, Pakistan's leading newsmagazine. Now a resident of Toronto, Canada, he is a regular contributor to *Chowk*, an interactive online magazine that caters to overseas Pakistanis, Indians, and other South Asians.

Organizations to Contact

The editors have compiled the following list of organizations concerned with the issues featured in this book. The descriptions are derived from materials provided by the organizations. All have publications or information available for interested readers. This list was compiled on the date of publication of the present volume; the information provided here may change. Be aware that many organizations take several weeks or longer to respond to inquiries, so allow as much time as possible.

American Civil Liberties Union (ACLU)
125 Broad St., 18th Floor, New York, NY 10004-2400
(212) 549-2500
e-mail: aclu@aclu.org • website: www.aclu.org

The ACLU is a national organization that works to defend Americans' civil rights guaranteed by the U.S. Constitution, arguing that measures to protect national security should not compromise fundamental civil liberties. It publishes and distributes policy statements, pamphlets, and press releases with titles such as "In Defense of Freedom in a Time of Crisis" and "National ID Cards: Five Reasons Why They Should Be Rejected."

American Enterprise Institute (AEI)
1150 17th St. NW, Washington, DC 20036
(202) 862-5800 • fax (202) 862-7177
website: www.aei.org

The American Enterprise Institute for Public Policy Research is a scholarly research institute that is dedicated to preserving limited government, private enterprise, and a strong foreign policy and national defense. Articles about terrorism and September 11 can be found in its magazine, *American Enterprise*, and on its website.

Anti-Defamation League (ADL)
823 United Nations Plaza, New York, NY 10017
(212) 885-7700 • fax (212) 867-0779
website: www.adl.org

The Anti-Defamation League is a human relations organization dedicated to combating all forms of prejudice and bigotry. The league has placed a spotlight on terrorism and on the dangers posed for extremism. Its website records reactions to the September 11, 2001, terrorist incidents by both extremist and mainstream organizations, provides background information on Osama bin Laden, and furnishes other materials on terrorism and the Middle East. The ADL also maintains a bimonthly online newsletter, *Frontline*.

Center for Strategic and International Studies (CSIS)
1800 K St. NW, Suite 400, Washington, DC 20006
(202) 887-0200 • fax (202) 775-3199
website: www.csis.org

The center works to provide world leaders with strategic insights and policy options on current and emerging global issues. It publishes books including *To Prevail: An American Strategy for the Campaign Against Terrorism*, the *Washington Quarterly*, a journal on political, economic, and security issues, and other publications including reports that can be downloaded from its website.

Council on American-Islamic Relations (CAIR)
453 New Jersey Ave. SE, Washington, DC 20003
(202) 488-8787 • fax (202) 488-0833
e-mail: cair@cair-net.org • website: www.cair-net.org

CAIR is a nonprofit membership organization that presents an Islamic perspective on public policy issues and challenges the misrepresentation of Islam and Muslims. It publishes the quarterly newsletter *Faith in Action* and other various publications on Muslims in the United States. Its website includes statements condemning both the September 11 attacks and discrimination against Muslims.

Institute for Policy Studies (IPS)
733 15th St. NW, Suite 1020, Washington, DC 20005
(202) 234-9382 • fax (202) 387-7915
website: www.ips-dc.org

The IPS is a progressive think tank that works to develop societies built around the values of justice and nonviolence. It publishes reports including *Global Perspectives: A Media Guide to Foreign Policy Experts.* Numerous articles and interviews on September 11 and terrorism are available on its website.

International Policy Institute of Counter-Terrorism (ICT)
PO Box 167, Herzlia 46150, Israel
972-9-9527277 • fax 972-9-9513073
e-mail: mail@ict.org.il • website: www.ict.org.il

The ICT is a research institute dedicated to developing public policy solutions to international terrorism. The ICT website is a comprehensive resource on terrorism and counterterrorism and features an extensive database on terrorist organizations, including al-Qaeda.

Islamic Supreme Council of America (ISCA)
1400 Sixteenth Street NW, Room B112, Washington, DC 20036
(202) 939-3400 • fax (202) 939-3410
e-mail: staff@islamicsupremecouncil.org
website: www.islamicsupremecouncil.org

The ISCA promotes Islam in America both by providing practical solutions to American Muslims in integrating Islamic teachings with American culture and by teaching non-Muslims that Islam is a religion of moderation, peace, and tolerance. It strongly condemns Islamic extremists and all forms of terrorism. Its website includes statements, commentaries, and reports on terrorism, including *Usama bin Laden: A Legend Gone Wrong* and *Jihad: A Misunderstood Concept from Islam.*

Middle East Media Research Institute (MEMRI)
PO Box 27837, Washington, DC 20038-7837
(202) 955-9070 • fax: (202) 955-9077
e-mail: memri@erols.com • website: www.memri.org

MEMRI translates and disseminates articles and commentaries from Middle East media sources and provides original research and analysis on the region. Its Jihad and Terrorism Studies Project monitors radical Islamist groups and individuals and their reactions to acts of terrorism around the world.

United States Department of State, Counterterrorism Office
Office of Public Affairs, Room 2507
U.S. Department of State
2201 C St. NW, Washington, DC 20520
(202) 647-4000
e-mail: secretary@state.gov • website: www.state.gov/s/ct

The office works to develop and implement American counterterrorism strategy and to improve cooperation with foreign governments. Articles and speeches by government officials are available on its website.

War Resisters League (WRL)
339 Lafayette St., New York, NY 10012
(212) 228-0450 • (212) 228-6193
e-mail: wrl@warresisters.org • website: www.warresisters.org

The WRL, founded in 1923, believes that all war is a crime against humanity, and advocates nonviolent methods to create a just and democratic society. It publishes the magazine *The Nonviolent Activist*. Articles from that magazine, as well as other commentary and resources about September 11 and America's war against terrorism, are available on its website.

Websites
American Liberty Partnership
www.libertyunites.org

The American Liberty Partnership, founded in response to the September 11 attacks, is a collaborative effort of leading Internet companies including AOL Time Warner and Microsoft. The website provides information to interested Americans on relief efforts, charity organizations, and charitable giving.

The Cartoon Web

www.cartoonweb.com

The official website of the Cartoonists & Writers Syndicate features the work of cartoonists from over fifty nations. These cartoons are placed in subject categories, which include "U.S. Under Attack," "U.S. Strikes Back," and "Anthrax."

Daryl Cagle's Professional Cartoonist Index

http://cagle.slate.msn.com

This website, assembled by cartoonist Daryl Cagle, features the work of more than fifty cartoonists and bills itself as the world's largest collection of newspaper editorial cartoons on the web. The website is continually updated; teachers' guides and lesson plans using political cartoons are also available.

For Further Research

Books

Yonah Alexander and Michael S. Swetman, *Usama bin Laden's Al-Qaeda: Profile of a Terrorist Network*. Ardsley, NY: Transnational Publishers, 2001.

Peter L. Bergen, *Holy War, Inc.: Inside the Secret World of Osama bin Laden*. New York: Free Press, 2001.

Noam Chomsky, *9-11*. New York: Seven Stories Press, 2001.

Martha Crenshaw and John Pimlott, eds., *Encyclopedia of World Terrorism*. Armonk, NY: Sharpe Reference, 1997.

Laura K. Egendorf, ed., *Terrorism: Opposing Viewpoints*. San Diego: Greenhaven, 2000.

Philip B. Heymann, *Terrorism and America: A Commonsense Strategy for a Democratic Society*. Cambridge, MA: MIT Press, 1998.

James F. Hoge Jr. and Gideon Rose, eds., *How Did This Happen? Terrorism and the New War*. New York: Public Affairs, 2001.

Jessica Kornbluth and Jessica Papin, eds., *Because We Are Americans: What We Discovered on September 11, 2001*. New York: Warner Books, 2001.

Bernard Lewis, *What Went Wrong? Western Impact and Middle Eastern Response*. New York: Oxford University Press, 2001.

Jon Ronson, *Adventures with Extremists*. New York: Simon and Schuster, 2002.

Barbara Shangle, ed., *Day of Terror: September 11, 2001*. Beaverton, OR: American Products, 2001.

Strobe Talbott and Nayan Chanda, eds., *The Age of Terror: America and the World After September 11*. New York: Basic Books, 2002.

Periodicals

David Aaron, "The New Twilight Struggle," *American Prospect*, October 22, 2001.

Michael Albert and Stephen R. Shalom, "September 11 and Its Aftermath," *Z Magazine*, October 2001.

Jonathan Alter, "Blame America at Your Peril," *Newsweek*, October 15, 2001.

Samir Amin, "U.S. Hegemony and the Response to Terror," *Monthly Review*, November 2001.

Benjamin R. Barber, "Beyond Jihad vs. McWorld," *Nation*, January 21, 2002.

Max Boot, "The Case for American Empire," *Weekly Standard*, October 15, 2001.

George W. Bush, "War on Terrorism: Homeland Security," *Vital Speeches*, December 1, 2001.

Business Week, "Keep America's Gates Open. Just Watch Them Better," November 19, 2001.

David Carr, "The Futility of Homeland Defense," *Atlantic Monthly*, January 2002.

Congressional Digest, "War on Terrorism," November 2001.

Economist, "The Day the World Changed," September 13, 2001.

Richard Falk, "Defining a Just War," *Nation*, October 29, 2001.

Fortune, "Eleven Takes on Terror," November 26, 2001.

Futurist, "The New Age of Terrorism: Futurists Respond,"January/ February 2002.

John Lewis Gaddis, "Setting Right a Dangerous World," *Chronicle of Higher Education*, January 11, 2002.

Adolfo Gilly, "The Faceless Enemy," *NACLA Report on the Americas*, November/December 2001.

Todd Gitlin, "Blaming America First," *Mother Jones*, January/February 2002.

Lee Griffith, "Terror and the Hope Within," *Other Side*, January/February 2002.

Michael Howard, "What's in a Name?: How to Fight Terrorism," *Foreign Affairs*, January/February 2002.

David E. Kaplan and Kevin Whitelaw, "The CEO of Terror, Inc." *U.S. News & World Report*, October 1, 2001.

Muqtedar Khan, "Understanding the Roots of Muslim Rage," *Canadian Dimension*, November/December 2001.

James Kitfield, "Ending State Terror," *National Journal*, October 2, 2001.

Charles Krauthammer, "The Real New World Order," *Weekly Standard*, November 12, 2001.

Lewis H. Lapham, "Drums Along the Potomac," *Harper's Magazine*, November 2001.

Michael Lerner, "The Case for Peace," *Time*, October 1, 2001.

Brink Lindsey, "Poor Choice—Why Globalization Didn't Create 9/11," *New Republic*, November 12, 2001.

Richard Lowry, "Profiles in Cowardice," *National Review*, January 28, 2002.

Wayne Madsen, "Why Wasn't Bush Warned?" *In These Times*, October 15, 2001.

W.J.T. Mitchell, "911: Criticism and Crisis," *Critical Inquiry*, Winter 2002.

Chris Mooney, "Holy War," *American Prospect*, December 17, 2001.

Daniel Pipes, "Who Is the Enemy?" *Commentary*, January 2002.

Earl D. Rabd, "The Semi-Apologists and the War Against Terrorism," *Midstream*, November 2001.

Sabeel Rahman, "Another New World Order? Multilateralism in the Aftermath of September 11," *Harvard International Review*, Winter 2002.

David C. Rapoport, "The Fourth Wave: September 11 in the History of Terrorism, *Current History*, December 2001.

Romesh Ratnesar, "What's Become of Al-Qaeda?" *Time*, January 21, 2002.

Richard Rhodes et al., "What Terror Keeps Teaching Us," *New York Times Magazine*, September 23, 2001.

Matthew Rothschild, "The New McCarthyism," *Progressive*, January 2002.

Linda Rothstein, "After September 11," *Bulletin of the Atomic Scientists*, November/December 2001.

Arundhati Roy, "New World Disorder," *In These Times*, November 26, 2001.

Benjamin Schwartz and Christopher Layne, "A New Grand Strategy," *Atlantic Monthly*, January 2002.

Nelson D. Schwartz, "Learning from Israel," *Fortune*, January 21, 2002.

Teen People, "Teens at Ground Zero," December 2001.

Evan Thomas, "The Day That Changed America," *Newsweek*, December 31, 2001.

Jay Tolson, "Early Drafts of History," *U.S. News & World Report*, January 14, 2002.

Howard Zinn, "The Others," *Nation*, February 11, 2002.

Index